Crucial 60 seconds, elites' power of persuasion

關鍵60秒
菁英式說服力

鄭家捷——著

書泉出版社 印行

獻辭

本書完成，有賴於雲林科技大學應外系同學的參與，提供了觀察與研究的對象，特別是 2018 年级郭文倩同學的有趣文章，本人於此特致謝忱。

Your persuasive power is decided by your ability on spotting issues from observation and analysis of all relevant and important facts, followed by a clear utterance of a simple conclusion supported by sound reasoning as well as perception procured from placing yourself in the position of the other person.

你的說服力是建在對於所有重要與相關事實上所做的觀察和分析，在找出的爭議點之後，清楚地說出具有正當支持的理由並考量同理心所做的簡單結論。

My motivation to write this book

Thirty years ago when I was in Saint Louis Law School, one day a good friend of mine asked me one question. "John, what is the difference between students in Saint Louis Law and Harvard Law?" I told him that they were in Harvard because they were more intelligent and studied harder. He said, "Not exactly, they already knew what they would do in the future when they were 12 years old when we only knew how to play baseball." Ten years later, my friend, by his keen observation and strong persuasive power, became a very famous football agent in the U.S., building his own empire with his empty hands. As an old Chinese saying goes, "ice of three inches thick cannot be made overnight." If you are weak in your power of persuasion, such weakness probably has lasted a long time and certainly cannot be cured overnight.

My motivation to write this book is simple, to build up the students' ability on persuasion in speaking, debating, writing and negotiation. I have taught English speech, debate and writing in college and have worked as an international attorney for over ten years. In the past ten years, I have noticed that many students with a high English proficiency, including some from mainland China, can neither talk nor write on topics assigned as those found in ILTS and TOEFL. When I inquired further, I was informed that they had spent time and effort in high school on being trained to read and listen rather than write, not to mention to deliver a speech on certain topics. To my surprise, they have never learned how to write even in their Chinese class either. In many cases, they had great difficulty in giving opinions. Most of them have no problem with their English proficiency. English is a tool helpful in communicating with foreigners and exchanging ideas. They spent plenty of time on learning English to achieve a high English proficiency, but they have never learned how to form their opinions by observing and formulating ideas. In their process of learning, they failed to understand that English is a tool rather than their final goal in the future. As an intellectual, you have to be able to express your own thinking and opinion. Your own opinion is the first step of training in persuasive speech, debate, writing and negotiation. What is more important here is that prior to discussing your own opinion, you have to be trained on providing descriptive facts or information from your observation.

The problem on how to establish an opinion is not limited to college students but encountered by business persons as well. In the past ten years, I worked as an international attorney to help some local companies with their international disputes including overseas litigations, mediations and settlements. In a business world, power on persuasion is important. To persuade others to accept what you say, which is an opinion with a conclusion, you must take a position first. To form an opinion, facts must be carefully observed, clearly described and be further analyzed. This task is the first priority in the management of any business decision, especially in disputes. This process requires a series of logical organization. Logical organization starts from a clear description of facts resulting into a well elaborated opinion subsequent to a logical analysis. Quite unfortunately, many business persons do not have sufficient training in this field. In many occasions where business disputes are involved, people who are in charge of this responsibility cannot give a clear description of relevant facts, not to mention spotting issues with a possible proposed solution. I am not referring only to a junior level regarding customer service, but also to a senior management level on this point. I hope this book can help some students as well as business persons who need help in their writing, speaking and negotiation.

前言

我寫這本書的動機

三十年前，我還在美國聖路易大學法學院讀書的時候，有一天我的一個好朋友問我一個問題，「我們的學生跟哈佛法學院的學生差異在哪裡？」我告訴他哈佛的學生他們比較聰明，也比較用功。他說「不完全是，哈佛的學生當他們 12 歲時就知道他們將來要做什麼，而我們 12 歲的時候只知道怎麼打棒球」。十年之後我的朋友，憑著他的敏銳觀察力和說服力，變成美國非常有名的足球經紀人，空手建立了他自己的王國。就像中國的成語所說：「冰凍三尺，非一日之寒。」任何問題不是一個晚上造成的。如果你的說服力是薄弱的，這個問題可能已經存在很久，當然也不可能在一個晚上就解決。

我寫這本書的動機起因很簡單，幫助學生在說話、辯論、還有談判上建立說服的能力。我在大學裡面教授英文演說、辯論、英文寫作以及從事國際律師業務超過十年的時間。在過去的十年當中，我發現學生們包括一些大陸學生即使有了很好的英文能力，也很難針對特定的議題發表談話或寫作，比方像雅思或是托福的口語或是作文題目。當我進一步詢問的時候，我才被告知他們在高中時花了很多時間在閱讀和聽力訓練，而非寫作，更不用談對於特定的議題進行演說。我甚至很驚訝的發現他們也沒有學過中文作文。事實上，在很多場合他們跟外國人交談是有很大的困難，但他們絕大部分英語水平並沒有問題。英文是一項幫助溝通或是交換想法的工具，學生們花了很多的時間學習英文甚至達到優異的英文能力，但是他們從來沒有學過如何觀察、整理想法以及形成他們自己的意見。在他們的學習過程中，他們忘記了英文只是一個工具而不是他們未來最後的目標。身為一個知識分子，你必須有你自己的想法和意見，而你自己的想法就是訓練具有說服力的演說辯論和談判的第一步。而更重要的是，在討論你自己個人意見之前，你應該要被訓練的是如何客觀的描述你所觀察到的事實和資訊。

如何形成一個意見？這樣的問題並不限於大學生，也包括了一些商務人士。在過去的十年當中我也以國際商務律師的身分，幫助了一些當地的公司處理他們國際糾紛，包括訴訟案件、協調與和解。在商業世界，無論任何情況，說服別人是很重要的工作。要達到說服的目的，意見，其實也就是結論，必須要先建立。要建立一個意見，事實必須小心的觀察以及清楚的陳述，這是處理任何商業糾紛第一件要做的事情。這需要一個邏輯的組織。邏輯的組織就是從清楚的事實描述開始，經過邏輯的分析而形成清楚解釋的意見。很不幸的，許多商務人士在這方面並沒有足夠的訓練。在許多商業糾紛的場合，負責處理糾紛的人員常常不能夠對於相關事實清楚的描述，更不用找出可能的爭議以及提出可能解決的辦法。在這一點上，我不只是說客戶服務部門的資淺階層，也包括資深的管理階層。我希望這本書對於寫作、說話以及談判上有所需要的學生以及商務人士，能夠有所幫助。

目錄 contents

Chapter 1 Introduction 緒論

Focus 本章大綱

1.1 Introduction／本書介紹

1.2 Training on asking questions and exploring possible answers／提出問題與尋找答案的訓練

1.3 Training on giving an opinion／提出意見的訓練

1.1 Introduction

This book is a compilation of my teaching experiences in college during the past 10 years in Taiwan on speech, debate, negotiating and writing. From the experiences accumulated, it seems fair to say that the curriculums on these subjects are built in a pyramid diagram with skills of speech laid as the foundation, with debate in the middle, and finally, with negotiation placed at the top. Therefore, a good negotiator is no doubt able to master all skills on communication including those on speech and debate. A good negotiator is a good debater and a good debater is always a good speaker. It is not necessarily true in reverse order. Clearly, any learner of negotiating must start from the basic skills on speaking. Unfortunately, most training programs or books on building up strengths on negotiation have failed to see this. Many books adopted in colleges on negotiation are written from research viewpoints and mainly focus on analysis and discussion of theoretical perspectives, which might work well for researchers, but probably are inappropriate for beginners in terms of building up their practical ability, because they are not written from observations of the practical experiences and techniques applied within a business world.

1.1 本書介紹

這本書蒐集了我過去在大學教授演說、辯論、談判、寫作課程十年的教學經驗。從所累積的經驗而論，這三個科目是建立在一個金字塔的模型架構，以演說爲根基，中層則是辯論，而談判則是最上層的結構。因此，一個好的談判者，毫無疑問地可以精通各種溝通，包括演說、辯論的技巧。一個好的談判者是一個好的辯論者，一個好的辯論者也一定是一個好的演說者，反之則不一定是如此。很明顯的，任何學習談判的人必須先從演說的基本技巧開始學起。很遺憾，絕大部分關於談判的能力訓練課程或書籍並沒看到這一點。許多在大學裡面所使用的談判書籍，是從研究上的看法寫出的，主要是以學說角度進行分析與討論，對於研究人員很有幫助，但若是以培養初學者實際能力而言並不是很適合，因爲他們並不是從商業界的實際經驗角度和實用技巧來觀察。

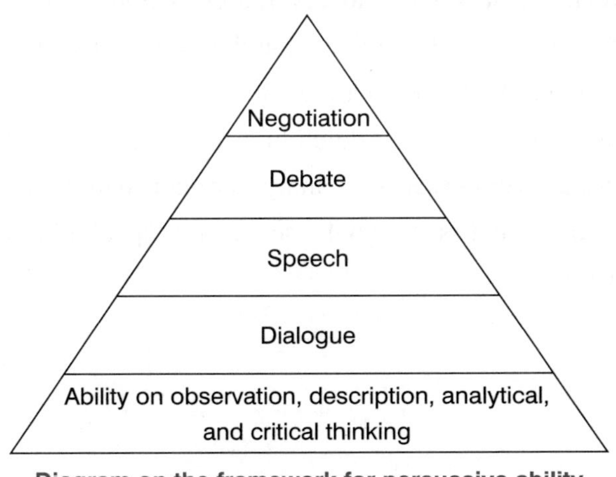

Diagram on the framework for persuasive ability

Knowledge is power as said by Sir Francis Bacon in 1597. Knowledge is gained by asking questions. If no question is asked, then there will never be any answer. Therefore, skepticism is the origin of knowledge. Skepticism is not limited to denial only but also includes doubt that is entertained in the mind. Once a question is asked, possible answers will be explored, proposed and examined. That is why a hypothesis should always be presented at the beginning of a research for exploration either in academic institutions or corporations. The gap between a question and a plausible answer might be bridged by an appropriate methodology, that is, logical reasoning, the so-called analysis. The reasoning process is subject to challenges covering both pros and cons, a type of confrontation and defense, a form of debate so to speak. This process is what we call critical thinking. Therefore, the purpose of advanced education, if aimed at problem solving, should train students to ask questions or, to be more precise, right questions. From the interaction between teachers and students in a classroom on the questions examined, with research conducted and possible answers explored, students may gradually learn a logical reasoning process piloted by teachers in establishing and defending their arguments. This book will discuss the very essence of analysis rather than on the debating technical rules. That is the goal I set for my speaking, debate and writing classes.

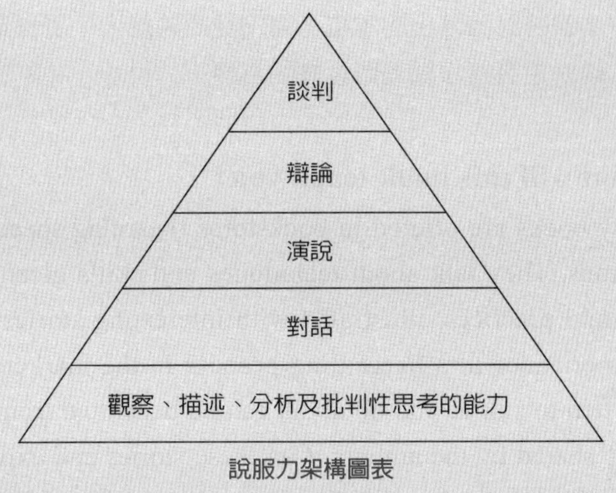

說服力架構圖表

「知識就是力量」英國的培根爵士在 1597 年如此說，知識是由所提問的問題當中而獲得。如果不問問題，那永遠不會有答案。因此，懷疑是一切知識的起源。懷疑主義並不限定在否定，他還包括心中的懷疑。當一個問題被問到的時候，可能的答案就會被探求、提出還有檢驗，這就是爲什麼在學術界或是公司裡面，一個假設應該在研究一開始的時候就被提出。而問題與可能的答案之間的鴻溝就是被適當的方法所連結起來，也就是邏輯論證的方式，所謂的分析。說理的過程是會被挑戰的包括正反的看法，因此挑戰是一種對抗與防禦，也就是辯論，這個過程我們稱它爲批判性思考。因此，高等教育的目的如果是在於解決問題，應該訓練學生提出問題，或是更精確一點說，提出正確的問題。透過老師與學生在課堂上的互動來檢驗研究問題，探尋可能的答案，學生們可能逐漸學習到由老師所領航邏輯性論證的過程來建立與防衛他們的說法辯詞。這一本書將討論分析的本質，而不是辯論規則。這也是我對我的演說、辯論還有寫作課程所設立的目標。

(1) What will this book teach you?

Many books are offered in bookstores regarding speeches and negotiations. They talk about techniques and skills gleaned from theories and practices, illustrated with interesting stories on personal experiences in a bargaining process in the market. People like to listen to stories and no doubt can be benefitted from the experiences shared by the authors. Can these stories and experiences help to build up negotiating skills required in business? To explore further, can these easy and fast learning skills really help those who have no ability in regard to speaking or analytical thinking?

(1) 這本書會教你什麼？

書店裡有許多關於演說跟談判的書籍，他們從許多學說與實驗中取得的技巧，搭配在市場上討價還價當中的個人經驗的有趣故事，喜歡聽故事的人當然可以從作者的經驗中學到很多，但這些故事跟個人經驗能夠幫忙建立在商場上所需要的談判技術嗎？更進一步地探討，這一些簡單與學習快速的方法能夠真正幫助那些不能夠開口說話也無法分析思考的學習者嗎？

If we view a good negotiator as the person who is able either to reach a good deal or to place himself/his team in a better position through communication, then we no doubt can say that a good negotiator should be a good communicator. In fact, a good negotiator should be someone who is more than a communicator. Why? Simply looking at any good sales person regardless of what products or services he is touting, he is certainly good at making ideal deals with his counterparts. He is not only good at expressing himself but should also know his subject matter, both strengths and weaknesses and possible issues that are involved. He should have done good research with an ability to analyze and evaluate the information gained in order to see the big picture and to know where he stands. To see a big picture and know where he stands, he must identify with his potential competitors in business and quickly evaluate both strengths and weaknesses on both sides. He knows the possible arguments to be presented by his counterparts and the rationale that stands behind those arguments. He could easily spot his opponent's weakness of an argument to his own advantage and, at the same time, to make a reasonable and strong argument for the position he takes and make a good defense on the weakness he has. He could thus increase his own bargaining power by exposing his opponent's weaknesses. Negotiators expect challenges and confrontations and therefore acquire a ability on attack and defense, that is, skills on debate. Without any training on debate, your strengths in negotiation will be weakened by an experienced opponent and your weaknesses be exposed and exaggerated. Simply speaking, a negotiator needs good skills on making arguments through analysis. He is more than a communicator.

如果我們認為一個好的談判者是可以透過溝通達成很好的交易，或是將他自己置於更有利的地位當中，那毫無疑問的我們可以說好的談判者就是一個好的溝通者，但事實上，好的談判者應該超越一個好的溝通者，為什麼呢？看一看那些優秀的銷售員，不論他賣的是什麼產品或是服務，他可以跟他的對手達成有利的交易，他不僅僅善於表達自己，而且明白他的主題、優點與缺點，還有可能的爭議點。他應該做好研究，以他的分析能力過濾所獲得的資訊來看到事情的全貌，知道他自己的立場，找出可能的競爭者，並且評斷雙方各有的優缺點。為了看到事情的全貌並且知道他自己所處的位置，他必須知道他的對手可能提出什麼樣的說法及為什麼會這麼說。他可以把對手的弱點變成自己的優點，並且同時宣揚自己的優點，為自己的缺點辯護。好的談判者可以透過找出對方的弱點而因此增加他的談判籌碼。談判者可以預見挑戰和對抗，因此需要攻擊防守能力，也就是辯論能力；沒有辯論的訓練，在談判中你的強項一定會被有經驗的對手削弱，而你的缺點也一定會被放大。簡單而言，一個談判者需要有很高明的技巧，透過分析進行辯論。他超越了一個溝通者的角色。

Some professional books, for example, the book *Negotiating* written by Philip O'Connor et al. and published by Longman of the fifth edition in 1998, which is based on research of the Harvard Negotiation Project, offers complete procedural training with emphasis on the practice of pattern sentences used in the hypothetical cases to help beginners get familiar with steps from relationship building to a conclusion of an agreement (i.e. relationship building, agreeing procedure, exchanging information, questioning, options, bidding, bargaining, and finally, settling and concluding). These steps offer excellent guide lines on the negotiating procedure for learners to follow. But the question here is what if the learners have some difficulty in expressing his ideas in a clear and persuasive manner in the beginning? What if he cannot make a good evaluation of the whole situation and pinpoint the issues, which are the essential qualities required of any shrewd businessman as mentioned in the preceding paragraph? Even if he does have these essential qualities, then how can he convince his counterpart to accept the message he delivers? Those books which offer guidelines on procedures obviously neglect the demand of new beginners needing to improve their thinking process and skills on expression and persuasion. In fact, few books offered on the market observe the fundamental training on the power of persuasion.

有一些專業書籍，例如：1998 年依據哈佛研究計畫 Philip O'Connor 等所撰寫出版的《談判》（*Negotiating*），提供了談判完整程序上的訓練，強調對於虛擬案例中慣用句型的練習，用來幫助初學者熟悉程序。從關係的建立一直到合約的簽訂（關係建立，談判程序確認，交換訊息，提問，方案選擇，出價，協商，合約簽訂）這些步驟提供了初學者在談判程序中絕佳的指導原則，但這裡的問題是，如果初學者在一開始就不能夠清楚而且帶有說服力的表達他的想法呢？或是他沒有辦法對整個的情況做好判斷來抓住爭議點，而這些能力都是精明的商人所必須具有的。就算他有了這些分析判斷能力，他又如何去說服他的對手接受這些訊息？那一些提供程序指導原則的書籍，很顯然的忽略對於初學者對思考訓練、表達技巧以及說服力能力提升的需求。事實上，目前市面上很少有書籍談到說服力的根本訓練。

What exactly is a negotiation and what skills are required of a negotiator? A negotiation is a persuading process to convince your counterpart to reach an agreement. It is communicating with a person whose interest might be different or often contrary to yours. It is unrealistic to expect a shrewd professional to be deceived by some trivial tricks to enter a deal unfavorable to his own interest in a zero sum game.

談判究竟是什麼？對於一個談判者他需要什麼樣的能力？談判是說服你的對手達成協議的一個過程，他可能是跟一個利益與你完全不同甚至相反的人的溝通。在一個零和遊戲當中，要和一個精明的專業人士達成一項對他非常不利的協議，是遠遠超過一些簡單技巧所能夠做的。

(2) The relation between abilities required on speech, debate and negotiation

The above diagram of a pyramid has best explained the relation between speech, debate and negotiation. It is not difficult to picture a negotiation, whether in a business or a political context, that the negotiator should communicate a free flow of expression of his ideas supported by a framework solidly built on effectively organized facts interpreted under logical analysis. Therefore, a good negotiator must be a good debater and a good debater must be a good speaker, although it may not necessarily be true in the reverse order (a good speaker is not necessarily a good debater and a good debater is not necessarily a good negotiator). Why so? In a speech, the speaker gives a speech to convince the listeners without any content being examined, while in a debate, the content will be examined by the opponent through questions asked. However, it is still the audience that both the speaker and debater will attempt to convince, and there is no difference on this point between a speech and a debate. There is no need for a debater to convince his opponent. In a negotiation, all skills mentioned above regarding the speech and debate are required of a negotiator except that the negotiator must convince his counterpart whose interest could be potentially contrary to the negotiator's, especially in a zero sum game. That is why negotiation is the supreme form of art in all communications.

(2) 演說、辯論和談判所需能力之間的關係

前述金字塔圖案已經對於演說、辯論還有談判的關係做了最好的解釋。我們並不難看到一個談判場合，不論是與商業或是政治有關，談判者需要非常流暢的表達他基於一個架構所支持的想法，而這個架構是由事實的有效組織，在邏輯分析下所做的詮釋上。因此，一個好的談判者必須是一個好的辯論者，一個好的辯論者必須是一個好的演說者，雖然反之並不必然（好的演說者並不必然是一

個好的辯論者，一個好的辯論者並不必然是一個好的談判者）。在一個演說中，演說者在演講企圖說服聽衆，而內容並不會被檢驗。但是在一個辯論中，內容會被對手透過質詢的方式檢驗，但是演說者和辯論者都是企圖要說服聽衆，在這一點上演說和辯論兩者是沒差別的。辯論中辯論者不須說服對方。在一個談判中，談判者除了需要具備演說和辯論的能力，談判者更必須說服他的對手，而他的對手的利益可能跟談判者完全相反，特別在一個零和遊戲當中。這就是爲什麼談判是溝通的最高境界。

In negotiating where both interests are involved, confrontation cannot be avoided. When a confrontation arises, debating skills are required. This is because demolishing an argument of your opponent can weaken your opponent's bargaining power and thus increase yours. Therefore, a weaker party in negotiating, especially, needs training in debate. However, in a negotiation, both sides are looking to reach an agreement through discussion. This changes the whole scenario for debating. Since an agreement is desired, a compromise is necessary. Confrontation and compromise are the essential differences between debate and negotiation. A compromise connotes an idea to yield to an opponent's needs to a certain extent. When yielding is necessary, a decision based on a full analysis of weaknesses and strengths of both sides in light of the situation as a whole must be conducted, and this is the essential training in a debate class. Many popular books written by some famous authors on negotiation fail to see this difference and have difficulty in drawing a distinction between debate, negotiation and communication.

在雙方利益都牽涉其中的談判場合，對立是免不了的。當對立發生的時候我們就需要辯論的能力。這是因爲打敗對方的論點可以削弱他談判的籌碼，因而增加我們自己的籌碼。因此，在談判中較弱的一方特別需要別人的訓練。但是在談判中雙方需要透過討論達成一個協議，那這就改變了整個的情況而與辯論不相同。既然雙方想要達成協議，妥協就是必須的。對立和妥協主宰了辯論與談判的不同。一個妥協指出了對於對手的需要進行某種讓步的概念。當需要進行讓步的時候，一個基於整體環境考量，對於雙方優缺點的完整分析的進行，是辯論訓練中最基本的要求。許多有名的談判暢銷書作家沒有了解到這些差異，而在辯論、談判以及溝通上的區別有很大的困難。

Many books on negotiation observe an agenda and procedure commonly practiced in the western world. They are very helpful to any who are already fluent in utterance and well equipped with abilities on fact organizing, issues spotting, as well as, reasoning with a deep perception regarding arguments from both sides (e.g. strengths and weaknesses on mutual positions) as well as some experiences regarding the use of tricks. But not much help can such training be given to beginners who have no aforementioned basic skills.

許多談判的書籍著重於西方人經常使用的議程還有程序，他們對於那些已經善於表達、具有組織事實能力、抓住爭議點、有論述能力，以及能對雙方論點（兩邊優缺點）深入了解，甚至有些玩弄技巧經驗的人會有幫助。但是這一類的訓練，對於那些不具有前述能力的初學者，是沒有多大的助益。

This book is going to offer some basic training to build up the learners' persuasion power on speech through interpretation of facts and to argue through reasoning in a cause and effect structure, by which a counter argument can be thoroughly examined. These essential skills are required of all managers who have to make a sound business judgment within their responsibilities and therefore must be familiarized by any student who aspires to be a good negotiator in the future. Fair to say, these qualifications are also highly demanded of any business person.

本書會提供初學者基本訓練，透過對於事實的詮釋，還有使用因果架構建立論點，並且用以檢查對方論點來提升他們的說服力。這些基礎能力是所有要做正確商業判斷的經理人必須具備的條件，因此也是對於任何想要在未來成爲優秀談判者的學生必須熟悉與需具備的能力。持平而論，這些特質在任何商人身上也都是極其需要的。

The first problem faced by our college students on the training of power of persuasion is that they seldom ask questions. If no question is asked, then no possible answer will be explored. This is a process of critical thinking. Unfortunately, our high school education aims at helping students to cram knowledge and information into their brain to prepare for their college entrance exam. Therefore, the first lesson requires the students to appreciate the difference in their educational goal between that of college and that of high school.

在訓練大學生說服力首先碰到的問題是，他們很少提問。如果不提問那就不會去尋找可能的答案，這也就是一個批判性思考的過程。很不幸的，我們的高中教育最主要在以填鴨教育的方式幫助學生準備大學入學考試。因此，第一件的功課就是要學生能夠了解大學教育與高中教育目的的不同。

1.2 Training on asking questions and exploring possible answers

(1) Differences between the educational purposes of high schools and colleges

Low wages and high unemployment rates among newly college graduates in Taiwan have become a hot topic for discussion on this island in the past seven years. Many have raised doubt on the value of a college degree for the payoff seems far less than what is expected, especially in light of huge student loans approximating to NTD $400,000 for each one owed by the great majority at the time of their graduation, and a college degree is no longer a guarantee for a lucrative job, probably not even a stable one. It is interesting to note that, on the one side, many graduates cannot find jobs well above NTD$ 25,000 a month and, on the other hand, enterprises constantly complain that there is not enough labor in the market to meet their needs. A container should hold water. A winter coat should keep us warm. A car should run. Detergent should wash our clothes clean. Any merchandise we buy should reflect the value that we are paying for it and the value is decided by the function we are expecting from the item we purchase. It seems that what is produced in school is not what the business world is looking for. Such a shortage of qualified labor thus raises a question, what is the purpose of our college education? What kind of students are we expecting to make?

1.2 提出問題與尋找答案的訓練

(1) 大學教育與高中教育目的的差異

在過去七年的時間，大學生的低薪以及高失業率，已經成為臺灣的熱門話題。大家對於大學學歷的價值產生了懷疑，在考慮到每一個人畢業的時候學貸有高達四十萬臺幣，而他們的收入卻遠低於他們的期待，大學學歷已經不再是一個收入優渥的保證，甚至工作還不能穩定。一個有趣的現象是，一方面，很多畢業生不能找到一個月超過兩萬五千塊錢的月薪，另一方面，企業界不停地抱怨市場上沒有適合的勞力來滿足他們的要求。一個水桶要能裝水，一件大衣要能在冬天保溫，一輛車應該跑得動，洗衣精也要能夠把衣服洗乾淨，我們所買的任何商品，都應該反映出我們所付出的價值，而這個價值是由這件物品是否具備我們所期待的功能來決定。看起來學校所生產的並不是企業界所需要的，對於合格人力的欠缺產生了一個問題，什麼是我們大學教育的目的？我們期待教育出什麼樣的學生？

In Taiwan, instruction by teachers in a classroom is prevalent in the great majority of high schools. Students in classrooms are taking notes and seldom asking questions. Generally, in the whole learning process, only the teachers' voice is heard with little few students participating in any discussion. Students are crammed with knowledge and information from books and subsequently are required to give standard answers in any exam they take. Once they are in college, most of them still follow the same practice, fed with information from the book and instructed to memorize all. Four years of such training in college make them good followers and few know how to ask questions, not to mention seek solutions to problems encountered. No doubt, the ability to solve problems encountered in our future lives is the most important task for our survival or even success.

在臺灣，絕大部分的中學都是採用老師講授的方式，學生在教室裡做筆記，很少做任何發問，通常在這樣的學習過程只聽得見老師的聲音，很少有學生參與討論。學生們從書本上學習到填鴨式的知識，接著在他們所參加的考試上面填上標準答案，一旦進了大學，絕大部分的人還是遵循著相同的學習方式，被灌輸著書本上的知識以及被要求牢記知識。四年大學訓練，使絕大部分的學生變成好的跟隨者，很少人知道如何發問，更不要說對於所碰到的問題找到解決的辦法。我們可以毫無疑問地聲稱，解決我們未來生活上所遭遇的問題是最重要的工作，關係著我們的未來生存甚至成功。

Logically, before any person can solve a problem, he must be aware of the existence of the problem. If you don't see a problem, you will never find an answer. If we don't see as a problem what Marco Polo has experienced (that is, to spend two years of travel by walking from Europe to Asia) as time consuming and tiring, airplane and cars would never have been invented and produced. Once a problem is recognized and identified through observation, then possible theories or even solutions can be proposed, examined and probably established by an application of sound methodology. In other words, the ability to solve problems seems to be what distinguishes college education from that of high schools. They need to have their own opinion. Unfortunately, both systems follow the same practice. Therefore, there is very little difference on the performance between college graduates and high school graduates in terms of problem solving.

邏輯上來說，在一個人解決問題之前他必須了解問題的存在，如果你看不見問題，那你永遠找不到答案。如果我們不把馬可波羅當年花了這麼多的時間和精力從歐洲旅行到亞洲來當成一個問題的話，我們永遠不會有飛機和汽車。當我們透過觀察而找到並且確認一個問題的時候，我們就可以透過使用健全的方法來提出檢驗甚至建立可能的學說或是方案，也就是說，解決問題能力的培養是區分大學教育以及高中教育重要的分野，他們應該有自己的意見。很遺憾的，兩個制度都使用相同的教育方式，因此在解決問題上，大學畢業生跟高中畢業生幾乎沒什麼差別。

Currently, our college students are still following their practice learned from high schools. They sit silently in the classroom. Still only the teachers' monotonous voice is heard with no participation by students in class discussion. No thinking process can be observed on the students' learning. Their performances again are evaluated in the tests based on how much information is crammed into them and memorized. Under such system, few students can be equipped with skills on tackling problems they will be confronted with in the future. They rely only on instructions. Fair to say, most are only good followers with no ability to even identify a problem.

現在我們的大學生依然按照著高中的方式在學習，他們沉默地坐在教室裡面，我們只聽到老師單調的聲音而看不見學生參與討論，我們看不到學生們在學習當中所表現出來的思考過程，他們的程度依舊是按照他們可以從書本上背誦了多少知識來決定。在這樣的制度下，很少學生能夠學習到在未來應付問題的能力，他們只是依賴著老師的指令，他們只是好的跟隨者，沒有能力來確認一個問題。

College education in fact has far exceeding amounts of information crammed into students to memorize with the potential of this information and knowledge becoming antiquated as time goes by while the power to solve problems is not. The aforementioned teaching style is seriously flawed because our students are made only as followers who cannot solve problems. They cannot solve problems because they cannot identify issues. Issues cannot be identified because they are never asked to observe, to think, to analyze, to consider all other possibilities supported by pros and cons. They can only be crammed with information well prepared by teachers and are asked to memorize all knowledge and information that could be quickly outdated.

大學教育事實上遠遠超過對於知識的背誦，因為這一些知識和資訊會隨著時間過去而變得陳舊不堪，但是解決問題的能力卻不會。前述學習的方式也是很大的問題，因為它使學生變成跟隨者而沒辦法解決問題。他們不能解決問題因為找不到爭議點，找不出爭議點是因為他們從來不被要求觀察、思考、分析與考慮正反兩方的各種可能性。他們只是填鴨式地記憶書本上所有的知識，而這些知識很快地會隨時間過去而變得不堪使用。

The mentality as a follower remains the same once these students graduate from college and start their career in a business world. They expect that instructions given from their supervisors can be clear enough on every step so that they can act accordingly without using their brains. As a result, when they encounter problems in their work and are demanded to find solutions, they have difficulty in dealing with both their supervisor and customer in expressing themselves either in speaking or writing. They go to libraries or book stores expecting to find a divine book that can help to solve their problem as quickly as possible. In reality, this is not possible. What you speak or write is from what you think. What you think is from your observation and analysis. Therefore, when you cannot speak or write, you have to examine which part of this process went wrong, that is, your observation, analysis or expression. Very few popular books in the current market try to explore this field. That is why many learners who read those books still do not have any perception of their own problem because they still remain as followers in their mentality.

當這些學生從大學畢業，開始工作的時候依然保存著一個跟隨者的心態。他們期待來自於主管的指令在每個步驟上是清楚的，然後他們照做即可而不需要使用他們自己的頭腦。當他們在工作上碰到問題並且被要求尋找出答案的時候，他們對於主管與客戶，在說和寫的表達上就會發生困難。他們到圖書館或者書店希望找到一本神奇的書可以盡快一次解決他們的問題。實際上，這是不可能的事情。你所說的或所寫的，是從你腦子裡面出來的。而頭腦裡的東西則是來自於你的觀察和你自己的分析。因此當你沒有辦法說或寫的時候，你必須檢查這個過程在什麼地方出了問題，是在觀察、分析還是在表達上。現在市場上的暢銷書很少在這一方面進行探討。這就是爲什麼這麼多初學者看過那些暢銷書之後，依然對於自己的問題缺乏了解，因爲他們依然保持跟隨者的心態。

Therefore, college education in Taiwan which has serious concerns with their capability in future careers, in my opinion, should make a revolutionary change by giving students more opportunity to observe and think critically, followed by practice in the real business world. During their practice, each actual confrontation will demand solutions from the students. In their process of searching for a solution, students will learn how to examine the facts in the real situation, spotting issues with a thorough analysis on pros and cons and, hopefully, arriving at an answer that is more strongly built. They will be tested hard. Once such thinking process is established, students will be much better prepared confidently to face challenges encountered in their future career.

因此，與他們未來就業職場專業能力密切相關的大學教育，我認爲應該有個革命性的變革，透過給學生觀察，和進行批判性思考的機會，然後將這些學習應用在商業世界裡面。在這種練習當中，從眞實世界來的挑戰會要求學生們解決實際的問題。在尋找答案的同時，學生們會學習在眞實的場合如何檢驗事實，透過正反兩方的完整分析找到爭議點，然後我們希望找到更爲堅強的答案，他們會被更嚴格的考驗。當這樣的思考過程被建立起來的時候，學生們對於未來工作上的挑戰，他們會更有自信的從容面對。

(2) To judge a tree from its fruits

Interpretation subsequent to facts will give a message leading to a conclusion.

(2) 由果實來判斷樹的好壞

事實加上詮釋就會產生訊息和結論。

Partial facts, if interpreted illogically, could create an unreasonable message, consequently an absurd conclusion.

部分的事實，加上扭曲的詮釋，產生的訊息自然也是荒誕不經，結論尤其荒唐。

Critical thinking demands that facts, if given, must be relevant, full and complete. A partial fact is only half a truth and therefore a lie.

批判性思考要求的就是，要談事實，就得是全部相關的重要事實，部分的事實只是部分的眞相也就是謊言。

The reasoning process must be logical, attending to the cause and effect sequence. A conclusion made under such process carries the value for reference.

論證的方式必須是邏輯、講究因果關係，這樣所得的結論才有參考的價值。

What terrifies us is that many people who receive a high education, regardless their age, still make judgments according to their emotions and ideologies.

可怕的是，許多接受過高等教育的人，不問年紀，仍用情緒、意識型態做決定。

They already make a conclusion in their minds according to their emotions and ideologies and then they search for the facts and reasoning process necessary to reach that conclusion.

他們先依情緒和意識型態決定了結論之後，再尋找一些適合他們結論的事實和相關的論理過程。

More than that, they are peddling their emotions in the name of logical thinking.

不但如此，更驚人與不可置信的是，他們在所謂的理性思考名義下，販售他們的情緒。

Emotions, especially negative personal emotions, carries no value at all. It is even a liability and a deficit. These liars intend to shift their debt to their followers.

情緒，特別是個人的負面情緒毫無價值！甚至是一種負債。這些說謊者，企圖把他們的負債移轉到他們的追隨者身上！

If no one accepts their peddling, they will further twist the facts and reasoning in order to succeed in their sale.

如果賣不動，販賣者不惜在事實和論理上更進一步動手腳，爲了達到銷售的目的。

The revolutions in Russia and China, rising of the Nazis, wars in Korea, Vietnam, and the Middle East, including the recent conflict between India and Pakistan, are all of same nature encouraging hatred and revenge, even brothers kill brothers.

俄國的革命、納粹的崛起、中國的共產革命、韓戰、越戰、中東戰爭，以及最近的印巴衝突，都是鼓勵仇恨和報復，甚至是自家人互相殘殺。

How to judge then?

如此怎麼判斷？

The Bible says, good trees bear no bad fruit and bad trees bear no good fruit. By the fruit, one can tell if the tree is good or not.

聖經上說，好樹不結壞果子，壞樹也不會結好的果子，樹的好壞從它所結的果子就可知道。

Those who encourage to tell lies and to engage in quarrels, division, hatred and killing for revenge are so called bad fruits. Good fruits are honesty, virtue, patience, love your neighbor as the Bible tells us.

那些鼓勵你說謊、紛爭、分裂、仇恨、流他人血的就是壞的果子，好的果實是善良、誠實、忍耐、愛人如己，如聖經上所述。

Therefore, young people, be alert to those tricky sales talks and make your own judgement according to the fruits they are peddling. Great loss shall come upon you if you trust in their legend which, in reality, is a tree replete of poisonous fruits.

所以，年輕人，注意那些販售的話術，從結果去判斷！否則神話說一堆，卻是充滿毒果的壞樹，得不償失。

(3) Important notes

1. Many students are expecting to expedite the process of learning and that, hopefully, one divine book can improve their speech, debate and writing skill within a short period of time. Such expectation is quite unrealistic because there is no such immediate one stop-shop for all you need. All distinguished athletes in the arena have their strict training for quite a few years under good instructors. Merely good instructions will not help you become a good swimmer. Persistent practice is necessary. This book can offer you a new perspective on learning, mainly from the angle of problem solving. To solve problems requires good observation, followed by spotting problems, analyzing the issues as well as the background information, thus resulting in the proposal of a solution. All these are founded on logical thinking. Training on observation

and analysis through logical thinking requires persistent practice as necessary as any good athlete will do over a period of years in their training field. Therefore, users of this book should not hold unrealistic expectations that skillful mastery of speech, debate and writing can be procured without any long term practice.

2 A problem on expression

If English is your second language and your expression in English is not fluent enough, the first problem to be clarified here is to find out if the difficulty on expression is raised from your language barrier or your thinking process. The rule of thumb for evaluation by a teacher is to ask students to express his thought in his native language (e.g. mandarin). If his thought cannot be made clear in his own mother tongue, a teacher should know that the student's problem is probably on his thinking process rather than his English proficiency. Therefore, the first task at this stage for a trainer is to understand the nature of a problem and then subsequently train a student to express his thought in a logical process with a clear utterance in his native language instead of merely forcing his expression in a language that he is not familiar with.

(3) 重要訊息

1 很多學生，期待加速他們的學習過程，希望有一本神書可以在很短的時間內改進他們演說、辯論以及寫作的技巧。這樣的期待有些不切實際，因為沒有這樣的東西可以一次滿足你全部的需要。

在運動場上，所有出色的運動員，都必須接受優良教練長達幾年的訓練。僅僅只有好的教導是沒有辦法讓你成為一個優秀的游泳選手。持之以恆的練習是必須的。這一本書可以提供給你在學習上一些新的看法，主要是從解決問題的角度來看事情。解決問題必須要有好的觀察，接著是找出問題，分析爭議，最後才是解決方案的提出。所有的這些都源自於邏輯思考。觀察和透過邏輯思維分析上的訓練，須要持之以恆的練習，就像那些優秀運動員在運動場上經年累月的訓練是一樣的。因此，這本書的使用者不應該有一個不切實際的期待，認為不需要長時間的練習，就能夠熟悉於演說、辯論、寫作及將來談判上技巧的使用。

2 一個表達上的問題

如果英文是你的第二外語，當你用英文表達不流暢的時候，應該要釐清的第一個問題的是，這究竟是英文流利上的問題，還是你思考上的問題。對於老師而言，簡單判斷的標準就是要求學生以母語（例如中文）表達他的想法，如果學生使用母語依然不能夠把想法表達清楚，這個老師就應該知道學生的問題可能是在於他的思考層面而不是他的英文流暢度。因此對一個訓練者，在這個階段工作就是要了解問題的本質，接著訓練學生使用母語，以邏輯的過程與清楚的表達展現出他的想法，而不是只單單要求學生使用一個他不熟悉的語言進行表達。

(4) Questions

Try to describe in your own words what you have visualized from a speech, a debate and a negotiation. Can you describe the key features for each occasion (e.g. What is the background? What topic or issues are they talking about? What people do you see? What are they doing? What are their purpose? How are they interacting with each other?) Share your experience in some real cases.

Speech, debate and negotiation are all forms of communication. The term communication generally denotes the idea of expressing and exchanging either opinions or information. Are they only seeking exchange of either opinions or information? If more than that, what does a speaker, a debater or a negotiator hope to achieve? How do you define a successful speech, a debate or negotiation? What are the skills required of a successful speaker, a debater or a negotiator? What is the common denominator among all three? What are their differences? Which requires more difficult skills and training? Why so?

(4) 問題

請試圖以你自己的話描述一下，你在演說、辯論還有談判看到了什麼，你可以描述每一個場合所看到的角色嗎？（例如：什麼背景，他們在討論什麼樣的主題或是爭議點？你看到哪些人？他們在做什麼？他們的目的是什麼？他們彼此如何互動？）分享一下你在實際場合的經驗。

演說、辯論和談判都是溝通。溝通這個字就表示表達或交換意見，或者是資訊，但是他們僅僅只是交換意見和資訊嗎？如果不只的話，那一個演說者、辯論者，他們希望達到什麼目的？你如何定義一個成功的演說、辯論或談判？一個成功的演說者、辯論者或談判者，需要什麼樣的技能？這三者有相同的部分嗎？他們又有什麼不同呢？哪一些比較困難？爲什麼會如此？

1.3 Training on giving an opinion

(1) The importance of having an opinion

Many oriental students tend to be reserved and prefer to stay quiet in their classrooms. They don't talk much. When asked in public to express their opinions on certain issues, they have little to say, generally only a few words (e.g. yes or no) with giggling. In the case where their English is not fluent, they really seem slow in responding, and thus, give an appearance of having low intelligence. Such a first impression, if created, could seriously tarnish their image in a classroom. However, merely talking in public will not necessarily win any substantial support from others unless the opinion shows some value (e.g. correct spotting of issues using good analysis). Therefore, in a classroom, students need to be trained to talk in public to deliver good opinions. The very same can be applied to a business occasion. A business person who is slow in response or lack of ability to bring forth good reasoning in support of an opinion is not able to persuade and therefore is likely to be regarded as incompetent.

To give a good opinion is important not only in a classroom but also in any working environment. An opinion is referring to a judgment formed subsequently to the evaluation of the information received including facts observed. In an office, an employee who has no opinion on certain issues appears as if he cannot make any judgment, possibly creating an image that he is not capable of managing the assigned work. Similarly, failure to object to a client's unreasonable complaint may signal a complete surrender to the client's request in a negotiation. Fair to say, a good opinion or a judgment shows a person's merit. Silence or a reserved expression could cast doubt on a person's ability.

1.3 提出意見的訓練

(1) 意見的重要性

許多東方學生在課堂中習慣保持沉默，他們很少說話。在當衆詢問他們對於問題是否有意見的時候，他們說得很少，通常只有簡短的幾個字（例如：是或不是），接著傻笑。如果他們的英文不夠流利的話，他們眞的看起來反應非常遲鈍，也因此看似智商不高。如此的第一印象如果形成的話，會很嚴重拖累他們在班上的形象。但是能夠面對群衆說話，並不代表你可以贏得支持，除非你的意見能夠展現出一定的價值（例如：正確地找到爭議點與進行分析），所以在課堂上學生們應該被訓練表達好的意見。在商業場合也是相同的情況。一個商人如果反應遲鈍或者欠缺說出好的理由來支持他的意見的能力，是沒有辦法進行說服，也很容易被認爲是欠缺能力的。

表達好的意見在課堂以及在工作場合都很重要，所謂的意見就是對於資訊包括所觀察的事實，經過分析而下的判斷。在辦公室裡面，一個員工對於一些議題不表達意見，表示他沒有能力做一個判斷，可能導致出他無法勝任所交付的工作這樣的形象。同樣的，對於客戶不合理的抱怨不能提出反對的意見，那只能任由對方予取予求。所以我們可以很公平的說，好的意見或判斷，表示一個人的價值。沉默或是保留，可能會對一個人的能力產生懷疑。

(2) How an opinion is formed and challenged

To reach an opinion on certain issues, one must take a position. Without a position taken, an opinion will not be formed and, simply speaking, there will be no conclusion. It is only a process of information sharing. For the purpose of this book on training on the power of persuasion in speech, debate and writing, students are urged to take a position in their opinion. To have an opinion is therefore of the first importance in the training of persuasion.

(2) 意見如何形成與被挑戰

在一些議題上面要形成一個意見，那就必須要提到立場。沒有立場也就沒有意見。簡單來說，如果沒有結論，那整個過程就只是分享訊息而已。本書的目的在訓練說服力，所以學生在演說辯論或是寫作上必須要有結論，要有立場。表達意見是訓練說服力最重要的工作。

Everyone can have an opinion. Even a fool can talk. Complaint is a typical form of an opinion given and is made when we feel unfairly treated as we sometimes experience in our community, shops, restaurants, work places or government branches. If no complaint is made when a protest is necessary, our silence will generally be interpreted as an acceptance of such unfairness and, as unfairness continues, our grievances will most likely continue into the future. Besides, if no complaint is made now, why should it be made later? When time is of essence in many cases requiring protests, silence could result in a serious consequence in a business world (e.g. legal right forfeited or bad image created).

每個人都可以有意見，即使傻子也能說話。抱怨是非常典型的意見型態，通常在我們覺得不被公平對待的時候所產生的，例如：在社區、商店、餐廳、工作場合或是政府部門所經驗到的一些事情。如果在該抱怨的時候不抱怨，我們的沉默往往會被當作接受這些不公平的事情，而當不公平的事情繼續時，抱怨的情緒會延伸到未來。此外，如果你現在不抱怨，那爲什麼以後還要再抱怨呢？在許多具有急迫、時間性的案件當中，保持沉默往往會在商業界導致很嚴重的後果（例如：法律上權利的喪失，或是不好的形象因而形成）。

When we make a complaint, reasons are necessary. The better the reasons are given, the stronger a case is built. However, merely a loud protest without any good reason is not enough, which in most cases, is like a mad dog barking, consequently creating only a bad image. No one will take a complaint seriously unless it is supported with good reasons. Therefore, opinions, in order to be convincing, must be supported with good reasons.

當我們進行抱怨的時候，必須要有理由，理由愈好我們就愈有立場，否則僅靠大聲且無理取鬧，只是像一隻瘋狗在狂叫，造成負面的形象而已。沒有人會把抱怨當一回事，除非這個抱怨有很好的理由，所以一個意見要讓人能被說服，必須要有好的理由。

Opinion means a judgment is rendered on certain issues raised from a set of facts or information. If there is no opinion, there won't be a position held and no work of persuasion can be engaged. Opinion is therefore delivered with either a yes or no as a conclusion is supported with a reasoning process and is the first step in the work of persuasion. As we have explained, the goal of a speech, debate and negotiation is aimed at persuasion. To form an opinion is therefore the first task of priority in training the many Taiwanese students who, in many cases, are used to the instruction approach from their high school education. They must learn to voice their opinion publicly, starting from this classroom.

意見就是對於一些由一組事實或資訊當中所產生的爭議所做的判斷。如果沒有意見，那就表示沒有立場，也就不會有任何說服的進行。意見的表達以是或否作爲一個結論，而這個結論，是由說理的過程來支持，而且是說服工作的第一步。如同我們所解釋的，演說、辯論和談判的目的都在說服。在訓練已經習慣於高中單純由老師講授課程的教學方式的臺灣學生，形成意見是最重要的工作，他們必須從這個教室開始學習公開的表達他們的意見。

The power of an opinion is decided by the strength of the reasons given. A complaint made to an airline about their service on luggage handling should be stated with good reasons, probably with photos provided. The same procedure is applied to a complaint to a government agency or even to a court. Generally, the merit of the case depends on the strength of the reasons. The strength of the reasons is centered on the crucial point of a dispute. A crucial point can only be spotted in light of sufficiency of the relevant verified facts organized in a logical cause and effect sequence. Persons who have a complaint, if possible, should state a brief description with a simple explanation on what damage has been caused and explain by the 6 W's why the airline should take the responsibility (e.g. what, when, where, who, how and why). Photos used as evidence are always helpful. Reliable facts explained with good reasons will expedite the claim for compensation and probably will earn you respect as well. A bad complaint written with only an emotional expression will be dubbed as unreasonable, outrageous and rude and probably will be consequently ignored.

意見的力量是由後面原因的強度來決定。一個對航空公司關於行李托運方面的抱怨，應該要提出好的理由甚至提供相片。對政府部門甚至對法院提出的書狀都應該使用相同的方法。通常一個案件的價值取決於理由的強度，而理由的強度則在於對爭議事件要害之點的掌握。而要害之點只有在經過足夠確認相關的事實之下，依邏輯方式進行因果關係的組合之後才能發現。抱怨的提出應該先精簡陳述，述明簡單的理由，說明是什麼損害，而且按照 6W 的方式解釋爲什麼另外一方需要承擔責任（發生了什麼事、何時、何地，是誰、如何發生、爲什麼發生）。提供相片當作證據總是有幫助。值得信賴的事實附上好的理由會加速與加強賠償的請求，而且也可能贏得尊敬。一份糟糕的抱怨信充滿著情緒字眼，會被冠上不合理、過分、粗魯的稱號，最後可能無疾而終。

However, one serious problem here should be mentioned and avoided. Many students are used to starting their speech and writing with "in my opinion". As noted earlier, an opinion is referring to a judgment formed subsequently to the evaluation of the information received or facts observed. Since an opinion by its very nature is an evaluation and judgment, the foundation, that is, the fact and information, on which a judgment is made, should be mentioned at first so that people will be able to know what facts or information you are evaluating. When you start your statement with "in my opinion" at the beginning without referring to the information or facts evaluated, people feel puzzled unless they already have some prior knowledge on the subject discussed. Therefore, logically, the term "in my opinion" should be avoided at the beginning, but used subsequently to the introduction of information or facts to be evaluated.

然而，有一個嚴重的問題這裡應該提一下而且避免。許多的學生習慣以「我認爲」當作他們演說或是寫作的開場白。就像前面所提到的，一個意見就是對於所收到的資訊或是所觀察到的事實所下的一個判斷。由於意見本質上就是一個評價與判斷，而這個評斷的基礎，也就是事實與資訊，應該在一開始先說明，這樣其他的人才知道你在評斷什麼樣的事實與資訊。當你以「我認爲」當作開場白，而沒有先提到你所判斷的資訊或事實的時候，人們會感到困惑，除非他們事前已經了解這個主題。因此「我認爲」這個字眼，邏輯上應在一開始的時候先避免，並在介紹完受評斷資訊與事實之後再使用。

(3) Cultural consideration on opinion forming

Our college students are not used to sharing their opinions in classrooms. They tend to stay quiet. Why do oriental students tend to stay silent in classrooms and remain so in their work place at a later time? Culture does matter on this issue. In a typical oriental classroom, instruction is still prevalent and students are required to take notes with few questions asked. The teachers seem to be the only actors in a classroom. The learning process involves little discussion and is rather passive. Students receive information from their teachers which, most likely, result in following their teachers' opinion. If we agree that an opinion is a judgment of information received, then stating a sound opinion requires consideration on both pros and cons in an issue, using a further defensive position as well as challenging another's opinion. This is a form of confrontation resulting from a doubting mind, so to speak. To confront especially an established system (e.g. authority) with doubt (which is the very essence of the western culture and the root of the theory "check and balance" leading to separation of powers) is not a part of the oriental culture. That is to say, to help students to establish their own opinion is to encourage them to raise doubts probably followed closely after their subsequent challenge of authority. It is therefore not acceptable by many in a society who collectively view obedience, harmony and respect as virtues.

(3) 意見形成上的文化考量

我們大學生不習慣在課堂上表達自己的意見，他們不說話。為什麼東方學生習慣在課堂上如此？而且在他們未來的工作場合上也是如此。文化是有影響的，在典型的東方教室裡，主要還是老師在說，學生在聽，不會問問題。老師是課堂上唯一的主角。這樣的學習過程很少討論，而且很被動。如果我們同意意見是對於資訊所做的判斷，那一個好的意見必須要考慮到在一個爭議點上的正反，進而要防衛自己的論點，以及挑戰別人的論點。這種對抗來自於懷疑的態度，對抗一個現有的制度，例如權威，是西方文化的基本精神，而且是權力制衡的根本，進而發展出三權分立，而這本身不是東方文化的一環。也就是說幫助學生建立他們自己的意見，也需要鼓勵他們表達懷疑，隨後就是挑戰權威。這種方式在將服從、和諧以及尊敬權威當作美德的集體主義社會，不容易被接受。

Simply speaking, to ask a student to give his opinion is to ask him to form his own thinking. When a disagreement arises in situations where persuasion is necessary, he must know how this disagreement occurred, that is, he must know what questions to ask. To ask questions, he must have some doubt in his mind. For the reasons stated above, a teacher must ask students to raise doubt in form of questions. That is why forming an opinion is the first task in a classroom that is learning persuasion. Students must remember by heart that a good opinion is an important proof of their own merit.

簡單而言，要求學生表達意見，就是要求他們要有自己的想法。在遇到有不同想法的場合需要進行說服的時候，他必須知道這些不同想法是如何發生的，也就是知道如何提問。他們必須知道如何去問問題。要求他們問問題，他們心中必須產生懷疑。基於上述原因，老師必須要求學生，以提出問題的方式表達他們的懷疑。這也就是爲什麼學生們首先必須要先有意見才能學習說服。學生們必須牢記，好的意見是你本身價值的重要證據。

Many issues in our family, school and society are appropriate topics for the training of establishing students' opinions, ranging from choices of a college to go to, school uniforms, corporate punishment for abortion, capital punishment and homosexual marriages. Public opinions can form a policy leading to a future change of law. If no new opinion is given, there will be no change in the future. College students should be exposed to such training prior to their entry into society.

在家庭、學校和社會有很多的議題是很適合討論的主題，比方說應該去念哪間大學？學校是否應該穿制服？學校可否准許體罰？一直到墮胎、死刑的存廢以及同性婚姻的問題。公共意見可以形成一個政策，導致將來法律的改變。如果沒有新的意見，那在未來就不會有改變。大學生應該在他們進入社會之前，接受這樣的訓練。

Chapter

2

Training on conversation

對話的訓練

◀◀◀ Focus 本章大綱

2.1 Importance of a conversation／對話的重要性

2.2 How to keep a conversation moving?／如何使對話進行？

2.3 Elements of conversation／對話的要件

2.4 Factors affecting a conversation／影響對話的因素

2.5 Other notes added for conversation training／關於對話訓練的其他要點

2.1 Importance of a conversation

As mentioned earlier, speaking power is a foundation to build abilities on debate and negotiation. A person who has difficulty on conversation probably cannot do well on speech either. Conversation is an interaction regarding the stating of a fact or an opinion by a speaker and a reaction from a listener with answers or questions. Interaction in a good conversation is pleasant and friendly and continuously free flowing.

My teaching experience shows that a learner who can do well in speech generally has no problem with conversing with others. In the negotiating class, the first lesson starts with relationship building. Having a good conversational ability is surely beneficial to relationship building. Try to imagine you are in a limousine with an important foreign customer whom you just picked up in an airport and it will take approximately an hour and a half to arrive at your company. How do you feel if you both do not talk and stay silent all the way until you both arrive at the conference room?

2.1 對話的重要性

在前面曾經說過演說的能力是辯論以及談判能力的基礎。一個在對話上有困難的人可能對於演說也很難駕馭。對話是一種互動，由說話者陳述一個事實或是意見，而聽話者以回答或是追問的方式進行反應。好的對話互動是愉快以及友善的，而且不斷持續的在進行。

我的教學經驗顯示出一個初學者如果能夠做好演說的話，通常在他與別人的對話能力上是沒有問題的。在談判課程中第一堂課就是從建立良好關係開始的。好的對話能力當然對於建立良好關係是很有幫助的。想像一下你剛剛在機場接機，一個很重要的外國客人，你跟他在一輛車子裡，需要一個半小時的路程到達公司，如果你們兩個在車上一路都不說話，保持沉默一直到會議室爲止，你的感覺如何？客人的感覺又是如何？

Speech is not limited to a formal occasion in a public place. It is a form of communication, or even a conversation, requiring ample interaction between a speaker and his audience. A pleasant conversation between people who first meet can create a good first impression and create a friendly climate for a following event such as a negotiation. As an old saying goes, “a good start is half of the way to future success.” That is why the first lesson in a negotiation class starts with relationship building, mainly centering on nurturing one’s ability to carry on a conversation prior to the starting of a formal negotiating procedure. Similar to negotiating training, a good impression and a friendly climate are also important for a successful speech.

演講並不限於在公衆地方的正式場合，它是一種溝通，甚至是需要演講者與他的聽衆具有互動的對話。在初次見面的當下，一個良好的對話可以創造出很好的第一印象，以及爲將來的談判創造出友善的氣氛，如成語所說：「好的開始是成功的一半」，這就是爲什麼談判課程的第一件事情是從建立良好關係開始，而建立良好的關係就在於培養談判之前所應該有的對話能力。與談判訓練相似，良好的第一印象還有友善的環境對於成功的演說是很重要的。

Try to picture a conversation between two old college acquaintances meeting unexpectedly in an airport. Their conversation probably can cover any topic including any issue involving a sensitive nature. On the contrary, a conversation between two strangers seems very limited, sometimes accompanied with uncomfortable anxiety and stress. Sometimes, both want to end their conversation as quick as possible. What makes such a difference? Two old acquaintances already knew each other and probably there has been a certain level of trust formed between them from the past. Their conversation can occur naturally with a free flowing exchange of information. Conversation with a stranger is more difficult because they do not know each other. There has been no prior understanding between them from the start, and thus, the trust between them may be limited.

想像一下兩位大學時代的好友在機場不期而遇，他們可以談論任何東西，包括具有敏感性質的話題。相反的，兩個陌生人的對話會非常侷限，而且會有不自在的緊張與壓力。有的時候兩人都希望對話能夠儘早結束。這一種差異是怎麼造成的呢？兩個老朋友早就互相認識，他們有過去建立的信任，他們的對話可以自然交換著訊息。跟陌生人的對話比較困難，他們一開始並不認識對方而且彼此不互信。

No doubt, there is a thick block of ice between strangers. If a person cannot break the ice encountered in a conversation, it is quite doubtful if he can break the icy atmosphere in a speech generally found at the very beginning. It seems that a person who cannot manage a conversation probably will not be a good speaker either. For this reason, the first task of speech training is to know how to develop good conversation.

毫無疑問的，陌生人彼此之間有道非常高大的冰牆，如果在對話中不能打破這道冰牆，我們也很懷疑他有沒有辦法打破在演講開始時的冰凍氣氛，看來一個人如果不具有進行良好對話的能力，可能就沒有辦法成爲一個好的演說者，因此訓練演說的第一步，就是要訓練良好的對話能力。

2.2 How to keep a conversation moving?

The ability to engage in a conversation with the people we first meet is important. As mentioned earlier, two hours of silence in a car will make you and your overseas client feel quite uncomfortable and possibly cause unnecessary stress and anxiety, which will likely create a negative image and some hindrance for the upcoming business negotiation. Many have this problem. They do not know how to interact with people probably because they are shy or nervous. The other party can undoubtedly sense their uneasiness which will soon affect the proceeding of a conversation. Therefore, an ability to engage in a conversation smoothly and naturally without pauses and silences is important on any business occasion; the main core is in relationship building and is the very first lesson necessary in a negotiation class.

2.2 如何使對話進行？

與初次見面的人進行對話的能力是非常重要的。如同前述，你和你的外國客人在車內當中保持兩個小時的沉默會讓雙方感到不舒服，產生不必要的壓力與焦慮，對於之後要進行的談判容易產生不好的影響。許多人都有這個問題。他們不知道如何與別人互動，可能是太害羞或太緊張。另外一方很容易感覺到這樣的不自在，而這一種不自在會很快地影響到後面對話的進行。因此，進行平順而自然並且沒有中斷和沉默的對話能力，在商業場合是很重要的，這個是建立良好關係的核心，而且是談判課程的第一步。

In fact, a good conversation starts from a good impression and can help to build up trust and create a friendly environment. Proper attire can speak for his status and taste. Eloquent language uttered elegantly speaks of one's family and educational background. A well-organized self-introduction helps others to know you in a relatively short time. When people learn more about you, they generally trust you more. Transparency through honesty always helps to build up trust. Your name and job title reveal what you do, a sense of responsibility and probably achievement. Direct eye contact shows your honesty and sincerity, sometimes your determination as well. Proper gestures can emphasize your message. Do not overdo it or you may come across as being over-exaggerated or aggressive. The key term here is sincerity and honesty. Without such, no trust can be built. Once a good impression is established in the first meeting, it can be easier to move onto the core part of a conversation.

事實上，良好的對話來自於良好的印象，而且可以增進互信，適當的穿著可以表明他的身分地位與品味，優雅的態度以及高尚的文字可以說明他的教育背景，組織完整的自我介紹幫助別人在很短的時間內了解你，當他們愈了解你，他們就愈相信你，你的名字和工作職稱表示你的職業，也就是你的責任甚至是成就的一種訊號。直接的眼神交流表示出你的誠實和眞誠，有的時候甚至是你的決心，適當的手勢可以增強你的訊息，但是不要太過度強調，要不然你看起來很誇張甚至具有侵略性。這邊的關鍵詞是眞誠和誠實，沒有這兩項就沒有信任。一旦初次見面形成良好的印象之後，我們就可以較容易進入到對話的重點部分。

2.3 Elements of conversation

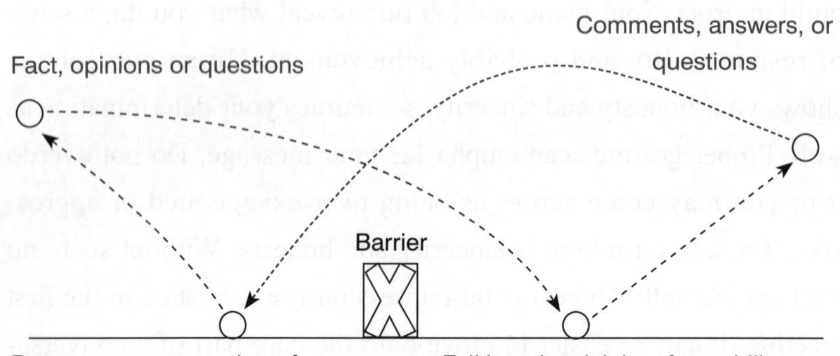

A moving conversation is indispensable for creating good interaction. A conversation is composed mainly of two parts: the first, the stating of a fact or an opinion by a speaker, and the second, questions, answers and comments presented by a listener. A moving conversation generally means that all parties involved are constantly talking and listening with questions asked and answers provided, like a Ping-Pong game. In a Ping-pong game, it is the light weight ping-pong ball on which both players focus. As long as the ball is hit, a game will continue and remain interesting to all audiences. If you want to continue the game, you have to focus on the ball and take correct action in hitting the ball. Therefore, the party who initiates a conversation, in expectation of the other's response, should be certain that the content of his statement falls into the vicinity that the other is capable, willing and ready to comment, answer or question. The other party, if entertaining a desire to continue the conversation, should comment, answer or question as returning the ball back into the category that the first party is capable, willing and ready to respond. If you want to continue the game, you have to focus on the ball and take correct action to hit the ball and, most importantly, make sure that the ball falls into the vicinity that the other party is capable, willing and ready to answer, comment or further question.

2.3 對話的要件

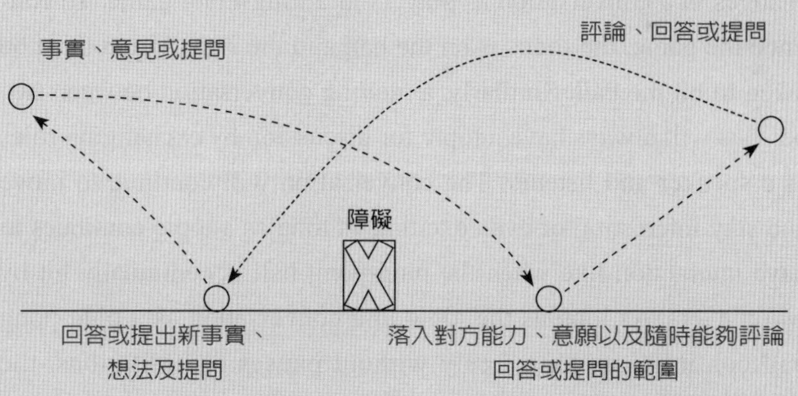

一個持續性的對話，對於形成一個好的互動是不可或缺的。對話主要包括兩部分：第一，說話者的陳述事實或意見；第二，受話

者的詢問以及回答。一個持續性的對話，通常是所有各方都能持續進行表達與聆聽，並且詢問與回答像是打乒乓球一般。在一個乒乓比賽中，小小的乒乓球是雙方選手注意的焦點。只要互相擊中乒乓球，比賽就會繼續，對於觀眾來說，比賽就會十分的精彩有趣。因此開始對話的一方，如果期待對方有所反應，應該要確認他說話的內容是落在對方能夠、願意而且隨時可以評論、回答或是提問的範圍內。對方如果也有這樣的意願繼續對話，那他的評論、回答或是提問也應該像打乒乓球一樣，落在另一方能夠、願意而且隨時準備反應的範圍內。你如果願意繼續這樣的對話，那就必須專注在球上而且採取正確的動作擊中乒乓球，更重要的是，確認乒乓球是落在對方能夠、願意而且立即回答，評論或是進一步詢問的範圍內。

A good conversation is very much like an interesting Ping-Pong game. Roles as a speaker and a listener constantly have interchanges in a conversation as players in a Ping-Pong game. To continue the game, the focus is on the ball and the right action must be taken to hit the ball. Similarly, a moving conversation between two persons will always have a topic for discussion by exchanging roles as a speaker and listener. The conversation will continue to move and stay interesting or even exciting as long as a topic continues to have interaction like when the ping-pong ball is continually hit by two players. As long as the topic in a conversation as a ping-pong ball continues moving freely without pauses or hesitations, the whole conversation will be stimulating rather than insipid.

一個好的對話就像一個很有趣的乒乓球比賽。在一個對話中說話者和受話者的角色，就像在乒乓比賽中的選手不斷互換。要讓比賽繼續，注意力必須是在集中在乒乓球上，而且選手要採取正確的行動打中球。同樣的，一個持續的對話要有一個可以討論的主題，然後說話者跟受話者的角色可以互換。對話能夠持續而且很有趣，甚至令人感到振奮，只要討論的主題能夠像乒乓球一樣，在討論中有來有往。只要這個對話的主題能像乒乓球一樣不斷地在自由運動而無中止或遲疑，那整個對話就會有趣而不至於無聊。

A conversation can continue better in a friendlier environment with fewer pauses and thus create a good interaction. Remember that appropriate questions asked show interest in what the other side has said and will bring more energy to the conversation. Therefore, listening with attention and understanding of what the other person says is of chief importance.

對話在一個友善的環境下能夠較順利的進行，也比較少中斷，因此形成比較良好的互動。要記得，提出適當的問題表示對於別人所說事情感興趣，可以對交談帶來更多能量，因此，專注的傾聽與了解對方說話的內容極其重要。

2.4 Factors affecting a conversation

In a conversation, interaction is important. None wants to stay for a monotonous conversation. A conversation will be difficult to continue without a comment, opinion or a question from the other party. If there is no comment, opinion or question given by the other party, it could mean that he is not interested in this conversation or, in a worse situation, he does not agree with what he has heard but simply shows his disapproval by staying silent. It is therefore necessary to elicit some words from the other party, may it be a comment, an opinion or a question. Asking a question and expecting an answer could be a good start as long as the question is neither intrusive nor inappropriate. Once the other party answers, his reply generally will contain some information that you either can go further by asking for more information or by commenting. In a few occasions, I have talked to some students who are either reserved or tend to remain quiet, and the conversation would terminate within seconds. The better approach here seems to ask some questions and probably to answer your own question yourself, more like giving an opportunity to state your own opinion. I have also noticed on some occasions that some hosts on radio or TV prefer to ask questions, waiting for a response from the guests. It could be embarrassing if the guest does not answer timely or give an answer beyond a host's expectation. If a host must ask questions, the question should be phrased to limit the answer according to the host's expectation.

A friendly attitude will help to relax any nervousness. If a speaker stays reserved, the other party can easily sense that in the atmosphere and might respond in the same manner and uneasiness will soon surface. If a speaker looks friendly, presenting a smile and a warm greeting, the other party might respond in the same way. It always takes two to tango. Our emotions and attitudes can be quickly sensed by the other party and reflected by the other's behavior as that in a mirror.

A common weakness in some people in their communication is that they are only interested in expressing their own opinion while paying no attention to what others say (e.g. feedback). Some of them even constantly interrupt another's conversation with their words. Such behavior is not only impolite but also offensive. Their primary objective in this conversation tends to voice their opinion as much and strong as possible. They seem to believe that the louder their voice is, the more powerful their opinion will be. An occasion like that is no communication at all. It is a unilateral expression of an opinion, a form of military order from a superior officer to soldiers.

2.4 影響對話的因素

在一個對話當中互動很重要，沒有人想爲了一個無聊的對話而停留。一個對話很難繼續，如果對方沒有接著提出評論、意見或者是問題的話。不提出評論、意見或是問題，這可能表示對方對於這個對話沒有興趣，或是更糟糕，他根本完全不同意他剛剛所聽到的，只是沒有表達不同意而已。所以我們必須讓對方說出他的看法、意見或是讓他提問。我們自己提出問題並且期待對方的答案也可能是一個好的開始，只要是問題並不尖銳或不適合的話。一旦對方回答的時候，他的回答通常會包含一些訊息，然後說話者可以更進一步地問一些更多的訊息或是評論。在一些場合，我曾經與學生對話，那些學生的話並不多甚至傾向於保持沉默，那對話很快就會終止。這個時候比較好的方法，可能是我們自己提出問題然後自己回答，比較像是給我們自己一個陳述我們自己意見的機會。我也注意到有一些其他的場合，像是收音機或是電視上有一些主持人喜歡問一些問題然後等待來賓的回答。如果來賓沒有即時回答或是給了一個出乎意料的答案，情況可能很尷尬。如果一個主持人必須要問問題，問題應該斟酌一下字句，將答案限定在主持人的期待當中。

友善的態度可以幫助放鬆他們緊張的情緒。如果說話者本身話也不多，對方可以很容易的察覺而且可能也會用相同的方式應對，那令人不舒服的場合很快就會出現。如果說話者看起來友善，帶著微笑與溫暖的問候，對方可能也會以相同的方式做反應。這種互動是相互的，對方可以很快察覺我們的情緒和態度，而且就像鏡子一樣，從對方的行爲可馬上反映出來。

有一些人的共同問題是，他們只對於表達自己的意見有興趣而並不在乎其他人說些什麼（反饋）。甚至有人不斷地打斷別人的談話，表達自己的意見。這其實也是非常不禮貌且引起別人反感的一件事情。這類對話的主要目標傾向於用力並且盡可能地說出他們的意見。他們似乎相信聲音愈大，意見愈有力量。這樣的場合並沒有任何的溝通。他只是單方面的表示意見，也只是一種軍事上上級軍官對士兵的命令而已。

A short description of certain locations for sightseeing, traveling experiences, food, movies, celebrities or sports news can be a good start for the people who are not familiar with each other because the general public usually has such experiences or knowledge. It is advised that conversation at this stage should not go into issues of a sensitive nature, e.g. privacy, political or religious issues. If your counterpart talks about his traveling experience in Japan, you can show your interest in what he says by asking further questions. For example, does he have any friends there or how did he find some places he wanted to visit? Questions like this also can help your counterpart to continue talking.

簡短的描述一些景點、旅行經驗、美食、電影、娛樂名人或是電視新聞，對於彼此並不熟悉的人可能都是很好的開始。因爲絕大部分的人都有經驗或這方面的知識，這個階段的對話應該避開具有爭議性的問題，比方說隱私、政治或宗教問題，假如對方談論他在日本旅行的經驗，你可以透過進一步發問來表示對他所陳述的事實感興趣，例如：他在那邊有朋友嗎？或是有找到那些他想去的地方嗎？這樣的問題可以讓對方繼續他的談話。

Laughter always makes people more relaxed. Some comments made with a good sense of humor often liven up the atmosphere and make listeners feel more comfortable. Be careful with using sarcastic remarks because they might cause some unpleasant feelings if not used appropriately. Avoid jokes with insulting remarks. Cheap jokes will downgrade your own value. A word fitly spoken is like apples of gold in a setting of silver (Proverbs 25:11). You are always welcome as long as you are friendly, pleasant and respectful in your words. A conversation is successful at this stage as long as the other party is willing to talk or ask questions later. Some sensitive questions as mentioned concerning privacy, politics and religions should be avoided. If asked, they should be asked in an objective manner with a mild and inoffensive nature. For example, a statement that "Your government is an authoritarian regime" is rather judgmental and sounds quite offensive. Instead, as suggested in Philip O'Connor's book, *Business Negotiating*, a statement "Do your people have a right to vote for your president?" or "How long is a term for your president?" sounds more objective because it is only acquiring a fact. Since an opinion shows evaluation of facts with a judgment, when an opinion is given to a person when meeting for the first time, one should be careful. Facts are more objective, but they can always be managed to produce in the end a desired result as planned. For example, the inquiry into people's right to vote for their president implies the suggestion that their government is an authoritarian regime. Simply speaking, questions asked should be made in a fact inquiring style rather than an opinionated one, especially avoiding any sarcastic remarks.

笑聲可以讓人們感到放鬆，具有幽默感的評語可以讓周遭的氣氛變得活潑，也能讓聽者放鬆。用到諷刺性字眼的時候要小心，因爲如果不適當使用的話很容易造成不愉快的感覺。避免一些有侮辱性字眼的笑話。廉價的笑話只會讓你自己的價值降低。就像聖經箴言所說的，合宜的話就像金蘋果在銀網子裡面。你如果友善樂觀以及在你的話語上受人尊重，那你總是受人歡迎。只要另一方願意說話或是發問問題，對話在這個階段就是成功的。有些敏感問題像是隱私或宗教應該要避免。如果提到的話，他們應該用客觀溫和而且不冒犯人的方式來提問，例如：你們的政府是威權政府嗎？這句話比較具有評斷性而且聽起來有冒犯的感覺。取而代之的，應該就像是 Philip O'Connor 在《商業談判》一書中所建議，如果以另一個形式來替代，例如：你們的人民有權利選出你們的總統嗎？或是你們總統的任期有多久？這兩句話聽起來比較客觀，因爲他只是在詢問一個事實，既然我們認爲意見就是對於事實衡量之後所產生的判斷，那我們就要小心將意見表達給初次見面的人，事實總是比較客觀，但是事實也可以被操弄來達到我們所想要的效果，例如：藉由詢問人民是否有直選總統的權力表達對於威權體制的暗示。簡單說，問題應該以詢問事實的方式提出，而不是具有評斷性的意見特別是諷刺的方式。

Questions by a listener, when appropriately asked, show his understanding of the speakers' content and demonstrate that the listener is interested in continuing the conversation. To be appropriate, a listener's questions generally should be relevant to the topic. Bear in mind that interest is the fuel to drive the whole conversation forward. A speaker should always bear in mind that no one likes staying around for a boring conversation. When a speaker is talking, you should pay heed to what he says without doing something else as the attention should always stay on the ping-pong ball in a game. A rather small thing, it seems, but should be attended to with great care.

聽眾所提出的問題表示他們對內容的了解程度，也表示出他們對於對話的興趣。聽眾的問題通常是跟主題有關聯的，要記得興趣是使整個對話能夠進行的動力。沒有人喜歡無聊的對話，當講者在說話時你應該注意聆聽而且不做其他事，就像乒乓球的選手把注意力放在球上一樣，這是一件很小的事情，但是要很小心。

During a conversation, roles of a speaker and a listener are continuously being interchanged. Reactions to each other is essential for good interaction at this stage. The speaker can very much receive the feedback from the listeners and vice versa, e.g. if they show interest or if they feel bored. Some people enjoy talking constantly without listening to what the other person says. Some are even worse, dominating a conversation all the way without even giving any opportunity for the other parties to talk. It is a conversation full of intrusion.

No one wants to stay for such conversation. In fact, it is no conversation at all. The speaking is done in a dictatorial style. Such dominance in a conversation must be avoided. The feedback could be delivered in an unspoken manner. Their eyes can indicate the level of their interest. A speaker must be alert enough to observe their interaction including silent messages. If necessary, the speaker should adjust the direction of the conversation either by changing the topic, adding some interesting facts or asking the listeners some questions to obtain their opinion. Observe especially the importance on "empathy". Empathy means one has the capacity to place oneself in another's position. Empathy can put us into other people's shoes and give us more understanding of their situation. This is especially important for a well-trained debater and a negotiator because such capacity can help him grasp a better understanding of another's position and thus prepare well for an effective argument. Comments made with a precise evaluation, but without empathy, can be quite judgmental. Judgmental words could be offensive, making it hard to win any support. No one likes to be judged. With such an understanding, we can communicate better with a greater power of persuasion.

在一個正在進行的對話，講者與聽者角色不斷的互換。對於另外一方的反應，是良好互動的一個要素，講者可以從聽者得到回饋，反之亦是如此，例如他們表達了興趣或是覺得無聊。有些人喜歡不停的講話，從來不聽也不注意其他人說了些什麼，甚至可能從頭到尾都是他一個人在講，根本不給別人說話的機會。那是一個充滿打擾與侵犯的對話。

沒有人喜歡這一種對話，事實上，這根本不是對話，只是一種獨裁式的說話方式。這種完全霸占整個對話的方式一定要避免。回饋可能並不以言語的方式表達，他們的眼神說明他們感興趣的程度，講者必須很小心來觀察他們的互動，包括那些沉默的訊息。如果有需要，講者應該改變問題，增加有趣的事實，或是對於聆聽者提出問題，詢問他們的意見，來調整對話的方向。特別注意到同理心的重要性，同理心的意思就是將自己放在別人位置上思考的能力。同理心把我們自己放在別人的角度，讓我們更了解其他人的情況。對於一個訓練有素的辯論者或是談判者非常的重要，因爲這樣的能力可以幫助了解對方的立場和想法，因此可以準備更有效的說法。具有精準判斷但缺乏同理心的評語，可能是非常具有評斷性，太過評斷性的字句可能會很容易冒犯別人而不容易贏得認同，沒有人喜歡被評斷。有了這樣的了解之後，我們就可以以比較具有說服力的方式來溝通。

Appropriate analogy is effective in persuasion. Learners are encouraged to use analogies in their training on conversation, speech, debate and negotiation. In my class observation, students who are better on drawing appropriate analogies (e.g. analogies that fit the need by the situation or individuals) seem better in grasping a better understanding and perception of another's situation and needs and therefore tend to have more empathy. On the contrary, students who have less empathy due to their lack of understanding of another's problem often have difficulty in drawing applicable analogies for persuasion.

適當的比喻在說服上是很有效的。初學者應當在他們的對話、演說、辯論和談判的訓練上儘量使用比喻。在課堂的觀察，那些能夠快速舉出適當比喻的學生（符合個人或是情況需要的比喻），通常能夠比較具有深度的了解他人的情況或是需要，因此也比較具有同理心。相反的，那些比較欠缺同理心的學生通常也比較不容易了解別人的問題，因此也不容易舉出適當的比喻進行說服。

Finally, what should be emphasized here is to carefully listen with understanding of what the other person says. Many quarrels are caused by misunderstandings. Quarrels from misunderstandings are somehow like fighting against an enemy that never exists. Why should we waste time and, and even more sillier yet, be hurt by this never existing enemy? If we analyze the whole process of a conversation, we should understand that a speaker utters what he has in mind and conveys his message to a listener. A listener, subsequent to his interpretation to what he has heard, responds to the speaker accordingly. Of course, the manner of such expression and response is also crucial. To have contempt for or despise someone can be easily drawn from some expression not intentionally made in an unfriendly situation. Misunderstandings somehow happen during this process, mostly in situations when either a speaker does not use appropriate terms to precisely express his thoughts (excluding his intentional provocation) or a listener fails to give correct interpretation or perception of the speaker's message. We cannot avoid quarrels if confrontation is intentionally made. However, there is no need to waste time and energy on an unnecessary fight caused by a misunderstanding, an enemy that never exists. We should eliminate such misunderstandings if possible.

最後應該要強調的是小心聆聽並且要聽懂別人所說的話。許多的爭執都是來自於雙方的誤解。由誤解所發生的爭執就像是跟一個從來不存在的敵人進行戰鬥。我們爲什麼要浪費時間，很愚蠢的被這個從未存在的敵人所傷害呢？如果我們分析一個對話的整個過程，我們應該明白一個說話者說出他心中想說的事情而且將訊息傳遞給聽者，而這個聽者在詮釋他所聽到的事情之後，進而做出反應。當然表達和回應的態度也非常的重要。在一個不是很友善的情況當中，一些不經意的表達很容易被解釋爲輕視或是不友善。而誤解就是在這個過程當中發生的，大部分發生在講者並沒有使用適當的字眼，正確地描述他的想法（除非是特意激怒對方）之外，或者是聽者沒有對於講者的訊息給予正確詮釋或是眞正了解講者的意思。如果對抗是故意製造的，那我們沒有辦法避開爭執。但是對於因爲誤解所產生的爭執，我們沒有必要浪費我們的時間和精力跟一個從來不存在過的敵人進行戰鬥。我們必須盡可能的消滅這樣的誤解。

Correct understanding of another's statement and precise expression of our own ideas require a good ability on perception and a good ability on perception requires a sense of logic. Doubtful statements with ambiguous meanings should be placed in a logical sequence for examination. Such logical sequence is framed under a cause and effect analysis which will be further elaborated on in the section regarding debate. Simply speaking, a listener should ask himself this question, why did the speaker make such a statement? What facts are the basis of his conclusion? How did he make such an interpretation of a fact? What reasons do the speaker use to reach his conclusion? To go further, what is the speaker's interest in the position held? To avoid misunderstandings is important in communication. It takes good sense of logic and experience to decipher from a framework of cause and effect the meaning of a speaker's statement as well as his possible interest and, mostly importantly, wisdom to respond accordingly.

In addition, for a negotiator at the international business level, good understanding and perception of cultural differences are essential to avoid misunderstandings. The very same statement or gesture could mean respect in one culture while represent a totally different meaning in another. Some gestures are appropriate in a western society while it may seem offensive in a conservative region or vice versa. There is no certain rule to follow. A few years ago, a young male high school student wore a Nazi uniform to participate in a Taiwan demonstration to protest against some governmental action. Not long after, a whole class of students in one high school in Taiwan dressed in Nazi uniforms for the parade at their school anniversary. Such acts immediately drew attention and concern from the Israeli representative office in Taiwan (similar status as an embassy). Learning experiences by reading some books, magazines or even watching movies will help to gain such knowledge to avoid conveying the wrong message.

正確了解別人的話語以及精確描述我們的想法，需要有好的理解能力，而好的理解能力需要邏輯感。當對別人的話語有疑問的時候，應該對這樣的話語以邏輯的順序進行檢驗。這樣的邏輯順序是建立在因果架構之下，這一部分我們會在辯論章節進一步的說明。簡單來說，一個聽者應該問自己這個問題，爲什麼講者會說出這樣的話？他所下的結論是以什麼樣的事實作爲他的立論根據？他如何對一件事實進行詮釋？他使用什麼樣的理由達到他的結論？更進一步的，在這樣的結論之下，他有怎麼樣的利益？避免誤解，在溝通上是很重要的事情。我們必須要有好的邏輯感和經驗，透過因果關係的分析，來了解別人說話的意思、他可能的利益以及更重要地用我們的智慧來進行反應。

除此之外，對於一個國際商場上的談判者而言，對文化差異的深度了解是避免誤解發生非常重要的事情。同樣的一句話或是手勢，對於一個文化來說表示尊重，可是可能對另一個文化而言就表示完全不同的意義。有一些在西方社會適合的表達，在其他比較保守的區域，可能就非常不適合，反之亦然。沒有固定的規則可以遵守。好幾年前在臺灣，有高中男生在示威抗議的時候穿著納粹的制服，不久之後也有一個高中的班級，全班在校慶的時候打扮成爲德國納粹參加校慶遊行，這些舉動當時都立刻引來以色列駐臺辦事處（相當於以色列大使館）的關切。我們只能說儘量從書本雜誌甚至看電影的經驗中，獲取相關的知識來避免傳達錯誤的訊息。

2.5 Other notes added for conversation training

If we agree that a person's attire can speak for his status and taste, then felicity with properly mannered words can build up a person's value. We like honest and trustworthy people, those who hold the right or same values as ours. We like their use of good gestures and proper eye contact for making expressions. A person's attire very much speaks where he is from and who he is. We like people who have pleasant personalities and who are easy to talk to. We like to listen to those who show great knowledge on the subject matter and know what they are talking about. We prefer to hear from those who show keen observation and present his views with a good sense of humor. No one likes to talk to a boring person. A conversation made with humor could help to thaw the ice and probably will further win you their good impression if made with honesty, patience, trustworthiness and a pleasant personality along with proper gestures and good eye contact. We especially are fond of those who can ask us good questions deserving of our effort on thinking, probably helping to sort out our current problems.

2.5 關於對話訓練的其他要點

如果我們說一個人的衣著可以幫他的地位和品味加分，適當的態度以及優雅的言詞可以增進一個人的價值。我們喜歡誠實值得信任的人，我們也喜歡那些具有正確觀念與我們價值觀相同的人。我們喜歡他們使用適當的手勢以及眼神交流來進行表達，一個人的衣著說明他從哪邊來、他是誰，我們喜歡有樂觀個性、好交談的人，我們也喜歡聆聽那些對於主題有充分知識而且知道在說什麼的人。我們傾向於聆聽那些敏銳觀察而且以幽默方式呈現觀點的人，沒有人喜歡跟一個無聊的人說話。具有幽默感的對話，可以融化溝通上的冰層，也可以增加他們對你的印象。如果你的表達可以呈現出你的誠實、耐心、值得信賴的程度、樂觀的個性，以及你的手勢及眼神交流。我們也特別喜歡那些會詢問值得我們思考的問題的人，而那些思考可能可以幫助我們脫離困境。

In a conversation with a stranger, it is not appropriate to inquire into another's privacy. The better approach seems to talk about yourself or comments on your observation of certain facts in a humorous way and then ask for the others person's opinion. If all the aforementioned characteristics are the ones that we like to see in a person we talk to, why not build up ourselves according to that image? The rule of thumb to judge if a conversation is successful is to see if your counterpart is willing to stay around for further talks. Sometimes, someone asks you a difficult question beyond your knowledge. In that case, it will not be appropriate to pretend that you are an expert. It is easy for an expert to find out that you are not truly as knowledgeable as you claim to be. The better approach is to lead the conversation into a direction where you have a better knowledge of and one you are more comfortable to talk about.

在與陌生人對話當中，詢問別人的隱私，並不恰當。比較好的方式就是討論你自己，或是以幽默的方式評論一些你所觀察到的事實以及問問他們的意見。如果上面所說的一些優點特質是我們希望在好的說話者身上看到的，那為什麼我們自己不朝這個方向，建立那些特質呢？判斷一個對話成不成功，簡單的標準就是看對方願不願意繼續這個對話。有時候有些人會問你不熟悉的問題。在那樣的情況之下，最好不要假裝你是一個專家，因爲這很容易讓其他人看出來你並沒有你所聲稱具有的那些知識。最好的方法還是把話題帶到你比較了解而且可以比較輕鬆談論的領域。

The final point to be noted here is the importance of understanding the other person's position or problem so that patience can be shown. No one likes to communicate with someone who is inpatient and has a lack of understanding to what we are talking about. It is not only a waste of time, but could also possibly lead to frustration as well as conflicts and anger. In order to be patient, it will be helpful to be understanding of the other party's position with a good perception regarding the crux of their statement. Good perception requires wisdom which can only be procured through years of experiences in dealing with people and accumulated, especially, from mistakes made. Once we can have a better understanding to their problems, we will know their difficulty and tend to have more patience. Communication will be made much easier if your listeners feel you are more understanding with empathy.

The most important factor in building up the power of persuasion lies on the capability to place oneself in another's position. Such capability is far more essential than your ability on analysis and utterance. I once asked a senior manager in a large corporation why he always cared so much about the slight difference in a salary paid to a new employee. He told me that, in his eyes, every new employee was a long term liability for his corporation in the next 30 years. Any trivial amount will be accumulated into a huge sum in 30 years. This is the difference in making a good judgment between a high ranking manager and a new employee. Once we place ourselves into his shoes, we will understand better why his decision is made regarding a new employee.

If you can manage a conversation effectively, you can move on to next level of speech.

最後一點要注意的是了解別人的立場或者是問題的重要性，有了這樣的了解才能夠有耐心。沒有人喜歡與沒有耐心以及不了解我們問題的人溝通。那不僅僅是浪費時間，而且可能造成衝突以及憤怒。要有耐心，我們必須要能夠了解別人的立場以及問題核心。深入了解問題需要智慧，而智慧是要長年累積與人們接觸的經驗，特別是從錯誤學習。一旦我們能夠了解別人的問題，我們就能夠知道他們的困難，所以我們會有更大的耐心。一旦你的聽衆能夠看出來你的善解人意以及同理心，溝通上會容易很多。

建立說服能力最重要的因素就在於換位思考的能力。這樣的能力遠比你分析和說話的能力來得重要得多。我曾經問過一個大型公司的高階經理人爲什麼他總是在乎對於新進人員薪水的些微差別。他告訴我，在他的眼裡，每一個新進人員都是公司未來三十年的負債。任何些微的差距在三十年後都會累積成爲可觀的數字。這就是一個高階經理人與新進人員在判斷上的差別。一旦我們能夠換位思考了解高階經理人的想法，我們就可以了解爲什麼他們對於新進人員薪水設定的決定。

如果你可以掌控對話，你就可以進入到演講辯論的階段。

Chapter

3

Speech Training
演說訓練

Focus 本章大綱

3.11 A note on self-introduction／關於自我介紹的一些看法

3.12 Narration/Description of facts／事實的敘述

3.13 Further elaboration on the interpretation of facts／對於事實解釋部分進一步的闡述

3.14 The following are some advice with a few tips based on the past practice from students／下列事項是依據學生們過去的表現列出以下建議

3.15 Sample speech and writing at the intermediate level／演說和中級寫作示範

3.16 Summary／摘要

3.17 Impromptu speech／即席演說

3.18 Observation in a classroom／課堂觀察

3.19 The application of the approaches learned from this chapter／本章方法的適用

3.1 Some basic messages for this chapter

One graduate once shared with me his experience of a job interview. A few applicants were waiting outside a room, busy with cramming information from notes into their brains, including their autobiographies and some answers to possible questions asked. Six applicants were called into a small room at the same time and each gave their self-introduction. Most seemed to be uttering to themselves the information crammed into their brains, stuttering and hesitating, afraid of making mistakes. Such stutters and hesitations seemed especially worse when questions were asked by the interviewers. The whole process at this stage has turned into an interrogation rather than a conversation between the interviewers and applicants. Some applicants could not even reply to simple questions under this pressure and apologized to the interviewers for their failure to answer. Of course, they have to say farewell to a possible opportunity of a bright career. Very often, your merit will be decided by your words uttered in a few minutes on an occasion like a job interview or a business presentation. Their experience with a job interview reminds me of my early days of study in the U.S. Some foreign students were quite intelligent and brilliant in their paper exams but neither skillful nor fluent with their oral expression. They were slow and hesitant in their communication. Such hesitation with pauses or even silence often left an impression that they had low intelligence and thus tarnished their image in the whole class. People did not like to work with them as a team for fear that they would receive a low grade. It's fair to say that what you say will determine what opportunity will be available to you, whether in school or in a business world.

3.1 關於本章的基本訊息

曾經有個畢業生跟我分享他找工作的經驗。房間外面有好一些應徵者在等待。在等待的時間不斷看著小冊子，上面寫著密密麻麻的資訊，他們正用最大的努力要記下來，包括他們的自傳，還有對於一些可能被詢問問題的答案。六個人被同時叫進了那小房間，然後每一個要自我介紹。大部分的人從他們的腦子裡面背誦出那些資訊，有些口吃而且遲疑深怕犯了錯誤。在被問到一些問題的時候，這樣的口吃與遲疑看起來更糟糕，整個的過程到了這個階段開始變成一個拷問而不是口試員與應徵者的對話。有一些應徵者在這樣的壓力之下甚至不能回答一些簡單的問題因而對於口試員進行道歉。當然這些應徵者必須對可能帶給他們光明前途的機會說再見。通常你的價值會被你在幾分鐘之內所說的話來決定，例如工作面試或是商業簡報。他找工作的面試經驗讓我想起我早年在美國讀書的那段時間。有一些外籍學生在他們的筆試上表現得很好，但是在他們的口語表達上並不流暢，溝通上顯得緩慢和遲疑。這樣的遲疑、中斷或是沉默常常讓別人留下他們並不聰明的印象，因此在整個班上的形象是受損的。同學們不喜歡跟他們做團體工作，深怕成績會受到影響而不佳。平心而論，不論在學校或商業界，你所說的會決定你的機會有多少。

Similarly, some students could not talk or write their speech in writing class. To cure a disease, we always need to have a correct diagnosis prior to giving the right medication. To solve this problem, it is imperative to identify what exactly their problem is. Is their problem on English proficiency or something else? The rule of thumb, in my opinion, is to ask students to give a speech or writing in their own native language. If they do not have any problem on expressing themselves in their own mother tongue, then their problem is probably on their English proficiency. If they cannot do that in their own mother tongue, then the first problem they encounter is definitely on their forming and organizing their thought.

同樣的，有些學生在他們的演說還有寫作課，沒辦法開口也沒辦法寫作。醫治疾病我們必須有一個正確的診斷才能給出有效的藥物。要解決學生們的問題，我們必須確認他們的問題在哪裡，也就是他們的問題究竟是在英文的流利程度還是其他的問題。我認爲簡單的判斷規則就是要求學生以他們自己的母語進行演說或是寫作，如果他們以自己的語言在表達上沒有問題的話，那他們的問題可能是在英文的流利程度上；但是如果以自己的母語他們都不能進行這樣的表達，那表示他們所碰到的第一個問題一定是在形成以及組織他們的想法上。

(1) Formulating Process on Expression

When we talk and write, we convey to others what we have in our minds. What we have in minds is from what we have observed. We organize and evaluate what we have observed and give our opinion to others in a form of writing and/or speech. This very basic pattern shows how writing and speech is established. For this reason, the training of beginners should start from a description of facts including information received followed by an evaluation before an opinion is given to others (i.e. writing or speech). Description of facts is the first task prior to explaining how a concept and an idea are formed. The description of facts is also important in a business world; may it be a claim for damages or promotion of products. Without a clear description of facts, neither writing nor a speech can proceed. Unfortunately, most students in their high school neither learn nor are aware of this basic concept in their writing classes. Therefore, they don't know where to start and what they should put on paper, not to mention discussing the reasons for supporting the different views. Training on the skills regarding the description of facts is the first priority for students and business persons in learning writing and speech.

Facts, once clearly and concisely described, should be skillfully interpreted by a speaker. Interpretation of facts will produce a message. Same facts, if interpreted differently, will lead to different conclusions. Therefore, training on the description of facts followed by good interpretation leading to a convincing message is the main task of this chapter. Simple facts interpreted give rise to a message leading to a conclusion. The following example will demonstrate the application of the above mentioned principle.

(1) 表達形成的過程

當我們說話或寫作的時候，我們把心中的想法表達出來。我們心中的想法是從我們的觀察中所獲得的。我們把我們所觀察的，加以整理以及評價之後，用寫作或是演說的方式，對別人表達出我們的意見。這反映出演說和寫作基本的模式。因為如此，在訓練初學者時，應該從描述事實開始，這包含所接收的訊息，接著是對於事實的評價，然後將所形成的意見轉達給其他的人。對事實的描述是在解釋概念與想法形成之前所必須先做的工作。對商人來說，對於事實的描述也非常重要，不論是在請求損害賠償或是對於貨物的銷售而言。如果不能清楚描述事實的話，寫作和演說也不能進行。很不幸的，絕大部分的學生在高中寫作課的時候並沒有學過也沒聽過這樣的概念。因此他們不知道如何開始，也不曉得寫些什麼東西，遑論解釋不同觀點的原因。對於學生和所有的商務人員而言，不論在演說或寫作，描述事實技巧的訓練是非常重要的。

一旦能夠清楚扼要地描述事實，講者接著需要熟悉對事實的解釋。事實的解釋會產生訊息。同樣的事實，如果經過不同的解釋，會產生不同的結論。因此本章的目的就在於訓練學生對事實的描述、解釋並且產生具有說服力的訊息。簡單的事實經過詮釋，產生訊息而導致結論。下面的例子將示範上面原則的使用。

Formulating Process on Expression

Observation → Brain → Thinking process (analysis) → Expression (writing and speaking)

All expressions whether in speaking or in writing are given from the information in brains. Information is acquired from observation from what have been heard, seen and read and is expressed subsequent to analysis through thinking process in the brain.

表達形成的過程

觀察 → 大腦 → 思考過程（分析） → 表達（說寫）

所有的表達，不論是說或寫，都是由腦中的資訊傳遞出來。資訊是透過我們所看見、聽到以及閱讀而取得，並且經過我們思考過程而分析再進一步表達。

Example 1

People remember special gifts or presents that they have received. Why? Use specific reasons and examples to support your answer.

Demonstration

When we mention special gifts, we tend to think of tangible and high valued gifts that we can see and touch. In fact, some special gifts are intangible and, interestingly enough, the person who gives this gift probably does not even know that he has ever given such a precious gift.

Thirty years ago, I was in high school and had to commute by train to school. Commuting students were offered an especially cheap rate on their monthly tickets for the ordinary train service. Such ticket holders were not allowed to take any express service and any violator would be required to pay a penalty. However, young students like a challenge and to be adventurous. I sometimes did that to feel that I earned a sense of achievement, an experience full of excitement.

I remember that I was caught once and was required to pay a large fine. I did not have that much money, so I asked help from my dad. He gave me the money to pay for the penalty and told me not to do that again because that was not honest behavior and would be despised by others. Not long after that, I did that again and was caught. When I asked help from my father, we had a serious fight. I retorted furiously and told him that such violation was not a matter of a serious nature and could be easily solved with money. When I raised my voice loud to show my reluctance to listen, he hit me with a light stick. He told me that if he did not teach me well, someday in the future someone would give me a serious lesson. The very moment he told me this message, I stopped being angry because I suddenly realized the potential cost I may have to pay for my stupidity in the future. At that moment, I understood the importance of self-discipline regarding right values.

Nowadays, parents give tangible or even high priced gifts to their beloved children to show their affection. Are those gifts carrying a special meaning to influence their children's future life to move toward the bright side? For me, I cherish many lessons my father gave to me thirty years ago. His words showed wisdom, special enough to guide me as a compass in every stage of my life even after my career as a teacher. Wisdom can avoid evil and lead to prosperity and is more precious than any tangible asset that parents can give to their children in this world.

範例一

人們記得他們所收到的特別禮物，爲什麼？請用明確的理由及例子來支持你的答案。

示範

當我們提到特別禮物的時候，我們傾向於想到那一些有形並且是高價值的禮物，我們能看得見，摸得著。事實上，有些特別的禮物是看不見的，而且非常有趣的是，那些送給我們這樣禮物的人甚至不知道他曾經給了我們如此特別的禮物。

三十年前，我還在念高中的時候，我必須搭火車上學。通勤的學生可以用特別便宜的票價買普通車的月票，但是，拿這種月票不可以搭乘高等車班，要不然會被罰錢。年輕的學生喜歡冒險和刺激，我有的時候會做這些事情來尋求一種成就感，一種充滿刺激的經驗。

我記得我曾經被抓過一次，然後必須支付一筆高額的罰金。我當時沒有那麼多錢，所以我請我父親幫忙。他給了我那一筆錢支付罰款，並且告訴我不要再幹這樣的事情，因爲那是不誠實的行爲，會被別人瞧不起。沒多久之後，我又再做了一次，又被抓到了，當我要求我父親幫忙的時候，我們爭吵得很激烈。我很生氣的回嘴，並告訴他這樣的違規並不是什麼嚴重的事情，並且可以用錢輕易的解決。當我拉高我的聲音表示我不想聽他說話的時候，他打了我一頓。他告訴我如果在家裡面他不好好教訓我的話，將來出去，我就等著被人教訓。當他告訴我這個訊息的時候，我不再生氣了。我突然了解到，將來我的愚蠢可能要付出的代價，在那個時刻，我明白了正確價值觀下的自我要求。

現在這個時代，父母親們把看得見、摸得著的高價值禮物送給他們摯愛的小孩來表達對他們的愛。這樣的禮物眞的有特別的意義足以影響到他們的一生，朝向正面的發展嗎？對於我而言，我珍惜著我父親三十年前給我的教訓。他的話，充滿著智慧，非常的特別，像是個羅盤針一樣，在我當老師之後，引導了我生活中的每一個步驟。智慧，能夠趨吉避凶，勝過父母親在這世界上所可以給予他們的孩子任何看得見的禮物。

Example 2

Share with your classmates your experience in a traffic jam.

Demonstration

No one likes to be caught in a traffic jam especially on holidays. Instead of enjoying a well-planned trip, monotonous time probably coupled with complaints from passengers in a small compact space among endless queues of vehicles on a freeway could make a supposedly good mood depressed. However, such time of impatience could be transformed into a precious moment of memories years later.

範例二

請跟同學們分享你塞車的經驗。

示範

沒有人喜歡被塞車堵在路上，特別是在假日。塞車的時候沒有辦法享受已經計畫好的旅程，在高速公路上無止境的車陣當中，無聊的時間伴隨著乘客們的抱怨，會使得原來很好的心情變得非常沮喪。然而，幾年後，這種不耐煩的時刻，將轉化爲一段珍貴的回憶。

Thirty years ago, my family went back to central Taiwan from the north to see my grandmother. Both of my parents together with my brother and sister, a total of five, were in a compact car. It was a Chinese new year time, so the traffic was really bad, full of vehicles going south. The regular two-hour trip lasted over five hours. We got off the freeway and tried to take a detour through some country roads, hoping that traffic would turn better. But it did not. In fact, it was worse because of the many stop lights at the intersections. We were complaining all the way to our destination. The six-hour trip was strenuous and was not pleasant at all.

三十年前，我和家人從北臺灣回到中臺灣去看我外祖母。我父母親以及弟妹共五人擠在一個小車子裡面。那是新年的時候，交通很擁擠，高速公路上充滿了回南部的車子。平常兩個小時的車程變成了五小時。我們後來先下了高速公路想要找一條替代道路，希望交通可以方便一些，但是其實不然，事實上變得更糟糕，因爲有很多交叉路口以及紅綠燈。我們不停地抱怨直到我們的目的地。全部六個小時旅程變得很辛苦而且毫無樂趣。

Now my grandmother and both of my parents have passed away, no more in this world. My sister lives in the U.S., ten thousand miles from this island, and we seldom see each other. What was so unpleasant and intolerable in that little compact car now seems like a beautiful and precious memory. It was a beautiful picture of a family reunion that no money could buy. I miss my parents and I wish I could spend time with them again. But now all are history and memories.

如今，我的外祖母和我父母親都已經過世了。我妹妹住在美國，離臺灣有萬里遠，我們也很少見面。小車子裡一些不太愉快甚至不容易忍受的事情，現在看起來變成一幅金錢買不到，美麗而且珍貴的家庭和樂團圓照。我很想念我的父母親，也希望我還能夠有時間跟他們在一起，但是這一切都成爲歷史以及回憶。

Life is interesting, something unpleasant at this moment could turn into something precious in the future. Unfortunately, we do not have that prescience to see the future. Probably a difficult time or an unpleasant event encountered with your family, friends or coworkers could become a souvenir with great value in your future life. Think about it. We are saying farewell to the present moment and those who are around us. So cherish each moment that you can hold in your hand and enjoy to the full extent.

人生很有意思，這個時刻不愉快的事情，未來可能變成非常寶貴。很不幸的，我們沒有那樣預知未來的能力。現在你跟家人、朋友或是同事之間不愉快的時刻或事件，也許在將來成爲你生命中非常有價值的紀念品。仔細想想，我們對於現在這個時刻以及我們周遭的人正在道別。所以把握你手上的每一時刻，盡情地享受吧。

These two short writings have demonstrated some simple and basic steps from observation to expression shown either in a speech or writing. On the level of structure, each is composed by the description of fact followed by writer's interpretation of the facts containing a message leading to a conclusion, which will be discussed in details in the following sections of this chapter.

這二篇短文示範了在演講以及寫作上，從事實的觀察到表達上的一些簡單和基本步驟。在結構的層次上，每一篇文章的組成是由對於事實的描述，之後是作者對於事實的詮釋，接著是作者藉由對事實的詮釋所帶出的訊息，最後是所引導的結論，而一些如何準備的細節會在本章的章節討論。

3.2 Purpose of Speech

What benefit can be procured from speech training?

There are various forms of speech entertaining different purposes such as informative and persuasive speeches. The most influential in the field of communication is the persuasive speech, because a speech, if made persuasively, can help to establish a positive relation with others leading to our future success in a career. For this reason, this chapter is confined to the discussion of persuasive speech. Readers should also be aware that the general principle elaborated here in this chapter can be used as a guideline for the training of students in a writing class at the intermediate level regarding their ability on the narration of facts as well as that on interpretation of facts that is presented with a message calling for the readers to take some action.

3.2 演說的目的

從演說訓練中可以獲得什麼樣的好處？

演說有不同形式各有不同目的，例如：告知式演說或是說服式演說。在溝通的領域內，最具有影響力的是說服式演說，因爲一個演說如果具有說服力，是可以幫忙建立與其他人的正面關係，導向我們未來在事業上的成功，基於這個理由，本章將討論限定在說服式演說。讀者也應該了解在本章關於演說部分的原則，也可以應用在中級寫作上，訓練學生對於事實陳述、解釋以及將訊息帶給讀者以呼籲他們行動爲目的的寫作。

In other words, a good training on speech will help learners to build up their ability on observation and description of relevant facts followed by a clear narration containing a message leading to a persuasive conclusion. The essence is to connect facts with a message for persuasion. Simply speaking, a message is a product and a fact is a vehicle to deliver the message. Once the skill is procured from constant training, the students' power on persuasion will be enhanced to a great extent.

換句話說，一個好的演說訓練可以幫助學生增強他觀察以及描述相關事實，解釋事實以及帶出訊息，引導出極具說服力結論的能力。重點就在於結合事實跟訊息達到說服目的。簡單來說，訊息是產品而事實的使用是傳送產品的交通工具。一旦從訓練中獲得這樣的能力，學生在說服上的能力將大力的加強。

Some may wonder whether they really need to learn how to make a speech because only a few people in their lifetime will ever have an opportunity to give a speech. True! Their doubt is not unfounded. What can we see in the instance of a speech? In a typical scenario, we see a speaker and an audience and their interaction, i.e. a speaker is talking to the audience. In fact, only few people will have those opportunities to speak to an audience. But if you really examine the elements of a successful speech, you will find that the building up those abilities will help your communication whether in your career or daily life. This is because the strength of a speech lies on the ability of persuasion. Such ability is highly desirable in an interaction with people. Good ability on persuasion helps to build up a positive relationship with people whether in a career or in a group. In fact, the content of a good speech, if put into a written form, is good writing as well as, probably at an intermediate level, for training purposes aiming at persuasion. Writing at an intermediate level aiming at persuasion demands a student to skillfully describe and interpret relevant facts, followed by a certain message delivered for persuasion. This approach is easy to learn and can be effectively applied in writing whether in school or for a business occasion. Therefore, skills learned in this section should be beneficial to all people including both high school and college students as well as those who have business needs.

有些人很懷疑，他們眞的需要學習如何演說嗎？因爲只有很少的人在他們一生中會有機會進行他們的演說。確實是如此，他們的懷疑不是沒有理由的。在一個演說的場合我們可以看到什麼呢？在一個典型的演說場合，我們看到一個演說者還有聽衆以及他們之間的互動，也就是一個演說者在對一群聽衆說話。事實上確實只有很少的人有這樣的機會跟一群群衆說話。但是如果你仔細檢查一個成功演說的要件，你會發現到這些能力的增強，不管在你的工作上或日常生活上，對你的溝通能力是有很大的幫助。這是因爲說服的能力決定了演說的強度，而這一種能力，在於人們的互動當中是非常受到歡迎的。強而有力的說服力可以在工作上或是在團體內增強正面的人際關係，好的演講內容如果把它變成書面的形式，也會是一篇程度很好的中級寫作文章，如果這個文章的目的是在作爲說服力的訓練。寫出一篇具有說服能力中級寫作的文章，學生必須具有描述和解釋相關事實的技能，之後再傳遞一個訊息達到說服性的目的，這一種方法很容易學習，而且可以有效地應用在作文，不論是在學校或是在商業場合，因此在這一部分所學習的技巧，對於高中生跟大學生以及有商業需要的人都是非常有幫助的。

Speech is more than talking. A fool may talk but a wise man speaks. Speech is an oral expression of thoughts and emotions and is directed to an audience or a listener with a conveyed message. Generally, a speech is directed at a topic and is made for the purpose of persuasion. One thing to be noted here is that the general principles suggested in this chapter can be used as guidelines for training of writing at an intermediate level if we confine writing of such level to a student's ability to narrate facts followed with an interpretation containing a message.

演說不僅僅是說話。傻瓜也會開口，但是智者能夠談話。演說是口頭的方式表達出想法以及情感，而且將訊息傳遞給聽眾，通常來說演說是針對主題，而且是具有說服性的目的。這邊要注意一點，若是我們將中級寫作的目的，定在學生們對於事實描述的解釋，並且將訊息傳遞的能力，那麼這一章所作的建議也可以拿來當作中級寫作訓練的基本原則。

What role does the purpose of a speech play?

演說的目的扮演什麼角色？

In a typical speech, we see a speaker and an audience and their interaction, i.e. a speaker is talking to the audience. As speakers, we like people to listen to us, to believe the facts we state, to heed our shared message and, if possible, to accept the opinion we conclude with and to act according to what we suggest. It is therefore a process of persuasion to convince the people of the delivered message and to act accordingly. The power of persuasion is important because it can create a good image, build up proper interaction, make people follow you, and lead people to believe in what you suggest and thus help to achieve your goal. Fair to say, the power of persuasion is able to gather influence in making you successful in a career as exemplified by famous politicians, lawyers and businessmen, etc.

在一個典型的演講當中，我們看到一個演講者與聽衆還有他們之間的互動，也就是演講者對著一群群衆說話。身為演說者，我們希望人們傾聽我們、相信我們所說的事實、注意我們所傳遞的訊息，而且如果可能的話，接受我們所下的結論，而且按照我們建議的去實踐。因此，演說是一個說服的過程，讓大家相信我們所傳遞的訊息，並且實踐我們所建議的事情。說服力很重要，因為他可以建立好的形象，增進適當的互動，讓人們跟著我們，而且引導他們相信我們所說的，進而達到我們的目標。很公平的說，說服力可以凝聚力量，讓我們在事業上成功，就像許多有名的政治家、律師和商人一樣。

In a speech, the purpose is the most important because it will decide which direction to go, what position to take, who your audience will be, what facts will be selected and how these facts will be interpreted, what message will be conveyed, and what action you will call for in the conclusion. In fact, the purpose is the first question that we should ask in all actions we undertake. Why did we make this speech? What is the purpose of this writing or negotiation? Why should we make this decision and take this action, such as which college to attend or which job to take? Why did we make this investment and why did we take this loan from a bank? No action can be satisfactorily completed without a purpose being clearly ascertained at the beginning. Purpose can always explain well why you plan to take whatever action and therefore is also important in examining the advice on what means we should take and the reasoning process on how to be prepared. A clear purpose will tell us if the means that we take is consistent with our purpose. For example, we are willing to work hard for making money because we believe that money can help improve our lives. But a problem happens when we devote too much time and effort on our work, while at the same time, spend much less time with our family and friends. Some even lose their health. At that point, we need to ask what is the purpose of making more money and then examine the approach to be taken to fulfill that purpose. If our purpose is to make our life happy, then are we still happy with the money earned at the cost of losing either our health or our pleasure with family and friends? This result, obviously, does not match with our purpose in the beginning, revealing the flaws with whatever means we took. Such examination of the means by checking it with the purpose can be applied to our speech as well. Facts used should be consistently interpreted with the purpose of the speech decided on in the beginning. It is interesting to note that I often question a student after he gives his speech, "What is the purpose of your speech?" Surprisingly, some of them don't know. Other questions, such as, "How is your speech related to your topic?" "Why did you use this fact?" and "Is your interpretation related to your purpose?" are all helpful in examining whether your reasoning is consistent with your purpose. If a student cannot successfully form a connection between his purpose and his content (e.g. facts and interpretation), then the speech has deviated from its original purpose and will fail in persuasion. This common mistake is often found in a job interview when an applicant is a new graduate from school, where the interviewee's purpose should be emphasizing one's professional background, diligence, loyalty, etc.

Once a purpose is ascertained in the beginning, we will move to the next stage on how to prepare a speech.

在一個演說中，目的是最重要的，因爲目的可以決定方向在哪、立場是什麼、誰是你的群衆、要挑選什麼樣的事實、事實如何被陳述以及產生什麼樣的訊息，最後要呼召什麼樣的行動。事實上，在我們所採取的行動中，目的是我們首先應該問的問題。爲什麼我們要做這個演說？這一篇寫作或是談判的目的在哪裡？爲什麼我們要做這樣的決定？採取這樣的行動？例如：爲什麼去念這所大學或接受這份工作？爲什麼要做這個投資？爲什麼要向銀行借這筆錢？如果一開始不能確認目的的話，那沒有工作可以滿意地完成。目的可以充分的解釋你爲什麼採取這樣的行動，因此，目的在檢驗一些所建議的方法，以及論理的過程是很重要的。一個清楚的目的可以告訴我們，我們所採取的方法是否與目的相符合。舉例而言，我們願意勤奮的工作來賺錢，是我們相信金錢可以改進我們的生活。但是當我們在工作上花了太多時間和精神，而同時卻忽略了我們的家人與朋友，問題就會發生，有些甚至犧牲我們的健康。一旦如此，我們就必須檢驗賺錢的目的以及為了達到那個目的所採取的方法。如果我們的目的，是讓我們的生活變得更快樂，那在失去我們的健康以及與家人朋友相聚的時候，我們依然能快樂嗎？這樣的結果顯然不能夠與我們最初的目的相符合，因而顯示出我們所採取的手段的缺點。這樣以目的來檢驗所採取的方法，一樣可以適用在我們的演說當中。對於演說中使用事實所做的詮釋，必須與演說的目的相符合。這裡有個有趣的註記，我通常會在一個學生演說後詢問他：「你演說的目的是什麼？」令人驚訝的是，有些人會沒辦法回答這個問題。至於其他的問題比方說：「你的演說和你的主題有什麼相關？」「你為什麼使用這個事實？」以及「你對於事實的詮釋是不是與你的目的相符合？」這些問題都有助於檢驗你的論理過程是不是與你的目的相符合。如果一個學生沒辦法很成功的建立目的與內容的關聯性（例如：所使用的事實與對事實的詮釋是否與目的相關聯），那他的演說，就偏離了原先的目的，而達不到說服的效果。這樣共通的毛病也常常發生在社會新鮮人的求職面談上，這類面談的目的應該是強調專業背景、勤勉以及忠誠。

一旦演說的目的確定之後，我們就可以至下一章節討論如何準備一篇演講。

3.3 Facts and interpretation

Fact	Interpretation of fact	Message	Conclusion
	Opinion		

Facts standing alone does not mean much. People tend to remember facts better. Facts can carry some meaning and exert power of persuasion only after being interpreted. The same facts differently interpreted will result in different consequences. A bottle half full of water is also a bottle half empty. An optimistic mind is pleased with it half full while a pessimistic mind feels sorry for the imperfection. Therefore, it is a matter of interpretation decided by the different perspectives taken. The same facts differently interpreted give a different meaning and thus exerts various power. A fact on killing a person, if construed as a murder, could result in a death penalty. Nevertheless, if successfully interpreted and corroborated with evidence as an act of self-defense, the accused will be acquitted. Similarly, a fact that a dog is killed does not carry much meaning. However, if an old dog is killed by police simply because of its faithful propensity to guard its homeless master against arrest, then the story will be different and will call for the public's sympathy. Facts need interpretation to be powerful and persuasive.

3.3 事實與詮釋

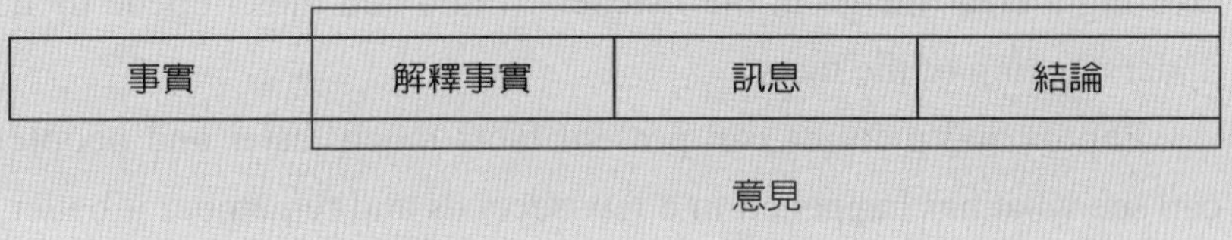

事實	解釋事實	訊息	結論

意見

單純的事實，沒有什麼意義，人們傾向記得事實。事實只有在被詮釋之後才有意義，才能夠產生說服的力量。同樣的一組事實，由於不同的詮釋會導致不同的結果。一個瓶子半滿的水也同時是半空的。樂觀的人爲這半滿的水而感到樂觀，而悲觀的人卻爲他的不完美感到惋惜。因此，這是所採取的角度以及解釋的問題。同樣的事實因爲不同的解釋會有著完全不同的結果，因而產生不同的力量。一個殺人的事實如果被解釋爲謀殺可以導致死刑，但是如果可以成功地以證據合理詮釋是自衛的行爲，就會使得被告無罪釋放。同樣的，殺掉一條狗的事實，沒有太大的意義，但是如果一條老狗，因爲牠很忠心，看守著他無家可歸的主人，拒絕警察的逮捕而被殺掉的話，整個故事就會不一樣，能夠召喚大眾的同情。事實需要被詮釋才會有力量具有說服力。

However, description of facts either in writing or speaking is not an easy job if we want our listeners to understand those facts easier and to remember them better. Generally, it takes time to read and understand verbal descriptions. Upon receiving the information from either writing or speaking the facts, the listeners will gradually construct an image from such information as if he is looking at a photo or watching a film. Therefore, vague descriptions including unskillful language are similar to blurs on a photo and will hinder creating a clear image in the listeners' mind and thus impede their understanding of the facts.

Photos and pictures can present facts much faster and people can see what has happened in a few seconds and remember it better and longer. In fact, images in the pictures or photos are more effective than the description presented in writing and speaking. European churches in the Middle ages told illiterate farmers the stories from the Bible with paintings. Currently, many advertisements appeal to potential customers through interesting and colorful photos, films and pictures. They hope their customers can come to know their products easier and remember them better. They are promoting their products by selling the images they create.

In the U.S., some elementary school teachers teach pupils writing by asking the children to draw a painting first and then the pupils have to tell the whole class what their paintings are about. This approach has successfully intrigued the pupils' imagination and constructs their ability to describe facts (i.e. an image). In fact, the description of facts can be made much easier if an image can surface first in the speaker's mind and then the description is made accordingly.

但是，以寫作或是演說的方式來描述事實並不容易，如果我們想要我們的聽衆能夠更容易地了解，更方便他們記憶的話。通常，要了解字面或是口頭上的描述需要花時間。在收到關於事實方面的訊息的時候，不論是書面或是口頭，聽眾通常會藉由訊息在他們心中建立起一個形象，就像他在照片或是影片中能看到的影像一樣。因此模糊的描述，包括不熟練的實用語言，就像是相片上的汙點一樣，會阻礙聽眾在他們的心中建立起一個清晰的形象，因此也妨礙他們了解整個的事實。

相片圖畫或影片能夠將事實快速的展現出來，人們可以在幾秒鐘之內看到發生了什麼事而且便於長期記憶。事實上，相片圖畫或影片的形象比起寫作或是演說的描述更有效率。歐洲中世紀的教會常常使用圖畫展現出聖經上的故事來教育那些不識字的農民，現今世代，許多廣告也使用有趣及色彩繽紛的相片、影片或是圖畫來吸引潛在消費者，他們希望他們的消費者能夠更容易地了解他們的產品，也方便他們記憶。他們利用銷售他們所創造出來的圖像來達成促銷的目的。

在美國，有些小學老師在教導他們學生作文的時候，先要求他們畫一張圖，然後小學生們必須要告訴全班他們畫了什麼東西。這樣的方式很成功地激起了學生的想像力，以及描述事實的能力（也就是這個圖像）。事實上，描述一個事實會變得容易許多，如果演說者能夠在心中先架構這樣的形象，接著再依照這樣的形象來描述。

Thirty years ago, a Marlboro man advertisement showing a cowboy in the wild west (photo as a fact) spoke for manhood, strength and courage against the wild nature (interpretation of a fact). A pack of Marlboro cigarettes is for real tough man (conclusion). This is an interpretation of the fact, a picture of a cowboy in the wilderness. An advertisement with a similar approach can be seen all the time everywhere. The interpretation is related to how you explain the facts shown. High school students in their writing tests are often shown a few pictures and are required to describe what they see and create a story from those pictures. This is training the student's ability to observe, describe and produce a persuasive message. Facts that happened can be conserved in our brains in a form of pictures and therefore the training of one's ability on verbalizing a story from pictures is the very basic training on the power of persuasion.

三十年前，Marlboro man 的廣告出現了在美國西部荒野的一個牛仔（事實）。為了對抗蠻荒而顯示出眞正男人的氣息、力量以及勇氣（詮釋事實）。Marlboro 是一包給眞正勇敢男人的香菸（訊息），想要成為眞正勇敢的男人就必須抽Marlboro 香菸（結論）。這就是對一張牛仔在西部原野的相片，一個事實的詮釋。相同方式的廣告無論何時何地都看得見。事實的詮釋是跟你如何解釋那些展現出來的事實有關。高中生在他們的考試中常常看到一些圖畫，然後需要描述他們看到什麼，而且要說出一個故事。這就是對於學生觀察事實，描述事實還有提供具有說服信息能力的訓練。而事實的發生是可以以圖像的方式存在我們的腦海當中，因此看圖說故事，是對於說服力的最基本訓練。

An interpretation of a fact is also a reasoning process. Reasoning refers to a process like a bridge connecting a point from the beginning to the end, a purpose and a conclusion, so to speak. In other words, the purpose should be consistent with your position held in a conclusion. If your purpose is to make sales on your products, then your reasoning should move in the promotional direction by emphasizing the advantages and benefits of your products, probably comparing the disadvantages of your competitors' products. If your purpose is applying for a job positon, then your introduction should be to build up your image on a professional level for landing that job. In either case, you should emphasize your advantages more. Your disadvantage, if ever mentioned, for example, in a job interview, should be used as a contrast (e.g. the experience learned from mistakes as a new beginner or too much dedication to work without observing your own health) to corroborate your fitness or strengths for achieving your purpose. So many times, I have noticed that students fail to take a firm position and emphasize their strengths in their conclusion at the end of their speech. They elaborate in their speech a good story with interesting details. Good stories always make a speech interesting, grasping the full attention of the audience and helping them to remember your speech better. To my surprise, in their conclusion, they gave no firm position and left all the decisions to the audience because they were trying to look "fair". No position taken in a conclusion means that no action is called for. No action called for means that a speaker is not intending to persuade. If a speaker is not intending to persuade, then what message can be conveyed to the audience through simply an interesting story? The whole speech is only giving information. If that were the case, then the message sent to the listeners is basically “forget what I just said”. The whole story is wasted and the purpose of that speech has failed in terms of persuasion. If no action is called for in the conclusion, the whole purpose of a speech fails unless your speech is merely for providing information or entertainment.

詮釋事實是一種論理的過程，論理的過程是把開始與結束之間，也就是目的與結論，銜接起來的橋梁。也就是說目的應該符合結論所持的立場。如果你的目的是要販賣你的產品，那你的說理過程就應該朝向推銷的方向強調產品的優點和好處，甚至是把對手的缺點作爲比較。如果你的目的是在找一份工作，那你的自我介紹就應該建立你的專業形象以及強調你的長處。在這兩種情形都應該強調你的優點，就算提到你的缺點，例如在應徵工作的面談，也應該用來當作一個反襯（比如相對於初學者，從錯誤當中所學習的經驗或是太投入工作而不重視健康），用以支持你的適合性或是優點來達到你的目的。有很多次學生們在他們演說的結論中並不採取確定的立場，他們給了一個充滿有趣細節的美好故事。好的故事總是讓演說很有趣味，可以抓到聽衆們的注意，而且讓他們容易記得。但讓我覺得驚訝的是，在他們的結論中，他們並不採取確定的立場，他們讓聽衆們做決定，因爲他們試著想看起來很「公平」。如果不在結論中確定立場，表示你不期待他們做什麼。如果你不期待他們做什麼，表示你不想說服。如果你不想說服，那你究竟給了聽衆什麼樣的訊息？整篇演說或文章只是在提供資訊而已。眞的是如此的話，那演說者所傳遞給聽衆的訊息，無非是「請忘記我剛才所說的」，整個故事就因此浪費掉。以說服而言，整個演說的目的是失敗的。如果演說的結論並不要求行動，那說服的目的是失敗的，除非你的演說只是在提供資訊或是爲了娛樂而已。

A similar mistake is found in some students' writings in high schools on a topic requiring discussion of the uniform issue. After completing their strenuous work of lengthy pages, no positions were presented in their conclusion. In a paper on discussing the school uniform code, one student in his conclusion advised the readers to make their own decision because either views were valuable and both have advantages and disadvantages. Everyone knows that any decision has pros and cons and can be made either way for whatever reason. When no action is called for and the readers feel free to make their own decision, all his effort in writing is in vain because neither any research nor any discussion is needed for a conclusion like that. If no action is called for, then the whole purpose of persuasion fails, whether in writing or given as a speech.

類似的錯誤，也發生在一些學生們討論關於學校制服議題的寫作上，在他們筋疲力盡的研究之後寫了長篇的報告，但在他們的結論中並沒有採取任何立場，一個學生建議讀者們可以自行決定，因爲各有利弊，看法也都各有價値。每一個人都知道任何論點都會有正反兩面，也都各有理由，也就是說他在寫作上所有的努力都是白費的，因爲不採取立場的結論，根本不需要任何研究或討論，如果不呼籲任何行動，讀者可以自由採取行動，說服的目的就達不到，不管是寫作或是演說。

We should also take notice that some people might play a trick by trying to appear unbiased by introducing some biased evidence, e.g. photos of an Arab and a photo of car explosion with a caption, "What do you think?" The question seems to be conveying an unbiased mind but the evidence does not. In fact, it is misleading for the purpose of persuasion.

我們也需要注意到有些人可能會玩弄一些技巧，他們試圖看似公正，但卻使用具有歧視性的證據。例如把一張汽車爆炸的相片與一張阿拉伯人的相片放在一起，然後下面出現一行字問：「你認為如何？」問題看似中立但是證據並不中立。事實上，他是為了達到說服的目的（恐怖分子都是阿拉伯人），而特意使用具有誤導性的證據。

One thing to note here, purpose in a speech or a commercial advertisement should be straightforward so that your listeners can immediately grasp your message. Some commercials on TV are probably intentionally made creative in some parts or retain beautiful models to catch the public's attention and are successful as expected. But, interestingly, consumers only remember the creative part or that pretty models of that commercial but fail to remember what products the commercials are promoting as a result. Some students have similar problems with their speech. They spend a good deal of time and effort to conjure up a story but fail to give an important message at the end. The audience does not know what the speaker is driving at? In fact, this type of problem may often surface in our daily conversation. These are distractions and should be avoided. If your listeners do not even know the main message of your speech or purpose of your promotion, regardless how creative it is, then you are simply wasting your time and effort.

這邊要注意一點，在演說或是商業廣告上，目的應該直接了當，這樣你的聽衆才能夠快速了解你的訊息。有一些電視的廣告可能是爲了吸引大家的注意，因此在一些情節上故意表現出他們的創意或是僱用了美麗的模特兒，而他們確實是一如期待非常的成功吸引了大家的注意。但很有趣的是，消費者只記得廣告有創意的部分或是美麗的模特兒，卻不記得這個廣告是在賣什麼產品。有些學生在演講上也有類似的問題。他們花了很多的時間和功夫來組織故事的事實部分，但卻不能夠在結束的時候給一個強而有力的訊息。聽衆不知道他的重點在哪裡？事實上，這樣的問題也在我們日常的對話當中發生。這些都是分散注意力的事情，應該要避免。如果你的聽衆不知道你主要的訊息或是目的，不管你有多少的創意，那你根本是浪費自己的精神和時間。

One thing to be noted here is that the principle of being straight forward with your purpose should be carefully applied in a negotiating situation. A client of mine once had a business dispute with a large retailer in the U.S. on the quality of the products his company sold. The retailer asked my client to come to America to discuss their new products. My client was very pleased and put great effort in preparing for his business presentation. When he attended the meeting, the presentation on the function of the new products only lasted a few minutes, and then the whole meeting was directed by the retailer on discussing the quality of one of the products they claimed to be defected and were seeking a possible compensation. My client was totally unprepared for this trick. Such a problem can only be foreseen and prepared for in advance, subsequent to a full understanding and analysis of the whole situation, and this will be elaborated on further in the fourth chapter on debate.

但是在這個地方要注意，對於你的目的直接了當的原則在談判上要小心的應用。我這有個客戶曾經有一次跟美國非常大的通路商，對於所銷售的商品有些爭議。這個通路商通知我的客戶到美國開會，他們想多了解新的產品。我的客戶非常高興，然後花了很大的功夫準備好介紹的產品。等他到了美國開會的時候，介紹產品的時間非常的短暫，整個會議幾乎就在討論產品的品質以及可能的賠償問題。我的客戶對於這樣的計謀完全沒有準備。這樣的問題只有在對於整體狀況充分了解與分析後才能夠預防以及準備。我們將在第四章辯論的部分會進一步的討論。

In preparation of a speech, ask yourself the following questions. Why am I giving this speech? What is my purpose? Who is my audience? What facts am I going to present? How do I connect my facts with my conclusion? What is my message? Are my facts relevant to the message? What issues am I bringing to the attention of the listeners? Are all the ideas or facts presented relevant and logically connected to each other in my speech? All these questions must be answered before a speech is given. The purpose will decide what facts will be introduced, what the issues are, how the ideas are connected, what message should be sent and what reasoning should be used. The purpose is the first task to be decided on in a speech.

在準備一篇演講的時候應該問到下列的問題：我爲什麼要做這個演講？我的目的是什麼？我的聽衆是誰？我要提供什麼樣的事實？我要如何將我的事實與結論連結？什麼是我的訊息？我的事實與訊息是否有關聯？我要對我的聽衆呈現什麼樣的爭議點？所有的想法和事實是不是都是相關的？而且彼此間是否有邏輯上的連結？這些問題在演講開始之前，都必須被回答，目的會決定需要提及什麼樣的事實，什麼是爭議點？想法如何連結？要送出什麼樣的訊息？以及該使用什麼樣的分析？目的是在演講當中最先被決定的。

The Gettysburg address as a very successful quintessence given by Abraham Lincoln in 1863, a period during the American civil war, contains only ten sentences with no more than 400 words. It is short, concise, yet powerful enough to call for the listeners' dedication and sacrifice to defend the belief and principles on which the U.S. Constitution was founded. How did Lincoln achieve his purpose? Take a look at the original context:

美國林肯總統在 1863 年，內戰仍在進行當中所做的蓋茲堡演說是非常成功的案例，他只有十句不到四百字，他很精簡但卻非常震撼，足以喚起聽者保衛美國憲法的決定，以及願意所做的犧牲。林肯怎麼達到他的目的呢？我們來看一下他的原文：

The Gettysburg Address

"Four score and seven years ago our fathers brought forth on this continent, a new nation, conceived in Liberty, and dedicated to the proposition that all men are created equal.

Now we are engaged in a great civil war, testing whether that nation, or any nation so conceived and so dedicated, can long endure. We are met on a great battle-field of that war. We have come to dedicate a portion of that field, as a final resting place for those who here gave their lives that that nation might live. It is altogether fitting and proper that we should do this.

But, in a larger sense, we cannot dedicate—we cannot consecrate—we cannot hallow this ground. The brave men, living and dead, who struggled here, have consecrated it, far above our poor power to add or detract. The world will little note, nor long remember what we say here, but it can never forget what they did here. It is for us the living, rather, to be dedicated here to the unfinished work which they who fought here have thus far so nobly advanced. It is rather for us to be here dedicated to the great task remaining before us—that from these honored dead we take increased devotion to that cause for which they gave the last full measure of devotion—that we here highly resolve that these dead shall not have died in vain—that this nation, under God, shall have a new birth of freedom and that government of the people, by the people, for the people, shall not perish from the earth."

蓋茲堡演說

八十七年前，前人來到這片大陸，開創了一個被認爲自由且致力於人人平等的國家。

現在我們正進行一場偉大的戰爭，考驗著我們或其他有著相同理念國家能否長存。我們在這遼闊的戰場相遇。我們將這戰場上的一部分奉獻出來給那些爲國家存亡所犧牲的勇士們，而他們值得這一切。

然而在更大的意義上來說，我們並無法貢獻，聖化，更不能神化這片土地。曾在這作戰，存活下來或犧牲了的勇士，都已聖化這片土地，且遠超過我們的微薄之力。世人不會記得我們所說過的話，但他們從不會忘記這群勇士在這所付出的一切。正確來說，是爲了活著的我們，他們致力於在戰場作戰。更確切來說，是爲了活著的我們，投身於這場戰事中。我們應更致力於令他們全力拼戰到最後一刻的那件事情上，我們在此下定決心不讓他們的犧牲成爲白費。在神的祝福下，這個國家將在自由之下獲得新生。這個民有、民治、民享的國家，將永存在這世上。

Lincoln's approach seems very simple, explaining the purpose of engagement in a civil war by telling the listeners "where we were from" (why this nation was built), "why we are here" (to memorize those who died for the cause of emancipation) and "where we are going" (to maintain a government of the people, by the people and for the people).

林肯的方法看起來很簡單，他透過告訴聽衆我們從哪來（爲什麼要建立這個國家），我們爲什麼會在這裡（紀念那些爲了解放黑奴所犧牲的人們），以及我們要往哪裡去（維持一個民有、民治、民享的政府），解釋了內戰的目的。

The focal point presented before the listeners is that "we should continue to maintain our forefathers' ideology by establishing a new government of freedom". But Lincoln did not ask the listeners to make their own decision. On the contrary, he made a decision in his speech for the audience to follow, in a tone of authority with persuasiveness built on deeds of their forefathers. His purpose for this speech is clear enough, so is the content with brevity. His attitude to engage in that war was with a strong conviction and an obviously strong determination, leaving no room for doubt by any American citizen of the entire country. If he would have left the choice for others to decide, he would never have achieved his purpose on calling for an action to take place because he would have sounded like he was wavering about his goal. If a speaker cannot be sure what he is talking about, he can never convince his listeners to follow what he suggests.

在聽者前面所呈現出來的重點是，我們應該維持我們前人所建立新自由政府的理想，但是林肯並沒有要求這些聽衆自己做決定，相反的，他在他的演說中，幫聽衆們下了一個決定讓他們來跟從，他帶著說服力而充滿權威的聲音是建立在前人們的行爲上，他演說的目的很清楚，內容也是一樣，他充滿確信及決心從事內戰的態度是很明顯而強烈的，對於所有美國人而言，沒有任何的懷疑的。如果他讓其他人自由地決定，恐怕就達不到他所呼喚的目的，因爲他聽起來會很猶豫不決。如果一個演說者不確定他所要的，那他永遠沒有辦法說服他的聽衆。

(1) Observation in a classroom

A cloud in the sky

As usual, I walked into my English writing class, the intermediate level. The goal of that class was to teach the students a persuasive writing style not quite different from a speech if put in a written form. The students are all sophomores. I simply followed the steps suggested by Dale Carnegie for an impromptu speech, presenting a story with a message calling for some action. Why did I use that approach in this class? Well, my idea was that if a student sends a clear message to the reader by telling a story elaborated with facts followed by good reasons, a purpose on persuasion would then be accomplished. Persuasion is the goal for writing and in giving a speech. It seemed easy but was quite difficult to achieve.

(1) 課堂觀察

天空中的一片雲

就像平常一樣，我走進我的英文寫作中級班，課堂的目的在訓練學生學習具有說服力的寫作，跟演講並沒太大不同，都是大二的學生，我依照著卡內基對於即席演說的訓練方式教導學生，也就是給一篇帶有訊息的故事，以召喚行動做爲結尾。爲什麼我會用這種方式呢？我的想法是，如果學生可以將一個清楚的訊息，透過一篇故事傳遞給讀者，而這篇故事能夠對事實以很好的理由加以闡述，那說服的目的就會達到。說服是演說與寫作的目的，看起來很簡單，做起來卻很難。

I often pay attention to the students in the first row. My professor in St. Louis University Law School told us in the classroom, "You guys, do you know what is the difference between students in SLU and Harvard? Harvard students take seats in the first row and SLU students prefer the last", quite sarcastically, yet true.

我對坐第一排的學生通常都會注意，我在美國聖路易大學的法學院教授曾說過，「你知道我們跟哈佛大學差在哪裡嗎？哈佛的學生喜歡坐第一排，而我們的學生喜歡坐在最後一排」，很諷刺卻很眞實。

Students here, in Taiwan, are used to the teachers giving instructions and the students prefer to use textbooks. They feel secure and comfortable with these tools. The monotonous tone of a teacher giving instructions makes the whole air in the classroom heavy and dead. As the teacher's voice carries on, few cannot hold their heavy head anymore but fall asleep with their head lying on their desk, probably because of their activities from the previous night. Some are chatting. Some are reading other books. Of course, you can always find a few still looking at you but lost into oblivion. Almost none takes notes. Interestingly, they don't take notes and they cannot remember either. That makes the teacher to constantly elaborate on the same principles. I often wonder if teachers are the only ones who gain progress in the course they teach. The classroom seems like a resting place for their tired bodies and souls.

這裡的學生習慣全部都由老師講授的方式，而且他們喜歡使用教科書。他們對於這些工具感到安全與舒適，老師們講課單調的聲音，讓整個教室的氣氛非常沉重，沒有任何的生趣。老師繼續講課，一些撐不住的學生就直接睡在桌上，也許前一天晚上太累了；一些在讀其他的書，當然你總是會發現一些學生眼神空洞的望著你。幾乎沒有人做筆記，有趣的是他們記不住又不做筆記，那使得老師不斷重複一樣的事情，我常懷疑整堂課下來唯一有進步的只有老師，整個教室就像是他們安置自己疲憊身軀與靈魂的場所。

Trying to get their attention during this class, I asked some questions to refresh their memory. "Can anyone give me an answer?" No one raises their hands. I ask again, still none. Probably this class is really the best place to rest their souls.

要引起他們的注意，我問一些問題來恢復他們的記憶，「有人可以回答嗎？」沒有人舉手，我再問一次，還是沒有。也許這個班真的是讓他們靈魂休息的最佳場所。

During a 10-minute break, life comes back to the whole class. I walk around the class to see what brought about their resurrection. All I heard was about their activities from the previous night, a tour somewhere, gossip about friends or some celebrities. Interestingly, now I know these are the topics that are able to hold their attention.

在十分鐘的下課時間，整個班上恢復了生趣，我在班上逛了一下，想看看是什麼讓他們又活了過來，我所聽到的是，他們昨天晚上的活動、到哪邊去玩了，或是討論朋友以及一些名人的八卦，我現在知道他們對什麼有興趣。

"Sir, should we know who our reader is when we write?" A girl approaches from behind with this question. I looked at her; a young girl who always sits in the first row, takes notes and asks questions. She showed me her work during break, asking for my opinion on how she could better improve her writing. The pages in her note book, full of scribbles, no longer seemed strong enough to withstand any further flipping. She was a good student by any standard in a crammed training course prevalent in Taiwan or in China.

「老師，當我們在寫作的時候，我們應該知道我們的讀者是誰嗎？」一個女學生從後面問我這個問題，我看了她一下，一個年輕的女孩子，總是坐在第一排，寫著筆記與發問，常常將作業在下課的時間拿給我看，希望我修改，筆記本上的紙張寫滿了字，看起來禁不起再次的翻閱，從華人填鴨式的標準來看，她是個非常優秀的學生。

"Oh!" I turned around and looked at her. In fact, I was puzzled by her question. Should we care about who our readers will be when we write? I remembered that story about Einstein who often got lost once he left home and could not remember his way back home. Just as that was something probably so simple and basic and, in my opinion, probably not worth my time to elaborate on. “Like hunting, shouldn’t you always find a target to shoot?” I answered.

「哦！」我轉過身來看著她，我對她的問題有點疑惑，當我們寫作的時候我們應該要知道我們的讀者是誰嗎？突然想起愛因斯坦的故事，出門以後常常忘記回家的路，有些事情可能太簡單了，以及如此的基本，所以我認爲根本不值得一提。「就像打獵一樣，你難道不應該先找到目標再射擊嗎？」我這樣回答。

In fact, she is not alone. Students under crammed training tend to follow the instructions given by their teachers. They rarely ask questions. Such training in Taiwan often extends from elementary schools to college level which, fair to say, focuses on memorizing information. The problem solving ability in the real world originates from the training of observing facts, spotting issues by analyzing the pros and cons together with their possibilities followed by proposing a feasible plan. No work can proceed unless we know where we are going. Once a direction is ascertained, we can decide what approach to take. Therefore, a purpose must be decided on at the very beginning.

事實上，她並不是唯一的一個。接受填鴨式教育的學生習慣於聆聽老師的講授，他們很少問問題，在臺灣這樣的訓練方式，從小學到大學都集中在資訊的記誦上面，真實的世界是要求解決問題的能力，這樣的能力是從事實中進行觀察、爭議點的掌握以及對可能性與正反的分析，接著提出可行的方案。除非我們知道要往哪邊去，否則我們沒有辦法進行任何工作。當我們確立方向之後，我們才能確立要採取哪種方法，因此，我們在一開始就必須決定目的是什麼。

A writing or a speech is directed at the listeners. Our goal is to persuade them with sound reasons. That is what we should bear in mind before we can proceed with our work. It is therefore a surprise to see that one of our best students under crammed training, who is capable of using complicated sentence structures embellished with beautiful vocabulary in her writing, produces no substance in her work because she cannot send out a message. She cannot send out a message because she does not know who her readers are? A hunter who does not know where his target is can only chase the wind. How can she ever write if she does not know whom she is writing to? Who her target readers or listeners are? Then what is the purpose of her writing? A good salesman should always know who will be his potential customers or he cannot make a sound business plan. From that moment, I realized that knowing your purpose and your audience is the very first priority to teach in a speech and writing class.

寫作和演說都是針對聽衆或是讀者。我們的目的是用好的理由去說服他們，這個是我們在開始工作前必須牢記在心的。因此很令人驚訝的是，看到我們在填鴨式教育下訓練出來最好的學生，他可以在他的寫作裡面中使用複雜的句型以及華麗的文藻，但卻不能傳遞訊息。他沒有辦法傳遞出一個訊息，因爲不知道讀者是誰。一個不知道獵物在哪邊的獵人，只能追風。如果一個作者不知道要寫給誰看，那怎麼進行寫作呢？誰是他的讀者或是聽衆？他寫作的目的在哪裡？一個優秀的銷售員應該知道誰是他的潛在客戶，要不然他是沒有辦法製作一個很好的商業計畫，遑論效果。從那個時候開始我知道了，了解你的目的以及你的群衆，在寫作課的第一堂課就必須告訴他們，那是非常重要的工作。

(2) Observation in a classroom

1 In a classroom discussion, a question is asked to all of the students. What is the purpose of doing a speech? Some answered that the purpose of a speech is to convey to others what we think. If that were really so, then no advertisement should pay attention to their content as long as a voice is heard and a promotion is made known to the public. It seems easy to assume that a speech is made for conveyance of our ideas only. But such answer is more likely to say that merely offering meals at a restaurant is good enough regardless of whether the meals offered will be sold or not. Is that really so? Are the customers always interested in the products we offer? In fact, consumers are only interested in the products they enjoy or need. Similar to making a sale to customers, in a speech, if we don’t know who our audience is, we can easily send out a wrong message to the

wrong people, similar to a situation where we sometimes text a wrong message by mobile phone to a wrong receiver. Similarly, you cannot sell your car to a person who is looking for a truck. We need to know who our audience is. A purpose in a speech will decide who your audience is and what they want to hear, what story to present and what message to use to call for their action. It is important for a beginner in a training process to remember what his purpose is in his speech.

(2) 課堂觀察

1 在一個課堂討論，問了大家一個問題，什麼是演說的目的，有的人回答，演說的目的是把我們所知道的告訴別人。如果眞的是如此的話，那廣告就不需要花工夫在他的內容上，只要聲音夠大，然後大家能夠知道有這樣的促銷就夠了。我們很容易假設演說就只是傳遞我們的想法，但是這樣就像是餐廳只提供餐點，而不管餐點是否會被購買。眞的是如此嗎？消費者對我們提供的商品一定會有興趣嗎？事實上，消費者只想購買他們有興趣或是需要的商品。就像是促銷商品一樣，在演講中如果我們不知道我們的聽衆是誰的話，我們很容易把錯誤的訊息傳給錯誤的人，就像我們使用手機把錯的訊息傳給錯的人。同樣的，你沒有辦法把你的房車賣給想要買卡車的人。我們要知道我們的群衆是誰，演說的目的會決定你的聽衆以及他們想聽些什麼，你又該呈現什麼故事，還有你要傳遞什麼訊息來呼籲他們的行動。初學者在演說訓練過程中，一定要總是記得他演說的目的。

2 Mirror image effect

It will be interesting to notice how the audience reacts to a speaker's performance including his expression, hesitation, doubt, confusion, passion, emotion, enthusiasm, etc. If a speaker is hesitant and shows confusion, the audience casts doubt on their faces. If he speaks firmly with enthusiasm and passion, the audience can sense the power and energy from his words, thus having better faith in the speaker. If a speaker talks slow with a boring tone, the audience is likely to yawn and look sleepy regardless how profound the message is. If the speaker is humorous, the whole atmosphere will be relaxing and the audience generally will respond with support by laughter and applause. If a speaker looks sad, the audience cannot look happy. A speaker is the commander of the emotions of the entire audience in a room. The reaction from an audience will generally reflect a mirror image of the speaker. Therefore, if you want your audience to respond with passion and enthusiasm, you first have to speak with passion and enthusiasm. If you want your listeners to believe what you say, you have to believe what you are preaching.

2 鏡中形象的效果

觀察群眾如何看待演說者的表現，包括演說者的表情、猶豫不決、懷疑、困惑以及他的熱情、情緒甚至熱誠等等，是非常有趣的事情。如果演說者很猶豫不決而且表現出困惑，群眾在他們的臉上就會顯示出他們的懷疑。如果他說話肯定並且帶著熱誠與熱情，聽衆可以感覺到他話語的那份力量還有活力，而且對他所說的也比較有信心。如果演講者以非常無趣的聲調，慢條斯理地討論他的介紹或是意見，群衆回報的，很可能打哈欠而且看起來非常疲憊，不管這個訊息多有意義。如果一個演講者非常幽默，那整個氣氛會是非常輕鬆而且聽衆會以笑聲與掌聲來做回應。如果演說者看起來悲傷，聽衆不可能看起來很快樂。一個演說者是整個會場裡面所有聽衆的情緒指揮官。聽衆的反應通常像是一個鏡子中的形象一樣。因此，如果你希望群衆以熱誠和熱情來進行回應，你必須自己也以熱誠和熱情來進行你的演講。如果你希望你的聽衆相信你所說的，那你自己首先要相信你自己所說的。

3 Anthony Robbins, a famous American charismatic speaker, says that emotion is the force of life. It seems true that determination is made more often with one's emotions rather than common sense. A smoker of 30 years may decide to quit smoking not because of his recent awareness of hazardous smoking but rather of a wish made by his granddaughter. A prodigal son may change his mind and move toward a right track of life probably because of love shown by his family or simply an admonition given by a stranger rather than his logical analysis of his weakness in his character. In fact, the addictive grandfather and this prodigal son may have known their problems for a long time and continued the same way of life for many years. Change came into their lives only when an emotion is born in their hearts. Emotions can produce force and force can change our life. Therefore, if a speaker can call upon the emotions of the listeners, he surely can

call the listeners to act. To create an emotion in their minds, the speaker must bring up the emotion probably through empathy or sympathy in his own mind. A speaker can pass on a fiery passion only when he has enthusiasm in his own heart first. A speaker must know his audience and try to connect his topic with that audience by creating the appropriate emotions. Once emotions are established, calling the audience to action will be much easier.

3 安東尼羅賓斯是一個非常有名而且具有領袖魅力的美國演說家，他說情緒是生命中的動力。這看起來似乎是眞的，決心通常都是由情緒而不是由理性所發動。一個三十年的老菸槍可能決定要戒菸，並不是因爲他最近才知道抽菸的害處，可能只是因爲他小孫女的一個期待而已。一個浪子回頭的改變心意，邁向正軌的生活，可能是由於家人對他的愛或是一個陌生人的勸告，而不是他對他自己弱點的理性分析。事實上，一個有菸癮的老祖父和這個浪子早就知道他們的問題，而且已經繼續這樣的生活許多年。他們生活的改變是由於他們的內心產生了情緒。情緒產生力量，而力量能改變我們的生活。因此，如果演說者可以引發聽衆的情緒，他就能夠使聽衆採取行動。要在聽衆他們心中製造情緒，演說者必須在他自己的心理以同理心或同情心製造出這樣情緒。一個演說者，只有當他心裡先有熱情的時候，才能將熱情的火焰傳遞出去。一個演說者必須了解他的群衆，而且應該試圖將他的主題與群衆以適當的情緒連結起來。一旦建立適當情緒的時候，呼籲群衆行動將會容易得多了。

3.4 Delivering a Message

Once a purpose is decided, we will know who our audience is and what action we will call for at the end. Everyone can forcefully present a conclusion but people will not be persuaded by a conclusion only. To persuade, a speaker needs to give the reasons and the reasons are made to support a message, the important idea, so to speak, which is delivered to the listeners. A sound reasoning process will be further discussed in the chapter regarding debates. Reasoning, in terms of persuasion, can be briefly contained in a story as an interpretation of a fact. The reason is simple. A fact refers to something, if authentic, that actually happened in the past and its existence cannot be challenged. A message drawn from a fact which actually existed in the past generally seems convincing and is easier for the listeners to accept. Of course, some deception, for example, on using partial facts to twist the truth will fall into the part related to interpretation of facts and will be examined in the chapter on debates.

3.4 訊息傳遞

一旦目的決定了以後，我們就會知道誰是我們的聽衆，以及在末了我們會呼籲什麼樣的行動。每一個人都可以大聲呼籲一個結論，但是人們不會被結論所說服。爲了達到說服的目的，演說者必須給理由，而理由是來支持那些傳遞給聽衆的訊息，也就是那重要的概念。如何給予一個好的理由？我們將會在下一章關於辯論的部分進行討論。論理，以說服力訓練而言，可以很簡短的說，就是對故事中的事實所提出的詮釋。理由很簡單，事實就是那一些過去發生的事情，一旦被證實，他們的存在是不容被挑戰的。從過去發生的事實所歸納出的訊息，看起來較具有說服力，也較容易被聽衆所接受。當然有一些技巧，例如：利用部分事實來扭曲眞相，是屬於關於事實解釋的部分，也一樣會在辯論的章節進行討論。

What is a message then? A message, as defined by the Merriam-Webster's dictionary, is an important idea contained in a speech. In fact, this idea should be important enough for you to persuade your listeners to take action to support your purpose. A message should be made consistent with the purpose of a speech and of a writing.

什麼是訊息？按照字典的定義，就是演說內容重要的想法。事實上，這一個想法應該是有如此的重要性，讓你能夠說服聽衆來採取行動支持你的目的，訊息應該和演說與寫作的目的相符合。

A message from a speaker is an interpretation by the speaker of the facts given; that is, what do the facts mean to the speaker? How should we view the whole event and what action does the speaker expect the listeners to take? For example, to produce photos regarding harm caused to the lungs from smoking is to present a fact with an interpretation. To claim that hazards are caused by smoking and therefore smoking should be avoided is the message presented to the listeners. To advise smokers to quit smoking and all restaurants to ban smoking is a call for action. This example shows a fact, a message elicited from the interpretation, and an action called for at the end. Interpretations from different perspectives could make the same fact leading to quite a different conclusion as we can see in the following examples. For example, to kill a stray dog is one thing. To kill a faithful dog which guards his homeless master against an attack is another. The same fact pattern of a dog being killed can give a completely different meaning and value. Similarly, a different conclusion can be reached from the fact that a bottle is half full with water. An optimist would feel lucky while a pessimist would view it negatively. In other words, the same fact will bring a different result if interpreted differently. Obviously, the interpretation determines the value of a fact.

演說者的訊息也就是演說者對於事實所提出的解釋，同時也表示事實對於演說者來說有什麼樣的意義。我們應該如何來看待整個事件，以及演說者期待聽眾採取什麼樣的行動，例如：提出相片顯示抽菸對於肺部所造成的傷害，就是提出事實以及對事實的解釋，聲稱抽菸所造成的傷害，因此，戒菸則是傳遞給聽眾的訊息；建議吸菸者戒菸以及所有餐廳禁菸，則是呼籲行動。這例子示範了事實訊息以及所呼籲的行動。而對於相同事實的不同詮釋，往往產生不同的結果，我們可以從下列例子看出這樣的情況。例如打死一條流浪狗是一回事，打死一條看顧無家可歸的主人的忠狗，因為牠不讓主人受到攻擊，則是另外一回事。同樣是一條狗被打死的事實，但是會有完全不同的結果。同樣的，裝了一半水的瓶子，也可以有兩種結論。樂觀的人覺得幸運，而悲觀的人，則用負面的態度來看待。換句話說，相同的事實會帶來完全不同的結果與價值，如果用不同的解釋方式，很顯然，對於事實的解釋，可以決定對事實的價值。

Without any interpretation given by the speaker, facts remain rather cold and hardly any action can be called on. A cold fact exerts little or no power of persuasion. In order to persuade, a speaker must give his interpretation of the facts and tell the listeners what he intends the audience to do, what action to take. An interpretation can make a cold fact become warm. Therefore, it is an important task to train students on their ability to interpret the facts in their story so that a message can be delivered to the audience.

如果缺乏演說者對於事實的詮釋，事實是冰冷的，而且很難引發任何行動。一個冰冷的事實產生不了說服力，要達到說服的目的，演說者必須賦予事實的解釋，並且要告訴聽衆應該怎麼做。對於事實的詮釋給予冰冷的事實溫暖。因此，訓練學生在說故事中對於事實的詮釋的能力，以便將訊息傳給聽衆是很重要的工作。

A few years ago, I was invited by a youth pastor to a church to give words of encourage to a group of high school students whose academic performances in school were below average, ranging from 10 to 50 on a 100 scale. After inquiring about their scores on some courses, I asked if they were willing to study hard? None raised their hands. Obviously, they did not like to study because they have no interest in it at all. Then I asked them again. "If I tell you today, you will be rewarded with 30 US dollars for each point earned above your score from your last test, are you willing to study?" They all raised their hands with no exception. Obviously, they can study and are willing to do so as long as there are incentives. In other words, they have full potential. They just need people to open their eyes to see their potentials. The fact in this case is clear. These students are all on the bottom of their class. This is an objective fact and cannot be rebutted. However, the result is not necessarily pessimistic if the fact is interpreted from a more positive angle. The result would be much worse if the same fact is interpreted negatively, for example, in an inquisitive tone, "Why don't you study harder? Why can't you do it while others can?" A different interpretation of the same facts will bring about a completely different message that will change the results. The message from my story is clear, even those who perform below average still have potential and are willing, ready and able to work hard as long as there are enough motivational incentives to intrigue their interests.

好幾年前，有一個教會的牧師邀請我對他們青少年團契演講，給予他們鼓勵。這些孩子們功課普遍不好，學校成績大概只有十分到五十分左右。在詢問他們課業上的表現後，我問他們是否願意用功，沒有人舉手，顯然他們不喜歡讀書，因爲他們沒有興趣。接著我再問他們一個問題：「如果我今天告訴你們只要你的分數每進步一分我就給你一千塊臺幣，你們願意讀書嗎？」他們全部都舉手了，沒有例外。很明顯，他們是能用功的，而且他們也願意，只要有足夠的激勵，也就是說他們潛力無窮，他們只是需要別人打開他們的眼睛看到他們的潛力。這個例子的事實很清楚，全部的學生在他們的班上都是後段生，事實是很客觀的而且沒有辦法被反駁。但是這樣的結果並不必然是悲觀，如果從一個較爲樂觀的角度來詮釋事實。如果同樣的事實是用較負面與質疑的口氣的態度來進行詮釋，例如：「爲什麼不好好用功？爲什麼其他人可以，你不行？」整個結果會變得更糟糕。對於相同的事實不一樣的解釋，會帶來完全不同的訊息而改變最後的結果。我的故事訊息清楚，即使那些書讀不好的人一樣有潛力，他們能夠願意而且隨時準備用功讀書，只要有足夠激勵他們的動機。

I also remember a skill my father used to convince me to undertake to develop my responsibility for my future career. When I was a junior in college, I lived with my parents and I usually got up at noon. My father was used to waking me up in the morning for school. It was not a pleasant thing for my sleep to be interrupted. Most of time, I told him that I had no class in the morning that day. After a few times, he could sense that I was not telling the truth. He did not rebuke me in either a loud or angry voice. He only asked me, “How would you view a young man of 20 years old like you that always gets up at noon with only half a day left after he gets out of bed? If a student has only half of the time to answer all the questions in an exam, do you think that he can prevail over others in their scores? Do you think that he will have high potential for his future career? If you don't go to school, what exactly are the other important things that you plan on doing with that time?"

我也記得我父親使用一項技巧來說服我承擔自己對未來前途的責任。記得我在大三的時候，跟父母同住，通常中午才起床，我父親會在早上叫醒我去上課，早上被吵醒不是一件太愉快的事情，大部分的時間我告訴他我沒有課，幾回之後，他感覺到我沒有說實話。他並沒有大聲或很生氣地責罵我，他只問我：「你如何看待一個跟你一樣二十歲的年輕人，總是在中午起床，而每天當他起床的時候，一天只剩下一半的時間，如果一個學生在考試的時候只有別人一半的時間可以作答，你認爲他可以考得好嗎？更重要的是，如果你不去上課，那你究竟有什麼更重要的事在進行呢？」

The fact here is clear. I often got up at noon and missed many of my classes. As a message, this fact through an interpretation of an analogy could naturally lead to possible consequences that I would never accomplish anything important in my future if I did not change my attitude and habit. The action called for is that I should change my attitude together with my habits and start getting up early to attend classes. My father successfully spurred my heart on with his message (i.e. a young man like me could never have a chance for future success) through an analogy because I could then see my weakness much clearer from his reasoning and analogy. He skillfully put me in his position to see my weakness and change my attitude on my responsibility toward myself.

這裡的事實很清楚，我通常在中午才起床，然後缺了很多課。這樣的一個事實經過一個對比的解釋，很自然的達到了一個可能的結果，而這個結果也是一個訊息，也就是我可能在未來很難成功，除非我改變我現在的態度還有習慣。這例子所呼籲的動作就是我必須改變我的態度以及我的習慣，並且開始早起以及到學校去上課。我父親很成功地使用比喻的訊息刺激了我內心的想法（像我這樣的年輕人，未來根本沒有成功的機會），因爲我能更清楚地看見我的弱點，他很有技巧地把我放在他的位子上，讓我很清楚地看見我的弱點，也改變我對責任的態度。

Another good example is my conversation with my father 30 years ago regarding my plan to study law in the U.S., which was rather expensive, strenuous and full of challenges. My father was in his 60's and I was only 25 years old, serving in the foreign service of Taiwan. I remember that we had a long conversation and he tried to convince me to stay in the Foreign Service for a stable life. I told him that he was in his 60's already and that he of course wished that everything would remain the same ten years from now. But I was only 25. If everything stayed the same with me ten years or, even worse, 20 years from now, I would feel very disappointed and upset about my total waste of time and effort. To maintain the status quo was a blessing to him but surely a curse to me. That was the message I gave to him and he accepted my explanation and was willing to support my studies in the U.S.

另外一個很好的例子，則是我在三十年前與我父親的對話，那是關於我想到美國去念法律，而這樣的計畫是很昂貴、很費力，而且充滿挑戰的，我父親當時六十多歲，而我只有二十五歲，正在臺灣的外交部門工作，我還記得我們談了很久，他試圖說服我留在外交部門有一個穩定的生活，我告訴他，他已經六十多歲，他當然希望未來的十年一切的事情照舊，但是我只有二十五，如果一切的事情在未來的十年甚至二十年都是一樣的話，我可能會對自己很失望，而且很難過，因爲我浪費所有的時間和努力。保持現狀對他來講是一個祝福，但是對我卻是一個詛咒，這是當時我給他的訊息，他接受了，並且願意資助我到美國讀書。

The fact used here is that I am 25 years old and my father is 60 years old, followed by an interpretation with the result being that I wanted to make changes for a better future while my father would rather continue to maintain a stable life during the next 20 years. The message naturally drawn from both the facts and interpretation is that if I want to have a better career in my future, I have to change. Of course all fathers wish their sons could have a bright future.

這裡使用的事實，就是我二十五歲而我父親已經六十歲，這個事實經過詮釋產生了這樣的結果，也就是我希望在未來能夠變得更好而我父親則希望在未來的日子維持不變，繼續有著非常穩定的生活。從事實以及詮釋所得到的訊息就是，如果我希望在未來有好的發展，我必須改變！當然所有的父親們都希望他的兒子有個非常美好的未來。

Another true story of a similar nature was told by my classmate who worked as a porter at a hotel during his summer break when he was a sophomore. He saw an American couple with their five-year old kid in a lobby. They needed to rush to the airport to catch a plane flying back to the U.S. The kid refused to leave because he did not finish assembling his Lego blocks in the lobby. My classmate asked me what our parents would do in that situation. I said that our parents probably would just drag us kids by force into the car. He told me that the father walked toward the kid and started to help the kid to assemble the blocks. The mother stopped the father and said, "Let him do his own job." The mother then walked to the kid and told him, "If you want to continue to assemble your blocks, then we will not be able to catch our plane flying back to the U.S. We will all get stuck here and you will not see any of your classmates and friends again back home." Once the mother finished her words, the kid immediately got up, packed his blocks and calmly left with his parents.

另外，我的同學也曾經告訴我一個類似的眞實故事。他大二暑假的時候到飯店去打工，有一天，他告訴我一件非常有趣的事情。他說在飯店大廳裡，看到一對美國夫妻帶著一個五、六歲的小孩，小孩子在玩積木，但是爸媽急著要趕飛機，小孩子卻不肯走，堅持要把積木拼圖拼完。我同學問我，如果是我們這邊的父母會怎麼處理這件事？我說，很簡單啦！強拉上車就好。他告訴我小孩子的父親，走過去幫小孩拼組積木，那個母親走過去立刻阻止小孩的父親，媽媽告訴爸爸：「讓小孩自己處理。」接著媽媽告訴了小孩：「你可以繼續組裝你的積木，但是我們會趕不上飛機，我們不能回美國，我們會留在臺灣，你再也見不到你的那些同學跟朋友。」小孩子一聽，立刻爬起來，把積木收拾乾淨，乖乖地跟著父母一起走。

This true story is about the different perspective on the method regarding the education of children. The fact is clear as mentioned above. The interpretation can be made that the father wants to help but the mother objects and she expects the child after her explanation to take the responsibility for the consequence. The message to the readers is that in terms of the education of children, patience with wisdom serves much better than the traditional physical punishment, only because the kid felt respected and gained more wisdom by understanding the nature and consequence of his action.

這個眞實的故事是關於對小孩教育不同的方式。事實很清楚如同前述。對於事實的解釋可以這樣來看，父親想要幫忙但是母親反對，而且她期待這個小孩子在她的解釋之後，應該要爲自己的行爲後果負責。對於讀者們的訊息就是，以小孩子教育而言，要有耐心並且要使用智慧，這樣的方法比傳統打罵教育好很多，因爲小孩子可以感覺到尊重以及透過對他自己行爲本質上的了解跟可能發生的結果，來學習到智慧。

The above examples also show a technique used in persuasion by putting a person into a position to see a possible future consequence resulting from what he is doing. If he is not ready to accept the possible result, then he must change his current track lest the undesirable result happens. This approach is quite effective in many cases because it opens the eyes of a person to see what problem might happen in the future. The above examples also reveal that a message in essence is not a conclusion. To make a conclusion is easy because anyone can do that, but it does not have enough reasons to make it persuasive. Therefore, merely a conclusion is not enough. You need a good message strong enough to convince the people of your conclusion.

上面的例子，也顯示出一種說服的方法，也就是把一個人放在一個位子上面，讓他可以看清楚他目前的做法將來可能導致的結果。如果他沒有接受這種可能的結果，那他必須改變目前的做法，免得發生他所不願意見到的結果。這種方法在很多情況之下是很有效的，因爲他打開一個人的眼睛，讓他看到未來所可能發生的問題。上面例子也顯示出一個訊息本質上就不是結論，下一個結論很簡單，因爲任何人都辦得到，但是結論少了理由就達不到說服的目的，因此單純一個結論是不夠的，你需要一個強而有力的訊息來說服你的聽衆相信你的結論。

The above stories have demonstrated some simple and basic steps from observation to expression shown either in a speech or writing. On the level of structure, each writing and speech is composed by the description of facts followed by writer's interpretation of the facts containing a message leading to a conclusion. These basic structures are easy to learn and should be constantly practiced.

前列的故事示範了在演講以及寫作上，從事實的觀察到表達上的一些簡單和基本步驟。在結構的層次上，每一篇文章或故事的組成是由對於事實的描述，之後是作者對於事實的詮釋，接著是作者藉由對事實的詮釋所帶出的訊息，最後是所引導的結論。這些基本架構很容易學習，而且應該經常練習。

Students should also bear in mind that the essence of the training at this stage is to connect facts with a message for persuasion. Simply speaking, a message is a product and a fact is a vehicle to deliver the message. Once a student is familiar with these skills, his power on persuasion will increase substantially.

學生也應當記住，重點就在於結合事實跟訊息達到說服目的。簡單來說，訊息是產品，而事實的使用是傳送產品的交通工具。學生一旦從訓練中熟悉這樣的能力，學生在說服上的能力將大力的增強。

In the past few years, I have seen some students with high English proficiency in their writing and oral expression as exemplified by their precise choice of vocabulary and the use of correct grammatical structure but were rather weak in delivering a good message. Few flaws in English could be found but the whole writing was lifeless like a flat coke. Such writing does not carry much value because there is no message but only beautiful words embedded in a complicated grammar structure as any sample sentence that could be found in a dictionary. Interpretation of facts makes a story interesting, and a message gives value and makes the whole speech and writing come alive.

在過去幾年，我看過很多在英文寫作以及口語表達上很優秀的學生，他們的用字精準，文法架構正確，但是在給予一個好的訊息方面相對薄弱，他們的英文表達上找不到什麼缺點，但是整篇寫作像是個沒有氣泡的可樂。這類單純表達英文字彙和文法的文章，就像任何字典的例句在寫作上沒有什麼價值。對事實的解釋使整個故事是有趣，而訊息則賦予了演說還有寫作價值以及生命力。

A speaker should always bear in mind that a fact will stay cold if no message is carried. No message can be carried if no interpretation is made. A cold fact becomes distant from an audience and does not exert much persuasive effect. A message is made and is directed toward an audience. A message makes a cold fact warmer, empowered with strengths in terms of persuasion and therefore serves as a bridge between a speaker and an audience.

一個演講者必須要記得，事實如果不帶有訊息的話，那是冰冷的，而事實如果不經過解釋，那是不能產生訊息的。一個冰冷的事實與聽衆有非常遙遠的距離，因而不容易產生說服力。對事實的詮釋而產生的訊息，可以使得冰冷的事實變得溫暖，對於說服力而言，能賦予生命力。因此他是演講者與聽衆之間溝通的橋梁。

The following examples demonstrate the application of the aforementioned principle regarding how a fact is described and interpreted with a message subsequently drawn and leads to a conclusion

下列的範例示範了上述原則的應用，也就是如何描述與解釋一個事實，而後產生了訊息到最後進入結論。

Demonstration 1, Smoking

Facts: A student who serves his compulsory military service is a non-smoker. But his colleagues are smokers and he feels that if he wants to be accepted by his friends, he has to smoke or his friends will make a mockery of him. He is therefore compelled to smoke because of peer pressure. I did have a similar experience 20 years ago when I worked for a large law firm. A group of my co-workers played basketball once a month and my mentor told me that I should go if I wanted to be accepted by those senior attorneys quicker. If I chose not to go, I would be taking a risk of being distanced from their group.

示範 1：抽菸

事實：有個學生他入伍服役而他不是個吸菸者。但他的同僚很多都是吸菸者，而他覺得如果要被他的朋友所接受，他必須抽菸，要不然朋友們會嘲笑他。由於受到同儕的壓力他因此而吸菸。二十年前我在律師事務所工作的時候，也有類似的經驗。我的同事們有一些一個月會一起舉辦籃球比賽，我的前輩告訴我，我應該去，如果我希望那些資深律師盡快接納我的話。如果我選擇不去，我就會有被他們疏離的危險。

Interpretation of facts: The two examples show peer pressure as a sign of tolerance and acceptance of which provides a ticket of admission to a new group. If you want to be a part of their group, you need to adapt yourself to meet their demands and accept their mode of behavior.

事實的詮釋：這兩個例子顯現出同儕的壓力是一種忍讓的表徵，接受同儕壓力提供了融入新團體的一張門票。如果你想成爲這團體的一部分，你必須調整自己，達到他們的要求，接受他們行爲模式。

Message: Peer pressure indeed is a form of burden, or a nuisance sometimes, but the acceptance of which will win an approval providing an access to the assimilation into the new group that you are interested in entering. If you desire to be part of that group, learn to adapt by coping with the peer pressure encountered.

訊息：同儕壓力事實上是一種負擔，有的時候甚至是一種困擾。

但是接受它能夠贏得一個認同，提供了融入你有興趣想參加的新團體的路徑。如果你想成爲這團體的一部分，那就必須學習應對所面臨的同儕壓力。

Conclusion: We accept the burden from such pressure and win our assimilation into the new group.

結論：我們接受這樣壓力所帶來的負擔，也融入新的團體。

Demonstration 2, Future plan

Facts: I studied law in college 30 years ago. During my first year, I found no interest in this field. Part of the reason was that the passing rate for the local bar exam was extremely low, probably below 2%, and the textbooks were too difficult to read and understand for an 18-year-old young man. Naturally, I couldn't stay focused and my entire mind was occupied with the idea of applying for a transfer to a different department.

示範 2：未來的計畫

事實：三十年前我在大學念法律。在第一年的時候，我對這個領域沒有興趣，一部分的原因是由於律師考試錄取率非常低，大概不到百分之二。使用的教科書對於一個十八歲的年輕人來說，不容易讀也很難理解。很自然的，我沒有辦法集中注意力，內心常常想轉到其他科系念念看。

In my second year, I took an interesting course and met a good professor. The course I took was American Torts Law and the professor was a California lawyer, quite different from other locally trained attorneys. The textbook of torts law was a compilation of American court cases followed by notes helping students to think and argue. Each case started with a description of facts followed by arguments raised by both parties. The courts' opinions were subsequently discussed and concluded at the end. When I read those cases, I almost could see the picture of what happened, like watching an interesting movie. Unlike the local approach, the American approach in this study did not ask for a standard answer but a plausible one. It is a learning process by leading students to think. The professor who taught this class was humorous and skillful in his story telling. He often shared his experiences of his studies and work in the U.S. I therefore developed an unquenchable desire to study law in the U.S. and become an attorney in the U.S.

在第二年的時候，我選修一個很有趣的課程，也遇到了一個很好的老師。我所選修的課程是美國侵權行爲，而老師是一個加州律師，與其他本地的律師有很大的不同。教科書是把美國法院的案例集合起來，然後有註解幫助學生思考與辯論。每一個案例從事實的描述開始，接著是雙方辯論的言詞。之後是法院意見的討論以及最後的結論。當我在閱讀這些案例的時候，我可以看到事情發生的景象，就像看一場有趣的電影一樣。跟本土的學習方式不同，美國的學習方式並不要求一個標準答案，而是一個合理的說法。這是一種引導方式的學習。教導這門課的教授很有幽默感，而且在敘說故事上很有技巧。他通常也會分享他在美國讀書和工作的經驗。我因此發展出無法遏止的渴望，要到美國學習法律以及成爲一名美國律師。

Interpretation of facts: A freshman in college cannot stay focused on his studies if he is not able to know what he would like to do in his future. Without a future plan, he has no direction, more like a boat sailing on an ocean without any destination.

事實的詮釋：大一的新鮮人，如果他不知道他將來想做什麼，很難全神貫注於讀書。沒有一個未來的計畫，他就不知道何去何從，就像在海上沒有方向的航行船隻一樣。

Message: Finding a model to follow can help a young person to find his future plan and show the direction to take and, therefore, can give strength to his effort to pursue his future goal.

訊息：尋找一個模範人物可以幫助一個年輕人找到他未來的計畫，而且提供他未來要走的方向，因此，可以給予他更大的助力來追求未來的目標。

Conclusion: Now I am a professor in a college and also a certified attorney in the state of New York. When I look back, I have to say, it is easy for any young person to get lost if he cannot set up a goal for his future. Many students cannot find any interest under a crammed pattern of education. From my own experience, I would say that it is important to find a model to follow. Once you have a model in your life, you will do your best to follow that model. In my case, a good teacher has helped me to develop a desire to follow his footsteps to become more like him. Therefore, I encourage young people to find your model and follow his footsteps.

結論：我現在是一所大學的老師，同時也是美國紐約州的律師。當我回頭一看，我必須說，如果年輕人沒有一個未來的目標，很容易迷失。許多學生在一個填鴨式的教育環境下，很難找到自己的興趣。從我自己的經驗來看，我必須說，尋找一個可以效法的模範是很重要的事。你一旦有一個模範，你就能夠盡全力追循這個模範。以我爲例，一個好的老師曾經幫助我發展出跟隨他腳步的渴望，可以變得像他一樣。因此，我鼓勵年輕人找到自己的模範，然後跟隨他們的腳步。

Demonstration 3, All of sudden

Facts: A student shared her experience with her sister's application for entrance to a college. Her sister was from a distinguished high school and she was determined to study finance. Unfortunately, her score was not good enough and her family had a meeting to discuss her sister's possible choice on studying a language. But when the result came out, her sister had decided to study Chinese literature and this decision had surprised everyone in her family because this major seemingly posed enough difficulty for her sister's future career.

示範 3：突然

事實：一個學生分享了她妹妹申請大學的經驗。她妹妹來自一個非常優秀的高中而且決定要念財務。很不幸的，她的分數沒有那麼好，她家舉行了一個會議討論妹妹將來可能要選擇念外文。但是，當結果出來的時候，她妹妹決定念中文，這個決定讓家人都很震撼，因爲這個主修對於妹妹將來的工作可能產生了很大的困難。

Interpretation of facts: She and her parents were suddenly surprised by the result of her sister's final decision. In fact, in our daily life, we could sometimes have sudden surprises from someone that we think that we know well. Someone got divorced, went bankrupt or even committed suicide.

事實的詮釋：這位學生和她的爸媽突然被妹妹最後的決定嚇了一大跳。事實上在我們的生活中，有的時候可能會被一些我們自認爲很了解的朋友們突然嚇了一大跳。有人離婚、破產，甚至自殺。

Message: A close relationship does not guarantee our understanding of the full truth. The moment that the truth is revealed, it often suddenly surprises us.

訊息：親密的關係並不保證我們了解所有事實的眞相。眞相揭露的那個時刻，通常帶給我們突然的震驚。

Conclusion: We should not assume that a close relationship will bring us a full understanding of the truth.

結論：我們不應該假設親密的關係可以讓我們知道所有事情的眞相。

Demonstration 4, DUI (driving under intoxication)

Facts: Taiwan has a strict law to punish those who are engaged in DUI. The law prescribes a maximum Blood Alcohol Concentration (BAC) limit and any reading above that limit will be prosecuted. Some jurisdictions in the U.S. have also a similar law to punish drivers engaged in DUI. However, the standard for prosecution is not based on the reading above the maximum limit but decided by whether the driver's ability is impaired by alcohol consumption. The driver who is suspected of DUI, once stopped by a police officer, must do certain acts required by the police officer to see if his physical function is impaired or not. If the officer finds that the driver, due to intoxication, is not able to consciously and correctly do what he is instructed to perform, then the driver is subject to punishment.

示範 4：酒駕

事實：臺灣有很嚴格的法律處罰那些酒駕的駕駛。法律規定酒測容許的最高數值，任何超過這標準的都會被起訴。在美國有一些州也有類似的規定，懲罰酒駕的駕駛。但是起訴的標準並不是根據酒測的數值而已，而是由駕駛身心受酒精的影響的程度來決定。駕駛人一旦被警察要求停車之後，必須做出警察所要求的動作，看看他身體的功能是否有受酒精的影響。如果警察確定這個駕駛由於酒精影響，不能夠很清醒而且正確的做出這些動作，那駕駛就會遭受處罰。

Interpretation of facts: The U.S. DUI law of some jurisdictions punishes drunk drivers whose functions are proved impaired by alcohol while Taiwan law has assumed that all drivers, once the BAC reading is above a certain limit, are impaired by alcohol. In fact, tolerance to alcohol may vary from person to person. A glass of wine may cause a great influence on one person while it may not affect another person at all.

事實的詮釋：美國一些州酒駕的法律懲罰那一些身體功能受到酒精影響不能正常駕駛的酒駕人士，而臺灣的法律假設一旦數值超過一定的限制，就是身體受到酒精影響，功能發生障礙，而不能正常行駛。事實上對於酒精容忍的程度，每個人都不一樣，一杯酒可能對於某人有嚴重的影響，但是對另一個人毫無影響。

Message: An assumption of a drunk driver's impairment in driving based on the reading of the BAC over a certain limit is not fair to those who have a higher tolerance to alcohol and thus are capable of driving consciously and safely.

訊息：基於酒測值高於標準而假設酒駕駕駛就已發生身體功能障礙，對於那些對酒精有高容忍度，並且能夠清醒而且安全開車的人而言，並不公平。

Conclusion: Taiwan DUI law should be made fair to prosecute those drunk drivers who proved to be impaired in their physical function to drive.

結論：臺灣酒測的法規，應該要更公平的去追訴那些已被證明他們身體功能受酒精的影響而發生障礙的酒駕駕駛。

Demonstration 5, Study abroad

In recent years, our university has an exchange program with other universities in the U.S. and Europe. A few of our students who study overseas do not improve their professional knowledge and language proficiency. Many of the foreign students who come to study in our university do not know Chinese but take some courses conducted in mandarin. They often exhaust themselves from parties and touring, and engage in activities for pleasure, making great noise sometimes which surprise or even annoy many of local students and residents. Their study overseas seems to be for fun only and they fail in their learning. They enjoy their vacation. One of the Spanish students once told me that these students were not like that in their homeland due to pressure from their studies. Besides, no one at home will know what they are doing while in a foreign land so remote from their home. Once they arrive in a foreign land, they are free and intend to do whatever they prefer, but dare not do in their homeland.

示範5：海外交換生

最近這幾年，我們的大學與美國和歐洲大學有一些交換的課程。我們在海外讀書的一些學生在他們的專業知識還有語言的流利程度上，沒有什麼進步。也有很多來到我們學校讀書的外籍學生並不懂得中文，但卻修習學校內一些以中文教授的科目。他們常常參加很多宴會旅遊，追求一些樂趣也很吵鬧，把自己弄得非常的疲倦，有的時候打擾了一些學生甚至當地的居民。他們的海外交換，看起來只是爲了享樂，在學習上是失敗的。他們非常享受他們的假期。有一個西班牙的學生告訴我，這一些學生在本國並不是如此，因爲讀書壓力很大。此外，家鄉的人不知道他們在離家如此遙遠的地方在做些什麼。一旦到了海外他們就自由了，喜歡做一些他們以前想做但是不敢做的事情。

Interpretation of facts: These international students seem unbridled in their activities during their overseas studies.

事實的詮釋：這些國際學生在海外讀書的時候，在他們的活動上是不受拘束的。

Message: It is what a person does at night rather than in the daylight that speaks for a person's true value.

訊息：一個人在晚上而不是白天所做的事情，代表了一個人眞正的價値。

Conclusion: Study overseas might be a great opportunity to observe a person's values, desire for learning and his expectation of himself.

結論：海外讀書可能提供了一個非常好的機會，觀察一個人的價值、學習上的渴望還有自我期許。

Demonstration 6, Puppy love

Facts: A girl in class recalled that her first love was in her kindergarten years. She liked a little boy only because she enjoyed watching him ride a bicycle, a pure love of innocence and simplicity without any other considerations. Now she is over 20 and love is no more so simple and innocent. It is the educational and family backgrounds, personality and financial status of the other side that she needs to take into account as well.

示範 6：初戀

事實：班上一個女孩子回想到她的初戀是在幼稚園的時候，喜歡一個小男孩，僅僅只是因爲她很喜歡看小男孩騎腳踏車的樣子，一個非常簡單、純粹而不考慮其他因素的愛情。現在她已經超過二十歲了，愛情不再是這樣的簡單與純粹，她必須考慮對方的教育和家庭背景、個性還有財務的情況。

Interpretation of facts: Love does not seem that simple as it used to be. Parents would like to find a right man for their daughter. A marriage should be ensured with stability and sufficiency for their future living, especially subsequent to the birth of children.

事實的詮釋：愛情看起來與以前不同。父母們希望幫他們女兒找到一個對的男人。一個婚姻應該保障穩定以及對於未來生活所需無缺，特別是有小孩之後。

Message: Love at youth is only a pure romance. Love between adults takes into account the need for future living and thus becomes a practical matter.

訊息：小時候的愛情只是單純的羅曼史。而成人之間的愛情，必須要考慮未來生活所需，因此變成實際的事情。

Conclusion: Puppy love, a pure romance of innocence and love, between adults generally leads to a marriage requiring the consideration of practical needs for their future living.

結論：小時候的愛情只是純粹的羅曼史。而成人之間的愛情通常會有婚姻，也必須考慮將來生活的實際需要。

The above demonstrations show the application of the form to the persuasive structure of an expression either in writing or a speech, that is, facts, interpretation of facts, a message to a final conclusion. Facts refer to a case that a speaker is going to introduce. Interpretation of facts focuses on the meaning of the facts and how the facts affect the related parties especially the relation between a cause and a consequence together with possible implications and inferences. A message is a principle drawn from the facts and interpretation. The conclusion is a combination of the facts and message, consequently making an affirmation of the principle drawn. For teaching purposes, it is effective training to build a student's ability on expression by learning how to prepare an expression through dissecting a speech or writing into four parts as facts, interpretation, a message and a conclusion. Once a learner is familiar with this structure, then a student can fluently give his expression either in writing or utterance.

前面範例顯示出上述格式的應用在具有說服力架構的演說或是寫作的表達上，也就是事實、對事實的詮釋、訊息以及最後的結論。事實就是演說者準備要談到的案例。事實的詮釋集中在所談到事實的意義、事實如何影響到相關人士以及之間的因果關係與可能的意涵及推論。訊息則是由事實以及對於事實的詮釋所歸納出來的原則。結論則是將事實與信息結合而以確認所歸納的原則為結局。以教學目的而言，透過將演說或寫作分成四部分學習（事實、對於事實的詮釋、訊息以及結論），對提升學生表達的程度是非常有效的訓練。一旦學生熟悉這樣的架構，就能夠很流暢的進行寫作或是演說的表達。

Once learners are familiar with the skills trained in intermediate writing on the observation of facts followed by a clear description with a message subsequent to sound reasoning that leads to a persuasive conclusion, then the students will move onto the next stage to build up their ability to examine the others' statements and make effective arguments, which falls into the category of advanced writing. Making an argument is the core of the subject of advanced writing.

一旦學生們熟悉中級寫作所訓練的技術，也就是對事實觀察之後所做的清楚描述，並且透過健全的說理提出訊息而產生具有說服力的結論之後，學生們就可以到下一階段學習建立如何檢驗其他人說法，並且做出有效地辯論，而這則是高級寫作的範圍。

Notes

1 The difference in writing between the intermediate level and the advanced:
The intermediate level offers training on description of facts with a clear message supported with good reasons. The advanced level requires training on arguments because an analysis of arguments on both sides is necessary. Students on an advanced level are expected to learn the skills of making an analysis on a debate and applying such analytical process in their advanced level of writing.

附註

1 中級寫作與高級寫作的差異：

中級寫作提供了對事實描述以及提出具有正當理由支持的清楚訊息。高級寫作要求辯論言詞的訓練，因爲在高級寫作當中，對於不同說法的分析是必要的。在高級寫作課程的學生，要學習辯論的分析方式以及將這樣的分析過程應用在高級寫作當中。

2 The most important factor in building up the power of persuasion lies on the capability to place oneself in another's position. Such capability is far more essential than your ability on making an analysis and utterance. I once asked a senior manager in a large corporation why he always cared so much about the slight difference in salary paid to a new employee. He told me that, in his eyes, every new employee was a long term liability for his corporation in the next 30 years. Any trivial amount will accumulate into a huge sum in 30 years. This is the difference in judgment between a high ranking manager and a new employee. Once we place ourselves into his shoes, we will understand better his decision in setting a salary for a new employee.

2 建立說服能力最重要的因素就在於換位思考的能力。這樣的能力遠比你分析和說話的能力來得重要得多。我曾經問過一個大型公司的高階經理人，爲什麼他總是在乎對於新進人員薪水的些微差別。他告訴我在他的眼裡，每一個新進人員都是公司未來三十年的負債。任何些微的差距，在三十年後都會累積成爲可觀的數字。這就是一個高階經理人與新進人員在判斷上的差別。一旦我們能夠換位思考了解高階經理人的想法，我們就可以了解爲什麼他們對於新進人員薪水設定的決定。

3 Ability to draw analogies is important because good analogies can help to explain your message and corroborate your position better. Learn to use an analogy that is helpful in selecting appropriate facts to corroborate with your message and position.

3 使用比喻的能力非常的重要，因爲好的比喻可以幫忙解釋你的訊息，有效支持你的立場。學生們應當練習使用適當的事實來支持訊息和立場。

3.5 To gain control at the beginning

The first lesson in negotiation is on establishing good relationships. Generally, it starts from a pleasant conversation including a self-introduction. Good relationship building in the beginning can help to build mutual trust to thaw the ice and further support the following process. Therefore, good relationship building is the first step in controlling a negotiation at the beginning. The situation for a speech is similar. Imagine that a speaker is five minutes late for the occasion. He rushes into the room and hurries to set up his laptop to be projected on the screen. His haste is an indication that he will lose control of the entire speech from the start. Quite a few times

I have seen this happened. The whole audience is somewhat like watching a show on a platform guessing whether this new recruit is able to finish a quick shower within three minutes as required in boot camp. Once a speaker loses his control at the start, it will take quite an effort to restore back to the status it should have been and thus possibly ruin his prepared presentation, not to mention his tarnished image.

3.5 在開始時候的掌控

談判的第一課就是建立良好的關係，通常他從一個愉快的對話開始，包括自我介紹。一開始的良好關係，有助於建立互信，進而能夠融冰並且幫助之後的談判過程。因此，良好關係的建立是控制談判的第一步。演說的場合也是類似。想像一下演講者遲到五分鐘，他衝進演講廳，急忙的設定他的電腦以及使用螢幕上的投影片，他這麼匆忙就表示失去控制場合的能力。我曾經看過幾次這種場合，全體的觀眾有一點像是觀看入伍的新兵能否在三分鐘之內完成他的戰鬥澡。如果一個演講者在一開始不能控制全場的氣氛，那要花很大的力量才能恢復他應該有的情況，因此可能搞砸了全部的安排，還不談這對他形象上的傷害。

On the contrary, an earlier control of the whole atmosphere will facilitate the subsequent flow of a speech, similar to good relationship building in negotiating. What is the difference between a speech presented to 50 strangers and that of 50 old acquaintances like a school reunion? There is, of course, more pressure in the former occasion. Such pressure is the source that freezes your free expression of ideas. A good interaction before a speech starts can help to thaw this ice and remove this pressure.

相反的，如果在稍早就可以控制全場的氣氛，而對於之後演講的順暢情況會有所幫助，就像是在談判一開始的時候，所建立良好的友善關係一樣。對於五十個陌生人的演說，以及對五十個畢業老同學的相聚講話，有什麼不同呢？在前者的壓力當然大一些，這樣的壓力可能會使你的表達有些障礙，演說前良好的互動，可以幫忙打破這些障礙，脫離這些壓力。

An early arrival can help a speaker to get familiar with the environment, ascertain normal functioning of his laptop and form good interaction with the audience. A good interaction, for example, chatting with some from the audience before the speech starts, can help the speaker to loosen up tension by gaining some familiarity with them and thus build up confidence. Once the speech starts, you can easily feel like talking to some old acquaintances and gain control over the whole atmosphere. Such control is important because it helps a speaker to talk more freely and smoothly, like a wild horse running freely in a prairie. On the contrary, late in appearance, as mentioned earlier, could result in you losing control of the situation because no good interaction is established at the start, not to mention the bad image formed with possible tension ensuing. In that situation, the speaker very often will be forced to catch up on his agenda, and the audience can sense the speaker's tension and haste. The speaker can easily feel like a defendant giving a testimony before a group of jurors.

提早到達會場，能夠幫助演講者熟悉環境，確認電腦的良好運作，以及與聽衆建立良好的關係。良好的互動，例如跟部分聽衆在演講前對談，可以讓演講者與他們熟識，進而放鬆緊張情緒，以及建立自信。當演講開始的時候，你可以輕易地感覺到你似乎在跟老朋友講話，而且可以掌控全場氣氛，這樣的掌控是很重要的，因爲他幫助演講者更自由以及平順的表達自己。像是在草原上奔跑的野馬一樣。相反的，如果像前述的情況遲到，很可能導致於你對場合氣氛的失控，因爲沒能夠在一開始建立良好的互動，更不用說對形象上的傷害。演講者在那樣的情況之下，常常要追趕他的議題，聽衆們可以感覺到他的緊張與急迫，演講者甚至有時候感覺像在陪審團前面作證的被告一樣。

Some people prefer to start with a joke to relax the atmosphere in the room. What if the audience will not laugh? What if you can only hear some dry laughter? Be very careful with such an approach because it requires quite a good skill with which only a few can master. Some prefer to ask the audience questions at the very beginning when a good interaction has not been established yet. A speaker should be alert of such practice as well. I have witnessed one speaker asking the audience a question, expecting them to raise their hands to answer. It turns out that no one did. Then the speaker goes even further, directing his question at a person in the audience and trying to force that person to answer and was, unfortunately, met with refusal. The whole air is all of sudden frozen below zero. What a great failure! It seems better to be careful with such technique unless a speaker has full confidence the whole audience will act according to what the speaker expects.

有些人喜歡在一開始的時候講些笑話緩和氣氛。如果大家不笑怎麼辦？如果你只聽到一些乾笑的聲音呢？使用這種方法要小心，因為只有少數人能夠熟練這個技巧。也有些人會在一開始就問一些問題，當彼此良好的關係還未建立的時候，演講者應該也須注意這個方法。我曾經看過演講者問群衆一個問題，希望他們舉手回答，但是沒人舉手，接著演講者指定一個聽衆並且強迫他回答，結果不幸該名聽衆拒絕回答，這個氣氛頓時降到冰點，非常失敗的演講。使用這種方式最好小心一些，除非演講者非常有信心，聽衆會按照演講者的建議去做。

Humor is a lubricant for the operation of both a speech and a negotiation. But humor could easily turn ironic if not used appropriately. Some speakers are not good with humor but blindly believe humor will help his speech. To intentionally make humorous remarks or gestures is rather artificial, probably favored by a few, and an audience can tell. A speech full of jokes with no link to any part of the purpose of that speech probably falls into this category, unless the speaker intentionally deviates from the topic as a break.

A trained mind can tell those jokes are quite intentionally made for winning laughter in a crowd.

幽默感是演講和談判的潤滑劑，但是幽默感如果不小心使用，很容易變成諷刺性的話語。有些演講者不善於使用幽默感，卻盲目地認爲幽默感可以幫助他的演說，特意製造的幽默感太過人工化，恐怕只有少數人喜歡而且聽衆們可以馬上聽得出來。演說裡面的笑話，如果跟目的沒有任何連結的話，就是這樣，除非演講者特意的使用這個笑話當作一個休息。受過訓練的人馬上可以聽得出來，哪些笑話是特意贏得群衆的歡笑。

Humor should come out naturally and sincere and in an inoffensive manner. If a speaker is not skillful in humor, do not try to force it. Such an attempt will lead to failure because it defies a speaker's ability and personality. People always prefer a speaker with a genuine, honest and pleasant personality.

幽默感應該是自然而眞誠，而且不應該不禮貌，如果演說者並不善於表達幽默感，那就不需要特意而爲，否則很容易失敗，因爲他與演說者的個性不合。人們通常喜歡眞誠、誠實以及樂觀性格的演說者。

When a speaker stands on a platform, he is the only object under a spotlight at that moment, attracting full attention of an audience and thus can affect the emotion of an audience. When he looks happy, the audience can feel his joy. When he shows sorrow, they can sense his sadness. When he vents his anger, the audience can tell immediately. If he is not well prepared, the audience can tell by his poor performance. If he looks nervous, the whole audience can easily sense his anxiety. If he tries pretending to be confident, the audience will notice his pretense. No one likes a pretender. A speaker on a platform is like an orchestra conductor, orchestrating the full emotions of the audience. Out of all the practices in my classroom, what can win the most praises and compliments are those who show their free flow of expression with true emotions portrayed in their message through clear, concise and well organized facts (e.g. stories) displaying good values with sincerity, honesty and ingenuousness. A speaker does not need facts full of intensity to build up the emotions of an audience. Very often, simple facts with a profound meaning will leave a strong impression of the speaker on the minds of an audience.

當一個演講者正在臺上的時候，在當下他是全場唯一的焦點，因此可以影響整個聽衆的情緒。當他看起來很快樂的時候，整個聽衆可以感受得到他的歡樂。當他感到難過的時候，聽衆也可以感覺得到他的悲傷。當他表達他的憤怒的時候，聽衆們也可以立刻察覺得出來。如果他沒有做好準備，聽衆可以看得到他不好的表現。如果他看起來緊張，全場聽衆也可以感覺到他的焦慮。他如果想要假裝很有自信，聽衆也不會太困難看得出他的虛偽。沒有人喜歡虛僞的人。在臺上演講者就像樂團的指揮一樣，他控制了全場的情緒。在課堂裡面的練習當中，能贏得最多讚美的是那些自然的真情流露，透過清楚、簡要及良好組織的事實（例如故事），並具有正確價值觀與誠實眞誠的態度所表達出來的訊息。時常，簡單但有著深遠含義的事實，可以讓聽衆們對演說者印象深刻。

3.6 How to conquer the fear when giving a public speech?

In a class discussion, almost all students have fear in speaking in front of their classmates. They lack confidence. They are afraid of creating a negative impression as a result of their speech and being looked down on. Simply speaking, they cannot control the situation, even if they know what to say. How to conquer fear is therefore an important task in the training of speech.

When a student is delivering a speech for the first time, he will feel nervous and probably cannot express himself clearly and fluently. Assuming he is making a speech on the same topic for the second time, he probably will fare better because he is familiar with the topic and he knows what problems he has encountered the first time and he is most likely to be able to overcome those problems. Assuming he is doing the same speech the third time on the same topic, he is highly likely to perform the task routinely and be quite familiar with all the ideas, freely expressing himself because he can now skillfully master the process and thus successfully convince people of his ideas. People generally have no fear in doing what he is skillful at and familiar with.

This example reveals the clue on how we can conquer our fear. We have fear in delivering a speech publicly because we do not have confidence. We do not have confidence because we do not feel that we have control over the situation. We are not able to have control over the situation because we are not familiar with the topic and we do not know the audience. In other words, fear is caused by the problem that which we do not foresee. To conquer that fear, we must know what to expect. Good preparation is essential.

A speaker should know what he is talking about once the content is well prepared. Familiarity with the content and the audience will help to lessen his fear in public speaking. Of course, we cannot possibly prepare all speeches well in every situation encountered. Therefore, the regular practice of daily conversation is important, since the ability in engaging in dialogue with others is essential in public speaking. As long as we like to associate with and talk to people, we will gradually pick up the necessary skills in conversation and the techniques in associating with people. Being familiar with people will help our communication with others and thus enhance our skill in public speaking.

3.6 如何克服公開演說場合的恐懼？

在一個課堂討論中，學生們表示他們對於在公開場合中演說是有恐懼的，他們缺乏自信，他們害怕由於他們演說的結果造成了負面印象，因而被否定，簡單來說，他們沒有辦法控制情況，縱然他們知道他們應該說些什麼東西。因此，如何克服他們的恐懼，在演說訓練中變成非常重要的功課。

當一個學生第一次演說的時候，他會感到緊張，可能沒有辦法很清楚並流利地表達他自己。假設，他對相同的主題進行第二次的演說，他大概能夠表現得更好一些，因爲他已經熟悉了主題，而且他知道他在第一次演說時所遭遇到的問題，他可能可以控制那些問題。假設他對於同樣的主題進行第三次演說，他非常可能將同樣的工作當作例行性事務，且熟悉所有想法並能夠充分的表達，因爲他可以很熟練地控制整個過程，並且能夠成功地說服別人相信他的想法。人們通常對於他所熟悉以及熟練的事務不會感到恐懼。

這個例子透露出我們應該如何克服我們的恐懼，我們對於公開演說感到恐懼是因爲我們沒有信心。我們沒有信心是因爲我們不覺得我們能控制場合，我們不能控制場合是因爲我們不熟悉主題以及我們不了解聽衆。換句話說，恐懼是由我們所沒有辦法預見到的問題所造成。要克服這樣的恐懼，我們必須知道會發生什麼事，而充分的準備是必須的。

一個演說者，如果是充分準備的話，應該知道他要談論些什麼東西。對於內容的熟悉以及聽衆的了解，有助於降低公衆演說時的恐懼。當然，我們不可能對於任何場合之下的演說都做有充分的準備。因此，藉由日常生活中的對話加以練習是很重要的，因爲與他人的對話能力，對於演說的訓練是極其必須的。只要我們喜歡與他人相處、說話，往往很快地就會學習到與人對話和相處的技巧。對於人情世故的熟悉，會幫助我們與他人的溝通，因此增加我們演說的能力。

3.7 How to intrigue interest through stories and examples

Many people love to watch movies or read novels. Movies and novels are a form of stories. We can see various figures in a certain environment involved in some events. People tend to listen to stories. especially those written with interesting twists and turns. Nevertheless, the focus is always on certain persons (e.g. protagonists) and the background is not complicated for the viewers and readers to understand and remember. Too many characters and intricacies could confuse the readers and viewers. A good movie tells a good story.

3.7 利用故事還有例子來刺激興趣

很多人喜歡看電影、讀小說，電影和小說都是一種故事，我們可以看到一些事件在特定環境裡面的一些角色，人們也喜歡聽故事，特別是那些特殊情節的故事，雖然如此，焦點總是在一些角色上（例如主角），而且背景並不會太過複雜，而使得觀眾難以記憶。好的電影講述著好的故事。

A good speech is not that different from a good movie. It requires a good story. Stories, whether fictitious or real, could be given in a form of examples excerpted from books, newspapers, magazines or personal experiences. But stories should not be limited only on the narration of facts alone. Every day we see many people walking on the streets or shopping in malls. Sometimes, we witness an accident on roads. But that is not a story. That is only a fact that few probably are interested in (parties involved, police officers and attorneys, etc.). But what if, as some TV program has shown, a man can tell you what he can infer from his observation of a pedestrian's outfit, such as his personality, job, his family background and probably even correctly guessing their names? Then there is a story, because these pedestrians are no more only cold facts on the street, because now someone can analyze these facts from some trivial details that we would never have noticed. We will soon develop an interest in following what will happen next. The inference is a form of interpretation based on the facts observed. Similarly, it is such an interpretation that makes the movie and novels interesting. The same rule applies to statistics obtained in surveys, which are boring and cold unless an interpretation can be given by an expert.

一個好的演講跟一部好的電影沒有什麼不同，它需要一個好的故事。故事不論是虛構或是眞實的，可以用書上、報紙、雜誌或是個人經驗的例子來呈現。但是故事不應該限定於事實的陳述而已，每一天我們在街上和商場裡看到很多人，有些時候我們在路上看到一個車禍，但是這並不是故事，只是極少人有興趣的事實而已（當事人雙方、警察還有律師等）。但是如果像一些電視節目，一個人可以從他對行人的觀察告訴你，個性、工作、家庭背景甚至可以正確的猜出名字，那就有故事可以談了，這些行人不再是冷冰冰的事實，因爲有人可以就細節對事實進行分析與詮釋，我們很快會有興趣知道下面會發生什麼事。這樣的推測基於所觀察的事所作的解釋，就是這樣的解釋使得這樣的電影或小說有趣。同樣的原則也發生在無聊且冰冷的統計數字上，除非這些數字可以由專家來解釋。

Interpretation of a fact helps to build up a story. All good stories contain a message. Remember that a speech is made to persuade the listeners to take action. For this reason, the narration of facts must contain a message for the listeners to tell what action to take. A story without a message remains only as cold facts exerting no power of persuasion. The purpose on persuasion of course fails if no action is called for.

對於事實的解釋，可以建立一個故事。所有好的故事都會帶著一個訊息，要記得一個演說是爲了說服聽衆採取行動的目的而存在。爲了這個理由，對於事實的解釋必須包含一個訊息，來告訴讀者他們必須採取什麼樣的行動。沒有訊息的故事，只是冰冷的事實而已，產生不了說服力，如果不呼籲任何的行動，那說服的目的是達不到的。

As mentioned earlier, a message from a speaker is procured from the reasoning from an interpretation of the facts given by the speaker; for example, what do these facts mean to the speaker? What is the conclusion? What is the connection between the beginning and the end? What does the speaker expect the listeners to see and what action is the speaker calling one to take? For example, to produce photos regarding harm to the lungs caused by smoking is to present a fact. To claim hazards caused by smoking (connection between the smoking and the harm as a result of reasoning) and therefore smoking should be avoided is the conveyed message to the listeners. To advise smokers to quit smoking and all restaurants to ban smoking is to call for action. Without such interpretation, action will not be called for and the facts remain cold, exerting little or no power of persuasion. In order to persuade, the speaker must give his interpretation to the facts and tell the listeners what he intends the audience to do, what action to take. Therefore, it is an important task to train students on their ability to tell a story with a message procured from the interpretation of facts to be conveyed to the listeners, thus calling on an action to be taken.

如同前述，演講者的訊息來自於他對事實的解釋，例如：這些事實對演講者有什麼樣的意義？什麼是結論？從開始到結束是怎麼連結的？演講者期待聽眾看到什麼？又希望他們採取什麼樣的行動？例如：提供抽菸所造成的傷害的照片，是提出一個事實，聲稱抽菸是會產生傷害的（抽菸與傷害之間的關係經過論證而產生的結果），因此戒菸應該是給聽眾的訊息。建議吸菸者戒菸以及所有的餐廳禁菸，則是要他們採取行動，沒有這樣的解釋是不會呼籲任何行動的，事實依然是冰冷，產生不了說服力，爲了達到說服的目的，演講者必須對事實提出解釋，以及告訴聽眾他希望這些人做些什麼事。因此，訓練學生透過事實的解釋說出一個故事來對聽眾傳遞訊息，是一個很重要的工作。

Practices in a classroom show that a good story could contain some facts exerting a conflict in the heart, which may attract attention from the audience. A student mentioned his experience with visiting his father in an intensive care room in a hospital. His parents divorced when he was little and he was raised alone by his mother. He hardly had any memory about his father. His father was once badly injured in a car accident and he went together with his relatives to see his father whom he rarely saw. He vividly described his observation in that intensive care room which he has never been before, including some horrific views that really shocked him. He told his classmates that one patient lost two legs and half of his abdomen and could only survive by a life support machine. The other one had really bad facial injuries and half of his face and part of neck was gone. He was shocked by what he saw. His father was placed beside the other two and his whole body was swollen like a pig due to an alcoholic problem. His grandmother and aunt were weeping. He stood there and was not moved by what he saw. He had no sorrow at all. According to him, he stood there like watching a stranger. He was raised by his mother alone and he seldom saw his father. He was not aware of any time that his father ever executed responsibility either as a husband or a father. They had no contact. The message he drew from this horrific fact was that without any interaction between a father and a son, the connection by blood alone does not mean anything to him at all. He suggested that parents should spend time and effort to show love to their children or the mere bond by blood alone does not create any love at all.

在課堂的練習當中顯示出，一個好的故事常常包含著具有內心衝突性的事實。有一個學生談到了他有一次探望在加護病房中的父親的經驗。他的父母親在他很小的時候就離婚了，他是媽媽單獨帶大的，對於他的父親，他幾乎沒有什麼印象。他的父親有一次車禍嚴重受傷，他跟他的親戚去探望他極少謀面的父親。他從來沒有去過加護病房，但他非常生動描述他在加護病房所看到的事情。他說，他看到一個病人失去了兩條腿，腹部的一半不見了。另外一個病人則是一半的臉和脖子不見了。他被這樣的場景嚇壞了。他的父親躺在這兩個病人的旁邊，由於酗酒的關係，整個身體腫脹得像一隻豬一樣。她的奶奶和姑姑都在哭泣，他站在那邊，但完全沒有任何難過的感覺。他說他站在那邊像是探望陌生人一樣。他是媽媽養大的，幾乎從來沒有見過他的父親，他也不知道他的父親何時曾盡過任何父親或是丈夫的責任。他們從來沒有過任何聯絡。從這樣可怕的一個事實，他說出一個訊息，也就是如果缺乏父親與兒子之間的一個互動，單單的血緣關係對他來說，不具有任何的意義。他告訴聽衆們，身爲父母親就應該要花時間也要盡力對自己的小孩把愛表現出來，否則僅僅血緣關係並沒有辦法創造出任何的愛。

His experience is rather unusual, illustrating a serious conflict in his mind which most people can hardly imagine. The facts are true and his feeling is also real. But all these facts and feeling are far beyond our comprehension. The horrific view mentioned in the beginning about what he saw in the intensive care room shocked most of his classmates. The indifference about his father's serious injury is far beyond our comprehension of a sound family relationship. He successfully drew everyone's attention in the classroom. The message he gave was profound, demanding our deep thought and inspection of our own family relationship. He successfully attracted our attention and pounded hard the message into our hearts.

他的經驗非常的特殊，說明了一般人很難了解他內心的衝突。事件是眞實的，他的情感也是眞實的。但是這些事實和情感都超出了我們的理解。他在加護病房所看到的景象讓同學們感到很震驚，他對於自己生父嚴重的傷勢毫無感覺也讓同學們感到驚奇，超出了我們對一般正常家庭關係的了解，他成功地吸引了整個教室的注意。他訊息的意義是很深遠的，要求我們更深層次的檢視我們的家庭關係。他成功地吸引了我們的注意力，以及將訊息用力地打進了我們的心中。

Another story is about my experience while studying in law

school in the U.S. during 1992. Training in law school in the U.S. is strict, especially the first year. Many American students were taking loans out for their studies. I remember that my classmate looked quite nervous in the student lounge after her finals because she was afraid that she could fail in her first year of studies. A week later, I saw her again and she looked quite relaxed and had a pleasant conversation with the other classmates. I thought she passed. In fact, she did not. She failed. Her failure during the first year of law school represented that she wasted one full year in school and the money she borrowed, approximately USD$ 30,000 in the early 1990's. It would be extremely difficult for any Oriental student to accept this result in terms of time and money invested, not to mention the loss of reputation and the expectations from home. Simply speaking, life is ruined. I asked my American classmate, how can she handle this difficulty that easy? His answer was very simple and short. "What can you do?" and he went further, "She failed and this is a fact already. There is nothing she can do to change it. Accept what has happened and move on." This short reply shows great wisdom in life. It is very true that mere regret and anger won't help any. Many times we refuse to accept what has happened, for example, failures in our work, business, marriage or loss of our health or beloved ones. We could spend all our time complaining, regretting or getting angry and yelling about the grievances received. But none of these will help because they won't change our future for better. The best policy seems to admit what has happened and move on, a fresh start, so to speak. Only then can our future be changed for the better.

另外一個故事是關於我在 1992 年於美國法律學院讀書時的經驗。美國法律學院第一年的訓練很嚴酷，絕大部分美國的學生是貸款。我還記得有次期末考結束以後，我在學生的休息室看到一個同學看起來非常的緊張，因爲她很怕考試不能過關被退學。一個禮拜之後，我又看到她了，她看起來非常的輕鬆而且和其他同學有說有笑。我以爲她考試過關了，事實上她沒有，她失敗了。她在法律學院念了一年以後的失敗，表示她浪費一年的時間且浪費了將近 30,000 美金的貸款。對於任何一個東方學生來說，很難接受這樣的失敗，時間和金錢的浪費，更不要說名譽的損失和家族的失望。簡單來說，整個生活毀了。我問了一個我的美國同學，她怎麼能如此輕鬆的看待這個問題？他的回答非常的簡單扼要，「你還能怎麼辦？」他接著說，「她失敗了，這已經是一個既成的事實，她沒有辦法再做任何事情去改變這個事實，只能去接受，而且重新出發」。這個簡短的回答顯示出生命中的大智慧。的確，後悔和憤怒是沒有用的。很多時候我們拒絕接受一個已經發生的事實，例如工作、生意或是婚姻上的失敗，甚至是失去健康或是所愛的人。我們可以花全部的時間去抱怨、後悔，生氣大喊我們不應該接受這樣的待遇。但這些於事無補，不能讓我們的未來過得更好。最好的方法，看起來就是承認已經發生的事實，然後重新出發，只有這樣，才能夠讓我們的未來變得更好。

The two examples used a story to illustrate a strong message. A story based on contrasted facts could easily build up intensity (e.g.

visiting a father in an intensive care room that a child has never seen or a girl's totally unexpected attitude toward her failure) and thus intriguing the interest of the audience wanting to find out what happened next. The audience will remember your story and message easier. Facts for giving such stories could be learned from our observations and memories from our own experiences or facts procured from newspapers, books, the internet or any other source.

這兩個例子都使用故事說明的一個強烈的訊息。一個建立在衝突性強烈事實的故事，很容易形成一個張力（例如一個小孩探望在加護病房從未謀面的父親，或是一個女孩子用令人不可置信的態度面對她的失敗），因此成功引起聽眾們的興趣想要知道接著發生了什麼事。聽眾會很容易記得你的故事以及訊息。故事所使用的事實，可以從我們或他人的觀察、記憶中的經驗，或是報章雜誌網路或其他來源的資訊。

3.8 The benefits of giving a story at the beginning

I remember a story told by a student in a speech class about her experience in an elementary school in regard to the uniform dress code. She remembered that a classmate in her elementary school once wore a pair of counterfeit sneakers to school. The little girl was from a poor family and her parents could not afford expensive items. When some of her classmates from wealthy families noticed what she was wearing, they made a mockery of that little girl. Some even hit her for the counterfeit shoes she wore. For this reason, she fully supported the uniform dress code in high school. Her description of the facts was very clear as we could picture the sneakers the little girl wore and the mockery uttered against her. The student successfully aroused the emotions in our hearts. In fact, the great majority of the people who heard this story felt sorry and sad for that poor little girl. I was deeply moved by her story as well. I was willing to buy a new pair of sneakers with a legitimate brand to give to that little girl if the speaker ever called for an action. Honestly, I used to believe that causal styles in high schools would encourage high school students to use their imagination and creativity and be beneficial to all children and teenagers. I changed my view completely ever since then. Her story was true and powerful and the facts were simple with no need for further elaboration. The facts already spoke for themselves. As long as her story remains vivid in my memory, I will always support the uniform dress code in high school. Therefore, can the readers see the strength exerted by powerful facts along with the built up of intensity given at the beginning of a speech?

3.8 在一開始講故事的好處

我記得一個學生在一場有關制服的演說課上分享了她在小學的

經驗。她告訴全班，在她小學時候，一個同學曾經穿了一雙仿冒的球鞋到學校。小女孩來自於一個窮困的家庭，她的父母親沒辦法買得起昂貴的東西。當有些富有的同學發現到她的仿冒球鞋的時候，他們嘲笑這個小女孩。有些學生甚至毆打她。爲了這個原因，她支持高中生應該要穿制服。她對事實的描述非常清楚，就像我們能看到那個小女孩穿的球鞋一樣，而且可以聽得到其他小孩子的嘲笑聲。這個演說者成功的激起我們內心的情緒。她的故事也深深的感動了我。我甚至願意自掏腰包買雙新鞋送給這個小女孩，如果這個演講者有要求任何行動的話。事實上，絕大部分的同學對那個小女孩感到難過。坦白說，我過去相信高中生的制服解禁，能夠鼓勵高中學生的想像力和創造力，對於所有小孩和青少年都很有幫助。從那時候開始，我完全改變我的看法。她的故事是眞實的而且非常有力量。她的事實是如此簡單，不需要再進一步的解釋。這個事實已經自我闡明。只要她的故事在我腦海裡面依然清晰，我就會支持高中生的制服規定。讀者們是不是也看得到，在一開始就提出具有震撼性、帶有強烈張力的事實所產生出來的力量？

A story: Wisdom in using a contract

A rich old man was dying. His son was traveling afar and would not be able to come back in time to see him. The old man had a slave and, in his last will, he gave all property to this slave in his house with only one reservation that one piece of property could be chosen by his son among all his estate when he returned home. When his son came, the rich man already passed away. The son was quite upset about his father's disposal of the estate and complained about why he could only choose one piece of property out of the whole inheritance. A slave was more than a son? The son then went to a rabbi for an answer.

一個故事：使用契約的智慧

一個老富翁，臨終之際。他的兒子正在遠方旅行，來不及趕回來見他最後一面。這個老富翁有一個奴隸，他在他最後的遺囑上面，將所有的財產，都給了這個奴隸，除了一項保留條款之外。這個保留條款規定，當他的兒子回來的時候，可以在所有的遺產裡面，挑一件東西，屬於自己。當他兒子回家的時候，老人已經過世。這個兒子對於父親處理遺產的方式，很不高興，並且抱怨，爲什麼所有的財產，他只能擁有一件。一個奴隸比兒子更重要嗎？這個兒子於是去找了拉比（猶太人的經學教師），來尋求答案。

The rabbi said to him that your father was a man of great wisdom. He wrote this will because he knew that you would not be able to come home in time. He needed to persuade the slave to stay to take care of him, not to steal his property and run away. Now you could choose for yourself one piece of property in your father's will, that is, the slave in your house. All the property of a slave's was his master's. Now you had regained all your inheritance.

拉比跟他說，你的父親，眞的是個有大智慧的人。他寫下這份遺囑，因爲他知道，你沒有辦法及時趕回來。他需要請這奴隸留下來照顧他，而不是將他的財產偷了以後逃走。你現在可以在你父親的遺產當中，選一件東西，那就是家裡的那個奴隸。奴隸的所有財產，都是他主人的。你現在已經獲得所有的遺產了。

This is a story that someone told me a long time ago. What do you think about a short story like this? Are you amazed at what a contract can do?

這個小故事是很久以前聽到的。你對於這個小故事有沒有什麼看法？你會很訝異，一份契約所能做到的嗎？

The above was my speech delivered in a training of international business persons regarding the importance of international sales contracts. Do you think a short story like this can intrigue their interest at the beginning and further make them appreciate the importance of a contract so that they will be more willing to devote their time in learning the subject? If you think the answer is positive, then you are admitting to the influence of persuasion that a good story can give to an audience.

上面的小故事，是我在對國貿人員關於國際契約訓練方面課程所使用的，你認為這樣的短篇故事，能夠在一開始就引起他們的興趣嗎？並且讓他們了解契約的重要性，因而更進一步願意學習這門課程嗎？如果答案是肯定的，那你就承認了好的故事在一開始就可以幫助達到說服聽眾的目的。

A good speech contains a good story and stories should not be limited only to the description of facts alone. Sometimes, we witness a violation of traffic rules, thus ending up with a serious accident. Even though, it is often a fact, not a story, lasting only as a short-term memory. But what if the accident is caused by a traffic violation (e.g. running through a red light) due to an international renowned Pizza chain store's express delivery policy resulting in a pedestrian's permanent paralysis and, by this policy, this company has earned billions of dollars in the past decades? Now how would an audience view this INTENTIONAL traffic violation? Would such narration help the audience to develop their interest in wanting to know what happened subsequently, and would the whole story regarding such a policy, probably as a plot, make them remember the whole event easier and longer and consequently make the speaker easier to present a message calling for the listeners' support to abolish the express delivery policy?

一個好的演說應該要有好的故事，而且故事不應該只限定在故事的陳述，有的時候我們看到，一些交通違規導致很嚴重的意外，雖然如此，這個事實通常並不是個故事，只存在於人們短暫的記憶，但是如果這個所造成交通事故的違規（例如：闖紅燈），是由於一個國際披薩外送店快送服務政策所造成的，而這家公司在過去的幾十年中已經賺進了好幾十億的美金獲利，那社會大衆會如何看待這個故意違規的事實呢？這樣，對於事實的闡述，是不是會增加聽衆們對於後續發展情況了解的興趣，以及整個的快送政策，也許是項陰謀，而使得聽衆們能夠將這個事件記得更容易一些，以及更久，乃至最後使得演說者比較容易呈現一個訊息，請求群眾對於廢除這樣政策的支持？

Similarly, sometimes we can see a dog that is killed by someone's neighbor. Such a fact is rather simple and generally will not call for much attention. However, a speech has made a case of this nature so unusual that people's view of a dog could be changed forever. A good case can be found in a speech given by George Graham Vest (1830-1904), a lawyer from the late 19th century in America, in his closing argument, A Tribute to the Dog, with only 375 words, speaking on behalf of all dogs, has earned all dogs laurels of loyalty and finally won the whole case. The speech is quoted as follows:

其他類似的情況，有的時候我們看到，有些人的鄰居打死了一條狗，這樣的事實很簡單，通常不會引起太多的注意。但是有一個演說，使得這樣的案例，性質變得如此不同，以致人們對狗的看法從此改變。這是因爲十九世紀晚期，在一項終結辯論中，所提出的演講，對狗兒致敬，內容只有三百七十五個字，爲全體狗兒說話，也幫忠狗贏得忠誠的冠冕，最後贏得了整個案件。演講內容如下：

Example: A Tribute to the Dog

"Gentlemen of the Jury: The best friend a man has in the world may turn against him and become his enemy. His son or daughter that he has reared with loving care may prove ungrateful. Those who are nearest and dearest to us, those whom we trust with our happiness and our good name may become traitors to their faith. The money that a man has, he may lose. It flies away from him, perhaps when he needs it most. A man's reputation may be sacrificed in a moment of ill-considered action. The people who are prone to fall on their knees to do us honor when success is with us, may be the first to throw the stone of malice when failure settles its cloud upon our heads.

The one absolutely unselfish friend that man can have in this selfish world, the one that never deserts him, the one that never proves ungrateful or treacherous is his dog. A man's dog stands by him in prosperity and in poverty, in health and in sickness. He will sleep on the cold ground, where the wintry winds blow and the snow drives fiercely, if only he may be near his master's side. He will kiss the hand that has no food to offer. He will lick the wounds and sores that come in encounters with the roughness of the world. He guards the sleep of his pauper master as if he were a prince. When all other friends desert, he remains. When riches take wings, and reputation falls to pieces, he is as constant in his love as the sun in its journey through the heavens.

If fortune drives the master forth, an outcast in the world, friendless and homeless, the faithful dog asks no higher privilege than that of accompanying him, to guard him against danger, to fight against his enemies. And when the last scene of all comes, and death takes his master in its embrace and his body is laid away in the cold ground, no matter if all other friends pursue their way, there by the graveside will the noble dog be found, his head between his paws, his eyes sad, but open in alert watchfulness, faithful and true even in death."

範例：忠犬禮讚

「各位陪審團：在這世上最好的朋友都有可能背叛你，成爲你的敵人。他細心照護的兒女都有可能不感激他的養育之恩。那些和我們最親密的人或我們所信任的人，都有可能背叛他們當初的誓言。一個人所擁有的財富可能會消失，可能在他最需要的時候消失而去。一個人的信譽可能因爲一個魯莽的行爲而蕩然無存。他人可能會在你成功時對你畢恭畢敬，但也會在你失敗時落井下石。

在這自私的世界，一個絕不自私、不背叛你的朋友就是你的狗。不管在主人成功發達，身處困境，健康或生病時，狗兒總是陪伴著他。牠會親吻主人的手，即使手上沒有任何食物。牠會舔舐主人在這嚴峻的世界中所留下的傷口。當窮苦潦倒的主人酣睡時，狗兒會像守護王子般的保護著他。當所有人背叛你離你而去，牠仍然會陪伴著你。當財富遠去，名聲支離破碎時，牠仍然會愛著你就像日升日落般永不改變。

當財富離牠主人遠去，在這世上無家可歸，無依無靠，一隻忠誠的狗只要求陪在他身旁，在旁保護他遠離危險，對抗他的敵人。當到了人生最後一刻時，死神帶走了牠的主人，他的身體躺在冰冷的地上，狗兒仍然陪伴在他身旁，不管主人的朋友是否各奔東西了。牠將頭趴在雙腳上，眼神散發出悲傷，但仍保持著警覺，至死不渝。」

A commonly seen civil liability case regarding damage of a property (e.g. life of a dog) has been transformed into a petition for respect and salutation to the man's best friend, a dog, an incarnation of loyalty. A mere stating of a fact that a dog is killed can never achieve that purpose. A good story can arouse our passion and shake our conscience to take action. The content of that speech clearly shows that what we need to learn is NOT to use a complicated grammatical sentence structure embellished with difficult vocabularies in either a speech or writing but a true passion emitted by some simple words that can shake our conscience! This speech sends us a clear message that facts need interpretation to become a story.

一個常見的關於財產的民事毀損案件（一條小狗生命的損失），變成了一項爲人類忠誠的朋友請命，也就是一條小狗，也是忠誠的化身。單單陳述一項小狗被殺的事實，永遠達不到這樣的目的。一個好的故事可以激起我們的熱情，震撼我們的良知來採取行動，這篇演講内容很清楚的顯示，並不是用一個複雜的文法或句型裝飾著艱深的字彙，我們要學習的是，在演説或寫作中不需要使用複雜的文法句型裝飾著艱深難懂的字彙，而是透過簡單字句，散發出來眞正的感情，來震撼我們的良知。這樣的演講給了我們清楚的訊息，事實是需要透過解釋，才能成爲一個好的故事。

The above two examples (i.e. the pizza express delivery policy and the tribute to the dog) have shown the importance of interpretation of facts which can generally help the audience to develop an interest to follow through to see what will happen next. It is such interpretation by which the author uses in making movies and novels interesting and speeches powerful.

上面兩個例子（也就是比薩店的外送政策還有對狗兒致敬）展現出對於事實詮釋的重要性，而這個重要性可以鼓勵群眾知道之後發生了什麼事情，同樣的，這也是作者的詮釋賦予電影和小說趣味性，也使得演講更具有說服力。

Interpretation of a fact helps to build up a story. All good stories contain a message. Remember that a speech is made for persuading listeners to take action. For this reason, narration of facts must convey a message to the listeners to tell them what action to take. A story without a message remains only as cold facts exerting no power of persuasion. The purpose of persuasion, of course, fails if no action is called upon.

對於事實的詮釋可以建立起一個故事，所有好的故事都有一個訊息。要記得演說的目的在於說服聽眾採取行動，爲了這個理由，對於事實的陳述和解釋必須包括一個讓群眾採取行動的訊息。沒有訊息的故事，只是冰冷的事實，產生不了說服力。如果不呼籲行動，說服的目的是失敗的。

3.9 Building up creditability through facts

Why and how can we build up creditability through the facts? The reason is simple. The existence of facts or events cannot be denied if their veracity is ascertained. Once a speaker's interpretation is premised logically on the undeniable facts, then he has a better chance to win on persuasion. Of course, the audience may raise questions about the speaker's interpretation or whether the whole truth was provided, but the audience cannot doubt the existence of verified facts. Fair to say, a speaker has built up his prima facie case (prima facie: at first sight) if he uses facts to build up his story until being challenged. Nevertheless, partial truth may affect the correct result of the interpretation. A story is composed of a set of facts and the message is made from the reasoning of the facts, a form of interpretation, so to speak. As mentioned, facts are un-deniable. Once facts are given in the beginning, certain creditability has been established. For example, a short video clip showed that a sturdy Taxi driver was pushing away two slender women has created a prima facie evidence (of course, subjected to a challenge by the introduction of contrary evidence) that the Taxi driver might have committed an assault. If no further evidence is produced to rebut, the taxi driver is highly likely to be convicted of assault and battery. However, evidence is not always equivalent to the whole truth. The whole truth, as revealed later by another clip, was that, two women were assaulting the Taxi driver first due to a quarrel about the Taxi fares and the poor driver was exercising his right of self-defense. He pushed away those women in order to protect himself from any further attack. The whole issue on whether the driver is committing an assault or engaging in any self-defense is a question regarding the facts. Partial facts have created damage to the Taxi driver's image because it does not reveal the whole truth. Partial truth is a form of lie and can lead to a twisted and biased conclusion.

3.9 透過事實建立起可信度

我們爲什麼以及如何能夠透過事實來建立一個可信度？答案很簡單，事實或是事件的存在不能被否認，如果它們的眞實性被確認的話。當一個演講者他的解釋是非常具有邏輯性，且建立在不可否認的事實的話，他會有比較好的機會進行說服。當然聽衆們可能會對他的解釋提出問題，或是質疑他有沒有說出全部的事實，但是聽衆們無法懷疑經過確認事實的存在性。很公平的說，一個演說者如果他使用事實來建構他的故事，他就已經建立了他的初步說法（所謂的初步就是第一眼印象），除非他被挑戰。雖然如此，部分的事實可能會影響到解釋所產生結果的正確性。故事是由一組事實所構成，而訊息是來自於對事實的論理，也就是一種詮釋。如同前述，事實是無法否認的，一旦在一開始先給出事實，某個程度的可信度就已被建立。例如：在一段簡短的影片中，我們看到一個長得高大魁梧的計程車司機，用力推擠著兩個瘦弱的女性，就很容易形成初步的證據（當然可以被其他相反證據所挑戰被推翻），這個計程車司機正在進行攻擊，如果沒有更進一步的證據被提出的話，這個計程車司機很可能會被判定觸犯了攻擊罪，但是證據並不總等於全部事實，之後的影片顯示出眞相是這兩位女性因爲計程車車費而跟司機吵架，首先動手攻擊，而這個司機只是行使他自衛的權利而已。他把這兩個女人推開，爲了防止他們繼續攻擊，究竟這個司機是觸犯攻擊罪，還是只是自我防衛，是個事實問題。部分的事實，對計程車司機的形象造成傷害，因爲部分的事實沒有說出全部的眞相，部分的眞相是一種謊言，會導致被扭曲以及充滿歧視的結論。

It is advised that when a story is given, in order to make a story more interesting and easier for listeners to understand and remember, the 6 Ws should be observed, that is, what, where, when, who, why and how. When the 6 Ws are used, remember not to confuse the listeners with too many intricacies. They must be relevant. In writings, any idea or facts presented must be relevant and connected somehow in the casual link. The same rule is applied here. Of course, a speech could be a little loose. Some jokes with good humor are always welcomed, but, of course, should be used with some caution. Thus, application of the 6 Ws can be less rigid when preparing a speech.

我們建議當談到一個故事的時候，爲了讓故事更有趣而且使聽衆更清楚，可以使用六個 W，也就是：什麼事情、在哪裡發生的、什麼時候發生的、誰做了什麼事、爲什麼做這事以及如何做這件事。當使用六個 W 的時候要記得，不要說了太多複雜且細節的事情，否則聽衆容易混淆。這些事情必須彼此相關。在寫作中任何提出的想法與事實必須有相互的關聯，而且在某個程度上要有因果關係上的連結。在演說中也是一樣。當然演說可能會比較沒那麼嚴格規範。具有一些好的幽默感的笑話總是受大家歡迎的，但是要小心使用。而在演說的應用上比較沒那麼嚴格。

According to Dale Carnegie's advice, examples, especially from true experiences, when told in a clear, simple and concise form of a sincere manner, are more likely to be quite convincing in calling the audience to act. This advice is very helpful.

根據卡內基的建議，當以非常清楚簡明的方式以及真誠的態度說出從實際經驗中的例子，是非常有說服力的，也比較容易使群衆採取行動，這是非常有幫助的建議。

Another important point to be noted here is that when a speech is made for persuasion, it is a form of advocacy. A speaker is allowed to prefer one side over the other. There is no need to balance the different positions in a speech. However, if a speaker is confident enough to elaborate on both views using good perception and analysis, corroborating his own position and pinpointing the flaws of the opposite views with convincing facts and reasoning, then there is no reason why the speaker should not do so. But this training falls into the category of debate which we shall make further discussion on in the following chapter.

另外要注意的一點是，當演講是爲了說服，那目的就是爲立場辯護，也是爲了自己的立場進行支持。演說者可以喜歡某種說法而不喜歡另外一種。演說當中並不要求我們做正反論述。但是如果演說者很有信心能夠以他的眞知灼見還有分析闡述正反不同的意見，並用具有說服力事實及論理更支持他的論點，而且找出對手的缺點，那沒有什麼理由他不可以這樣做，但是這樣的訓練是我們在下一章關於辯論的範疇才會談到。

(1) Observation in a classroom

1 On a topic “growing up”, students are required to share their story as a message delivered to an audience. Many students do not know how to start. Most complain that their college life is rather plain and boring, not as exciting as what they had expected when in high school. Since their lives are rather plain at this stage, they don’t have much to share. In this case, students are encouraged to explore the definition of the term “growing up”. One student said that “growing up” could be referred to as a concept of change. She then shares her experience regarding her study of one required course which she had no interest at all. Her scores on each regular test reflected her effort and interest on that course until one day she was fed up with the feeling of being a failure. She made up her mind to study hard and received a good score in the end. The story is true but rather plain because the message is weak. However, if she could share the reason why she decided to change her attitude, being that

one day she recognized as an established fact that this subject was a required course and she has to take it regardless she likes it or not, then the story will be more powerful because her attitude changed after she acknowledged as an established fact that it is a required course and she has to take it. Therefore, the message to the listeners is that if you want to make any change, you have to recognize what happens as a fact, regardless how unpleasant it may seem. The same set of facts under a different interpretation will give quite a different conclusion.

(1) 課堂觀察

1 在一個以「成長」爲標題的演說訓練中，學生們被要求分享一個帶有訊息的故事。很多學生不知道如何開始，大部分的人抱怨他們的大學生活非常的平淡與無趣，跟他們高中時候的想像大不相同，因爲在這個階段的生活太過平淡，他們沒有太多可以分享。一個學生說到成長本身就帶有改變的概念，接著他就談到，曾經有一堂必修課，他完全沒有任何興趣，每次平常考的分數反映出他不努力的情況以及對於這門科目毫無興趣，直到有一天，他對這樣失敗者的感覺感到厭煩，他下定決心用功，而且在期末得到一個好成績。這是個眞實的故事，但是有些平淡，因爲訊息很薄弱。如果他可以告訴聽衆他的態度爲什麼改變，是因爲有一天他認知到這門科目是必修課，而這是一個既成的事實，不論他喜歡與否，那整個的故事就會變得更有說服力。他態度的改變是因爲他承認了必修課的這項事實，他必須修完這門課。因此，整個訊息呈現出來的是如果你想進行改變，你就先必須承認已經發生的事實，不管它令人感到多麼不悅。相同的事實，如果詮釋的方法不同，會產生一個完全不同的結論。

2 A student came back from the U.S. and shared his experience in a writing class in the U.S. According to him, the professor who taught that course did not ask them to write in the beginning but rather required them to brief and summarize the articles they read. Training on summarization can help students to locate important ideas and find the logical relationship and connection between those ideas and how they are developed; for example, their background, their current situation, and their future direction. This is a good learning approach for any beginner who is imposed with the work study of new subjects or new responsibilities of research. We learn to write or speak by following another's model. Students can learn to understand the framework of a model through analysis and follow the approach taken by that model. It is in fact a common practice by a new employee, whether in a business entity or a government branch, to learn from the previous files how the work was processed and completed by former employees. In addition, forming a summary from studying previous materials is very good training for effective reading. Writing a summary helps students to observe, to imitate and to think.

2 一個學生剛從美國回來，分享了他在美國大學課堂上的寫作經驗。根據他說，教授這一門課的老師並不要求他們在一開始就進行寫作，而是要他們對於所念過的文章進行濃縮並寫成摘要。摘要的訓練可以幫助學生找出重要的概念，以及發現這些概念之間彼此的邏輯關係及聯繫，還有他們如何發展，例如：他們的背景、他們現在的狀況，還有他們的未來如何發展。這因此對於任何學習新的主題或被賦予新的研究責任的初學者而言，都是一個很好的訓練方式。我們從模仿別人的作品當中，學習寫作與說話。學生們可以透過分析模範作品的結構，進行學習，而且模仿作品所採取的方式。事實上這對於任何一個新的員工，不論是在公司行號或是政府部門，都是普遍的方式，讓他們從舊檔案中，學習工作應該是如何被先前的人所執行與完成。除此之外，把念過的資料進行摘要整理是對有效閱讀非常好的訓練方式。製作摘要的寫作能夠幫助學生進行觀察，模仿以及思考。

3 On the practice of giving a description of what the students have seen in a movie, some students start giving every detail which could easily last over 15 minutes. Generally, a question like this in class demands no more than two minutes. If a student continues in giving all the details, his answer could easily last, as mentioned, over 15 minutes. A simple, clear, and succinct description of facts with a simple introduction of the main structure of the story is enough, usually lasting no more than 3 minutes. Too many details will distract the audience's attention, take up too much time and also make the whole story difficult to understand, even failing to recognize the main theme of the movie.

3 在訓練學生對於所看過的電影進行描述的訓練上，有些學生開始講出所有的細節，這樣的描述可以很容易就超過十五分鐘。通常在課堂上這樣的問題，會要求不超過兩分鐘的描述。如果學生說出了全部的細節，他的答案會超過十五分鐘。一個簡單、清楚以及精簡的事實描述，和對於故事主要結構的簡單描述其實就夠了，且通常不會超過三分鐘。太多的細節會讓大家失去注意力，會花上更多的時間去陳述而且使得整個故事不容易被了解，甚至無法了解電影的主要架構。

4 A story containing a conflict as a point of tension will intensify and thus attract attention.

4 故事如果帶有緊張之點的衝突，會形成張力因而吸引注意。

5 It is helpful to establish a mental picture in your mind first, then narrate the facts according to the image.

5 先在內心構思一幅圖像，然後再依照這個圖像描述事實。

6 A skillful arrangement of the factual descriptions could lead an audience to reach a certain conclusion before an interpretation is provided.

6 具有安排技巧的事實陳述，可以在沒有詮釋的情況之下引導聽衆達到一個結論。

(2) A view from a corner of the class

By Guo Wenqian

"What are you up to these days?" asked professor Cheng as the school bell rings.

"Well, nothing interesting, still preparing for IELTS." I pushed my glasses up my nose and responded timidly. I am afraid of being seen as a boring nerd, but what I have done lately proves that I am exactly that, a nerd.

"Still? You want to get the top score?" he asked. I can hear a little bit of sarcasm in his voice.

"Nope, I just want to pass this exam and improve my English. I don't want to look like a fool when I study abroad."

"Hmm ... interesting! What do you think is the hardest part of IELTS?" he asked.

"Speaking. I am not talkative and impromptu speeches always freak me out." I responded without any hesitation.

I can see myself sitting across from a foreign examiner. In front of me, a topic card, a recorder and a timer lying on the table. The examiner stares at me with a friendly but fake smile, waiting for my 3-minute impromptu speech after a one-minute-preparation. My mind is totally blank. What should I talk about? How should I organize my words? "Time is up! You'll have 2 to 3 minutes to talk about the given topic." The calm voice of the examiner is like a verdict of death. "I ... I want to talk about ... " I squeeze out some words "about ... " I stammered. I woke up. A nightmare! The IELTS speaking test is like a nightmare to me.

"Have you asked yourself why you are afraid?"

"Yep, the preparation time for the IELTS speaking test is very short, only one minute, and some of the given topics are totally unfamiliar to me. I can't think of any stories when I get an unfamiliar topic."

"Examples?" asked Professor Cheng.

"Like this one." I pull out a topic card from my folder.

It states, "Talk about an exciting sports event you have attended or witnessed."

"That's it? That's way too easy!"

"How can it be easy?! I have never witnessed or attended any sports events! I tried to make up a story, but it seemed so fake!" I said surprisingly.

"Have you ever taken any P.E. exams?" he asked.

"Of course!" I replied. I am confused. What do P.E. exams have to do with sports events? They are totally different.

"Then, can you remember your experiences of taking a P.E. exam?"

"Well, there is one. Five years ago," I generated my thoughts and continued, "I attended a very important P.E. exam, and the result of the exam had a direct influence on whether I could enter the best high school in our city or not."

"Go on." Professor Cheng said, with an encouraging smile.

"I remember, a 200-meter run and a contest throwing a medicine ball were required." I answered confusedly. Come on, that wasn't an exciting event at all! But when I looked up, Professor

Cheng is still encouraging me to continue.

"How did you feel that day?" he asked.

"Well, I was nervous to death."

"Can you be more specific?"

"Hmm ... I was nervous to death and I felt butterflies in my stomach. There was a moment I wished I could just run away and forget the whole test."

"Better! But why were you that nervous?" he asked.

"Because ... because ... I was very bad at P.E. Even my primary school P.E. teacher could still recognize me after 10 years, because I was such a huge trouble in his class. I have never passed any P.E. exams. I was afraid that if I failed this exam, I couldn't enter the best high school which was my biggest fear at that time."

"So how was the exam?"

I searched the painful memory in my mind.

"The 200-meter run started first. I stood on the track with great fear in my mind, praying not to trap myself and fall down in front of hundreds of people like an idiot. When the examiner signaled us to run, I ran with all my strength. But still, I saw all the other examinees run passed me, and I was the last one who reached the finish line. Obviously I failed, but my nightmare wasn't over as later came the medicine ball throwing contest. I was so skinny at that time, and the ball was way too heavy for me. Without any doubt, I failed again."

"Has this event influenced your life?"

"Well, I didn't get to go to my ideal high school." What a painful memory!

"That's it?"

"Well, since then, I am determined to build up my body and exercise every day. I am athletic now. I can jog 5 km in 40 minutes and swim 40 laps in a swimming pool within an hour without feeling tired. Because the failure urged me to do so, I do not want to fail again just because I am not fit enough."

"That's a great story! It has every element of composing a story. Why did you think the topic is unfamiliar to you?"

"Because it's not what I think an exciting sports event should be. I think it has to be something like ... like ... football matches, basketball matches, swimming competitions and so on. Mine is just ... too ... " I paused and searched for the right expression, "ordinary and plain."

"Audrey, it's ridiculous! You have your own story which you never noticed and seen as boring!" He looked at me into my eyes and continued, "No matter whether you are chatting, writing, or making a speech, what others want to hear from you is your own story, feelings, opinions, not just some made-up stuff, or vague theories. Do you know what I mean?"

I nod. As a reader and a listener in an audience myself, I love listening to real stories and I hate those who always are babbling about theories or making up stories that are not convincing.

"You have to look inside yourself and try to spot stories of your own. And to do so, you have to experience more, observe more, and think more. If you shut yourself up and study all day long, you won't make any progress."

2. 課堂一角

郭文倩同學

「最近如何啊？」鄭老師的問候聲緊接著上課鐘響傳來耳邊。

「沒什麼特別的事，我還是在準備雅思的考試。」我推推我的眼鏡掩飾我的不安，我很害怕我看起來像個無趣的書呆子，然而我最近的所作所爲卻證明了我確實是個書呆子。

「還在準備啊？你想考滿分啊？」鄭老師問著，而我從他的語調中，感覺到了一絲嘲弄。

「不是啊，我只是想通過考試並增進自己的英文能力罷了，我不想在國外讀書時當個傻瓜。」

「嗯，眞是有趣。那你認爲雅思最難的部分是什麼？」

「口說吧，我不是一個健談的人，而且即席演講總讓我相當受挫。」我毫無遲疑的回答。

我看見了我自己坐在外籍考官對面。在我眼前，一張題目卡，一臺錄音機，和一個計時器就這樣擺在桌上。考官看著我，他臉上帶著友善卻虛僞的笑容，等待著我用一分鐘的時間準備三分鐘的即席演講。我腦中一片空白。我該說些什麼？我該怎麼組織？正當我還在思考時，考官冷靜的像是宣判死亡的聲音傳來我的耳邊，「時間到，現在你有二到三分鐘的時間來談談你所被指定的主題。」「嗯……嗯……我想談論……關於……關於……」我口吃的重複著「關於」，並努力的想講些什麼。突然間，我醒了。原來是場惡夢啊。雅思的口說部分，對我來說，確實是個惡夢。

「你問過自己爲什麼會害怕這部分嗎？」

「當然，因爲雅思的口說部分準備時間非常短，只有一分鐘，而且有些主題是我完全不熟悉的。對於我不熟悉的主題，我完全想不到該用什麼故事來闡述。」

「像是什麼主題啊？」鄭老師問著。

「像是這個。」我從資料夾中拿出題目卡。

上面寫著：「請談談你曾參與過或看過的精采運動賽事。」

「就這種題目啊，這也太簡單了吧。」

「這怎麼會簡單？我從來沒看過或參加過任何運動賽事！我試著要捏造一個故事，但好像太虛假了。」我驚訝地回答著。

「那你總該上過體育課吧？」他問著。

「當然。」我理所當然的回答，但我相當困惑，體育課跟運動賽事有什麼關聯？這兩件事完全不相關！

「好，那你還記得你上體育課的經驗嗎？」

「記得啊，在五年前的一個經驗。」我喚起記憶並繼續答著，「我上了一堂相當重要的體育課，課程考試的結果會直接影響我是不是能進入我們城裡最好的高中。」

「嗯，繼續。」鄭老師投以我一個充滿鼓勵的笑容。

「我記得在兩百公尺的距離跑當中還必須投球。」我困惑的回答著。拜託，這對我來說一點都不有趣。但當我看向鄭老師時，他依然投以我一個燦爛的微笑，鼓勵我繼續。

「你那時候感覺怎麼樣啊？」他問著。

「我緊張到快死了。」

「可以再明確一點嗎？」

「嗯……我緊張到快窒息了，我感受到我的胃在翻騰，在那一刻，我只希望我能逃跑並澈底忘記這場考試。」

「好點了，但你爲什麼會那麼緊張啊？」

「因爲……因爲……我非常不擅長運動，甚至我小學時的體育老師在十年後還是記得我，因爲我是他課堂中的大麻煩。我從來沒有順利通過體育考試項目過。我很害怕自己因爲沒通過體育考試而導致我不能進入最好的高中，那是我當時最畏懼的事情。」

「所以，那場考試如何？」

我在心中搜索著那慘痛的記憶。

「200 公尺距離跑先開始，我忐忑不安地站在跑道上，祈禱著自己別像個傻瓜般地在衆人面前被自己絆著了。當裁判鳴槍示意我們起跑時，我盡全力地向前跑，但一如往常的，我看著其他受測者紛紛超越了我，而我果然是最後一個到達終點線的人。很顯然的，我失敗了。但我的惡夢並沒有伴隨著 200 公尺距離跑而結束，隨之而來的是投球競賽。在當時，我非常的嬌小，所以那球對我來說是非常大的負擔，果不其然，我又失敗了。」

「這樣的經驗有影響到你之後的人生嗎？」

「嗯，我沒辦法進入我理想中的高中就讀。」多麼慘痛的一個經驗啊！

「就這樣？」

「在那之後，我就決定要好好健身，每天運動。現在，我是運動員了。我可以在四十分鐘內跑完五公里，在一小時內在游泳池裡游來回四十趟，而且一點都不覺得累。因爲這樣不愉快的經驗促使我這麼做，我不想再一次地經歷失敗，只因爲我不夠強壯。」

「這就是很棒的故事啦！一個故事該有的要素都有了，你怎麼會覺得你不熟悉這樣的主題呢？」

「因為這並不是我想像中刺激的運動賽事該有的樣子啊。我認為它應該像是……像是……足球比賽、籃球比賽、游泳競賽之類的。而我……我的經驗太……太…… 」我暫停了對話，並搜尋著適切的表達方式，「太過於平凡普通了。」

「奧黛莉，這太荒謬啦！你擁有一個被你視為無聊而從不曾注意過的故事呢！」他專注的看著我並繼續說著，「不論當你在聊天、寫作或做演講時，聽眾想聽的正是你自己的故事、感受和想法，而不是一些捏造的東西或是一些模糊不清的理論。你懂我的意思嗎？」

我點點頭。當我自己作為一個聽眾及讀者時，我確實喜歡聽眞實的故事，而且我相當討厭那些總是胡說八道或捏造故事的人，因為那一點都不具說服力。

「你必須了解你自己並試著點亮你的生命故事。而這麼做的方法是，你必須經歷更多、觀察更多，也要思考更多。如果你總是讓自己閉上嘴巴然後整天讀書，你永遠不會進步的。」

Comments

As shown in her statement, the speaking test in IELTS was the difficult part that she was not confident enough to manage because, according to her, many questions are beyond her personal experiences. When the examiner asked her about her experience in sports, she basically had to make up one. A made up story can seldom go smoothly with any free flow because there is no genuine feeling, not to mention any persuasion.

評論

就像她所說的，雅思口試部分是很困難的，而她沒有足夠的自信能夠應付，因爲根據她的說法，很多問題是在她的個人經驗之外，所以當口試者問她關於運動方面經驗的時候，她基本上是要創造一個說法。一個虛構的故事，往往並不流暢，因爲那沒有眞實的感情，更不要說說服。

The truth is that she does have some experience in sports. Every student is required to take P.E. in high school. In fact, the physical exercise test is part of the entrance examination in China with crucial consequences. Audrey gave a clear account of what had happened in her physical exercise exam days, such a failure prevented her aim at entering a better school. Interestingly, that failure did not stop at that very moment as a permanent flaw but, on the contrary, it brought a consequential change in her life forever. It turned out to be a blessing. Ten years have passed and she is still a fitness buff continuing her daily exercises. This is a truly great story encouraging all of us to avail ourselves of learning lessons from any failure in order to gain future success.

眞相是她確實在運動方面有些經驗，每一個學生中學的時候都有體育課，事實上，在中國大陸體育考試是入學考試的一環，考試結果是很重要的。學生很詳細的描述當天體育考試的情況，而這一項的失敗導致她不能進入更好的學校就讀。有趣的是，這項失敗，當下並沒有以終生的遺憾而告終，相反的帶給她未來生活完全改變。

這是一項祝福。十年已經過去了，她還是每天保持運動的習慣，依然身體強健。這是一個非常好的故事，鼓勵我們大家從失敗當中學習，走向未來的成功。

The topic for oral tests such as IELTS or TOEFL will not test your special knowledge. They only test your general knowledge. Talking about sports is not necessarily limited to topics regarding some professional athletic celebrity or events. Everyone has certain experiences with sports. Just recall your personal experiences or any of your friends'. You will have plenty to tell.

雅思或是托福考試的題目不會測試你的特別知識，他們僅僅測試你的一般性知識。關於運動的話題，並不必然的限制在一些專業的運動員或是特別的運動事件上。每個人對運動總是有些經驗，只要回想一下你跟朋友們的個人經驗，你就有很多故事可以分享。

Another important note here to be reminded of is that if you only have one minute to prepare for one topic as that encountered in a daily conversation with your customers, then you have to forget about organizing in the same way as preparing for a formal essay. One minute is only good enough for you to come up with a story organized with an interpretation that produces a message of persuasion.

另外一個重點，我們應該也要銘記在心的是：如果你只有一分鐘的時間準備一項主題，就像一般日常跟客户的對話，基本上你必須放棄爲了準備論文發表才有的架構。一分鐘的時間只夠你準備一個故事以及透過解釋故事所產生一個具有說服的訊息。

Exercise

What are some of the qualities of a good parent? Use specific details and examples to explain your answer.

A student shared with the whole class about his opinion about his father. His father is a strict person, tending to discipline his son with strict rules and harsh punishment. Once his father asked him not to stay up late and stop spending that much time on his mobile phone. He resented it and greatly complained because his father continued to do the same thing that he forbid his son to do. In other words, the father was asking his son to do something that he himself could never accomplish. Therefore, in his opinion, a father should be a model for his children by his conduct rather than by mere words. The whole class was surprised by his resentment in his speech against his father. He did not tell in his speech what good parents should act like but what they should not do.

The whole speech is fine and impressive indeed because it is composed of all the necessary elements as advised, such as facts, interpretation followed by a message and a conclusion. My advice here is an analogy could be added for corroboration. For example, if he could extend the content to include another common phenomenon in Taiwan, such as, many parents put their high expectations on their children which ends up being on them an unfair burden which the parents have never been able to fulfil in their youth (e.g. sending their children to crammed schools to get better scores in order to get into the best universities or acquiring higher skills to compete). The whole speech would sound more complete and powerful because the message from the first story has been further elaborated in the second story, which is a common social phenomenon in our society that parents use their children to fulfill a dream which they had never been able to achieve in their youth.

Another student claimed in her speech that good parents should respect their children as an independent entity rather than dictate to them as a parent's subordinate. She told the class that her parents always respected their children's decision to learn, for example, some skills such as playing a piano as she had always been interested in. She felt respect from her parents. My advice here is that another example could be introduced as a contrast. For instance, I know some cases that children are forced to learn to play the piano by their parents. It is not a pleasant experience because they are under pressure to do something that they are not interested in. Some resent it and some even end up with psychological problems. Objectively, these two cases seem to share the same fact pattern, i.e. children are learning to play the piano. But the former is out of a free will as an independent entity with a happy experience and the latter is out of compulsion as a subordinate leading to an unhappy ending.

An example as an analogy or a contrast could extend a message of the first example to the second for corroboration. Extending a message by applying and elaborating on other examples will make a speech or writing more persuasive and powerful.

習作

好的父母親的特質是什麼？請用細節還有例子來解釋你的答案。

一個學生在班上跟同學們分享他對自己父親的看法。他的父親是一個嚴格的人，傾向於使用嚴格的規則及嚴厲的懲罰來訓練自己的兒子。曾經有一次，他爸爸要求他不要太晚睡，而且也不要花過多的時間在滑他的手機。他內心非常的不滿，且有許多抱怨，因爲他的父親更晚睡，甚至也一樣在滑自己的手機，而這些正是他嚴格禁止自己兒子做的事情。換句話說，這個父親要求他的小孩去做一些他根本不能完成的事情。所以在他的意見裡面，一個父親在教育小孩子這方面，應該以身作則，而不是只用言語告訴小孩子應該怎麼做。整個班上對於他對父親的憤怒感到很訝異。他沒有說明什麼是好的父母親應該做的，反而是什麼樣的事情是父母親不應該做的。

整篇的演說還可以，確實令人印象深刻。因爲他包括了我們所建議所有需要的元素，像是事實，對於事實的解釋，以及訊息，還有最後的結論。我這裡的建議是，還可以再加上一個類比，作爲支持。例如；他可以擴充他陳述的內容，加入另外一種在臺灣很常見的現象，比如很多父母親對於他們的小孩有非常高的期待，希望他們的孩子可以完成父母親在他們年輕時所達不到的夢想，結果這樣的期待變成非常不公平的重擔（比方說將他們的孩子送進補習班，希望他們得到更高的分數，得以進入最好的大學，或是在補習班學得更好的技藝以謀求在競賽中的成功），整篇的演說會更完整也更有力，因爲第一個故事中的訊息會被第二個故事更進一步的詮釋，一個在我們社會中非常普遍的現象，也就是父母親利用他們的小孩來達到他們年輕時的夢想。

另外一個學生，在她的演說中，提到好的父母親應該尊重他們的孩子是一個個體，而不是以一個附屬的方式來命令他們。她告訴班上，她的爸媽總是尊重孩子在學習方面上的選擇，例如，她對學習鋼琴有高度的興趣，她感受到來自父母親的尊重。在這裡，我的建議是，我們可以加上一個反面的例子，比方說，我知道有些情況是父母親逼著他們的孩子去學習鋼琴，這並不是一個愉快的經驗，因爲他們的孩子被逼迫去學習鋼琴，有些孩子抱怨，有些甚至造成產生了心理上的問題。

客觀而言，兩個例子看起來有個相同的事實模式，也就是小孩子在學習鋼琴。但是前者是來自於獨立個體的個人選擇，經驗是愉快的；而後者，是來自於強迫，是一個附屬的地位，結局並不愉快。

一個比喻或是相反的例子，可以將前面例子的訊息延伸到第二個例子來增加整個演講或作文的說服力和力度。

3.10 Training beginners

The purpose of a speech, as we explain at the beginning, is for persuasion. To persuade, a speaker must have confidence. He should know his subject matter and present the message with good utterance and confidence. Any hesitation and slow response will generally cast doubt on the speaker's message (he is not sure about what he is talking about). In Taiwan, many students are reserved and do not like to talk in public (e.g. classroom). They are used to following a teacher's instructions without any form of doubt and taking notes rather than sharing their own views in public, not to mention presenting a different view which could be interpreted as a challenge against an authority figure. Even if they are asked questions regarding their own opinion, many have little to say and some won't even talk at all. In other words, students stay passive and generally tend to be quiet in a speech class. Once students refuse to talk, then the purpose of training them on speech will fail.

3.10 對於初學者訓練

就像我們在一開始所談到的，演說的目的在於說服。要能夠說服，演說者必須要有自信。他應該要了解他的主題，並且充滿自信與清楚的表達來傳遞訊息。遲疑以及過慢的反應很容易讓別人對於演說者的訊息產生懷疑（他不清楚他在說些什麼）。在臺灣很多學生比較沉默也不喜歡對公眾說話（例如：在教室）。他們習慣毫無疑問地接受老師們的指示，並勤作筆記而不願意公開表達他們的意見，遑論提出一個可能被視為挑戰權威的意見。當他們被詢問關於自己意見的時候，大部分的人說得很少，甚至根本不說話。換句話說，學生們傾向於被動，而學生們在演說課傾向於被動而保持沉默。學生們一旦拒絕說話，演說訓練的目的就失敗了。

Speech is a form of conversation, so are debate and negotiation. A good speech is a good conversation. For those who are reluctant to talk in public, they cannot hold a conversation with the public. If there is no conversation, then there is no communication. If there is no communication, the purpose of persuasion cannot be achieved. Therefore, as mentioned in the section regarding conversation, for those who hesitate to talk in public, they should be encouraged as the first step to engage in a conversation, talking freely and naturally without any required speech format. In my class observation, some students even tend to draft the content for some simple questions encountered in a daily conversation, whether it involves a self-introduction or some future plan. This should be avoided because, in reality, no one will draft the content for any daily conversation. Besides, preparation of the content for a simple conversation, of course, will delay the time of their response to the other party and thus may make their actions appear unnaturally slow (i.e. robotic) or even appear they lack intelligence. Students at this stage are encouraged to freely and naturally express their own views without being discouraged, even speaking on something trivial, because their confidence to talk in public is the first priority in such training. Once they can pick up the confidence to talk in public, then they can move to the next stage, the description of facts.

演說是對話的一種，辯論和談判也是。好的演說是好的對話，對於那些不願意在公眾面前講話的人，他們是沒有辦法跟群眾進行對話的。沒有對話就沒有溝通。沒有溝通，說服的目的就不能達到。因此，就像在前一章節所談到關於對話的部分，對於那些在公眾面前不願意說話的人，他們應該先把從事對話當作第一步，能夠自由與自然的不拘演講形式的表達。在我的課堂觀察中，有些學生對一些日常生活對話的問題，像是自我介紹或未來的規劃，甚至要先打草稿才能回答。這種情況應該避免，因爲在日常生活中，不會有人先打草稿再講話，而且先打草稿再說話，會耽誤反應的時間，會讓別人覺得說話者反應遲緩，甚至智商不高。學生們在這個階段應該被鼓勵自由與自然的表達意見，縱然是一些小事，因爲對公眾說話的自信是在這個階段訓練中的第一要務。一旦他們找到公眾演說的自信，他們就可以進行到下一步關於對事實陳述的訓練。

Some topics for practice at this stage:

*Self-introduction and why it is important

*My experience with English learning

*My vision for the future

*My change in the past three years

The above four topics are all related to the background of the student speakers within their full knowledge. They should have no problem on providing the information regarding themselves if they have enough confidence and ability to speak English to the public. If a student delivers the speech fluent in his own mother tongue but hesitant in English, then the student's problem is probably on English rather than expression.

在這個階段建議一些訓練習作：

* 自我介紹以及爲什麼自我介紹很重要

* 我學習英文的經驗

* 我的未來願景

* 我過去三年的改變

上述四個問題全部與學生自身有關，他們是全然了解這些訊息的。因此，在提供上述與自身有關的訊息上應該是沒什麼問題，如果他們有足夠的自信跟能力以英文表達的話。假若學生以他的母語表達沒問題，但是在英文表達上卻充滿遲疑停頓的話，那我們就知道他的問題是在英文而不是在於表達上。

3.11 A note on self-introduction

Self-introduction is important because you are offered with an opportunity to present yourself to the listeners. In a class of 35 students, when each is asked to give a 3-5-minute self-introduction, the whole process in class, including comments made by the teacher, could last over three hours. Students can easily feel bored with the same old content with only a slight difference with names and addresses. The same boring feeling can be found among interviewers when they face a good number of applicants applying for jobs. How can you make people remember your identity among all the applicants?

3.11 關於自我介紹的一些看法

自我介紹很重要，因爲你有一個機會可以對聽衆展現你自己。在三十五個學生的班上，每一個學生有三至五分鐘的時間進行自我介紹，整個過程加上老師的評論可能會超過三個小時。學生們對於除了名字與地址略爲相異而其他幾近雷同的內容容易感到厭煩。在那些面試很多應徵者的面試官身上，也可以找得到一樣煩悶的情緒。你如何讓聽衆們在所有人當中記得你的身分？

Most students don't know how to give an effective self-introduction. It is funny to see some who give their self-introduction without giving their names first. He still remains as a stranger to all as he finishes. Some talk about their family and where they are from, then they stop and seemed to pause for further instructions from the teacher. They seem quite timid and don't know how to go any further. Upon asking a question, some talk about their hobbies and music, probably their personality and future. It is rather an INTERROGATION by a teacher than a speech or a conversation. Even for those who can finish their story, most are as monotonous in their tone and content as they can be, more or less like watching a blade of grass slowly growing. Very few, if any, can give a good story to build up his image to be remembered.

大部分的學生不知道如何進行一個有效的自我介紹。有些人甚至很滑稽的忘了告訴大家他的姓名。當介紹完畢的時候，對於群衆，他依然是一個陌生者。有些談到他的家庭，還有他住哪邊之後就完全停止，等待老師的進一步指令，完全不知道該怎麼辦。經過提示，有些人談到他們的興趣，有些則是他們的個性和未來，看起來這根本是由老師在進行拷問，而不是一個演說或對話。對於那些能完成他們故事的人，絕大部分的音調和內容，是極其單調，幾乎像是在觀察小草生長一樣，非常少數的人能做到透過好的故事來增進他的形象讓別人容易記得。

Remember those applicants mentioned in the beginning of this chapter? Most of the applicants seemed to be uttering their crammed information from their brains, stuttering and hesitant, afraid of making any mistakes. Such stutters and hesitations seem especially worse when questions are asked by the interviewers. The whole process at this stage has turned into an interrogation rather than a conversation between the interviewers and applicants. Some applicants cannot even reply to a simple question under this pressure and apologize to the interviewers for their failure to answer. They are bound to say farewell to those good opportunities that could have been their future career.

記得在本章一開始所談到的那些工作的應徵者嗎？大部分的應徵者從他們的腦子裡面背誦出那些資訊，有些口吃而且遲疑，深怕犯了錯誤。在被問到一些問題的時候，這樣的口吃與遲疑看起來更糟糕，整個的過程到了這個階段開始變成一個拷問，而不是口試員與應徵者的對話。有一些應徵者在這樣的壓力之下，甚至連一些簡單的問題都回答不出來，因而對口試員道歉。他們是注定要跟他們未來良好的工作機會說再見。

Simply speaking, your purpose of talking will fail if none can remember who you are after your introduction. The question here is, how to make people remember you? Among all 35 students, whoever builds up his uniqueness will be remembered easier and longer. Such uniqueness could be related to special experiences from various times in different places. It could also result from a humorous expression stated by the speaker. In other words, the speakers must create something unique for the listeners to remember. What can be more interesting than facts is a story about you or your friends' true and special experiences? These true, interesting and unique experiences could come from descriptions of family relationships, travelling, future plans or hobbies. Proper details can intrigue the interest of the audience and help place them in the situation. Such self-introduction could give a good impression to any interviewer. The point here is that you should distinguish yourself from others or you are only one out of a group of ants.

簡單來說，如果在說完之後沒人記得你，你的自我介紹是很失敗的。在這邊的問題就是要如何讓別人記得你，三十五個學生當中最容易被記得的，以及記得最久的，就是那些具有獨特性的人。這種獨特性可能是來自於不同時間、不同地點的經驗，他也可能來自於演說者的幽默感，也就是說演說者必須有一些獨特性讓聽眾能夠記得，有什麼東西會比你或你朋友眞實並且特別的經驗來得更有趣的呢？這些眞實有趣以及特別的經驗可能是來自於對家庭關係的描述、旅遊的經驗、他未來的計畫，或是他的興趣等等。適當的細節可以讓聽衆聽得津津有味，置身其中。找工作的時候，採取這樣方式的自我介紹，可以讓面試官印象深刻。重點在於你不應該跟其他的人一樣索然無味，否則你就只是衆多螞蟻中的其中一隻。

3.12 Narration/Description of facts

Description of facts is important because a good description can provide not only information about what has happened but also show how and why it happens. Such information and reason are given so a decision can be made in the mind of the listeners. A court's decision regarding a fact description generally serves as a good example as being clear, relevant, logical, succinct and decisive (i.e. important) on the issue presented. The readers of a court's decision usually are able to understand what has happened in a given case (e.g. why a plaintiff sues a defendant). Of course, a court's decision is written with legal language often replete with jargons as well as complicated grammar. Nevertheless, students could follow the same framework regarding fact description but should write it in a plain English style.

3.12 事實的敘述

對於事實的敘述很重要，因爲好的敘述不僅能提供關於發生什麼事的資訊，同時也會顯示出事情是如何發生以及發生的原因。法院判決中關於事實敘述就是個很好的例子，這些敘述清楚、具有關聯性、有邏輯、精簡，以及在所呈現的爭議點上具有決定性（很重要）。看過法院判決的人通常能夠了解在一個案件裡發生什麼事（例如：爲什麼原告控告被告），當然，法院的判決所使用的法律語言通常充滿了法律術語以及複雜的文法，雖然如此，在事實表達部分，學生們應該以簡單英文的格式表達事實。

Example 1 of a summary of legal facts

An American buyer visits a seller in Taiwan. The seller has been engaged in the business of toy manufacturing for over 20 years and is a world-wide known supplier. The buyer visits the seller's factory and has a meeting with the seller's design team. Both parties sign the confidentiality agreement. The buyer, thereafter, shares with the seller's research team his design and the seller's team responds positively with the buyer's request. The buyer and seller communicate verbally and by e-mails many times. The seller's research team also shares their opinion on the design originally presented by the buyer and the buyer agrees with them. Therefore, the design is modified according to the seller's opinion. Both sides agree that the seller will pay USD$ 100,000 for tooling, and such expense will be amortized within the contract terms by the buyer with the quantity ordered (USD$ 1 for each unit). Finally, two months later, the buyer reaches an agreement with the seller's management on product specifications, price, method of payment, tooling and intellectual property rights, etc. A master agreement of two years is signed with details left to subsequent purchase orders.

法律事實摘要的例子

一個美國買家訪問在臺灣的賣家。賣家從事玩具生產超過二十年的時間，是一個國際知名的供應商。買家訪問賣家的工廠之後，與賣家的設計團隊開會，雙方簽訂了保密協定，買方因此將他的設計與賣方的研究團隊分享。而賣方的研究團隊對於買方的要求也都予以正面肯定。買方與賣方利用口頭與 email 溝通非常多次，賣方的研究團隊，同時也將他們在設計上的意見，與買方分享，而買方也同意他們的設計理念。所以，設計最初是由買方所提供，但是卻由賣方所修正。雙方同意賣方負責開模，費用是 10 萬美金，而這個費用會由買方在契約期限之內，按照訂單所購買的數量（每一個單位一美金），逐步攤還。在兩個月之後，買方與賣方的管理階層，就產品規格、價格、付款方式、模具、以及智慧產權部分達成協議。雙方簽訂主要供貨契約，期限兩年，細節部分則交由之後的訂單來處理。

Their relationship is running smooth at the beginning but later turns sour after a few disputes over the method of payment. According to the contract, the buyer will make quarterly T/T payments and a “set off” is allowed. In one event, the seller is demanding the buyer’s quarterly payment of USD$ 1,000,000, yet the buyer is claiming a “set off” of USD$ 150,000 because of the seller’s delivery in the past of non-conforming products. The buyer claims that such damages caused by delivery of non-conforming goods should be deducted from the quarterly payment. However, the seller is upset because the buyer is extremely picky with the quality of products, and the amount the buyer purchases yearly is only counted as 10%, USD$ 3,000,000, of the seller’s yearly turnover (i.e. USD$ 30,000,000 for a yearly turnover), but the amount the buyer rejects is about 15%, USD$ 750,000, of the seller’s total rejected goods of that year (i.e. USD$ 5,000,000).

雙方的關係一開始還好，但是在幾次付款上面的爭議之後，逐漸變差了。根據契約，買方應該在每一季結束的時候，用 T/T 來付款，以及雙方債權債務的「抵銷」是許可的。在一次場合當中，賣方要求買方支付當季貨款美金 100 萬元。但是買方主張抵銷美金 15 萬元，因爲賣方在過去交付了不合規定的貨物。買家聲稱這些不合規定的貨物造成的損害，應該從當季的貨款當中扣除。但是，賣家非常的不高興，因爲買家對於貨物的品質，極端的挑剔；再者，買家每一年所買的貨物，僅相當於賣家一年營業量（美金 3,000 萬）的 10%，也就是美金 300 萬，但是買家的退貨率卻高達賣家當年所有退貨率（美金 500 萬）的 15%，也就是美金 75 萬。

The seller is threatening to terminate the contract and to stop delivery. The seller also refuses the buyer’s request to return the moulds. The buyer is extremely angry with such “threat” because this might cause the buyer’s breach with many of his clients in the United States. The buyer therefore threatens to sue for breach of contract and for patent infringement, and both sides hold a meeting for a negotiation.

賣方威脅要終止契約，以及不再出貨。賣方同時也拒絕了買方將模具歸還的要求。買方對於這樣的威脅感到非常的憤怒，因爲賣方的行爲很可能會導致買方與其他美國客人的違約。買方因此也威脅要控告賣方違約以及專利侵權。接著雙方展開了談判的會議。

The above summary is an illustration in a plain English style with the logical sequence of facts describing a usual manufacturing pattern of a Taiwan company either as an OEM (original equipment manufacturer) or an ODM (original design manufacturer) followed by a possible dispute. The facts should be concise and relevant. Relevancy of facts is decided by the issue of law. Fair to say, whoever drafts a business letter regarding a dispute should have some basic concept on law. It is advised that the description of factual background should be written in a plain English style with a logical sequence for others to better understand it.

上面的摘要，是以簡單的英文以及邏輯的順序，描述了臺灣地區 OEM 或是 ODM 公司一般的接單與生產過程的事實，然後之後可能所發生的爭議。相關的事實，是由法律上的爭議來決定，平心而論，任何人起草一份關於爭議的商業書信，必須對於法律有基本認識和了解。在處理商業事件中，最好使用簡單的英文而且以邏輯的順序來表達事實的背景以及提出相關的爭議。

3.13 Further elaboration on the interpretation of facts

In a class practice on a speech topic "one thing that someone taught me", a student talked about her high school teacher's enthusiasm and dedication on teaching as well as her sympathy coupled with regular donations to help some poor students, but, quite unfortunately, she was later diagnosed with cancer that ended her life. At her funeral, the students wept and were sad for a long time. They encouraged each other to follow her spirit and deeds in the future. Her message is easily drawn from the facts given without any further elaboration. No elaboration was made because there was neither an issue nor conflict in the whole speech. Anyone who learns the facts at the beginning may immediately draw such conclusion.

3.13 對於事實解釋部分進一步的闡述

在課堂演講題目「曾經有人教我的一項功課」，一個學生談到她的高中老師在教學上充滿熱誠與奉獻，以及對於貧窮學生的憐憫甚至給予資助。很不幸的，之後她因罹患癌症而過世。在她的告別式中，學生們傷心難過，持續了很久的一段時間，他們彼此互相鼓勵，應該追隨這個老師的精神。這個學生的訊息不需要特別的解釋，從所提供的事實就很自然地看得出來。不需要特別解釋是因爲整篇的演說並沒提出爭議或是衝突點，任何人只要知道這些事實後，幾乎可以馬上知道相同的結論。

An issue or a conflict raised by a speaker can show the speaker's inquisitive level of mind, his perspective in seeing the facts given, and his perception of reality as demonstrated by his message, and probably his wisdom, as well as, taking the audience on his exploration of the difficulties that were encountered. For example, in the above case, one possible issue is asked, "If a good person like her high school teacher died in such a way, then why should we do good? Why did a good person die early in such a way? Why does a good guy finish last? Why should we do good? When the speaker shared this doubt/issue/conflict with the audience, the general public will have an interest in knowing what journey the speaker has travelled, what destination he has arrived at, and what he has found out? Many students have presented their views on the facts given in this speech. To sum it up, if any person only cares about how much payoff he can receive from his deeds, then he is rather a businessman because he only cares about profit, a form of self-interest. In the case given, the high school teacher never asked for payoff (e.g. what benefit can I receive from my dedication and sympathy in giving). In fact, she cared about the welfare of many students, especially the poor ones. She was dedicated to her teaching. She spent time on encouraging those who had learning problems. She helped the students who had financial difficulties. She was not wealthy but she definitely was a philanthropist. She had helped many. Those who have received her help will help others in the future. If her kindness is a seed, then we have no doubt in saying that she has planted seeds of kindness which have grown up into a forest to bring hope to this society for a better future. The whole society benefited from her good will and deeds and this is not something that a selfish person who only cares about self-interest can achieve. Therefore, the message is that if you only care about receiving payoff for yourself, then you should not give in the first place. However, for those who do enjoy satisfaction from improving the welfare of society, your giving and kindness is a precious seed toward our future.

演說者所提出的問題或爭議點能夠顯示出他內心的質疑程度、看事情的角度以及對眞實環境了解的程度。這些都是透過他的訊息還有智慧所展現出來，藉此帶領著群衆探索所遇到的困難，例如：在上述案件一個可能的問題就是，如果像她的高中老師這麼好的一個人卻英年早逝，那爲什麼我們還要做好事呢？爲什麼這麼好的一個人會這麼早過世？爲什麼一個好人總是最後一名？爲什麼我們要行善？當一個演說者跟聽衆們分享他的懷疑和衝突的時候，群衆們會很有興趣知道這演說者在他內心經歷了哪些旅程？他最後到了哪裡？以及他究竟發現什麼？許多學生在這個例子裡分享他們的看法，簡單歸納，如果任何一個人是因爲在乎他的回報而做了好事，那他就是一個商人，因為他只在乎利益，一種自我受益的形式。在這個案例裡，這個高中老師從來沒有要求回報（例如：我可以從我的服務或是憐憫得到什麼）。事實上，她在乎許多同學們，特別是那些貧困同學的幸福，她致力於她的教學，她花時間鼓勵那些在學習上有困難的學生，她也幫助那些在財務上陷入困境的學生。她並不富有，但她是一個慈善家。她幫了很多人，那些接受她幫助的人，將來會幫助更多的人。如果她的善良是一顆種子的話，那我們可以毫無疑問地說，她種下了許多善良的種子，而這些種子們已經長成了一片樹林，給了這個社會更多美好的未來。整個社會從她的善行得到利益，這並不是一個自私的人可以做得到的事情，因此，這個訊息就是，如果你只在乎自己的回報的話，你根本一開始就不應該給予，但是對於那些可以從改進社會利益當中得到滿足的人，你的善行和奉獻是給我們未來寶貴的種子。

The above case shows that even a simple fact can be interpreted as an exciting story as long as a strong message could be elicited from a profound and perceptive issue. A profound and perceptive issue can be found upon arrangement of facts in a logical sequence under a cause and effect framework as we will further elaborate in the next chapter. Under this framework, contrast is used for comparison between philanthropy and a business. The message is strong and tends to call followers. You do not need either complicated or exciting facts full of twists and turns to attract attention. A profound and perceptive issue with a wise message is enough to arouse the audience, draw their attention, answer their doubts, and call for their action.

上述的例子，顯示出即使是一個簡單的事實，也可以被詮釋爲令人振奮的故事，只要從它具有深度的爭議點，引導出強而有力的訊息。對於事實透過因果關係的架構與邏輯排列的安排，可以找出這樣意義深遠以及具有深度意涵的爭議點。在這樣的架構之下，慈善與商業進行比較而作爲對比。你不需要一個充滿曲折故事的複雜事實來吸引注意，一個具有深度的爭議點以及它所帶出具有智慧的訊息，就足夠喚起大衆、吸引他們的注意、解答他們的疑問以及呼籲他們的行動。

Another example is regarding a student's speech on "one thing you learned when you grew up". She mentioned her change within the past few years on her relationship with her friends. In elementary school, she had quite many close friends. They stayed together all the time. In high school, she had less. Now in college, she has even fewer. More gaps found in a friendship with others seem to be a necessary process in growing up. Only with a few can she build a bridge to form good connections. She finally gave the conclusion that independence is necessary and important in growing up. The experience she refers to seems quite familiar to most of us. If explored further, the fact revealed that her self-identity had been gradually formed. We were more homogeneous in elementary school and high school than we were in college. This is because, in the process of growing up, we slowly develop our own personality, values, judgments and preferences. All these developments make us distinct from others. These differences sometimes bring in disputes and conflicts. Such uniqueness contributes to our building a castle with a fence for a sifting purpose to keep away those whom we do not favor. It takes great patience, time and, most importantly, the wisdom to accommodate the differences, which are difficult for any teenager to do. Each is unique. Each has his own identity, like our own facial features, only a few look similar to each other. Consciousness of self-identity is therefore a mark of growing up and it could make you lose many old friends in one way while helping you to win some true good friends in another way. The very same fact, if interpreted with a deeper perception, could lead to a more profound meaning with better persuasion of the audience. The readers may find that the key terms here are on self-identity and uniqueness that can lead the whole speech and writing into a deeper level of perception with better persuasive power.

另外一個例子，是關於學生就「你成長中所學習到的一件事情」所做的一篇演講。她提到了她在過去跟朋友之間關係的轉變。在小學時候，她有很多好朋友常常在一起，到了高中的時候朋友變少了，現在到了大學，朋友更少。與朋友之間關係距離的形成似乎是成長的必須條件。她覺得只能跟很少數的人形成友好的關係。她的結論是獨立是必須的，而且對於成長來說是很重要的。她所提到的經驗對我們大家來說都很熟悉，如果更進一步探討，這一些事實顯示出她的自我認同正逐漸形成當中。比起大學，在小學和中學時代，我們跟大家更趨於相同。那是因爲在成長的過程當中，我們逐漸發展出自己的個性、價值觀、判斷能力以及喜好。這些發展使我們與其他人不一樣。這些不同，有的時候會造成爭吵或是衝突。這些獨特性造成了我們建立了一座帶有圍牆的城堡，遠離了我們並不喜歡的對象。我們需要很有耐心，花很多時間，更重要的是要有智慧才能夠接受這些不同，這對於任何青少年來說是很困難做到的。每一個人都很特別，每一個人也都有他的自我，就像是我們臉部的五官一樣，只有少數的人看起來相似。因此對於自我的了解是成長的印記，讓你失去很多舊的朋友，但是另外一方面也同時幫你贏得一些眞正的朋友。同樣的事實如果以更深層次去做解釋的話，可以帶來更深遠的意義，也更影響聽衆，更能說服聽衆。讀者們在這裡可能發現關鍵字眼是自我認同以及獨特性，兩者將整篇演說或是寫作帶到更具有說服力的更深層次。

Another student wrote in her paper regarding her experience on the same topic that she was more opened to her friends when in elementary and high schools but became more reserved in college. This description is interesting. However, she unfortunately gave a rather weak message that she cherishes all friends in all stages of her life. In fact, a good interpretation can be drawn from this self-observation. At the elementary school level, she was actually younger and more fragile, but she was more opened with her friends. In college, she was stronger in strength, both physically and mentally, especially on her knowledge. Nevertheless, she trusts friends less, probably due to some unpleasant experiences. She could sense more insecurity and felt uncomfortable if her privacy was not maintained. Privacy seemed a necessary buffer in her friendship with others and should be respected. Such insecure feelings will get stronger as she grows older. An increase of knowledge and personal experiences as time went by opened her eyes to see herself as an independent entity, consequently with the necessity of keeping privacy in her friendship with others. Privacy is therefore a sign of growing up, representing independence and self-identity. The above shows that an in-depth interpretation of facts can bring some profound meaning to simple facts.

另外一個學生在相同的題目寫下她的經驗，在小學的時候，她對於她的朋友比較能敞開心胸，但到了大學，反而對朋友有所保留。這個描述很有趣。但是，她的訊息相對薄弱，因爲她說她珍惜她生命中每一個階段的所有朋友。事實上，我們可以從這樣的自我觀察中，抽取出更好的解釋。在小學階段，她年紀更小，事實上，也更脆弱，但是對於她的朋友，她卻能夠更敞開心胸。在大學的時候，不論在體能上或心智上，她都更爲成熟、更爲強壯，特別是在她的知識上。雖然如此，可能是由於一些不愉快的個人經驗，她不再信任她的朋友。如果她不能保有她個人的隱私的話，她會有更強烈的不安全感，且也感覺更不自在。隱私，在她與她的朋友交往中，成爲了必要的保護，而且應該要被尊重。這樣的不安全感，會隨著她的年紀增長，愈來愈強烈。隨著時間過去而增加的知識及個人經驗，打開了她的眼睛，讓她看見自己是一個獨立的個體，在她與朋友之間的交往，讓她必須要保留她的隱私。隱私，因此是一個成長的象徵，代表著你的獨立，以及自我的身分。上述的說明，顯示出對於事實具有深度的詮釋，可以對簡單的事實帶來深遠的意義。

Exciting facts in a story serve as a good start. However, it still requires a strong message to exert the maximum influence on the hearts of an audience. One student's writing had attracted my attention at the beginning of her writing. She lived on the fifth floor. One night someone shook her screen door. She was in shock because it was late at night and she lived on the fifth floor alone. This fact created a powerful effect in the minds of the audience because everyone wanted to know what happened. It turned out that her neighbor's cat jumped to her patio from her neighbor's patio. However, her message was quite weak because she could not elicit a good message from this unusual fact.

故事內容的精彩事實，會是一個好的開始，但是它仍然需要強而有力的訊息，來對聽衆的內心形成最大的影響。一個學生在她作文一開頭就吸引到我的注意。她住在五樓，有天晚上，突然有人敲她陽臺窗戶，她嚇了一大跳，因爲已經深夜了，而且她又一個人住在五樓。這個事實有個非常強烈的效果，因爲每個人都想知道後來發生什麼事情。原來是她鄰居的貓跳到她陽臺上，但她的訊息非常軟弱無力，因爲她沒有辦法從這麼不尋常的事實，引導出好的訊息。

3.14 The following are some advice with a few tips based on the past practice from students

1 Speech is a form of communication not much different from a conversation with others. How to keep a conversation moving is necessary for building a good relationship. If you cannot engage in a conversation, you probably will have a very difficult time in giving a speech. Therefore, how to keep a conversation moving is a necessary training for making a speech. When asked what kind of conversation that you have no desire to continue or even to listen to, the answers from students varied from direct sales to political talk shows on TV. The reason seemed obvious, those conversations are motivated or led either by self-interest or prejudices which are highly questionable in regard to their motives.

3.14 下列事項是依據學生們過去的表現列出以下建議

1 演說是溝通的一種型態，與對話並沒有什麼不同。良好關係的建立，有賴於好的對話能力，如果你缺乏對話能力，演講上你可能也會有困難。因此如何使對話流暢，是在訓練演說時，必須學習的功課。當人們被問到，哪種形式的對話是你沒有興趣的，答案從直銷到電視上的政治評論，理由看起來很簡單，這一類型的對話，他們的動機大部分是自私或是帶有歧視。

2 In the matter of persuasion, nothing is more important than building trust. Are you trustworthy enough on the topic and content of your speech/conversation? Put in another way, have your expertise, honesty, integrity and observation/reference of facts been doubted by the listeners? How to build trust? Assuming you are a direct sales person, how would you win trust from your potential customers?

2 在說服力這件事上，沒有任何事情比建立信任來得重要。對於演講的題目與內容，你值得被信賴嗎？換句話說，人們會對你的專業、誠實、人格、對事實的觀察及解釋感到懷疑嗎？你要如何建立信任？假設你是個直銷人員，你如何贏得你客戶的信任？

3 What is your goal in this speech? Who are your listeners/audience? And what do you attempt to accomplish in this speech? I did ask a question in my class. What is your purpose on writing? One young man gave a good answer, “To let others know what we think.” The answer is good because he does speak out on what young people have in their minds nowadays. They like talking. Actually, we do have some friends who enjoy talking like a chatter-box regardless of whether or not people like to listen. Many times, we simply want them to shut

up, to stay quiet for a while. But what is the reality? All of us are bombarded with all kinds of information every day from advertisements in the streets, magazines in the convenience store, or even news from our friends on FB or LINE. The truth is that we probably will ignore most information that we have seen or heard. You want to talk, but none will listen. Who wants to practice a drama that no one will ever watch or a book that no one will ever read? If you know that no one will read your work, you probably will never write it. In that case, the purpose of speech or writing has failed. Therefore, the purpose of speech and writing is made to persuade others. Students must bear in mind that the purpose of both speech and writing is for persuasion.

3 你演說的目標是什麼？誰是你的聽眾？你希望在這個演說中完成什麼事？我曾經在班上問過這樣的問題：「什麼是你寫作的目的？」一個年輕人這樣回答：「讓別人知道我們在想什麼。」這是一個很好的答案，因為他說出了現在年輕人的心聲，他們喜歡表達自己的想法。事實上，我們總有一些朋友很喜歡像留聲機一樣，話說個不停，不管其他人是不是喜歡聽。許多時候我們希望他們可以把嘴巴閉上，給我們一點安靜。但什麼是現實？我們每一天被各種不同的資訊轟炸，比如說這些來自於街道上、雜誌上，甚至是臉書、Line 上的資訊。事實是我們可能會忽略我們所看到或聽到的大部分資訊，你想說話但是沒人想聽，誰會演一齣沒人想看的戲或是寫一本沒人想看的書呢？如果你知道沒人會讀你所寫的書，那你可能根本不會動筆。在那樣的情況之下，演說或是寫作的目的就失敗了。因此，演講跟寫作的目的在於說服他人，學生們必須牢記這一點。

4 The conclusion is reached by the interpretation of the facts given. If only partial facts are given, then the whole conclusion will be reached according to the partial facts which will be far from the truth. One good example is from a clip of film taken by a student in a high school classroom showing that a female teacher rebuked a student in an unreasonably angry tone with a high pitched voice. What the film did not show was the provocative acts made by the student against the teacher. When the clip was shown on TV, great pressure from virulent criticism of society was directed against the teacher. If the whole complete film were shown, then the viewers would know the reason why the teacher reacted with such anger toward the student and probably would have a more favorable response toward the teacher. Another example, as discussed earlier, is a clip showing a TAXI driver pushing around a female guest outside his taxi. The female guest claims that the Taxi driver had committed assault and battery. But, according to a witness, the female initiate the attack first. The Taxi driver "pushing her around", in light of the attack by the guest, was really a form of self-defense. Partial truth therefore is a form of lie. If you want to tell the truth, you have to give the whole truth lest the conclusion be twisted.

4 結論是由於對事實解釋產生的。如果只有部分的事實，那依照部分事實所做成的結論與眞相可能相去甚遠。有一個很好的例子，就是曾經有一段影片顯示出一個中學的女老師正在用她非常高亢、憤怒、不理性的聲音責罵學生。但是這段影片並沒有顯示出這些學生們故意刺激這位女老師的行爲和動作。當這些影片在電視上報導出來的時候，社會上憤怒的批評當然就落在這個老師身上。如果整個影片完整播出，觀看者就會知道爲什麼這個老師會對這個學生這麼憤怒生氣，並且做出對這個老師較友善的看法。另外一個例子就是前面所說的計程車司機推開女乘客的事件，乘客說計程車司機觸犯了攻擊罪，但根據證人說法是乘客先攻擊，他之所以推開乘客是實行自衛。部分的眞相，本質上就是謊言。如果想說實話，那就必須說出全部的實話，否則結論是被扭曲的。

5 How much do you understand your listeners/audience? What background are they from and what are their needs? Try to picture yourself in the following scenario. How would you prepare for your speech or conversation?

5 你有多了解你的聽衆？他們的背景如何？他們有什麼樣的需要？試想一下下列的情景，你要怎麼準備你的演說或是對話？

6 What goal is your speech/conversation? What is the message you plan to send to your listeners/customers?

6 你演說或是對話的目的是什麼？你對聽衆所傳遞的訊息是什麼？

7 How to make the message convincing?

7 如何使訊息具有說服力？

8 What facts/stories could help you to send out that message?

8 什麼樣的事實或是故事可以幫助你傳遞這樣的訊息？

9 How to describe the facts in the form of examples or stories?

9 事實要如何以故事的方式表達？

10 Are the facts given simple, clear and relevant to the message for the listener's understanding? Rule of thumb, can your audience understand the factual background of your story after your first description?

10 所談的事實是否簡單、清楚並且與訊息相關而讓聽衆能夠了解？簡單的判斷標準就是，你的聽衆在你初步做完事實陳述之後，能夠了解整個背景嗎？

11 Are the facts given with the 6 Ws (when, where, who, what, how and why) and in proper timing or logical sequence? Will the listeners feel confused by your description of facts?

11 事實部分是否有使用適當的時間以及邏輯順序以六個 W 的方式

呈現出來？（什麼時間？地點？是誰？做了什麼事情？如何做？以及爲什麼做？）

12 Are the facts given related to the message entertained or full of red herrings or too complicated for comprehension? Facts so remote and redundant will distract the listeners' attention and affect their comprehension of the connection between the facts and the message it contains.

12 所給的事實與訊息相關嗎？或是充滿一些不重要的部分或是太過複雜很難被了解？事實如果太遙遠或是太複雜很容易分散聽衆的注意力，進而影響到他們對事實與訊息的連結。

13 Will an opposite example, if given, help the listeners to remember the message better with this contrast?

13 如果有相反的例子，是否能夠幫助聽衆更記得你所要傳遞的訊息？

14 Are there any statistics, data or other examples of a similar nature necessary to be added in order to make your speech more persuasive?

14 是否能加上任何的統計資料或是其他類似性質的例子，讓你的演說更具有說服力？

15 Are you fluent with your language? Does your style, manner and demeanor help to win trust from your audience, and the words precisely describe your thoughts for your listeners' understanding? Is there any barrier on the communication aspect or in their understanding?

15 你所使用的語言是否流暢？你的風格、態度還有行爲能否贏得群衆信任？你的話語能否準確表達你的想法而讓聽衆們充分了解？溝通上或是他們的了解上是否有障礙？

16 What is your conclusion? Is it well connected with your topic and goal? Is the message persuasive enough in light of your facts and interpretation?

16 你的結論是什麼？你的結論是不是與主題和目的有很好的連結？以所提出的事實和對事實的詮釋而言，你的訊息是否具有足夠的說服力？

Exercise

1 You are asked to give a self-introduction in an interview either for a job or for admission to a college.

習作

1 你在一個面談當中被要求自我介紹，爲了要找一個工作或是要申請學校。

2 You are talking to a group of high school students stating why they should apply to this college.

2 你在告訴一群高中生爲什麼他們應該申請這一所大學。

3 You are selling your motorcycle/car to a potential buyer, either a garage owner or a lay person.

3 你正在推銷你的二手摩托車或是汽車，對象是車行老闆或是一般的人。

3.15 Sample speech and writing at the intermediate level

Demonstration 1 (Chinese version with English translation)

By Guo Wenqian

What is the purpose of living? The question has been hovering over my head for a long time without an answer. Today, the answer popped up when I devoured a gourmet meal in a classy restaurant. We live to please our mouths! All animals including human beings have come a long way fighting for food to appease their greedy mouths.

3.15 演說和中級寫作示範

範例一（中文寫作與英文翻譯）

郭文倩同學

活著的目的是什麼呢？這個問題已藏在我心裡好久了，但我一直不能解開這個謎。今天，在餐廳裡大口大口嚼著美食時，腦海中閃過一個念頭——活著為了一張嘴。不管是什麼動物，都為一張嘴而到處奔波，尋找能填滿這張貪婪的嘴的食物。

Animals often are grabbing, fighting or even killing each other for the satisfaction of their mouths. Human's mouths are much worse, becoming so picky and growing tired of the same delicious meal only after a few times. Then what do they do? They change cuisines like a magician playing with their tricks to please their mouths again and that is why the position of a cook was born. Sarcastically, not only the rich but also the poor must serve to the satisfaction of their gluttonous mouths.

動物們往往會因為這張嘴而互相搶食，廝打，甚至殘殺。人的嘴就更囂張了。這嘴不知好歹，一樣美食吃上幾天竟然厭了，不愛吃了，怎麼辦呢？人們便想方設法變著戲法似的變出各種各樣的美味佳餚來討好這張嘴。廚師這個職位不就是這樣來的？富人要伺候這張嘴，窮人照樣也要服侍這張嘴。

If we think it over carefully, we are all fools, aren't we? We work hard to make money and then squander most of our earnings on food to please our mouths. Who dare to claim that such satisfaction of our mouths is not our final destination in our lives? What a boring life! Instead of being so, why not practice philanthropy as all saints have done?

仔細想想，我們還眞愚蠢，不是嗎？人類去工作賺錢，最終還不是把最多的金錢投在塡飽這張嘴中？誰敢說我們活著的最終目的不是爲了一張嘴？多麼乏味呀！不如多做點善事，早日成仙算了！

Comment

This interesting speech is short, stating a question regarding the purpose of life followed by the exploration of a possible answer through observation of certain facts. As the old Chinese saying goes, nothing is more important than food. To eat is something that both rich and poor must do and the supreme form of satisfaction is represented by delicacies to serve the mouths of both rich and poor as a reward of their hard work, which, in its ultimate purpose, is no more than maintaining a life for human beings. An interesting analogy in comparison is drawn between animals and human in their desperate desire for food with the role of a chef as a peak point in this writing as the most interesting observant to the unquenchable hunger of the human's greedy appetite. The connection between each idea are natural, revealing no weakness in logic, flowing freely like spring water.

To analyze this simple speech, mainly three parts formed this amusing speech: a question at the beginning, the reasoning process on observed facts, and a conclusion. The words used are simple and the facts described are common, clear and vivid. The flow seems logical. What makes this writing amazing is her skillful reversal of cause and effect. Generally speaking, people eat because they want to live. But the author claimed that people live because they want to eat, somewhat absurd but an interesting interpretation in reversed order. Since the main purpose of living under her interpretation is to eat, examples and explanations ensued in this reversed structure are rather sarcastic because they show the negative side of human nature. What surprises me most is that this writing was written by Ms. Guo when she was only 10 years old.

評析

這一篇有趣的短文一開始以生存破題，接著對於特定事實的觀察，探索可能的答案。如同中國諺語所說，民以食爲天。不論貧富都得吃飯，而滿足口腹之慾的最高形式，就是由美味代表，這也是對窮人和富人他們辛勤工作之後的獎賞，而其最終目的也不過就是維持人類的生存而已。這篇文章，以動物作爲人類的對比作爲反襯，反映他們對於食物共同的渴望，之後再以廚師當作高潮，說明對於人類貪婪的口腹之慾的最佳觀察與諷刺。這篇文章的每一個想法之間的聯繫是很自然的，邏輯上並沒有弱點，表達上行雲流水。

分析這一篇短文，主要有三個部分，先以一個問題破題，接著是對於事實的詮釋，而後是結論。使用的文字簡潔，而所描述的事實是家喻户曉，清晰而生動。文章流暢也具有邏輯性。這一篇文章很令人驚奇的是作者熟練的倒果爲因。通常來說，人們因爲想活下去而想吃東西。但是作者聲稱人們是因爲想吃東西而活下去，有點荒謬也很有趣，但有反其道而行的解釋。因爲根據她的解釋，活著的主要目的是爲了吃，根據這樣反其道而行的結構所發展出來的例子和解釋，就顯得有些諷刺，因爲他們表現人性中比較負面的一面。最令我驚奇的是，這篇文章的作者郭同學，她寫這篇文章的時候只有十歲。

3.16 Summary

1 A speech is made for persuasion, and if no position is taken, then the whole purpose of a speech fails because no persuasion can be made.

3.16 摘要

1 演說的目的在於說服，如果沒有立場的話，整個的演說目的是失敗的，因爲沒有辦法進行說服。

2 A speaker fails in his speech if he cannot grasp the attention of the listeners.

2 如果演說者不能夠抓住聽衆的注意力，那他的演講是失敗的。

3 Stories used in a speech should be easy to understand and remember. The facts contained within it must be relevant.

3 演說使用的故事應該容易被聽衆了解，而且容易記憶。故事所提到的事實必須具有關聯性。

4 Stories should contain a message. A message is an interpretation made by a speaker on the facts, showing the speaker's views and values.

4 故事必須帶有訊息。訊息是演說者對於事實部分的詮釋，表達演說者的看法及價值觀。

5 A well prepared case can tell good stories, intrigued the listeners' interest to follow it and present issues for discussion under a complete framework of a topic, covering description and narration of relevant facts with a powerful message drawn leading into a forceful conclusion.

5 一個準備充分的案件，可以說好的故事，引起聽衆的興趣，並且藉此提出跟主題有關完整架構下所展現出來的爭議點，包括了對於相關事實的描述和詮釋，引出強力的訊息導致激發具有力量的結論。

6 Most importantly, stories, if flavored with humor, can easily intrigue the listener's interest and draw his attention to follow the speaker's suggestions.

6 最重要的故事如果帶有幽默感的話，能夠激起聽衆的興趣，抓住他們的注意，跟隨著演說者的建議。

7 The facts refer to something that actually happened in the past. An interpretation based on undeniable facts seems more trustworthy and reliable. Challenges can only be made on the interpretation rather than the facts on which the interpretation is based.

7 事實是提到過去所發生的事件。基於過去發生的事實所做的詮釋，看起來較値得被信任。可以被挑戰的是對於事實的詮釋而非事實本身。

8 Undeniable facts could be partial and therefore is not equivalent to the whole truth. A partial truth is a lie, though it is based on facts.

8 不可否認的事實，可能只是部分的事實，並不等於全部的眞相。部分的眞相是一個謊言，雖然它是建立在事實之上。

9 Examples, especially from true experiences, when told in a clear, simple and concise form with a sincere manner, can be

quite convincing and most likely will stir the audience to act.

9 如果是使用來自眞實經驗的例子，當以非常清楚、簡單扼要的方式並且以誠懇的態度描述時，是相當具有說服力的，很容易引起聽衆的共鳴。

10 A simple story can deliver a strong message as long as a speaker gives a good interpretation.

10 簡單的故事可以傳遞一個強烈的訊息，只要演講者給予一個好的詮釋。

3.17 Impromptu Speech

Training on impromptu speech seems like a good opportunity to offer students at this stage for building up their ability on persuasion through story telling. During the training, students are given a topic without much time to prepare, usually 5 minutes or less. Since time for preparation is very limited, students in this situation are advised to give a story with their own interpretation rather than a lengthy essay built on a sound framework replete with details and various perspectives provided. Students at this stage are simply to find some facts or events delivered with a message to call for an action. Always bear in mind that all speeches mentioned in this book are confined to the work of persuasion and nothing is more important than winning trust in the task of persuasion.

3.17 即席演說

即席演說給這個階段的學生提供一個非常好的機會，讓他們透過說故事的方式建立他們說服的能力。在這個階段，學生們有五分鐘時間準備一個題目，因爲時間很有限，我們建議學生談論一個故事並加上自己的詮釋，而不是用準備論文的方法提供一個充滿資訊、細節、面向的完整架構。學生在這個階段，僅僅需要找到一個事實或事件，傳遞一個訊息並進而呼籲行動。要記得在這本書所談到的演說的目的限定在說服，而說服的工作最重要的就是取得對方的信任。

Impromptu speech is good training at the beginning stage for new learners because it requires neither preparation nor special knowledge on any specific topic and the time length lasting only between 3 to 5 minutes, which, by its very nature, is close to our daily conversation with our friends, co-workers or family members. Unlike debate, there is little or no argument in this training. The only task imposed on the speaker is to give a short speech to convince the listeners in a controlled setting with a story containing a message. Once the students feel comfortable and skillfully apply this skill to meet their practical needs, then they can move on to a more advanced level of communication with a more complicated nature known as debate.

即席演說對於初學者是非常好的訓練，因爲他不需要任何先前的準備，也不需要對於這個特定的主題有先前的知識，時間大約三至五分鐘，在本質上很接近我們日常生活跟朋友、同事或家人的對話。它跟辯論不同，在演說訓練中沒有爭論的部分，演說者的責任就是給一篇短篇演說，在一個控制的環境當中，以帶有訊息的方式說服聽衆。一旦學生們可以很輕鬆自在而且熟練地使用這些技巧來達到他們的需要，那他們就可以進階到較爲複雜的溝通階段，也就是辯論部分。

Extra considerations for practicing impromptu speech:

即席演說練習上的其他考量：

1. How important is interaction between a speaker and his audience?

1. 演說者跟他的聽衆互動的重要性如何？

2. Is it good to ask the audience questions? What if the answer is not what you are exactly expecting? What if you do not see any response, complete silence?

2. 一開始就詢問聽衆問題適當嗎？如果他們的回答不是你所期待

的，該怎麼辦？如果你沒有看到任何回應，全場一片寂靜，怎麼辦？

3 How important is humor? What is the proper limit to the use of humor? What is the difference between humor and sarcastic remarks?

3 幽默的重要性如何？使用幽默有沒有適當的限制？幽默感與諷刺有什麼差別？

4 How important is eye contact? What message can you send out through eye contact?

4 眼神的接觸有多重要？你可以透過眼神的接觸傳遞什麼樣的訊息？

5 How important is your tone and gestures in your expressions?

5 你的音調和表達的手勢重要性如何？

6 How important is the simple language in your expressions? Does that help your audience to understand your message easier and clearer?

6 在你的表達中，淺顯易懂的重要性如何？那可以幫助你的聽衆更容易和清楚了解你的訊息嗎？

7 Is speech a form of performing arts?

7 演說是一個表演藝術嗎？

8 Do you observe the reaction from your audience as feedback? How do you adjust yourself according to their reaction?

8 你會注意聽衆的反應並當作一種回饋嗎？你會根據他們的反應來調整自己嗎？

9 Is your description of facts similar to reading an accounting book and thus making your listeners bored? Are there any twists and turns (e.g. conflicts in your story) to intrigue the listeners' interest?

9 你對事實的描述會像是在朗誦一本帳本，而使你的聽衆感到非常無聊嗎？你的故事曲折（例如：故事中的衝突性），而能夠引起聽衆的興趣嗎？

10 How do you control the whole atmosphere?

10 你如何掌控全場的氛圍？

11 Is the example given close to the experiences of the audience?

11 你所給的例子貼近他們的生活經驗嗎？

12 Do you laugh when you give jokes?

12 你說笑話的時候自己會大笑嗎？

13 How does your own background relate to your topic and thus affect your speech?

13 你的背景跟你的主題有關嗎？會不會影響到你演講的內容？

14 Do you look/sound nervous with ample hesitations and pauses in delivering your speech? What will be the message sent to your listeners?

14 你的演說會不會充滿著中斷與遲疑？那會給你的聽眾什麼樣的訊息？

15 Do you look trustworthy with the message given? Always remember that TRUST is the very crucial factor on the task of persuasion, which no amount of rhetoric can ever achieve.

15 你看起來值得被信任嗎？永遠要記得，信任是說服的最關鍵的因素，沒有任何言詞可以取代它。

More topics for practicing impromptu speech:
Car accident
My experience with different countries

How your idols affect you?
Cellphone
Unforgettable memory
The person who affects me the most
The most pleasant thing that I have done recently
Is it good to be independent?
How do you define a good life?
Something that I want to complete the most
Value from within
One thing that someone has taught me
One thing your friend did that has moved you the most
Why you want to attend college
How to solve pressure
My summer vacation
How are the teenagers of the current generation affected by the current social value on appearance?
My favorite book
Is it important to study overseas?
Part time job
The most valuable thing in your life
Breaking up a relationship
Travelling
How to manage fear

即席演說題目練習：
車禍

我在其他國家的經驗
你的偶像如何影響你
手機
難忘的回憶
影響我最多的人
我最近做過最愉快的事情
獨立生活好嗎？
你如何定義一個好的生活
我最想完成的事情
內在的價值
曾經有人教我的一件事
你朋友所做過最讓你感動的事情
為什麼你想上大學
如何解決壓力
我的暑假
現今的年輕人如何被現在社會價值影響他的外表
我最喜歡的書籍
國外讀書重要嗎
兼職工作
你生命中最有價值的事情
男女朋友的分手
旅行
如何控制恐懼

3.18 Observation in a classroom

1 When we speak or write, we do that from our memory. Our memory is made from our observation of facts (e.g. what we see, hear and read) stored in the form of pictures in our brain. When describing a fact, we retrieve from our memory the form of pictures and describe the facts accordingly. Therefore, the narration of a story starting from stating facts observed from our daily life is good training for students on their ability regarding both speech and writing. That is why a beginner should start their training with narrating a story from the pictures in his mind.

3.18 課堂觀察

1 當我們說話或寫作的時候，我們所說出或是寫下的東西是來自於我們的記憶。我們的記憶來自於我們對事實的觀察（例如：我們看見了什麼、聽到了什麼，或是讀了些什麼），而這些對事實的觀察是以圖片的方式記在我們的腦子裡。當我們描述一個事實的時候，我們會將這樣的圖片從記憶當中找出來，然後依照圖像描述事實。因此，以日常生活中所觀察到的事實來陳述一個故事，是對於學生在演說、寫作上一個很好的訓練。這就是爲什麼對於初學者，我們應該訓練他就心裡面所能看得見的圖像，進行說故事的演練。

On the level of writing, some teachers on YouTube advise brainstorming to produce ideas. Ideas, once produced, should be connected and organized with coherence and cohesion. Such coherence and cohesion, in my experiences, refer to putting descriptions into a logical sequence. A logical sequence requires that the entire ideas be placed in a cause and effect structure. In this structure, one idea is connected with another one. The facts used must be relevant. Irrelevant facts are redundant and therefore unnecessary.

在寫作的層次上，有些老師建議，利用腦力激盪的方式產生一些點子。一旦產生點子之後，點子彼此之間的連結和組織應該具有一致性與緊密性，這樣的一致性和緊密性在我的經驗裡，是跟與具有邏輯連貫性的陳述有關係。邏輯的連貫性要求以因果關係來呈現我們的想法。在因果關係的架構下，一個想法與另一個想法結合。所使用的事實必須有相關性。不相關的事實是多餘的，也因此不需要。

A topic sentence is important for it shows the main idea of the writing. If we are writing an essay on “a good student”, the very first image that surfaces in our mind is the very best students. We may brainstorm for ideas from their image and ask ourselves, What do they do?” They may study hard and earn good grades. They may have good attendance in all the classes. They may actively participate in class discussion and voice their opinions, get involved in activities to build up their interpersonal relationships, and may even serve as leaders in some student clubs. They seem to know well what they are looking for and probably have made future plans for their career. To sum it up, they know what they are moving toward and they work hard to achieve their goal. They know what they want at an early stage of life and they know how to fight for it. All these are required for future success and that is the purpose for their studies in school. Therefore, the main theme of this essay is that good students should know what their future goals are and are willing to work hard for their goal. A good topic sentence can be made as "A good student should know what his future goals are and are willing to work hard for it." Once a topic sentence is decided, then the following ideas and details for supporting it, as those stated above, can be used for elaborating on the topic sentence.

主題句很重要，因爲它展現了一篇寫作的主要想法。如果我們在寫一篇文章，題目是:「好學生」，我們內心所浮現的第一個印象，可能是那些班上最好的學生。我們可以想一想他們的影像，以及他們做了什麼事情。他們很用功讀書，而且成績很好。他們可能從不缺席。他們可能很積極的參與班上的討論，並大聲說出他們的想法，也很踴躍的參加活動，建立起他們的人際關係，以及擔任學生社團的領導幹部。他們看起來很清楚他們要什麼東西，也可能已經爲了他們的未來做好了打算。總而言之，他們知道他們要往哪裡去，而且他們很努力。他們在很年輕的階段，就已經知道他們要什麼，而且知道如何爭取他們想要的東西。這些都是未來成功的要素，也是爲什麼他們要在學校讀書的原因。因此，這篇文章的主軸就是，一個好學生應該要知道什麼是他們未來的目標，而且也願意爲了將來的目標努力工作，所以一個好的主題句可以這樣說：「一個好學生應該知道他未來的目標是什麼，而且願意努力爭取。」一旦我們決定了主題句，如同上述用以支持的想法和細節就可以呈現出來，對於主題句進行進一步的解釋。

Of course, good students could include those who have completed something quite unusual with profound meaning in our society; for example, form a student club to raise funds and organize activities to help those pupils in remote areas with their learning. In that case, it is the passion, sympathy, enthusiasm and leadership that make this student unique and a great asset to this school and society. Therefore, a topic sentence could be that "A good student should not only demonstrate his own merits in learning, but also apply his attitude and values toward the betterment of the pubic community." Please bear in mind that a proper topic sentence can be given only when a writer can produce a basic framework of his writing.

當然，好的學生也包括那一些曾經完成一些特殊並具有深遠意義的事情的學生，例如成立學生社團募款與組織活動幫助那些偏鄉地區的教育。在這種情況下，是他的熱情、同情心、熱誠還有領導力讓他變得如此獨特，也成爲學校和社會的一個巨大的資產。因此開頭主題句可以是，「一個好學生不只要證明他在學習上的成就，也要包括他對公眾事務的態度與貢獻價值。」要記得，寫作者只有在明白他寫作基本架構時，才能寫出適當的主題句。

A note on topic sentence

Many teachers emphasize the importance of a topic sentence in the beginning of writing. However, most students are puzzled on how a topic sentence is made. They are constantly told to write a topic sentence in a paragraph first and then find supporting ideas to elaborate the topic sentence. Since a topic sentence will show the direction of writing, the truth is, a topic sentence cannot be made unless a student has reached a conclusion on the topic of his writing.

Students should bear in mind that a topic sentence cannot be produced unless a conclusion of writing is ascertained. A conclusion cannot be ascertained unless a structure of writing has been established. A structure can be established only with a careful analysis and research (e.g. facts to be used, pros and cons on the issues and messages to be delivered) conducted regarding the topic of writing.

Simply speaking, a topic sentence can come into existence only after a writer knows the conclusion of his writing.

關於主題句的注意事項

許多老師強調在文章一開始主題句的重要性。但是大部分的學生對於怎麼寫主題句感到非常的疑惑。他們聽了很多，在段落一開始應該先寫主題句，然後再找出一些支持的想法來闡述這個主題句。由於主題句會顯示出文章的方向，所以眞相就是，除非已經對文章下了結論，否則是寫不出主題句的。
學生必須記得，除非你的文章結論已經確定，否則寫不出主題句。而結論是無法確定除非你已經建立起文章的整個架構。而架構的建立必須先對文章主題有詳細的分析和研究（例如要用什麼樣的事實、爭議點的正反論述還有要傳遞的訊息）。
簡單而言，學生已經有了結論以後才可能產生主題句。

Another example is an essay asking for your opinion on a question regarding whether a big factory should be built in your neighborhood. How do you make a topic sentence?
A question of this type is always a matter of choice. On a matter of choice, there is always an analysis made from the pros and cons. In other words, it is considering the cost and benefits in this matter. A big factory, especially a highly polluted one, can cause great bodily harm to local citizens. However, it may also bring a great opportunity of employment and thus create a huge economic profit to people in this neighborhood. For writers, a decision must be made and the topic sentence will show the main thrust followed by the development of our subsequent reasoning. If we take a position in opposition to the establishment of this factory in our neighborhood, we may start our topic sentence as “What benefit can we have if we win the whole world but forfeit our own lives?” This topic sentence

clearly indicates this case is a matter of a choice and a decision that must be made by analyzing the cost and benefits.

另外一篇的作文題目是，在你家附近將要建立一個大型工廠，你的意見爲何？如何開始一個主題句呢？
這一類的問題，總是關於選擇。在選擇這一件事情上面，總是要對於正反理由進行分析。換句話說，這樣的事情要考慮到成本與效益的問題。一個大型的工廠，特別是那些高汙染的，可以對當地居民的身體造成傷害，但是它也可以帶來豐富的就業機會，因此，對當地居民創造了鉅額的經濟利益。對於一個寫作的人而言，他必須做決定，而主題句會顯示出他的主軸，接著是理由的陳述。如果我們採取一個反對的立場，我們可以這樣開始我們的主題句：「我們贏得了全世界，卻賠上了自己的性命，這又有什麼益處？」這樣的主題句很清楚的說明了這種案件是個選擇問題，然後基於成本與利益的考量，而後做的決定。

2 At the end of this class, the students were asked to write an essay on the topic "What have I learned most in this class?" Many of them summarized what we have discussed above; for example, facts with elaboration followed by a message leading to a conclusion. However, there is one essay that drew my attention. She wrote "In this class, I have heard many impressive stories given by my classmates. Everyone has his own experience. Even for those who have similar experiences, they could come up with different messages because they see things in a different perspective. Everyone has his own personal experience and

ideas. None are the same. His expression can be unique and special if that can be made through his own thinking process." Such observation and comment is truly one of a kind, superior to her peers because she can correctly procure the essence of this class.

2 這堂課結束的時候，學生們被要求寫一篇文章，題目是：「這堂課我學習最多的事情」。許多學生把我們上面所討論的內容做摘要，例如事實經過詮釋產生訊息，最後達到結論。但是有一篇文章特別吸引我的注意。她寫到：「在這堂課我聽到同學們許多令人印象深刻的故事，每個人都有他自己的經驗。即使一些有類似經驗的人，他們由於從不同的角度來看事情，也可能會有不同的訊息出現。每個人都有他們自己個人的經驗還有想法，沒有人是一樣的。如果加以思考的話，每個人的表達可以是如此獨特！」這樣的觀察的評論，眞是非常獨特，超越過她的同學們，因爲她正確的學習了這一堂課的精髓。

3.19 The application of the approaches learned from this chapter

All writings and speeches originate from our observation of facts, something that has happened in our daily life. If no such observations were made, then there wouldn't be any writing and speech. Therefore, students should learn the very basics regarding the observation and narration of facts.

3.19 本章方法的適用

所有的寫作和演說來自於對事實的觀察，也就是我們生活當中所發生的事情。如果沒有這樣的觀察，就沒有辦法產生寫作和演說，因此學生必須學習對於事實的觀察和描述。

The narration of facts is important not only on an academic level but also in the business field. For any management of any business issue, from complaint letters, dispute and negotiation, the ability on narration of facts, is extremely important. Narration of facts tells what has happened, decisive on the issues regarding what the possible consequence will be and suggestive on the importance of this problem. All business men involved in a dispute must be aware of the importance of having a clear description regarding the facts leading to a claim of possible damages. Without a clear description of the facts regarding a possible defect of a product or the timing of a late delivery, no effective claim can be made. It is not too far off to say that the narration of facts is the first task for any beginner to learn, whether in schools or in business units.

對於事實的觀察不僅在學校裡很重要，對商業界也是一樣。任何處理商業問題，包括客戶抱怨、爭議以及談判，事實的描述是非常重要。事實的描述說明了發生什麼事，決定了可能會有什麼後果以及提示我們問題嚴重性。所有的商人在處理糾紛的時候，一定要很清楚地了解對於相關事實明確的陳述，以及之後如何索賠的重要性，如果不能夠清楚描述貨品可能的瑕疵或是遲延交貨，那是沒有辦法進行有效索賠的。所以可以很公允的說，對於任何一個初學者清楚陳述事實，不管在學校或商業界都是第一重要的工作。

As said in the prior sections, the facts alone may appear cold and it is the interpretation that gives warmth to the facts. The ability to elaborate and interpret is essential because such ability will decide the value of your facts.

如同在前面章節提到，單純的事實是冰冷的，但是事實的詮釋是有溫度的。對於事實的解釋以及闡述是非常重要的，因爲這個能力會決定你所提供事實的價值。

Some students have a problem with describing facts. A beginner probably has no problem in describing in mandarin what has happened in a car accident but might encounter great difficulty in describing it in English. One possible reason is that they are trying to translate it from Chinese to English. When you are describing facts, you are not asked to translate. A beginner (a student in this case) was asked to describe an accident she had experienced before. She had no problem in making such description in mandarin. When asked to mention the event in English, she became very slow in her response and speech. In fact, she was making a translation, trying to be careful with her choice of words and observing grammatical precision. Her slow response raised a lot of doubt as to whether she was able to make a complete description of what had happened because doubts were raised about her memory, narration, speech and even integrity caused by too many pauses and hesitations. Such doubts will hinder her from building the trust of others and cause others to question her creditability.

有些學生對事實的描述是有困難的，一個初學者在描述一個車禍事件時，以中文表達可能沒問題，但使用英文時可能會有困難。可能的理由是他們正想著如何把中文翻成英文，當你在描述事實的時候，你並不是在做翻譯，一個學生曾經被要求描述她所經歷的車禍，使用中文時並沒問題，但是使用英文的時候，她的反應和說明變得非常遲緩。實際上她正在做翻譯，盡可能地使用正確的字彙以及小心她的文法準確性。她遲緩的反應讓人懷疑她是否能完整地敘述曾發生的事，因爲大家已經開始懷疑她的記憶、描述與說明能力，甚至誠信，因爲有太多的中止與遲緩。這樣的懷疑很可能形成信任與可信度的障礙。

The narration of facts is not making a translation. A speaker, when asked to give what he has witnessed or experienced, must utter from what he has observed and what is stored in his mind. It is like a description of pictures according to what you have stored in your memory, mental pictures so to speak. Many high school teachers in their writing class try to ask students to describe what they have seen from a set of pictures. The purpose of such test is simple.

It is a test on a student's ability on narration of facts according to the pictures seen, further giving an interpretation of facts. This is a very basic form of training which should be performed with all beginners, whether in a school or in a business unit, in order to improve their ability to describe facts through interpretation.

對於事實的陳述並不是在進行翻譯，當被問到他所目擊或是經驗的時候，說話者必須說出他所觀察到的而且記得的，這就像是從你記憶中所存在的圖片所進行的描述。許多中學老師要求學生看圖說故事，這種訓練的目的很簡單，他是在測試學生根據圖片描述所看到的事實以及解釋事實的能力。這種基礎訓練應該適用於每一個初學者，不管是在學校或公司，用以提升他們描述並且解釋事實的能力。

When depicting what has happened, a speaker is suggested to refresh his memory first in a form of visual pictures in his mind. The speaker may further make a description according to the pictures seen. Not all the facts, but stating only those that are relevant, just as we don't describe a movie in full detail, or otherwise the listeners will lose their focus and cannot understand the main theme. The question on relevancy will be examined in the next chapter regarding debate. Each description is formed by sentences and the sentences are connected in a logical sequence. Try to give a sentence one at a time. In dealing with business disputes, no lie should be told BUT not all truth has to be revealed. It is a task left to the attorney to manage, but all businessmen at this stage have the responsibility not to escalate the problem by giving unfavorable facts at the expense of their own interests.

在描述發生什麼事情的時候，說話的人應該先以圖像的方式恢復一下他的記憶，接著再按照他心裡所看見的圖像進行文字描述。不需要提到所有發生的事情，只需要談到那些相關的事實，就像是我們不應該以鉅細靡遺的方式來描述一部電影，否則所有的聽衆會失去他們的注意，也因此不能了解這部電影的主軸。至於什麼叫做相關，我們將在下一章關於辯論的部分進行討論。每一個描述都是由句子組成，句子彼此之間應該有邏輯上的聯繫，一次只給一個句子。在處理商業糾紛的時候不應該說謊，但是沒有必要說出全部的事實，這當然是律師們的工作，但是商人在這個階段有這個義務，不應該說出不利於自己利益的事實使得情況變得更複雜。

Chapter

4

Debate

辯論

Focus 本章大綱

4.1 Why should we learn debate? / 我們為什麼要學習辯論？

4.2 Critical thinking resulting from doubt / 批判性思考源自於懷疑

4.3 Training of debate / 辯論的訓練

4.1 Why should we learn debate?

In a typical scenario of debate, you make a claim and defend the position you hold. In fact, a debate is a form of speech, except that in a speech, your statement will not be questioned, but in a debate, your statement is subject to an examination in a form of confrontation. If you know how to expose an opponent's weakness through questioning, you should be able to know what questions your opponents have prepared to expose your weaknesses and thus prepare yourself better in both statement making and in defense. Simply speaking, in learning about debate, the focus is placed on the "examination" of the statements of others. Such a question originates from doubt in the mind, which is, fair to say, the beginning of all knowledge. Defense in a debate refers to a statement supporting your claim previously made, your position held, when confronted. Everyone can make a claim. Unless you can make an effective defense of your claim, such claim carries no value. Defense requires evidence, often a form of facts with logical interpretation. Fact requires elaboration and interpretation as discussed in the last chapter.

How important is it to defend your position? It is important, very important. It happens every day on all levels of life. It is a thinking process requiring your examination of all aspects of an issue, vital for your future success. In college, graduate students and scholars defend their thesis. On the road, a police officer defends the ticket he issues. In a job interview, an applicant makes a claim on his merit and defends his claim against the questions asked. A government official makes a decision and defends his decision against any doubt. A sales person defends his sales talk all the time. In a court room, an attorney makes an argument and defends his position against any examination. In a political campaign, a candidate defends his claims and examines his opponent's weaknesses. Simply speaking, you make a claim and you defend it, and your value and merit depend on how successful you defend what you claim. If you cannot defend what you say or do, your claim will carry no value at all.

Most important of all, debating skill is the foundation of all negotiating ability. If you cannot debate, you cannot defend your interest either. If you cannot defend your own interest, you are incompetent in negotiating. Besides, in a negotiation, the opponent's weaknesses should be exposed through examination by debating and bargaining to your advantage. Without debating skills, it will be difficult to bargain to your advantage in a negotiation.

4.1 我們為什麼要學習辯論？

在一個典型辯論的場景中，你做一個聲明，然後爲你所採取的立場進行辯護。事實上辯論也是演說的一種型態，但是在演說中你並不會接受質詢，而在辯論中你必須爲你所說的接受質問。如果你知道如何以質問的方式暴露對手的缺點，那你也應該知道你的對手將準備什麼樣的問題來暴露你的缺點，因此，你可以在你的說法上做出更好的準備並且有能力防衛你的說法。簡單來說，在學習辯論中，重點在於檢驗其他人的說詞。這樣的質問是來自於心中懷疑，而懷疑是所有知識的來源。辯論中的防衛是指，當你被質疑的時候，你所用來支持前面所做的聲明以及所堅持立場而做的說法。每一個人都可以做一個聲明。但是除非你可以對你的聲明提出有效的防衛，否則這樣的聲明沒有價值。防衛你的聲明需要證據，然後再加以邏輯上的解釋。這一部分我們在上一個章節已經有很詳細的說明。

爲自己的立場辯護有多重要？很重要，非常的重要！這樣的事情在日常生活當中每一個階層都在發生。這是一個思維的過程，要求你思考一個問題所有的角度，對於你未來的成功有決定性的影響。在大學裡面研究生還有這些學者必須爲他們的論文進行辯護。在路上警察也必須爲他的開單進行辯護。找工作面試的時候，求職者聲明了他的優點特長，也必須爲他所聲稱的優點進行辯護，回答面試官的問題。一個政府官員也必須爲他所做的決定辯護並解答其他人的懷疑。銷售員總是爲他的說法辯護。在法庭裡，律師爲他所持的立場進行辯護，反擊對手的那些指控。選舉時，候選人爲他的政策辯護而且也同時檢驗對手的缺點。簡單來說，你做一個聲明，你爲你的說法進行辯護，而你的價值和本事就在於你爲你所做的聲明進行成功的辯護。如果你沒有辦法爲你所說或所做的進行辯護，那你的聲明就沒有價值。

最重要的是，辯論的能力是所有談判能力的基礎。如果你沒有辦法辯論，你就不能維護自己的利益。如果你不能維護自己的利益，你就沒有能力進行談判。除此之外，在談判當中，對方的弱點可以透過辯論被顯現出來，因此增加我們談判的籌碼。沒有辯論的能力，很難在協商當中取得我們最佳的利益。

4.2 Critical thinking resulting from doubt

The New Testament (Romans 3:4) says, “So that you may be proved right in your words and prevail in your judging.” (Romans 3:4) The key terms here are “your words”, which represents what you say, and “your judging”, which indicates a standard to be applied in evaluation, whether judging or being judged. What you say together with your standard adopted form the crucial elements of debate. How to achieve a prevailing status? The answer is easy, confronting and defending by debating as Apostle Paul did. You need to prepare for confrontation, either confronting or being confronted. Confrontation requires wisdom and courage and forms the very essence of the western culture and generally leads into arguments. Your value is proved by how you successfully defend your claim against any challenges.

4.2 批判性思考源自於懷疑

新約聖經（羅馬書三章四節）這樣說：「你責備人的時候，顯爲公義；被人議論的時候，可以得勝。」這個地方主要的字眼就在於「責備人」，這代表你所說的話，以及「被人議論」，這顯示在判斷上所使用的標準，不論在判斷別人或是被別人判斷，你所說的話以及所依據的標準構成了辯論最重要的部分。如何做得到得勝？答案很簡單，就是以辯論的方式進行質問與防禦，就像使徒保羅所做的一樣。你必須爲對抗做準備，或者質問別人，或者被別人質問。質問需要智慧以及勇氣，並且是西方文化的精髓。通常導向爭論。你的價值決定於擊敗那些挑戰，成功的防衛你的說法。

Confrontation originates from a doubt in the mind which is conducive to a modern concept in a political philosophical term "check and balance" as designed by Montesquieu, a political philosopher and a lawyer in the age of Enlightenment, incarnated in the separation of powers provided in the U.S. Constitution and represented by those modern democracies. Doubt in the mind connotes a question from an individual. Therefore, it is fair to say that confrontation, which originated from doubt, is a product of individualism, the foundation of all western civilization.

質問來自於心中的疑惑，產生了現代政治哲學上的新概念（權力制衡），並且以三權分立的方式存在，這是由啓蒙時期法國政治哲學家以及律師孟德斯鳩所提出，表現於現在的美國憲法與民主政治。內心的疑惑意指個人提出問題的概念。因此可以很公平的說，從內心疑問產生而來的質問，是個人主義的產品，也是西方文化的根基。

Once a doubt is raised, questions will be asked. When a question is asked, possible answers will be explored. The process of such exploration, similar to constructing a bridge that connects a question and an answer, is a process of building the analysis and persuasion. By this process, we are not necessarily guaranteed to find the answer but we can surely remove the impossible during our journey of exploration. This is what we call critical thinking.

一旦有懷疑就會提出問題。當提出問題的時候我們就會找尋可能的答案。這一種找尋的過程，就像是在問題與答案之間建立一個橋梁，也是建立分析與說服的一種過程。在這個過程當中，我們並不必然找到答案，但是我們可以排除一些不可能的選項，我們稱之為批判性的思考。

The term “critical” denotes the ideas of criticism and disapproval against an opinion made by others. Criticism is a judgment made with a conclusion. The person whose opinion is criticized needs to defend his reasoning and, in many cases, is required to pinpoint the weakness of the others’ opinions through reasoning as well (e.g. criticizing others). It is a process to find an answer, although the person who raises a doubt does not necessarily know what the answer should be. As Socrates said, he doesn't know the answer but he does know those who claim to have wisdom do not have the wisdom as so claimed. Raising doubt in a form of a question is the first step of reasoning and reasoning is a bridge between a question and an answer. Therefore, learning the process of reasoning, the so-called analysis, helps us to search out possible answers. Through this process of reasoning, the impossible is removed. It is a searching process based on a doubt leading to a confrontation which, in most cases, exists in a form of debate. All of the process is triggered from doubt in the mind and is followed by arguments in search for a possible answer, a form of confrontation. Fair to say, confrontation and debate are deeply embedded in a doubt arising from individualism, a practice so prevalent in learning knowledge in the western culture including both their academic and practical daily life.

「批判性」這個字眼，說明了批評與不同意別人的意見。批評就是判斷之後的結論。一個人意見受到批評的時候，需要防衛他自己得到此意見的理由，在很多情況之下，也需要提出理由指出別人意見的弱點。這是發現答案的一個過程，雖然提出疑問的人並不必然知道什麼是答案。就像蘇格拉底說的，他也不知道答案，但是他知道那些聲稱具有智慧的，其實並沒有他們所聲稱的智慧。以詢問問題的方式提出懷疑是論理過程的第一步，而論理過程是一個問題與答案之間的橋梁。因此學習論理，也就是所謂的分析，來幫助我們找到可能的答案。透過這個論理過程，不可能的選項被移除了。這是一個建立在懷疑之上的尋找答案的過程，而懷疑帶來對抗而存在於辯論的形式當中。所有的過程來自於內心疑問的發動，而後透過辯論來找尋可能的答案，也就是質問的形式。所以很公平的說，對抗與辯論是根深蒂固的建立在個人主義所抱持的懷疑之上，這也是在西方文化當中，學習知識上廣泛使用的做法，包括他們的學術界和一般的日常生活。

Analysis is a process of reasoning. It is reasoning rather than a conclusion to persuade. A conclusion made with no analysis carries no power of persuasion at all. Anyone can make a conclusion with a loud voice but only those who come up with reasons can persuade. It is easier to borrow money from your friends, family and banks for something with a justifiable cause rather than that for pleasure. They care more about the reasons than the conclusion. They might lend money to you on certain occasions but refuse to do so in others, even though the amount is the same. Therefore, we must learn the skills of reasoning. Reasoning is a process of carefully formulating information and facts into a logical sequence to show a cause and effect structure as we will elaborate further in the following sections.

分析是一個論理的過程，我們是透過論理而不是靠結論來進行說服，沒有分析的結論並不具有說服力。任何一個人都可以大聲喊出他的結論，但是只有那些可以說出足夠理由的能夠說服。無論對於你的朋友或是家庭甚至是銀行，有著正當的理由去向他們借錢要比為了玩樂而借錢來得容易。他們關心的不只在於你要借錢，更重要的是，是為了什麼借錢。他們可能願意為了某些原因可以借，但另外一些原因他們不願意借，雖然數額都是一樣。因此我們必須學習論理的技術。論理的過程是建立在依邏輯過程所謹慎建置的事實與資訊，進而顯示出因果關係的結構。我們將在下一章節做進一步的討論。

Of course, under some cultures, different opinions could be oppressed due to the operation of social systems ranging from family units to the whole political institutions. But in the western nations observing the freedom of individuals (the very product indispensable to individualism), oppression won't work. That is why, in the western perspective, the system of democracy is superior to all other political mechanisms because the governing has theoretically procured the consent of the governed. To gain consent, persuasion by communication either in speech or debate is necessary as commonly seen in the western political campaigns and court trials. During communication, opinions which cannot withstand challenges will not be accepted and thus carries no value in the minds of all listeners. For this reason, in a debate, subsequent to any speech made, challenges must be expected. The work of persuasion will fail if challenges cannot be successfully defeated.

This chapter will not be elaborating on the rules governing debate competition but rather exploring the questions on how to build a solid opinion through the reasoning process, skills on defense, and those on examination of arguments by others in the art of debate.

當然，在一些文化之下，不同的意見由於家庭或是政治體系的運作，而會受到壓迫。但是在尊重個人的西方國家（個人主義不可分割的產物），壓迫是沒有用的，這就是為什麼在西方人的觀點中，民主政治比其他的政體來得優秀，那是因爲統治者理論上取得了被統治者的同意。要取得被統治者的同意，透過溝通的說服是必須的。比方說在選舉中的演講，或是法庭中的辯論。在溝通當中，任何不能通過質疑的挑戰的意見，沒有辦法被接受，因此在聽眾的心中並沒有價值。為了這個原因，在辯論中，我們必須期待他人挑戰我們剛剛說過的話語。如果不能夠通過挑戰，說服的工作沒有辦法完成。

本章不會討論辯論比賽的規則，我們將探索如何透過論證的過程，建立一個有效的意見，以及防禦的技巧還有檢視他人的說法，也就是辯論的藝術。

4.3 Training of debate

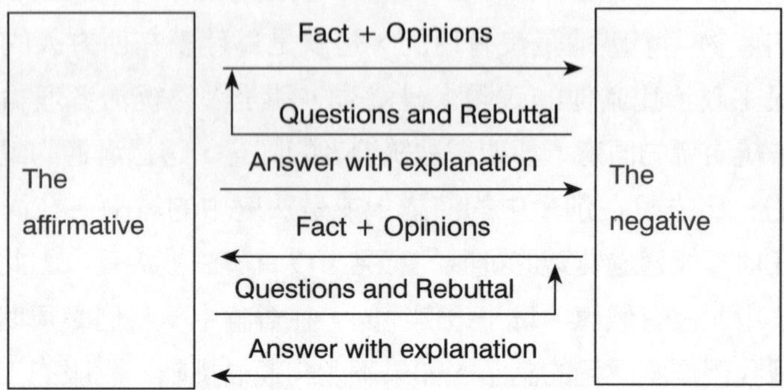

1. General composition of an argument

1 Difference between a speech and a debate

In the training of speech, students have learned how to narrate stories with a message delivered to an audience calling for some action as suggested by Dale Carnegie. A message in a speech is an opinion rendered by a speaker and generally will not be challenged. Different opinions or contrasted examples could be provided as either for discussion or for comparison to corroborate a speaker's position if necessary, but should be carefully applied so that his position will not be damaged by his contrasted examples.

4.3 辯論的訓練

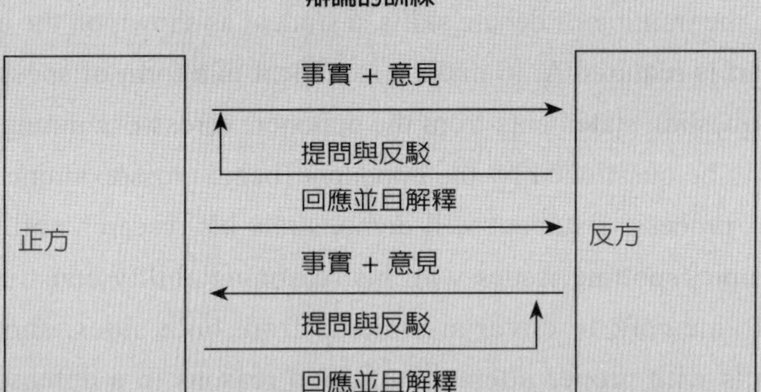

(1) 辯論的結構

1 演說與辯論的差異

在演說的訓練中，學生們已經依照卡內基的訓練方式，學習到如何敘說一個帶有訊息的故事，並且將之傳遞給聽衆，要求他們行動。演說的訊息，是演說者的意見，而且通常不會被挑戰。如果有需要的話，不同的意見，或是相反的例子，也可以拿來提供作爲討論或是比對，用來強化演說者的立場。但是要小心使用，這樣才不會損害他的立場。

However, a debate is different and more complicated. It is made in a form of advocacy subjected to examination by an opponent. Without such an examination, a debate is not that different from a speech. Unlike questions asked in a discussion style, the cross-examination in a debate by an opponent is made as challenges aiming at defeating the whole argument presented. Therefore, it is necessary to know how to defend and how to challenge.

On the training of debate skills, a student as shown on the above chart is required A. to make a statement in a form of speech, B. to question statements from the opponent (cross-examining) and C. to be questioned by the opponent (being cross-examined). In this process, a student will demonstrate his research ability on a topic, spotting issues with his reasoning ability constructing a framework to cover arguments from both sides, showing skills with proper utterance of good reasons in a defense and in a logical examination aiming at persuasion of an audience by defeating his opponents' argument as his final goal. One important thing to be noted here, research in debate should cover arguments from both sides expecting future challenges and reasons from your opponent. If research is only limited to the position held, then there will be a great risk of unknown danger resulting from any possible unexpected challenges presented by the other side. An introduction of demonstrations will be elaborated on in the following sections.

但辯論是不同且比較複雜，辯論是一種帶有立場的辯護方式，他必須受到反對者的檢驗。沒有這種檢驗，辯論與演說沒有什麼不同。在辯論當中對手所使用交互詰問的方式，並不是討論，而是一種挑戰，目的在摧毀對手整個的說詞。因此我們必須要知道如何防衛，以及如何挑戰。

在訓練辯論的技巧，一個學生就如上列圖示必須被要求：A：以演講的方式發出聲明；B：質問對手的聲明（交互詰問）；C：被對手質問（被交互詰問）。在這個過程當中，學生會證明他對一項主題的研究能力，以分析找出爭議點，並且建立包含兩邊不同看法的架構，以適當表達好的說詞進行防衛，並以邏輯檢驗對手看法的能力，以擊破對手的說詞爲最終目標。這地方要注意到的事情是，在辯論當中的研究，應該包含兩邊的立場，並且應當預見未來對手可能提出的挑戰及理由。如果一項研究只限定在某一個特定立場，那就會有來自於另外一種立場的未知危險。在後面章節我們會看一下示範以及更進一步的討論。

2 Refutation

In a debate, a speaker must challenge the opposite opinion by proving their flaws (not true) in argument. This is what we call refutation or, more precisely, a form of cross-examination.

Refutation is the essence of a debate. When both sides, if well prepared, give their opinion through facts logically reasoned ending with two conflicting views, the audience often cannot tell who is correct and thus feels confused. Refutation provides an opportunity for the better understanding of an audience on issues by examining the mutual arguments with revealed flaws if a refutation is well done. Without refutation, so called debate is nothing more than a form of persuasive speech with two opposite views that only perplexes the audience in the end. By refutation, especially in the form of cross-examination, flaws of an argument will be obviously and clearly revealed. For example, in a debate regarding whether corporal punishment in schools should be allowed, listeners will feel perplexed if no refutation by cross-examination is made because both arguments could be made upon certain persuasive facts including statistics organized under a sound framework with reasonable explanations. Arguments from both sides carry values and flaws. A speaker who supports corporal punishment cannot be expected to criticize his own views in the same occasion. Such flaws would be exposed by the questioning of the other side. The cross-examination of each other in this case would reveal the mutual weaknesses and flaws of the opposite arguments.

2 反駁

在一個辯論當中，一個演說者可以用證明對方論證上的缺點（不眞）來挑戰相反的意見，我們稱之爲反駁，或是更精確一點說，是一種詰問。

反駁是辯論的精髓，當已經充分準備的雙方透過對於事實，透過邏輯性的論證，產生兩種不同的意見，聽衆們通常無法判斷哪方正確，因此覺得困惑。反駁透過檢驗雙方辯詞的方式，提供了一個讓聽衆對於爭議比較好了解的機會，而這種檢驗可以顯示出辯詞上的缺點。如果沒有反駁的程序，那辯論只是一種具有說服性的演說，兩種不同的意見只是讓聽衆覺得困惑而已。透過反駁，特別是交互詰問，辯詞的缺點會很明顯而且清楚的顯示出來。例如在一個關於學校是否應該准許體罰的辯論題目，如果辯論雙方沒有互相以交互詰問進行反駁的話，聽衆可能會對雙方的理由覺得困惑，因爲他們的證詞可能都是建立在非常完整架構下，經過良好組織、非常具有說服力的事實，包括一些統計數字。兩邊的辯論都各有價値也各有缺點。我們不能期待支持體罰的一方，在同一場合批評他自己的論點。這種缺點只有透過另外一方以詰問的方式顯現出來。彼此的交互詰問是可以顯現出兩個不同論點的弱點和缺點。

To refute is to say that something is not true. When you claim that something that you heard is not true, you have to come up with explanations. Without good reasoning, people won't be persuaded by you loudly voicing your conclusion.

Good reasoning is basically sound interpretation in a logical manner of either evidence or information organized under an appropriate framework with precise issue spotting by a speaker. The whole key factor here is a logical ability in connecting each sentence and paragraph. What is exactly a logical ability? It seems to me no more than an analysis based on a cause and effect structure for the purpose of debating. The logical links of each concept in sentences and paragraphs must be tight enough to withstand any challenges within any reasonable expectation. How are these words, sentences and paragraphs connected? What are these links? Are they connected in a logical sequence? This brings up an issue on critical thinking. Demonstrations will be introduced and elaborated on in the following sections.

反駁就是聲稱某件事情並不眞實，當你聲稱某件你所聽到的事情並不眞實，你必須要提供說明，缺乏一個好的論證，人們是無法被你大聲的結論所說服的。

一個好的論證基本上就是演說者對於證據或是資訊以邏輯的態度在適當的框架之下，找出確實的爭議，提出合理的解釋。這個地方的關鍵就在於連結每一個句子和段落的邏輯能力。什麼是邏輯能力？對我來說就是爲了辯論的目的，在因果架構上所建立的分析。在句子與段落之間每一個概念的邏輯銜接，必須非常緊密，能夠對抗來自於合理期待中的挑戰。這些句子與段落如何連接？連接點是什麼？他們是否具有邏輯性的前後關係？這就產生了批判性思考的問題。在後面章節我們會看一下示範以及更進一步的討論。

How to make a refutation? Refutation is directed to a speech given by your opponent. A speech generally consists of facts and opinion as mentioned in the previous chapter. Facts are elaborated with reasoning as analysis leading to a conclusion. To make an effective refutation, a logical mind with a skillful ability on making a quick and effective summary of the information heard in a short time is required. The structure of a speech given by an opponent could be either well or poorly organized. Whatever the case may be, a debater should be able to make a quick and effective summary on the facts and reasoning heard. The speech heard should be quickly summarized and arranged under a clear and logical cause and effect sequence. The cause and effect sequence shows in the relation between a subject and an object linked by the verb used. Once a cause and effect sequence is clear, we should soon find either assumption made or standard used by the opponent for evaluation, which we will further elaborate in the following sections.

如何進行反駁？反駁是針對對方所做的演說。演說通常包括事實和意見，就像我們在前一章所說明的。事實以理由進行解釋，進行分析，進而導致結論。要做一個有效的反駁，必須具有邏輯的思考，並能在短時間之內對所聽到的資訊，快速與有效地進行摘要的能力是必須的。在辯論中對方所進行演說的架構可能是組織良好也可能是非常鬆散。不管如何，辯論者必須對於所聽到的事實和理由進行快速有效的摘要記錄。所聽到的演說應該迅速地以摘要的方式，將內容置於清晰的邏輯因果關係之下。因果關係的過程顯現於主詞動詞和受詞的關係當中。一旦因果關係很清楚，我們就可以很快地找到對方判斷所使用的假設和標準，這一部分我們會在之後的章節談到。

What is critical thinking? A doubt or simply a denial might be a good start, but it is not enough. Critical thinking, it seems to me, refers to a thinking process searching for an answer once a doubt is raised and a question is asked. Between a question and an answer, there is a methodology used as a bridge that is built on a reasoning process by which a standard can be ascertained and adopted. Critical thinking is a reasoning process searching for answers. A teacher's responsibility is therefore to help students to raise some doubt in their minds and help them to search for answers by training them on a reasoning process. According to Mr. Robert Boostrom in his book, Developing Creative & Critical Thinking, setting a standard is an essential step for thinking critically. A standard, as publicly well known, is used for judging and evaluating. Therefore, the power of judgment relies on the ability to ascertain whether a basis on which a standard formed is sound or flawed.

什麼是批判性的思考？一個懷疑或是一項否認可能是一個好的開始，但是絕對不夠。批判性的思考對我來說，就是一旦懷疑形成而且問題提出的時候，一個尋找答案的思考過程。在一個問題和答案間有一個橋梁，而這個橋梁就是方法，建立在論證過程之上，並且透過論證過程來尋找並且採用某個標準。批判性思考是尋找答案的論證過程，因此一個老師的責任是幫助學生在他們的內心提出疑問，並且透過論證的方法來尋找答案，根據 Robert Boostrom 教授在他發展創造性與批判性思考一書中，說到建立標準是批判性思考最重要的一步，眾所周知標準是用來判斷與檢驗的，因此，判斷的能力有賴於確認一個標準的基礎是否健全還是有缺點。

Critical thinking is an examination process starting from collecting and organizing the facts and information relevant to issues on which an opinion is based with a conclusion made through reasoning. Various factors such as partial truths and biased standards can always affect a conclusion. These flaws can be exposed by examining the relevancy and completeness of facts and information under a cause and effect structure in a logical sequence which will be elaborated on in the following sections.

批判性思考是從開始的蒐集、組織與爭議有關的事實和資訊，並透過對這些事實和資訊的論理過程而產生的意見的一個檢驗的程序。不同的因素，例如部分的事實或是帶有偏見的標準，總是會影響到結論。這些缺點可以透過因果關係的架構，在一個邏輯順序上，檢驗事實和資訊的相關性以及完整度來發現缺陷。我們會在下一章節進行討論。

3 Evaluating facts with a standard

In a debate, arguments from both sides on the same topic with different conclusions generally lead to a muddy fight, to only confuse the listeners. Training on debate should focus on finding flaws on both arguments rather than reaching a consensus, another important process with certain steps which should be further elaborated on in the training of negotiation. Unfortunately, many books in the current market on negotiation do not start from this basic training on debate.

3 以標準來檢驗事實

在一個辯論中，雙方針對同一個主題的不同辯詞以及不同結論，通常只會讓聽眾覺得更困惑。辯論的訓練應該集中在發現雙方辯詞的缺點，而不在於謀求一個共識，而共識這個部分很重要，應該是在談判的課程中更深入討論，有一定的步驟需要討論及訓練。很不幸的，目前市面上很多談判的書籍，不從一個基本的辯論訓練開始。

To reach a conclusion, a standard must be applied. As stated in the earlier sections, a conclusion is not that important because everyone can make a conclusion and voice his own opinion. Besides, the reasoning process is to persuade. Therefore, the most effective approach in an argument is to attack the standard used by an opponent rather than his conclusion. Once his standard as a foundation falls, the whole conclusion will collapse accordingly. For this reason, students at this stage must learn how to spot the weakness of an argument with close examination on the standard applied in order to find the very flaw. Some argument questions from GMAT are ideal for this practice.

要達到結論，我們必須採取標準，像前幾個章節所提到的，結論並不這麼重要，因為每一個人都能下一個結論而且提出自己的看法。除此之外，要達到說服的目的，必須依靠論理的過程。因此在辯論中最有效的方法，是攻擊對手所使用的標準而不是他所下的結論。一旦作為根基的標準倒下來的話，整個結論也會隨之傾倒。因為這個理由，學生們在這個階段必須學習如何嚴格檢驗對方所使用的標準，進而找出對方辯詞上的缺點。在這部分訓練上，GMAT 一些辯論的題目很適合練習。

We will examine a very simple question at the beginning. Try to find the flaw in the statement that "Since every student who earns an A has brought ball point pens for their test. Therefore, we should ask all students to carry ball point pens in order to earn an A." All students have no problem in telling the absurdity in this statement and it is easy to rebut by introducing a fact that some other students who bring ball point pens did not earn an A on that test. In other words, the fact that other students who brought ball point pens for their test did not earn an A has proved that there is no relationship between Grade "A" and a ball point pen. Carrying a ball point pen for the test is not a factor unique to the students who earned an A.

我們在一開始先檢驗一個很簡單的問題。試著找找看下面一句話的缺陷，「每一個得到A成績的學生，在考試的時候都帶原子筆。因此我們應該要求所有的學生，都帶原子筆參加考試，這樣他們就可以得到A的成績。」所有的學生都可以找出這句話的荒謬性，而且也很容易推翻它，也就是提出另一個事實，有其他帶原子筆的學生並沒有得到A的成績。換句話說，有學生帶著原子筆但沒有得到A的成績這項事實，證明了A的成績與帶原子筆之間並沒有關聯，帶原子筆參加考試並不是只有得到A成績學生的專有特色。

We will take a look at another simple question. Some claim that people who live in a rich area are successful in their business. Therefore, in order to make a successful business, we should move to a rich area. It seems true that that people who live in a rich area probably carry quite a profitable business. But the question here is that when did they move into that rich area, after or before they earned money? The answer is probably easy to tell. They moved into a rich area after they have money. This statement explains the causal link between a rich area and a successful business in reverse order. Another example similar in reverse order of a reasoning process can be seen such as "Rich people drive a sports car. Buy a sports car and you will get rich."

我們再來看另外一個簡單的問題。有一些人聲稱那些住在富有地區的人們都有很成功的事業，因此要讓事業成功，我們必須先搬到有錢的區域。絕大部分住在有錢區域的人們，通常都有很成功的事業這似乎是眞的。但是這裡的問題是，他們是什麼時候搬進這些有錢的區域？在他們有錢之前還在他們有錢之後？答案可能很簡單，他們有錢以後才搬進這些區域的。這一句話以倒果爲因的方式，解釋了有錢的區域與成功的事業的關係。其他類似的例子，像是「有錢人都開跑車，買一輛跑車你就會變得有錢」，這些都是同樣倒果爲因的例子。

We will further examine more difficult questions. For example, in a case claiming that an airline is the best choice for all business travelers due to being number one on its time rate (95%). Ninety-five percent on its time rate is a fact. To claim that the airline, as a company being the number one on its time rate, is the best choice for business travelers is a conclusion. This conclusion is based on an interpretation of a fact (95%

on-time rate) evaluated under a standard (on-time rate is the only standard to decide if an airline is the best choice). The conclusion of course is to call action to all listeners to use their service. This simple example shows a very typical judgment in our daily life by stating a fact, a standard, an interpretation of fact (e.g. evaluation under a standard) and a conclusion.

我們接著要檢驗一些更困難的問題。例如在一個例子當中，某一家航空公司聲稱由於他第一名的準點率（95%），因此是所有商務旅客的最佳選擇。95% 的準點率是一個事實。聲稱這一家航空公司因爲具有第一名的準點率，因此成爲商務旅客的最佳選擇則是一個結論。這一個結論是建立在對於一個事實的詮釋上，而這個事實是受到準點率標準的檢驗（準點率是決定一家航空公司是否最好選擇的唯一標準）。結論當然是要求所有商務旅客使用他們的服務。這一個簡單的例子透露出我們日常生活很典型判斷的方式，也就是說明一項事實，提出一個標準，以及對事實提出解釋（例如在一個標準之下對事實進行評價）和做出結論。

This example has illustrated the common pattern used in a debate including all promotions in commercials and political campaigns (claiming one is superior to the other). The supporter has made a conclusion that this airline is the best choice for all business travelers. The conclusion is made on a reason purely based on an irrefutable and convincing fact, that is, its 95% on-time rate. What is more interesting is that this claim uses its on-time rate, an irrefutable and very persuasive fact, as the only standard. Many beginners will find that this argument is very difficult to rebut because this statement seems to be stating facts only.

這一個例子說明了在辯論中常使用的模式，包括商業上的銷售以及政治上的選舉活動（聲稱比對方優秀），在這個例子中，支持者下了一個結論，也就是這一家航空公司對於所有商務旅客來說是最佳選擇。這個結論是建立在一個完全沒有辦法被反駁而且非常具有說服力的事實，也就是 95% 的準點率。更有趣的是，這一個聲明使用了準點率當作唯一的標準。許多初學者發現這樣的辯詞很難被反駁，因爲整個的聲明似乎只在闡述事實而已。

If we agree that an on-time rate is the only standard that should be adopted, we undoubtedly will accept that conclusion as true that this airline is the best choice for all business travelers. If we can establish a standard on other factors, for example, the safety, flight fare or service, this airline could be ranked at the bottom in choice if their safety rate is not good. In other words, the rank of the same airline could be changed drastically from top to bottom if we changed a standard for consideration, especially those factors unfavorable to the airline.

如果我們同意準點率是應該被採用的唯一標準，我們會毫無疑問的接受，這家航空公司是所有商務旅客的最佳選擇的結論。假如我們可以以其他的條件爲標準，例如：安全性、機票的價格或是服務，如果他們的飛安紀錄不好的話，這家航空公司的排名有可能墊底。換句話說，同樣的一家航空公司排名可能劇烈改變，從山頭跌到谷底，如果我們改變考量的標準，特別是那些不利於這一家航空公司的因素。

A very similar rule can be applied to a student's performance. If we define a good student as those who have achieved good scores, then the person who has the highest grades in class is a good student because grade is the only standard for consideration. However, if we change the standard to consider the attendance rate only, the position of excellence might be transferred to someone else. Simply speaking, by changing a standard, the whole conclusion for the very same fact could be changed.

類似的規則也可以應用在學生們的表現上，如果我們認爲只有那些好成績的才能夠稱爲好學生，那班上功課最好的一定是好學生，因爲成績是考量的唯一標準。但是如果改變標準，只考量出席率的話，那好學生的頭銜就可能會移轉給其他人。簡單來說，改變一個所適用的標準，對於相同事實所下的結論也可能會改變。

Another similar situation can be found in the working environment. Many companies in the Orient tend to consider loyalty of employees as the highest standard in evaluation while western companies will probably regard capability in professional performance as the top consideration. The result will be different if a different standard is applied even if the facts remain same. Therefore, a good debater rarely makes an argument on the conclusion especially in a business world. It only causes an unnecessary fight. They focus on changing the criterion in judgment by using good reasons.

另外一個類似的情況也可在一個工作的場合看見，許多在東方的公司傾向於以公司員工的忠誠度當作考核的標準，而西方的公司可能認爲專業能力的表現才是最重要的因素。標準不同，結果也會不一樣，縱然事實並未改變。因此，一個好的辯論者很少對於結論進行爭論，特別是商業事件，那只會造成不必要的紛爭。好的辯論者應該集中於以好的理由來改變判斷的標準。

Another GMAT type of example is related to a fact that people drink less Coke but more coffee as age increases. It is also a fact that more and more people will get older and naturally consumption of coffee will increase as time goes by. Therefore, more investment is suggested to be made in the future in coffee instead of the Coke company. The standard used here is that people prefer coffee as they get older and more and more people will get older. Under this standard, the conclusion could be quite correct because this standard is using a fact if such a fact is limited on literary meaning without any assumption introduced (i.e. more and more people will drink coffee as they get older). Nevertheless, any student who is intelligent enough will notice that the standard intentionally omits another important fact that is bound to happen, that is, old people will die while the younger generation will be born. In other words, there is an assumption implicitly included in the standard in this case that people who prefer coffee as they get older SHALL LIVE FOREVER and THAT THE YOUNGER GENERATION WILL NEVER INCREASE IN THEIR POPULATION. This is not true. People will die, so will their consumption. Younger generation will be born and increase in their population. In addition, the whole conclusion also will be changed if the birth rate goes up rapidly. The standard is seriously flawed because it is not comprehensive enough to include some crucial facts in the offing in making their standard.

GMAT 型態的另一個例子是有關於一項事實，人們年紀愈長，喝的可樂愈少，喝的咖啡愈多。而愈來愈多的人年紀會愈長，因此對於咖啡的消費隨著時間的過去也會愈來愈多，這也是事實。因此，未來的投資應該是放在咖啡而不是可樂。這個地方所使用的標準就是人們隨著年紀漸長愈傾向喝咖啡，而且愈來愈多人會老化。在這個標準之下，未來的投資應該是放在咖啡的結論可能是正確的，因爲這個標準使用一個事實，如果這個事實又限定在字義上，而不帶進任何的假設的話（也就是愈來愈多人年紀愈大他們就會選擇喝咖啡），如果文義只限定在字面上的意義而不做任何的推論的話。但是有一些聰明的學生可能已經察覺到，這個標準特意省略另一項必然發生的重要事實，也就是老年人會過世而新的一代會不斷的產生。換句話說，在他的標準有一個隱藏的假設，人們年紀漸長他們愈喜歡咖啡，而且他們會永遠活下去，而且新的一代人口並不會增加。這並不是事實。人們會死亡而他們的消費也會停止。而新生的一代會不斷的產生而人口增加。除此之外，如果出生率很快增加的話，整個的結論也會被改變，這一個標準有很嚴重的缺點，因爲它並沒有廣泛包括了其他重要即將發生的事實。

Here is another interesting example.

我們看一下另外一個有趣的例子。

Following appeared in a memorandum from the Director of Human Resources to the executive officers of Company X:

下面是 X 公司人力資源部門主管所提出備忘錄的一部分：

“Last year, we surveyed our employees on improvement needed at Company X by having them rank, in order of importance, the issues presented in a list of possible improvements. Improved communications between employees and management was consistently ranked as the issue of highest importance by employees who responded to the survey. As you know, we have since instituted regular communications sessions conducted by high-level management, which the employees can attend on a voluntary basis. Therefore, it is likely that most employees at Company X now feel that the improvement most needed at the company has been made.”

「去年，我們對於 X 公司的員工按照議題的重要性，調查出公司可能需要改進的議題。對於已經回覆的問卷認爲最優先的順序是管理部門與員工溝通改善的問題。衆所周知的，從那之後開始，我們有了管理部門所主導的溝通會議，員工可以選擇自由參加，因此，很有可能公司的員工現在覺得公司內部最需要改善的問題已經完成了。」

The statement made by the human resources director seems to make sense. The company has a serious problem on communication between top management and the employees. The director establishes regular meetings between the high level management and employees, a forum to talk to management. Since employees have a place to meet the management and an opportunity to talk, the director claims that the problem on communication has been solved.

人事主管所說的話聽起來有些道理，這一家公司的管理部門與員工之間有嚴重的問題，人事主管在管理部門與員工之間建立了經常性的會議，一個可以跟管理部門說話的地方。因爲員工有地方可以見到管理部門且可以有機會表達一些意見，這個主管聲稱溝通的問題已經解決。

The problem is on the term “communication” which denotes a concept of exchanging of ideas or information. There is no doubt that the director has provided a place and an opportunity for the employees to talk. But this does not necessarily mean that there will be an exchange of ideas, a form of mutual interaction. For instance, the meeting is held on a voluntary basis. Not all employees who wish to express their opinion will go. Even if they decide to go, they are not necessarily guaranteed to have a right on free expression. They could have the fear of revenge from their supervisors. Besides, top management will not necessarily respond to their questions or opinion. In other words, according to this director, once we have a session, we have communication. This director sets up regular sessions as a standard in evaluating the problem. But the true standard should be an exchange of ideas or opinions rather than sessions.

問題在於這一個字眼「溝通」，這個字說明了一個交換想法或信息的概念。毫無疑問的，這個人事主管提供了一個地方與機會讓員工來說話，但這並不必然說明會有意見的交換，一種互動的模式，例如：這個會議室採取自由參加的方式，並不是所有想要表達意見的員工都會去，即使他們決定去了，他們並不被保證有自由表達意見的權利，他們可能害怕被主管報復。除此之外，管理高層並不會搭理他們的意見或問題。換句話說，根據這個人事主管所說的，一旦我們有了會議，我們就有了溝通。這個主管以會議的存在爲標準，來衡量問題解決與否。但是眞正的標準應該在於意見的交換而不是會議本身。

We still can examine a few more similar examples so that readers may grasp a better idea on how to spot the flaws of an argument.

我們可以再檢驗一些類似的例子，讓讀者們對於如何找到這類辯論言詞的弱點有更好的概念。

The following appeared as part of an article in a trade publication:

下列是一份貿易期刊的部分內容：

“Stronger laws are needed to protect new kinds of home security systems from being copied and sold by imitators. With such protection, manufacturers will naturally invest in the development of new home security products and production technologies. Without stronger laws, therefore, manufacturers will cut back on investment. From this will follow a corresponding decline not only in the protection quality and marketability, but also in production efficiency, and this ultimately, a loss of manufacturing jobs in the industry.”

「我們需要更嚴格的法律來保障家庭防盜安全系統不被仿冒者仿冒以及銷售。有了這樣法律的保護，製造商很自然的會投資在新的家庭防盜產品的發展以及生產技術。沒有這樣嚴格的法律，製造商會因此降低投資，這樣會導致防盜品質以及市場銷售的相對衰退，而且也會在產品的銷售上面顯現出來，因此最後導致這個產業工作機會的喪失。」

This statement is urging protection of industrial products

by enacting stronger laws imposing harsher punishment on imitators so that business is more willing to invest more in this field. This statement sounds very irrefutable because it is based on a common belief that the intellectual right in an industry should be protected. How can anyone cast doubt on this statement? The problem lies on the specific characteristic of this product, the home security system.

這一部分的說詞是鼓勵制定更嚴格的法律，對於仿冒者加以更重的刑罰來保護工業產品，好讓企業在這領域更願意進行投資。這樣的說詞聽起來似乎無可辯駁，因爲它是建立在一個共通的信念，也就是智慧財產權需要被保護，我們怎麼去懷疑這樣的說法呢？這問題存在於產品本身的特質，家庭防盜系統。

Will a stronger law, if passed to impose harsher punishment on the imitators of the home security system, deter such infringement and thus help to further investment in this product? The answer probably is negative. It is because the purpose of those imitators is to illegally break into home security systems and there is no reason to assume that a stronger law will stop them from doing so. In other words, this statement assumes that those law breaking imitators will be deterred by harsher punishment. Besides, the function of the home security products is to prevent burglars from breaking in. The home security system is designed to protect the safety of a home, a person's sacred haven. This is the basic function of this system, the very fundamental value that consumers are bargaining for. If such products cannot serve this basic function, then there is no value. The value of this type of products rests on the people's satisfaction to the perfect performance of their function and it cannot be created by a stronger law. This example again shows that a seemingly iron cladded conclusion could be made on a basis of an irrefutable common belief or a fact.

我們有可能透過較嚴格的法律，對於家庭防盜系統的仿冒者給予更重的懲罰，達到阻止這類的仿冒行爲並且幫助對這類產品未來的投資嗎？答案可能是否定的。那是因爲仿冒者的目的是在於非法的破解家庭防盜保全系統，而我們沒有理由假設一個更嚴格的法律能阻止他們這樣做。換句話說，這個說法假設了嚴格的處罰會阻止這些已經違反法律的仿冒者。除此之外，家庭防盜系統的功能在於阻止盜匪的侵入，這樣的系統是設計保護一個家庭的安全，也是一個人神聖的避難所。這是這一個系統最基本的功能，也是消費者付錢所期待的最基本的價值。如果一個產品不能達到這基本的功能，那它就沒有價值，這個產品的價值在於人們對於其功能的完整展現，這不是能由嚴格的法律所創造出來的。這個例子再一次的展現，一個建立在無可爭辯的事實或是信念上的結論可以看起來是非常健全的。

The following appeared in the editorial section of a local newspaper.

下面是一份當地報紙社會評論的部分。

"The profitability of the Taiwan oil company, recently restored to private ownership, is a clear indication that businesses fare better under private ownership than under public ownership."

「臺灣石油公司最近剛恢復爲私人公司，它的獲利能力是一個很清楚的指標，私人企業比公營企業經營得更好。」

All conclusion and reasoning are contained in one sentence. Nevertheless, we still can make the following analysis. The conclusion is that this profitable company fares better under a private ownership. The reasoning is that the company is recently restored to a private ownership from a public ownership. This conclusion will probably make all sense without the key words "recently restored". The terms "recently restored" has indicated that this profitable company was publicly owned and it made a good profit. In other words, we can almost be sure that the company fares good when in public ownership. We are not sure if this company still could do well in the future but it did well under public ownership. Therefore, the conclusion is subject to some doubt.

這一個句子包括了所有的結論和論證。雖然如此，我們可以做下列的分析，這個結論是這一家具有獲利能力的公司以私人型態方式管理經營得更好，理由是這一家公司最近從公營改回私營。如果沒有這個重要字眼「最近恢復」，這個結論或許說得通。「最近恢復」就已經說明了這一家獲利良好的公司之前是公營事業，賺了不少錢。換句話說，我們幾乎可以確定這家公司在公營型態的時候營運良好，我們不確定這家公司在未來能不能做得好，但它確實在公營時做得不錯，因此這樣的結論是值得懷疑的。

The following appeared as part of advertisement for Mr. Chen, who is seeking re-election as a mayor.

下面出現在尋求連任的市長陳先生的廣告。

"Re-elect Mr. Chen, and you will be voting for a proven leadership in improving our economy. Over the past years alone, seventy-five percent of the city's workers have had increases in their wages, six thousand jobs have been created, and ten large international corporations have located their headquarters here. Most of the respondents in a recent poll said they believe that the economy is likely to continue to improve if Mr. Chen is re-elected. Chen's opponent, Mr. Hu, would lead our country in a wrong direction because Mr. Hu disagrees with many of Mr. Chen's economic policies."

「票投陳先生，你會選出改善我們經濟，能力已被證明的領導人。在過去幾年，百分之七十五的市民薪水增加了，六千個工作機會被創造出來了，而且有十家國際型企業的總部搬來了這，絕大部分的民調顯示他們相信經濟可能會持續改善，如果陳先生繼續當選。陳先生的對手，胡先生會將我們的經濟帶到錯誤的方向，因爲胡先生不同意陳先生許多的經濟政策。」

Chen's achievement has been proven by his accomplishments during his incumbency as mayor and therefore this statement sounds very convincing, seemingly hard to rebut. Chen seems to be a better candidate than Mr. Hu because Mr. Hu disagrees with many of Chen's economic policies. The statement is based on the one assumption that employment is the only issue of this state and there is no other approach but Chen's that can lead to prosperity. However, employment is unlikely the only concern for a city. There are probably other problems which could affect an electorate's vote, for example, issues on taxes, the environment, public safety, traffic, education, etc. Besides, to claim that Hu will lead the city in a wrong direction simply because he disagrees with many of Chen's many economic policies is to believe that Chen's approach is the only correct path leading to economic prosperity. The economy is a cycle and any future demand in the market could change rapidly regarding manufacturing that could probably replace labor with technology. A new mayor must have a perception and vision for the future of the city.

陳先生的成就已經被他市長任內完成的事情所證明，所以這一段話聽起來很具有說服力，而且很難被反駁。陳先生看起來比胡先生更適合，因爲胡先生不同意陳先生許多經濟政策。這樣的說法是建立在一個假設上，也就是這一市唯一的問題在於他們的就業，而且除了陳先生的政策之外，沒有其他的方法可以達到繁榮。但是就業不太可能是這一市唯一的問題，可能有其他問題會影響到市民的投票，例如：稅制、環境方面、治安方面、交通以及教育方面等等的問題。除此之外，聲稱胡先生會將這一市帶到錯誤的方向僅僅由於他不同意陳先生的許多政策，就等同於相信陳先生的方法是達到經濟繁榮唯一正確方法。經濟是一個循環，未來市場的要求可能會急速改變，由科技取代勞力，一個新的市長對於一個城市的未來必須要有遠見。

The above examples show a common pattern used in arguments, that is, facts are evaluated under a standard followed by a conclusion. All arguments above are very much following this pattern in reaching their conclusion. Therefore, to spot the standard used is essential in a debate and, of course, in a negotiation as well.

上面的例子顯示出在辯詞當中常用的共通模式，使用一個標準來評斷事實並且得到一個結論。所有上述的辯詞大致都按照這個模式，來達到他們的結論。因此在辯論中找出使用的標準是很重要的，當然，在談判中也是一樣。

As the above cases show, facts standing alone do not create much value. A mere change of standard will change the whole conclusion even if the facts still remain the same. One famous case describes the difference between an optimistic mind and a pessimistic one in commenting on a bottle half full of water. The optimist will say that we are lucky because the bottle is still half full while the pessimist will complain because the bottle is half empty. The very same fact can be subject to different interpretations, producing a quite opposite effect. Why can the same fact lead to such a difference? The answer lies in the standard used. For the optimist, the standard is that as long as it is not empty, it is good. For the pessimist, the standard is, unless a bottle is full, it is no good. The same fact will lead to a completely different conclusion simply because different standards applied. Another good example is the students' scores in schools. Some will say that B plus is good enough while others might think it is not good enough. The key word here is the STANDARD adopted.

上面的例子所顯示的單純的事實，並沒有太大的價值，改變了一個標準就會改變結論，縱然事實還是相同。一個很有名的例子就是，悲觀的人和樂觀的人對於半瓶水看法的差異性，相同的事實可以透過不同的解釋產生完全不同的效果，爲什麼相同的事實在結論上會有這樣的差異，答案就在於所使用標準的不同，對於樂觀的人來說，標準就是只要瓶子不空就是好事；對於悲觀的人來說，標準就是瓶子如果不是全滿那就不好。相同的事實會導致完全不同的結論，僅僅因爲使用不同的標準，另外一個例子就是學生在學校的成績，有的人認爲 B+ 已經很好了，但有些人認爲那不夠好，關鍵在於所採用的標準。

4 Cause and effect in a sentence

Cause and effect sequence in a sentence

There are many things that happen every day. Not all facts carry value. In a speech, facts require interpretation to give value and produce power through the message. In an argument, only those facts germane to an issue should be introduced. Facts important to certain issues could mean little in another issue. It is a comparative concept. In other words, an issue will decide what facts are relevant and important.

4 在一個句子中的因果關係

句子中的因果關係

每一天有許多事情發生，但並不是所有的事實都具有價值。在一個演說當中，事實必須經過解釋，透過訊息才能夠產生價值和力量。在辯論當中只有那些與爭議相關的事實應該被提及，對於某些爭議重要的事實可能對另一個爭議不具有什麼價值。這是一個相對的概念。也就是說，一項爭議會決定什麼是相關而且重要的事實。

Issues are contained in arguments. Arguments are made on

a set of facts with reasons centering on issues followed by a conclusion. An issue will be decided by the standard used for evaluation. If a standard can be shaken, the whole conclusion will be reversed. Therefore, it is necessary to find out what the issue is and what standard is applied. To find an issue, it is very helpful to arrange the facts in a logical sequence, the so called, cause and effect analysis.

辯論當中會包含議題。辯論是基於事實，進而對議題論證，而導致結論。一項爭議會被所使用的標準進行評斷。如果標準發生動搖，整個結論可能會被推翻。因此我們有需要去找出什麼是爭議以及所使用的標準。將事實按照邏輯順序排列會有助於爭議的發現，也就是所謂的因果分析。

Arguments are made on a set of facts. The most common question encountered in any argument is "WHY". Analysis on a cause and effect process is very helpful to answer that question. Facts or information organized in a logical sequence can show a cause and effect structure, for example, why did this happen, what it was, what it is, and what it will be.

辯論是基於某些事實。最常問到的問題是「為什麼」。因果關係的分析非常有助於找出這樣的答案。將事實或是資訊透過邏輯順序的整理，可以顯示出因果關係的架構，例如：為什麼會這樣發生？過去是什麼？現在是什麼？以及未來是什麼？

The following sentences show a cause and effect relation. It is quite easy to understand and readers must get themselves familiar with such sentence pattern for their future learning of analysis.

下面的一些句子顯示出了因果關係，這些都很容易了解，讀者們應該熟悉這樣的句型以便將來學習分析。

Examples of cause and effect show how one thing can affect another.

因果關係的例句，顯示一件事情如何影響另外一件。

Examples on the cause and effect can be found on an online dictionary.

以下這些因果關係的例句是你能在網路上找到的。

We received seven inches of rain in four hours. - The underpass was flooded. Many buffaloes were killed. - Buffaloes almost became extinct.

過去四小時累積了七英吋的雨量，造成下水道積水。很多水牛因此淹死，導致瀕臨絕種。

The streets were snow-packed and icy. - Cars needed more time to stop.

街道上覆滿了雪，導致車子需要更多時間來煞車。

He broke his arm. - The doctor put it in a cast.

他斷了手臂，所以醫生將他的手臂接了回去。

I flipped the light switch on. - The light came on.

我將電燈的開關打開，燈就亮了。

An oil spill. - Many deaths to wildlife.

因石油外洩，造成許多野生動物死亡。

Cause and Effect Examples in Sentences:
When water is heated, the molecules move quickly, therefore the water boils.

因果關係的例句：
當水加熱時，分子會快速移動，因此會有水滾的現象產生。

A tornado blew the roof off the house, and as a result, the family had to find another place to live.

龍捲風吹走了房子的屋頂，因此這家人需要另找住處。

John made a rude comment, so Elise hit him.

約翰給了個很不禮貌的評論，因此艾爾西打了他。

When the ocean is extremely polluted, coral reefs die.

因爲海洋遭受嚴重的汙染，珊瑚因此死亡。

I had to get the mop since I spilled my juice.

因爲我打翻了果汁，所以我需要拿拖把將地板拖一下。

Tsunamis happen when tectonic plates shift.

當板塊移動時會產生海嘯。

Fred was driving 75 in a 35-mile zone, therefore he got a speeding ticket.

佛雷德在限速 35 英哩的地區卻開到 75 英哩，因此收到超速的罰單。

Maria didn't follow the recipe correctly, so the cake did not come out as expected.

瑪麗雅並沒有確切按照食譜上的指示，所以蛋糕並不是所預期的那樣。

The weather forecast called for rain, so he took his umbrella.

天氣預報表示會下雨，所以他帶著傘。

Because of a price increase, sales are down.

因爲價格上漲，所以銷售量降低。

Water is formed when two hydrogen atoms and one oxygen atom combine.

當兩個氫原子和氧氣結合，就會產生水。

The batter couldn't hit the softball because he didn't keep his eyes on the ball.

這名打者打不中壘球，因爲他的眼睛並沒有跟著球。

When the manuscript is edited, the company will publish it.

將原稿編輯好後，公司便會發行出去。

Since the electricity went out for most of the day, the ice cream in the freezer melted.

因爲幾乎斷電一整天，冰箱裡的冰淇淋都融化了。

As the wind speed increases, the sail boat moves faster.

當風速加快時，船也會行駛得更快。

When nuclear fusion stops or starts, a star explodes.

當核融合停止或開始時，星星便會爆炸。

Wind is produced when the surface of the Earth is heated unevenly.

當地球表面受熱不均時，便會產生風。

Because of inflation, the dollar is worth less than before.

因爲通貨膨脹，貨幣變得不像以前那樣値錢。

Read more at http://examples.yourdictionary.com/cause-and-effect-examples.html

請參考
http://examples.yourdictionary.com/cause-and-effect-examples.html

All the sentences above show a cause and effect relation of a phenomenon, explaining why an event happens and how they affect each other. To make a sentence with a cause and effect structure is the first task in the training of analysis.

上面所有的句子都顯示出一個現象的因果關係，解釋了為什麼一個事情影響到另外一件事情，以因果關係造一個句子，是在分析訓練當中最初要學習的工作。

5 Cause and effect in a paragraph

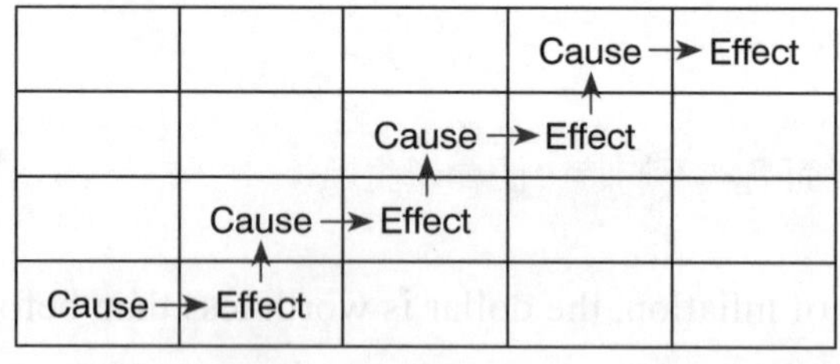

A sentence can only explain the causal relationship between a subject and an object. An argument in most of the cases demands a reasoning process composed of a few sentences in a logical sequence to bridge the gap between the beginning and the end or a question and an answer. An argument is mainly consisted of two parts, proposition with reasons for a position (including defense) and questioning.

Please be noted that such logical and causal connection applies not only to sentences but also concepts and ideas.

5 段落中的因果關係

段落中的因果關係

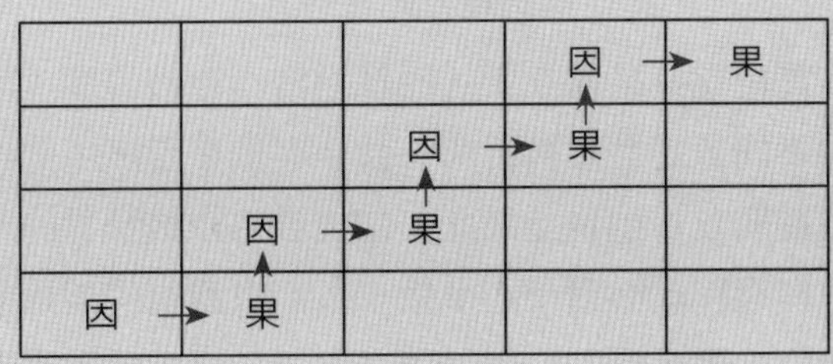

一個句子只能夠解釋主詞跟受詞之間的因果關係。在絕大多數的情況中，一個辯詞需要好幾個句子，按照邏輯的順序所組成的論理過程來建立起開始和結束或是問題與答案之間的橋梁。一個辯詞主要有兩個部分，提出理由支持一項論點（包括論點的防衛），以及進行質問。

請注意這樣邏輯和因果的聯接性不只應用在句子上，同時也呈現在概念和想法上。

Unlike a regular speech, which is a form of advocacy in nature and often is not subject to challenges; an argument is subject to challenges which sometimes are similar to an interrogation in a criminal proceeding even among friends. When a challenge is expected, reasons presented in support of a position should be made with carefully prepared information including facts arranged under a logical framework to meet possible challenges. We have studied the cause and effect relationship in a sentence structure. Now we need to see how each sentence connects and affects each other under a framework built on a cause and effect structure. The following examples will demonstrate how a conclusion is reached through reasoning by a cause and effect structure, the so-called analysis.

演說的本質是支持某種立場，而且通常不會被質問；而辯論與一般的演說不同，是需要被質問，甚至與刑事程序中的拷問有些類似，即使在朋友當中也是如此。當挑戰可以被預見的時候，支持立場的論理過程就必須小心準備，包括以邏輯的架構整理事實來面對可能的挑戰。我們已經看過了句子結構中的因果關係，現在我們要來看一下在一個因果關係結構當中，句子如何連結而且彼此互相影響，下面的例子會示範如何透過因果關係架構的論證過程來達到結論，也就是所謂的分析。

Examples demonstrated for the better understanding of a logical arrangement of sentences:

使學生比較了解經過邏輯安排的範例：

Example 1

Statement: "Loss of nail on a horseshoe results in an end of an empire."

A One missing nail damages a horseshoe.

B A damaged horseshoe causes a horse to be killed in a battle-field.

C A horse killed in a battlefield causes the death of a military general.

D The loss of a military general causes a war to fail.

E A failed war ends the whole empire.

F Therefore, one missing nail on a horseshoe could bring an empire to an end.

範例一

聲明：「丟失了一隻馬蹄上的釘子導致了一個帝國的結束。」

A 一個丟失的釘子，損失了一個馬蹄鞋。

B 損失了一個馬蹄鞋，損失了在戰場上一匹馬。

C 戰場上損失的一匹馬，導致一個將軍的死亡。

D 一個將軍的死亡，輸了一場戰爭。

E 輸了一場戰爭導致一個帝國的滅亡。

F 因此丟失了一隻馬蹄上的釘子可能結束了一個帝國。

Explanation

This is a very simple form of events in a cause and effect sequence, which begins as something trivial and ends as something important, to help the students to better understand. There is a connection between each sentence. The former is closely connected with the latter with an inference leading to the next sentence finally resulting in a possible outcome. Objects of the former sentence have turned to the subjects of the latter sentences with a verb linking the two, indicating their causal relationship. Each sentence shows how it affects the latter and how the latter is affected. All the sentences in the paragraph are linked, showing a clear cause and effect connection.

解釋

這是一個非常簡單的事件，依因果關係的順序來看，從不重要的開始到重要結尾，使得學生容易了解每一個句子之間都有聯繫。前者與後者緊密相連，以推論導致出下一句，最後達到可能的結局。前一個句子的受詞變成下一個句子的主詞，兩者以動詞連接，說明了它們的因果關係。每一個句子顯示出它如何影響下一個句子以及下一個句子如何受到影響，這一段落的所有句子都被聯繫起來，顯示了因果連結。

Example 2

Statement: “Staying humble can help us make progress.”

A Staying humble can help us heed some good advice.

B Good advice can help us to procure the necessary knowledge, skills and good attitude in life for the improvement of our weaknesses for a better future.

C The so-called progress has connoted an improvement for a better future.

D Since staying humble can improve our life for a better future and a better future is a form of progress, staying humble can help us make progress.

範例二

聲明：「保持謙卑能夠讓我們更進步。」

A 保持謙卑能夠讓我們注意到一些好的建議。

B 好的建議能幫助我們得到一些對於生活必要的知識技能與好的態度。

C 所謂的進步就已經意涵著改進，而且有著更好的未來。

D 既然保持謙卑可以改進我們生活有更好的未來，而更好的未來本身就是一種進步，所以保持謙卑可以讓我們更進步。

Explanation

The reasoning here requires an elaboration of "staying humble", leading into an inference on heeding advice and gaining knowledge which are helpful in making progress in our future. The whole paragraph shows a cause and effect connection by linking together all the sentences to explain how "staying humble" can reach the status of "making progress".

解釋

這裡的論證過程需要對於「保持謙卑」進行解釋，而這樣的論證引導出一個推論，也就是注意別人的建議並且取得知識，而這些可以幫助我們未來更進步。整個段落顯示出所有句子因果的聯繫，並且解釋了「保持謙卑」如何「進步」。

Example 3

Demonstration on forming a liability for a traffic violation case

If a woman runs through a red light and hits a pedestrian, we can conclude that she should be responsible for the injury caused. Now we have a fact that she ran through a red light and hit a pedestrian. How can we prepare a claim for her liability? "She is negligent." This statement is the conclusion. How was this conclusion reached (i.e. why is she negligent)? Of course, it is made in light of some facts, for example, she ran through a red light and hit a pedestrian. Probably it is better in this occasion to give a more complete picture by explaining that the driver's regulatory responsibility is to stop a car before a red light and she failed to do so. Besides, there is no other justification for her failure to do so (e.g. emergency).

範例三

交通違規案例責任的示範

如果一個女人闖了紅燈撞到了行人，我們應該下一個結論，她對所撞到的行人應該負責。現在我們有這樣的事實，她闖了紅燈撞了行人，我們要如何提出她應該負責任的理由呢？「她有過失」這句話是個結論，這句話如何達到的（爲什麼她有過失）？當然，這個結論是依據一些事實所做出來的，例如：她闖了紅燈撞了行人。可能在這種情形下給一個比較完整的說明解釋駕駛人法律上的責任，在紅燈前必須要把車停下來，但她並沒有做到這一點，此外，她沒有正當理由不能這麼做（例如：緊急事故）。

To put the whole description in a logical sequence in the reverse order starting from the conclusion:

She should be liable for the injury to the pedestrian (the conclusion).

She should be liable for the injury because she was negligent in causing this accident.

She was negligent in causing this accident because she failed to stop her car before a red light (a fact).

A driver should stop before a red light according to the traffic rules (regulation).

She violated the traffic rules and hit the pedestrian (causation, i.e. breach of a law resulting in an injury).

She therefore should be liable for the injury caused to the pedestrian.

把所有的描述，從結論按邏輯的順序倒推回去，會有以下的句子：

她應該對行人的受傷負責（一個結論）。

她應該對受傷負責，因爲她的過失造成了這個意外。

她的過失造成這個意外，因爲她沒有在紅燈之前停下車（一項事實）。

一個駕駛依照交通法規應該在紅燈之前把車停下來（法規）。

她違反交通法規撞到行人（因果關係，也就是違反法規撞到行人）。

因此她應該爲撞到行人負責。

Explanation

A similar approach is used. There is a link between consecutive sentences, showing a good cause and effect connection. The interchange between subjects and objects in consecutive sentences can be constantly seen. In an analysis, such causal link is very important. If a link is missing, there will be some difficulty in explaining the cause and effect relationship. It is like a chain with one ring well connected with the next in a good sequential order. Under this sequential order, an evaluation can be easily made to see if the information inserted is relevant or not and, if relevant, what is the role of this information that is placed in the whole cause and effect structure (e.g. its importance).

This negligence case shows a very simple form of a legal claim with both facts and law presented, together with the analysis ending in a conclusion. Facts must be relevant and material. The relevancy and materiality of evidence are decided by the legal rules. Legal rules, when applied to the facts, must be explained in an analysis, e.g. how the facts fit into the category of negligence. In a negligence torts case, the liability is found if four requirements are met:

- Ⓐ Duty of care: The driver is under a duty of care as a reasonable person in driving and he should exercise his care in following traffic rules such as watching pedestrians and stop lights.
- Ⓑ Breach of duty: The driver should stop her car when the stop light is on but she failed to do so resulting in her breach of duty.
- Ⓒ Injury or damages: The driver's failure to stop her car before the stop light results in hitting the pedestrian and causing injury.
- Ⓓ Causation: The accident would not have happened if the

driver did not fail to stop her car before the stop light. There is causation between the driver's violation of the traffic rule and the pedestrian's injury.

E No defense is raised by the driver: There is neither contributory negligence nor assumption of risk on part of the victim, etc.

Simply speaking, an analysis requires an explanation for the reason you said so. A student who is used to the instruction style often has a difficult time in explaining things. Generally speaking, following instructions is much easier than explaining and questioning things. This is a weakness in the college education in Taiwan. In a legal case where a rule is applied, you have to explain why the requirement is met by applying the rule to the facts. Analytical skills on explaining the reason is seldom practiced in Taiwan colleges. Explaining the reason is fundamental when training on the power of persuasion. A mere conclusion will not persuade.

This practice of analysis can also be applied to other civil cases including cases regarding a breach of contract whether on a domestic or an international level. Such skill is also very helpful in debating and negotiating.

解釋

這邊也使用類似的方法。上下兩個句子都有連結表示一個很好的因果關係。我們不斷看見在兩個句子主詞與受詞變化交換使用。在一個分析中，這樣的因果連結非常重要，如果連結斷掉的話，那將會不容易解釋因果關係。這就像一條鐵鍊。每一個環節跟另一個環節具有順序的連結著。在這樣的連結順序中，我們很容易判斷訊息是否相關，如果有關聯的話，整個的訊息是否在完整的因果關係一下進行排列整理。

這一個過失侵權案件，顯示出法律訴訟在事實、法律適用、分析還有結論的最簡單的形式。事實必須相關而且重要。而證據相關性和重要性是由法律的內容來決定。我們必須解釋法律的規則如何應用在事實上，例如所發生的事實爲何構成過失侵權。過失侵權法律的責任會產生，如果下面四個條件滿足的話：

A 注意的義務：這個駕駛人在開車的時候，有按照合理的人的標準行使注意的義務，遵守交通規則，例如注意行人以及紅燈停車。

B 違反注意的義務：駕駛人在紅燈亮起的時候應該停車，但是她沒停車導致了她違反她注意的義務。

C 人身或是財務的損害：駕駛人闖紅燈導致撞傷行人。

D 因果關係：如果駕駛人沒有闖紅燈，行人不至於受傷。駕駛人的闖紅燈與行人的受傷之間是有因果關係的。

E 駕駛人沒有抗辯的理由：這一部分是說受害人並沒有過失也沒有自願承擔危險等等。

簡單而言，所謂的分析就是要求解釋理由原因。一個習慣在課堂上只聽老師上課的學生，通常叫他解釋會有困難。一般來說，叫他單純的聽課要比叫他解釋或提問來得簡單得多。這也是臺灣大學教育的一項弱點。在一個法律案件中，法律適用就是你必須解釋爲什麼事實是符合法律的要件。解釋原因是訓練說服力最基本的訓練。我們沒有辦法只靠單純的結論去進行說服。

這樣分析的練習一樣可以適用在其他商務民事案件，包括違約的處理，不管是國內或是國際貿易層面。這一種思維的方式，對於談判或辯論極有幫助。

Example 4

Statement: "High school students in Taiwan should wear uniforms in school."

- A School is established for educating students and students attend school for learning.
- B Often a high school in Taiwan accommodates thousands of students with limited human resources apportioned among a great many of the faculty members and administrative employees.
- C Thousands of students require good management by the school on allocating a very limited amount of human resources to educate students and for the students' learning.
- D An outfit is a person's statement of style and status showing taste and family background, whether good or bad, rich or poor, which most likely causes some comparison among all the students between each other.
- E Some comparison among all the students will be especially escalated if casual wear were allowed because students may very well tend to appeal to their peers' attention on the superior quality and style of their outfits which may speak on their exquisite taste and wealthy background.

F Comparison regarding superior quality and exquisite taste require a great effort of time, attention and money for all the students which are unrelated to either the purpose of a school's education or students' learning while, at the same time, possibly inflict harm on the dignity of those students who are from poorer families. Casual wear therefore will bring an unnecessary burden to many students and thus bring some difficulties to the management of the school.

G A uniform means the same style and quality, very much indicating equality for all the students in terms of education and learning.

H A uniform means that no burden of comparison will be caused between the students among their outfits and a school therefore does not need to allocate limited human resources on the issues arising from the students' outfits but rather focus on the students' learning.

I Therefore, uniforms should be required in high schools in Taiwan.

範例四

聲明：「臺灣中學生應該在學校穿制服。」

A 中等學校的目的在於教育學生，而學生上學的目的在於學習。

B 在臺灣通常一個中等學校有好幾千名學生，而可以被教職員使用的資源是很有限的。

C 幾千名的學生需要學校在分配有限的資源於教育學生和學生學習上，要有良好的管理。

D 一個人的衣著是他的風格還有地位的聲明，顯示出他的品味與家庭背景，不管好或壞，富有或貧窮，都很容易造成學生之間的比較。

E 學生之間的比較會加劇，如果學生們可以穿便服的話，因為他們很可能傾向於以衣著的高尚品質風格，吸引同儕的注意，並且聲明他們的極佳品味以及富有的家庭背景達到比較的目的。

F 而衣著的高尚品質風格與學生極佳品味這一類的比較，需要學生們大量的時間和金錢，與學校教育或學生學習的目的沒有關聯，同時也對來自貧困家庭的學生自尊上造成傷害。穿便服因此會帶給很多學生不必要的負擔，因此也對學校管理造成一些困擾。

G 制服表示了相同的風格與品質，也大致上表達了在教育和學習上學生們平等的意味。

H 制服表示了一間學校不需要把有限的人力資源放在管理一些由於學生比較所產生的問題，而能夠更集中於學校的教育。

I 因此中學生應該穿制服。

Explanation

This is an advocacy which means that the position together with reasoning only speak for the one side. The first three points state the purpose of both the school's education and the students' learning followed by the limited resources requiring effective management of a school. Links from the fourth D to the F point are established on the relationship between the subjects and objects in a consecutive order of sentences with the verbs indicating the nature of their actions. Often, an object of the former sentence turns into a subject in the next sentence and thus forms the connection between the two consecutive sentences. Students must observe the causal connection between each sentence, the so-called analysis (i.e. reasoning process), which is very important in establishing both an argument and a writing in any persuasive style either in the academic or business world.

解釋

上面的說法是一種辯護式的說法，理由以及立場都只倒向一邊。前三點從學校教育的目的以及學生學習目的開始，接著說明是學校有限的資源是需要學校有效地管理。從第 D 點開始到第 F 點，每個依照順序所排列出來的句子，主詞與受詞之間靠著動詞進行聯繫說明了關係的本質。通常前依據的受詞變成下一句的主詞然後形成前後兩句的連結，學生必須注意到每一個句子的因果連結，也就是所謂的分析（論證過程），而分析對於建立辯證以及具有說服性的寫作是非常重要的，不論在學界或是商業界。

Aside from the above explanation on the cause and effect reasoning process of the sentences, it should be noted here that this paragraph is made in a form of an argument with quick reference to the background information (e.g. the purpose of education as well as the current situation in all schools such as limited resources) in order to present an issue for discussion. The background information is provided for better understanding of an issue and the reasoning process. It must be relevant and important in deciding on an issue in a case. Generally, a concise summary is enough for building up a framework. Details can be provided at a subsequent stage.

除了上面關於句子方面因果論證的解釋之外，也須注意到這一示範是以辯論的方式提出，並且大略提及背景資訊（例如學校教育目的還有目前學校有限資源的現況）以便提出爭議點。背景資訊的提出讓我們更了解爭議以及論證過程。它必須是相關而且對於決定爭議是很重要的。通常在建立架構的時候，摘要概述是足夠的，細節總是可以在之後的步驟補上。

As stated in the preceding paragraph, an argument involves a proposition and an examination of the opposite argument. Such training on a cause and an effect analysis is effective and efficient in preparing a proposition for an argument and making an evaluation of arguments presented by the opposite side. Under a cause and effect analysis, the connection between all sentences and ideas are linked in a logical sequence as rings in a chain. They must be well connected with each other. One missing ring can break the whole chain. By applying this analysis, a debater will quickly notice the weak link in his argument and will be able to mend his weakness in time. By examining the opposite argument, using the same analysis, any weakness regarding factual relevancy and logical connection can be quickly exposed as well.

就像先前的說明，一個辯詞包括提案以及對於反方說法的檢驗。這種因果關係分析的訓練是在於提出辯詞以及檢驗反方說法的評斷上非常有效率。在一個因果關係的分析中，所有句子與想法的連結是像鐵鏈的環扣以邏輯的順序接連起來的，彼此之間必須做好強而有力的連結，失去了一個環扣會使整個鏈條斷裂。使用這種分析的方式，一個辯論者可以很快地發現他辯詞當中薄弱的連結，因此能夠及時修正他的缺點。而依靠這種方法來檢驗對手的證詞，對方所提的事實是否相關以及邏輯上的缺點也會很快地顯現出來。

Example 5

"Be slow to fall into friendship, but when you are in, continue firm and constant."

—Socrates

A A firm and constant friendship requires good trust.

B Good trust can be established by good understanding.

C Good understanding of each other requires a long time.

D It requires a long time because two persons as strangers in the beginning are probably from different backgrounds with different personalities and values.

E To form trust with understanding and the acceptance of each other's differences takes more time.

F Once trust is formed, friendship is established upon understanding each other and the acceptance of differences and is therefore real and firm.

G A real and firm friendship with trust and understanding is therefore rare as a diamond found among rocks.

H Therefore, such precious trust should be constantly continued in and stayed in.

範例五

「不要太快建立友誼，但是當你建立起友誼的時候，應該堅定而且持久。」

——蘇格拉底

A 一個堅定而且持續的友誼需要良好的信任。

B 良好的信任是建立在適當的了解上。

C 彼此之間適當的了解需要長時間。

D 彼此之間良好的了解需要長時間，因爲兩個人在一開始的時候可能是來自於不同背景的陌生人，有著不同個性及價值觀。

E 基於了解以及接受不同之處進而形成的信任，是需要花時間的。

F 信任一旦建立，友誼是建立在互相了解並且對於差異性的接受，因此是眞實而且堅定的。

G 一個基於信任與了解因而眞實與堅定的友誼，就像在岩石當中的鑽石一樣的稀少。

H 因此，這樣珍貴的信賴應該繼續下去。

This is a reasoning process with a cause and effect connection applied. The sentences in the main part are connected together with an explanation to show how they affect each other and finally lead to the conclusion.

這個是應用因果連結的論理過程，主要部分的每一個句子互相連結，而且解釋了他們如何影響彼此的結論。

Example 6

"The only true wisdom is in knowing you know nothing."
—Socrates

- A Wisdom is defined in the Merriam-Webster dictionary as "knowledge that is gained by having many experiences in life".
- B To claim that we learn by experiences is to admit that we learn by mistakes.
- C To claim that we learn by mistakes is to admit that we gain knowledge from mistakes we make.
- D To gain knowledge from mistakes means that we have to recognize mistakes we make.
- E To recognize the mistakes we make is to stay humble.
- F Therefore, when we stay humble, we learn new knowledge and that is wisdom.
- G To claim to know something is to claim that no mistakes were made on something that we know.
- H Such arrogance will deny learning of new knowledge.
- I To deny learning new knowledge is to deny wisdom.

For this reason, a person should always stay humble and claim that he knows nothing in order to learn wisdom.

範例六

「眞正的智慧在於承認無知。」

——蘇格拉底

A 在 Merriam-Webster 字典中，智慧被定義爲生活當中許多經驗所得到的知識。

B 聲稱我們從經驗中學習就等於承認了我們從錯誤中學習。

C 聲稱我們從錯誤當中學習，就等於承認了我們從錯誤中得到知識。

D 從錯誤當中得到知識說明了我們承認所犯的錯誤。

E 承認我們所犯的錯誤就是保持謙卑。

F 因此，當我們保持謙卑，我們學習新的知識，那也就是智慧。

G 聲稱我們知道一些事情，就是聲明在我們所知道的事情上不會犯錯誤。

H 如此高傲的態度會否決學習新的知識。

I 否決學習新的知識就等於否決新的機會。

爲了這個原因，一個人必須保持謙卑，而且聲明他是無知的，這樣可以學習智慧。

Example 7

Statement: Democracy by the majority is not the best political governing mechanism to observe people's interest in terms of efficiency and effectiveness.

Ⓐ The democracy by a majority vote in the current world is represented in the form of "one person, one vote".

Ⓑ The notion of "one person, one vote" connotes the idea of equality, a very symbol of individualism.

Ⓒ The government is organized for the interest of the people.

Ⓓ Serving the best interest of the people requires officials with good character, integrity, intelligence, and solid training together with useful experiences which demand a long time of nurture and observation followed by a strict screening process.

Ⓔ A vote by the majority does not guarantee the selection of such talents for management.

Ⓕ A vote by the majority does not guarantee the selection of such talents for management because a person who is elected under a democracy only represents a fact that he has procured the consent from the majority of the governed who vote, partial of the common public.

Ⓖ Voters who give consent, due to their variance on intelligence, education, training, interest and experiences, does not necessarily know how their best interest as a whole can be served. (e.g. how to lay the foundation and governing form for a nation and how to build long term prosperity).

Ⓗ The voters' limitations are probably caused due to their lack of perception to the social issues and ability to discern the qualification of the candidates required for the positions.

Populism is good evidence as a product from recent democracies.

I As Socrates has put it, a vessel engaged in a sea voyage needs a captain with good knowledge and experience on sea-faring. A captain with neither such knowledge nor experience cannot manage the task of managing a boat on sea.

J Administration is a mechanism similar to a vessel engaged in a sea voyage, requiring a knowledgeable and experienced captain to manage the vessel.

K A knowledgeable and experienced government management can surely be selected through some other screening mechanism under a long term of nurture, observation, tests of their character, integrity, intelligence, solid training and useful experiences necessary to carry out their responsibility.

L The current democracy in the world under equality only sanctifies the consent of the governed and it does not have a screening process to monitor the selection of suitable candidates for their position.

M Besides, according to Socrates, democracy is a perfect system only for a perfect people and we are not perfect.

N Therefore, democracy by the majority is not the best political governing mechanism in terms of efficiency and effectiveness.

範例七

聲明：以效率和效能來說，民主的多數決並不是保護人民利益最好的政府管理方式。

A 現今世界上民主多數決，表現出來就是一人一票的方式。

B 一人一票的概念，指出了平等的觀念，個人主義的基本標誌。

C 政府是為了人民的利益而組織的。

D 要能夠服務人民最佳的利益，就必須有具有道德品行、頭腦、能力、良好訓練以及有用經驗的政府官員，而這需要長期的培養與觀察以及嚴格挑選的程序。

E 多數決的投票並不保證能夠選出這樣有才能的官員進行管理。

F 多數決的投票並不保證能夠選出有才能的官員進行管理，是因為一個民主制度所選出的人，只表示他取得有投票權的被統治者的同意，也就是部分的公民。

G 投票表示同意的公眾有可能受限於腦力、知識、教育、訓練、利益和經驗，並不必然知道如何可以達到他們全體的最佳利益，例如，國家應該建立在什麼樣的基礎之上，有什麼樣的制度以及如何建立起長期的繁榮。

H 這種受限可能是由於他們並沒有對社會議題深刻的了解，也不具有認知哪些候選人能夠具有勝任他們職位的能力。民粹主義就是最近民主制度的負面產物的證據。

I 就像蘇格拉底所舉的例子，航行在海上的船隻需要一個具有航海知識與經驗的船長。不具有這樣知識與經驗，是無法操控一條在海上航行的船隻。

J 政府的管理就跟海上航行船隻的操控一樣，需要有知識與經驗的船長掌控。

K 我們透過一些長時間的培養、觀察的考核機制，審核道德品行、頭腦、能力、充足訓練以及有用經驗的累積，可以確定選出具有知識和經驗的政府領導階層，確保他們能夠執行責任。

L 現今世界上的民主制度只看重於被統治者的同意，並沒有一個嚴格的篩檢機制來監控候選人是否適合該項職務。

M 再者，蘇格拉底也提到民主制度，只有對完美的人來說是一個完美的制度，而我們並不完美。

N 因此，以效率和效能來說，民主的多數決並不是最好的政府管理方式。

The above is only a demonstration of reasons made in a logical sequence (cause and effect structure) to support the statement that democracy is not the best governing mechanism in terms of effectiveness and efficiency. The whole purpose is on persuasion. Readers must bear in mind that even a statement may withstand all challenges and sound quite persuasive, such persuasiveness does not guarantee the truth. By applying the same reasoning principle, students may try to write reasons in a logical sequence in support of a proposition as to why democracy should be respected and adopted as a typical form of a government.

上面的例子，是將理由以邏輯的方式排列（因果關係的架構），用以主張民主以效能而言的話，並不是最好的政治機制。整個的目的是在說服。讀者必須要記得，縱使一個說法可以抵抗所有的挑戰，而且聽起來很有說服力，但這樣的說服性並不保證這個說法一定是對的。學生們也可以使用上面的論理原則，嘗試以邏輯的方式寫出理由來支持爲什麼民主應該被尊重而且被採納，當作一般政府的型態。

A counter argument may claim that democracy is the most effective and efficient in governing because it provides the stability to the whole political and social system as compared to those in an oligarchy system and that autocracy is generally susceptible to control of the limited few with absolute power leading to absolute corruption. Once corruption happens and grows into a calamity beyond control, a revolution is likely to happen and all stability will be lost. When stability is lost, there won't be any so-called effectiveness and efficiency. Therefore, check and balance is required. Separation of powers as seen in the U.S. Constitution is the architype of modern constitutions and can work well in curbing expansion of governmental powers in the executive, legislative and judicial branches so as to prevent corruption. Therefore, democracy is the best political system in guaranteeing effectiveness and efficiency on a long term basis.

我們也可以提出另外一方面的說法，來聲稱民主在管理上是最有效率和效能的方法，因爲民主制度相對於少數人所把持，容易產生絕對腐敗的專制制度，比較上對整個政治與社會系統提供了穩定性。一旦發生腐敗而且蔓延成爲不受控制的災難，就容易產生革命，因此失去穩定。一旦失去穩定性，就不會有所謂的效率和效能。因此權力制衡是需要的，在美國憲法裡面的三權分立，就是現代憲法的主要型態，而且在控制政府於立法、司法、行政的濫權用以防止腐敗有相當的效率。因此，民主制度在保障效率和效能上，是最好的政治制度。

The above arguments from both sides have reasons to support their positions and are all evaluated under the same standard, that is, effectiveness and efficiency. Readers must remember that a counter argument could adopt a different standard and thus change the conclusion. If we shift the standard from effectiveness and efficiency to an individual's choice and dignity, the conclusion will be different.

兩邊的說法都有支持的理由，而且都在相同的標準下進行判斷，也就是效率和效能。讀者們必須記得反對的一方可以採取不同的標準，因此改變結論。如果我們將標準從效率和效能改成個人的選擇和尊嚴，結論也會因此不同。

If we apply a different standard in the interpretation of democracy, we will see a different conclusion as shown from the following example.

Democracy is still regarded by the western world as the best form of government. The reason is simple. Western philosophy is mainly based on individualism which is deeply inculcated in the minds of all westerners. Individualism is also closely associated with some social issues such as homosexual marriages, abolition of capital punishment, abortions, freedom to bear arms, the right against illegal search and seizure, even including the theory regarding the fruit of a poisonous tree (i.e. evidence from an illegal search cannot be used in courts), etc. Individualism is to a great extent related to the respect granted to a choice by an individual. Under a society formed under collectivism, personal choice or interest must yield to public order, safety or interest. As mentioned in the earlier section, the same fact if evaluated under a different standard will lead to a different conclusion. It is the standard applied that decides the conclusion. Once a standard changes from the consideration on effectiveness and efficiency to respect granted to an individual's choice, then the whole conclusion changes. Democracy will surely become the best system under individualism if it were made as the standard for evaluation. Why one standard should be preferred over the other in application is a question that takes into account many considerations regarding the social, historical and cultural perspectives. In many cases, it is based on the consideration of interest. There is no absolute answer to some social issue as appears in the above. However, what is always required in the matter of persuasiveness is a demand for good reasoning to effectively persuade.

我們如果以不同的標準進行詮釋民主制度，那就會產生不同的評論結果，就像下面的例子一樣。

民主制度依然被西方世界認爲是最好的政治制度。理由很簡單，西方哲學主要建立在深植西方人內心的個人主義，個人主義與一些社會議題密切相關，例如：同性戀婚姻、廢除死刑、墮胎、擁有槍枝、免於非法搜索和逮捕的權利，甚至包括毒果樹理論（也就是非法調查證據不可以作爲呈堂證供）等等。個人主義在很大的範圍內與對個人的選擇尊重有關。在集體主義的社會，個人的選擇或利益必須在公共秩序安全和利益之下。如同前述，同樣的事實在不同標準之下會有不同結論。所適用的標準會決定結論。一旦標準從效率和效能改變成爲對個人選擇的尊重，整個的結論就會改變。民主制度依照個人主義，如果個人主義是評斷的標準的話，當然會變成最好的制度。爲什麼一個標準在適用上應該優於另一個標準？是有很多在社會、歷史文化方面的考量。在很多情況下是基於利益的考量，對於上述的一些社會議題並沒有決定的結論，但是在說服力這件事情上面，我們確定需要的是好的論理能力。

Example 8

Statement: Human evolutionism regarding the explanation on the existence of life is not true.

A It is a generally accepted scientific conclusion that in a material world, a nothing cannot be brought into existence. No one including any scientist can ever provide any conclusive evidence that nothing can produce something into existence.

B Life in this world is something already in existence and is full of various forms.

C Something in existence cannot be brought from nothing, as a scientific conclusion has indicated.

D A life therefore cannot be brought into existence from nothing.

E Evolutionists claim that life can be brought into existence from nothing.

F Therefore, evolutionism regarding the existence of life brought from nothing is not true.

範例八

聲明：進化論主義關於生命的存在，是不正確的。

A 這是舉世所接受的科學定律，在物質世界中，是不可能無中生有的。任何人包括任何的科學家都不可能提出具有任何結論性的證據，證明物質能無中生有。

B 世界上的生命已經存在而且具有各種形式。

C 已經存在的物質是不可能無中生有的，這是科學的定律。

D 生命因此不可能是無中生有。

E 進化論者聲稱生命可以無中生有。

F 因此進化論主義關於生命的存在，是從無中生有是不正確的。

The whole reasoning is structured under a syllogism, for example, all men are mortal, Socrates is a man so Socrates is mortal. The whole argument is made against evolutionism upon one premise as the standard, that is, existence of something cannot be brought from nothing. In fact, current science cannot produce any evidence that nothing can be made into existence by any scientific means, not to mention life. In other words, life could be brought from nothing is only an assumption, a bold scientific proposition, so to speak. A very similar approach can be applied to a discussion on the existence of rationality.

本題全部的論證過程是建立在三段式論法之上，例如：所有的人都必死，蘇格拉底是人，所以蘇格拉底必死。所有關於反對進化論的論證是建立在以一個標準爲前提，也就是說，任何事物的存在不可能從無到有。事實上，現在的科學沒有辦法提出任何證據可以以任何科學的方式無中生有，更不要說生命。換句話說，從無到有只是一個假設，一個大膽的科學提案。同樣的論證方式也可以應用討論在人類理性的存在。

Example 9

The past has passed and therefore there is nothing but bygone times. This is a fact. The future has not come and is not in existence either. This is also a fact. Since both the past and the future do not exist, therefore there is no such existence of them in the NOW.

A The statement that the past has passed and therefore the past does not exist is made on the premise of the existence of the current time.

B The statement that the future has not come and therefore is not in existence either is made again on the premise of the existence of the current time as well.

C Both statements are made on the premise of the existence of the current time.

D Therefore, the existence of the current time has not been denied by the non-existence of both the past and the future.

範例九

過去已經過去，因此並不存在，這是事實；未來還沒有來臨，因此未來也不存在，這也是事實。既然過去跟未來都不存在，所以現在也不存在。

A 過去已經過去，因此過去不存在這樣的說法，是建立在現在存在的前提之上。

B 未來還沒有來臨因此並不存在，這個說法再一次也是建立在現在存在的前提之上。

C 這兩個說法都是建立在現在存在的前提之上。

D 因此，過去與未來都不存在的事實，並未推翻現在的存在的事實。

If the past and the future do not exist, how can the current time exist? The conclusion reached seems quite persuasive and difficult to rebut. The flaw lies on the assumption which is implied in the statement to be examined. In fact, the non-existence of both past and future is premised the existence of the present time, which is implicit in the time sequence in this example. Readers must remember that evaluation is made under a standard and a standard often is created under certain assumptions.

如果過去和未來都不存在，那現在如何存在？這樣的結論看起來很有說服力而且很難反駁。這說法的缺點就在於假設，而這個假設是隱藏在要受檢驗的說法裡面。事實上，過去和未來都不存在的說法，是建立在現在存在的前提上，而這個前提是隱藏在本題的時間順序內。讀者必須記得，任何一個判斷都是基於某個標準，而這個標準常常是基於某種假設而創造出來的。

Example 10

If God is perfect, why do we still have so many tragedies and disasters in this world?

A In the book of Genesis, God created the whole universe within seven days.

B On the seventh day, God finished the work he had done and he rested on the seventh day from the work he had done. So God blessed the seventh day and hallowed it because on it God rested from all his work which he had done in creation.

C God created light and separated light from darkness on day one.

D God created light again on day four, sun in the day and moon in the night. Day and night formed a day of 24 hours that we know now.

E Obviously, light referred to in the beginning is not the light emitted from the sun and the moon which were created on the fourth day.

F In other words, the seven days in which God created the whole universe including all creatures probably were not seven days of 168 hours under the standard day of 24 hours. The day of light and darkness from day one to day seven probably refers to a regular cycle from creation and chaos, rather than 24 hours a day by sun and moon.

G On the sixth day, God created Adam and Eve. And the Lord God commanded the man, saying, "You may freely eat of every tree of the garden; but of the tree of knowledge of good and evil you shall not eat, for in the day that you eat of it you shall die."

H As mentioned above, seven days of creation does not mean a day of 24 hours but God's cycle from light to darkness.

I Therefore, when God told the man that he should die on the six day if he ate the fruit, it did not mean that the man should die within the sixth day measured from the 121st hour and 144th hour since the beginning of creation. Rather, it means that the day cycle from light to darkness.

J Jesus in his defense on working on the Sabbath said to the Jews, "My Father is always at his work to this very day, and I too am working." (John 5:17) Obviously, God and Jesus had not stopped working since the very beginning of creation.

K In light of the reference to Genesis on the seventh day, God finished the work he had done and he rested on the seventh day from the work he had done. This could mean that the seventh day has not come yet because Jesus said that God and he have not stopped working.

L Therefore, do not let anyone judge you by what you eat or drink, or with regard to a religious festival, a New Moon celebration or a Sabbath day. These are a shadow of the things that were to come; the reality, however, is found in Christ. (Colossians 2:16-17) In reference to these two verses, some figures and events in the Old Testament are the foreshadowing of the New Testament.

M The Lamb in the Old Testament foreshadows Jesus.

N In Genesis, Adams and Eve committed sin in the Garden of Eden and were clothed with garments of skin to hide their shame. Skin from animals is perishable, therefore high priests in the Old Testament gave sacrifice for the Jews regularly so that their sins could be forgiven.

O In the New Testament, Jesus gave himself as the sacrifice once and for all. Christians will be clothed with a garment washed in white by the blood of the Lamb referring to Jesus as the sacrifice and their sins could be forgiven forever.

P The events and figures in the Old Testament are only foreshadows of what came in the New Testament.

Q The seventh day for God's resting his work has not come. We are in the night of darkness of the sixth day.

R The whole testament, both old and new, tells the story about man from the beginning of sin and ending with the perfection of the Kingdom of God.

S Therefore, the answer to the question that "If God is perfect, why do we still have so many tragedies and disasters in this world?" is that, we have not entered the seventh day of the true Sabbath for a complete rest. We are still in the process of perfecting ourselves till the seventh day comes.

範例十

如果上帝是完美的，爲什麼在這個世界上我們還有這麼多的悲劇和災難？

A 在創世紀，上帝在七天之內創造了整個宇宙。

B 在第七天，上帝完成了他的工作而且歇了他的工。上帝祝福了第七天而且使它爲聖，因爲在第七天上帝歇了他所有創造的工作。

C 上帝在第一天創造了光明，而且將光明與黑暗分開。

D 上帝在第四天又創造了光，白天的太陽和晚上的月亮。白天和晚上構成了我們所知道的一天 24 小時。

E 很明顯的，一開始所提到的光明並不是指第四天太陽所發出的光。

F 換句話說，上帝在七天之內創造了整個宇宙包括所有的生物，並不是說以一天 24 小時爲單位的七天 168 小時。第一天的光明與黑暗可能是說經常性創造與混亂的循環，而不是由白天太陽和晚上的月亮所構成的一天 24 小時。

G 在第六天，上帝創造了亞當和夏娃。上帝告訴這個人：「你可以吃花園裡面所有的果子，除了能夠分辨善惡的知識果子你不可以吃，因爲你吃的那一天你就會死亡。」

H 就像前面所說的，七天的創造並不是說一天 24 小時，而是指上帝從光明到黑暗的循環。

I 因此，當上帝告訴那個人，你會在吃果子的當天死亡（如果是第六天他吃了果子的話）所謂的當天那並不是說那個人必須在從創造起算的第 121 小時至第 144 小時內死亡。而是指從光明到黑暗第六天的循環的時間。

J 耶穌在爲安息日工作所做的辯護，告訴那些猶太人：「我的父親一直到今天都在工作，而我也在工作。」（約翰福音五章 17 節）。很顯然的，上帝和耶穌從創造的那一天起，一直都沒有停止工作。

K 在創世紀，上帝完成他所做的工作而且在第七天歇了他的工，這可能表示第七天還沒有來臨，因爲耶穌說上帝和他到現在並沒有停止工作。

L 所以，不拘在飲食上，或節期、月朔、安息日都不可讓人論斷你們。這些原是後事的影兒；那形體卻是基督。（歌羅西書二章 16-17 節）參考這兩段經文，舊約聖經的一些人物和事件是新約聖經的預兆。

M 舊約裡面所提到的羔羊就是指耶穌。

N 在創世紀，亞當和夏娃在伊甸園犯罪之後穿著獸皮的衣服遮蓋他們的羞恥。獸皮是會毀壞的，因此在舊約的大祭司必須爲猶太人不斷地獻祭，這樣他們的罪才能得到赦免。

O 在新約聖經，耶穌一次獻上自己，基督徒穿上了羔羊的血所洗淨的白袍。羔羊也就是耶穌，還有那些基督徒他們的罪可以永遠得到赦免。

P 在舊約的事件和人物都只是在新約聖經裡即將來臨的事情和人物的縮影。

Q 上帝在第七天歇了他的工的日子一直還沒有來臨，當今的我們正在第六天黑暗裡等待第七天的來臨。

R 所有的新約和舊約聖經談論的是，人的故事從一開始的犯罪到最後上帝完美國度的降臨。

S 「如果上帝是完美的，爲什麼在這個世界上我們還有這麼多的悲劇和災難？」因此這個問題的答案，也就是我們還沒有進入到第七天安息日達到完全的安息。我們還在將我們自己變得更完美的過程當中，一直到第七日眞正安息日的降臨。

The whole reasoning here is divided into four stages. Firstly, a distinction is drawn on the definition between "light and darkness" as a cycle of indefinite time and "day and night" as 24 hours since the sun was created in the fourth day. Secondly, the sixth day that Adam should die therefore is NOT interpreted in a literary meaning from 121st hour to 144th hour since the day one of the creation but in a perspective referring "light and darkness" as the sixth cycle. Thirdly, by the words from Jesus that God is still at His work, we know that we have not entered the seventh day, the true Sabbath. Fourthly, we may conclude that we are still in the sixth day through a perfecting process.

整個的論理過程分成四個階段。第一個階段，先指出定義上的差別，以太陽是第四天才創造，所謂 24 小時的「白天與黑夜」，有別於創造初始所謂「光明與黑暗」，不確定時間循環的一天。第二階段，亞當在第六天必須死亡，因此不應該就字面上解釋，在創造始初的第 121 小時到 144 小時之間，而應該是「光明與黑暗」第六個循環的角度來詮釋。第三個階段，耶穌曾經說過「我的父親到現在還在工作」，我們因此知道我們尚未進入到第七天安息日。第四個階段，我們因此能夠做出我們依舊仍在第六個循環「光明與黑暗」第六天的結論。

The above examples show how sentences and paragraphs are formed and connected under a cause and effect sequence. By such approach, we can easily find out which part, whether factual or from reasoning, is relevant and decisive, and has not, but should be, filed in this logical sequence. We are also able to tell the degree of the importance and relevancy of a fact or a reason already shown in our argument as well as that in the opponent's. Such approach is REQUIRED OF a lawyer to examine the sufficiency and relevancy of facts, determine the weight of evidence, establish his argument, and study the rebuttal of his opponent, followed by his preparation for a counter argument.

上面的一些例子，顯示了句子以及段落在因果聯繫上，它們如何組成與銜接。這樣的方法我們可以很輕易地找到哪些並沒有顯示出來但卻應該顯示出來的事實或理由。我們也能夠判斷在我們或是對手的說辭上所談到的事實或是理由的重要程度與關聯性。這是每一個律師所必備的能力，用來檢驗事實是否有足夠完整性與關聯性，也決定證據的重要程度，並建立他的說詞以及檢查對方的說法並進而準備他的反駁。

As some readers have noticed, these paragraphs have contained issues raised from topics discussed. Examination and discussion of the issues spotted will establish a framework on which arguments can be made and arranged in a logical sequence. The ability to spot an issue is essential whether in a debate or negotiation and therefore is crucial on building up the power of persuasion.

Remember, a framework can only be constructed with prepared arguments when issues are found.

有一些讀者可能已經注意到這些段落包含了一些爭議點。檢驗以及討論這一些爭議點可以建立一個架構，在架構上可以用邏輯順序準備以及安排說詞。找到爭議點的能力，不論在辯論或是談判是極爲必須的能力，因此在建立說服力上，必須具有迅速找到爭議點的能力。

要記得，一定要先找到爭議點才能建立整體的架構以及準備好辯詞。

6 Issue and a focal point

Each example from the above shows a reasoning process underlying a persuasive proposition through forming connections between sentences. In fact, prior to the establishing of such a connection, there is an issue (if there are arguments on two opposite views) or a focal point (if there is only a statement) on each example, that must be spotted, whether explicit or implicit, and this issue will subsequently lead into a decisive adopted standard in the outcome of each question. For instance, in example four regarding school uniforms, the issue spotted in the reasoning aspect was the insufficiency of human resources for the educational and learning purposes related to the management of a school (an undue burden to the school). All reasons in example four that are given in support of the proposition are centered on the issue leading to establish as a standard the "wise allocation of the limited resources for the educational and learning purposes". That means, before any analysis can be made, the issue must be ascertained. In a debate, each issue demands an analysis covering the pros and cons.

6 爭議點與中心點

上面的例子顯示出透過建立句子之間的聯繫，形成論證的過程，進而達到具有說服力的提議。事實上，在建立這樣的聯繫之前，每一個例子都有一個爭議點（如果有二種不同看法的爭議）和中心點（如果只有一句話），不管是明示性或暗示性的，我們都必須將它們找到，而這些爭議點會引導出一個所採用的標準，用來決定每一個問題的結果。例如在第四個關於學校制服的例子，在論證過程中所找到的爭議點，是學校在教育與學生學習管理方面人力資源的不足（對於學校過大的負擔）。在第四個例子所有支持提案的理由都與這個爭議有關，進而引導出建立的標準，也就是：「爲了教育與學習的目的，應該善用有限的資源」。這說明了在一個分析之前，爭議必須先被確認，在辯論當中，每一個爭議點都要求包括正反兩方面的分析。

In example three regarding the car accident, the issue is on the driver's negligence (no negligence, no liability) and the claim on negligence is supported by the reasons given. In example two, the key point presented is to have a better future as a common feature to connect the reasons provided. In example one regarding a horse shoe, a very basic consecutive reasoning step was applied. The focal point implied is that one careless mistake can cost us way beyond our imagination. Without such an issue or focal point, inference cannot be established. Such a focal point must be decided on before an inference can be made. To sum up, an argument should contain at least two fundamental parts, the issue and reasoning (analysis or inference) aspects. The issue should be ascertained before any analysis can be made.

在第三個車禍的例子，爭議點是在於駕駛者的過失（沒有過失就沒有責任），並且過失的主張透過理由進行分析獲得支撐。在第二個例子中關於保持謙卑能幫助進步，所提出的中心點就是以光明的未來為共通點進行連結。在第一個關於馬蹄的例子，這是最典型的逐步推論過程。中心點是暗示的，一個不小心的錯誤所付出的代價可能超乎我們想像。沒有這樣的爭議點或中心點，推論可能沒辦法被建立。我們必須先確認中心點才能進行推論。簡單來說，一個爭辯當中必須包含至少兩個主要部分：爭議與論理步驟（分析或推論）。在任何分析或推論進行之前必須先找出爭議點。

Example 5 was a statement made by Socrates regarding friendship. Our task is to build a bridge to connect the beginning and the end through inferences. The focal point here in this analysis is a matter of trust and a trust takes a long time to be built. Once trust as a focal point is ascertained, we can reasonably infer that a long time is necessary and such trust, if ever procured, is precious as a diamond and of course should be cherished and kept for a long time. In other words, trust as a focal point may bring up all these inference in the reasoning aspect. Of course, there are many other bridges that could lead to the conclusion. This reasoning aspect only serves as one of many possible connections.

第五個例子是蘇格拉底所說關於友誼的話。我們的工作在於透過推論建立橋梁連接頭尾。在這個分析的中心點是信任，而信任需要長時間才能建立。一旦確認信任是中心點，我們可以合理的推論長時間是需要的，而且一旦信任可以被取得，像是鑽石一樣珍貴，應該被珍惜並且長時間保存。換句話說，以信任當作中心點可以帶來論證過程中的所有推論，當然也可以有其他橋梁能夠達到這樣結論，這邊的論證只是許多可能連結之一而已。

Example 6, again, is a statement from Socrates. The dictionary is referred to for the definition of wisdom. The key part in the definition for our use for inference is “the knowledge gained from experiences”. Therefore, the inference can start from either knowledge or experience. The terms experience and knowledge, when connected together, implies making mistakes. Everyone makes mistakes, the only difference is that some accept and learn while some stubbornly refuse. The former reveals wisdom while the latter, ignorance.

第六個例子又是蘇格拉底所說的話：「眞正的智慧在於承認無知。」我們使用的字典找出了智慧的定義，而定義中主要的部分是「從經驗當中所學到的知識」。因此，我們可以從知識或是經驗進行推論。而經驗與知識這兩個字眼隱含著犯錯的意思。每個人都會犯錯，差別只是在於有的人承認，有的人頑固的否認。前者顯示出智慧，而後者則顯示了愚蠢無知。

In an argument, challenges are expected. For this reason, each sentence in the reasoning process should be made logically with a link established to show the cause and effect connection as a well-connected chain involving all the inferences. Oriental students generally are weak in making such an analysis. Such reasoning process is very similar to any mathematical proof process. Each step should be reasonably made with a causal link to the next step, as a mathematical proof process that we learned from high school. The familiarity with such approach will help students to form a strict logical reasoning ability to establish their argument, defend their position, and examine the veracity of the opposite argument. Remember that it is through the reasoning process rather than the conclusion that the audience is persuaded.

在一個辯論中，對手的挑戰是可以被預期的。爲了這個理由，論證當中的每一個句子，應該很有邏輯的鎖鏈連結起來，以顯示出推論之間的因果聯繫。東方學生這樣的分析能力通常比較不足。這樣的論證過程非常接近於數學的證明題，每一個步驟都應該合理的與下個步驟有因果聯繫，就像高中所學到的數學證明題一樣。對於這種方法的熟悉，會幫助學生建立邏輯能力，進而建立他們的辯詞，防禦他們的立場，以及檢驗對手說法的合理性。要記得，說服靠的是論理過程，不是結論。

7 Examination of an Argument:

In the preceding section, we have discussed an application of cause and effect in a sentence, consecutive sentences, and a framework of an argument. All the ideas in the sentences should be connected under a cause and effect framework. Such analysis can only proceed when an issue or a focal point is established. Now we can also apply the same approach in examining the argument proposed by our opponent.

7 對於辯詞的檢驗

在前一個段落，我們已經討論了把因果關係應用在單一句子、連續的句子，以及整個辯詞的架構。句子之間所有的想法應該以因果關係聯繫起來。這樣的分析只有在爭議點或中心點被建立起來的時候才能進行，現在，我們能夠使用同一個方法來檢驗對手的辯詞。

To examine an argument, the first attention should be given to a conclusion. Conclusion shows the position taken and is important especially when an argument is crammed with much information followed by either complicated or lengthy reasons, which can easily confound the readers, ending with misunderstandings. Bear in mind that all reasoning including the analysis and inference direct where the conclusion goes.

檢驗一項辯詞首先要注意一下結論。結論顯示出所持有的立場，而且很重要，特別是當辯詞充滿了訊息，而論理過程冗長又極其複雜，使得讀者充滿疑惑甚至誤解。要記得所有的論理中的分析與推論都朝向著結論而寫。

Then we need to analyze the reasoning process by which the conclusion is reached. Try to put all the ideas into a logical sequence to see if they flow as the aforementioned demonstrates. Are the ideas in each consecutive sentence well connected in a logical sequence? Are all the rings logically connected without any lapses between them? What is the focal point or the issue found in this flow of inferences on which reasoning is being centered? The focal point is important because all reasoning given is centered on either the focal point or an issue. Once either a focal point or an issue can be established, the whole framework of an argument and a defense can be built. A correct spotting of an issue in an argument generally requires a good perception of the argument on both sides. A focal point or an issue, once pinpointed, will lead to establishing the standard to apply. In that case, an adoption of a standard is generally a matter of choice. The solving of an issue requires a standard. Therefore, a standard must be adopted to include all judgments mentioned or an evaluation cannot be made. The issue is closely connected to a standard. Once a standard is found, then ask yourself how are the ideas under that specific standard connected to support the focal point. Each sentence is a statement and it should make sense. Any good reasoning is like rings in a chain that are well connected without any lapses between them. Therefore, a careful examination directed at the formation of the connections between each sentence could reveal possible flaws in an argument.

接著，我們要分析達到結論的論理過程。請試圖把所闡述的想法，依邏輯順序展示出來，用以觀察它的演進過程，就像前面那些例子一樣。每一個上下的句子的想法是不是都以邏輯上的因果連接呢？所有的環節都具有邏輯的連接性而沒中斷嗎？在這個推論過程中，什麼是論證的爭議點或中心點？中心點很重要，因爲所有的論證過程是集中於所有的爭議點或中心點，一旦能夠建立中心點或爭議點，整個辯論或是防衛的架構就得以因此而建立。在辯詞中找出爭議點通常表示對於雙方辯詞的深刻了解。一旦被找出來中心點或爭議點，就能導致標準的建立。那樣情況之下，標準的建立和採用只是選擇的問題而已。解決一項爭議需要一個標準，因此在所有的判斷中都會有使用的標準，要不然是無法進行評斷的。爭議點與標準有密切的關聯，一旦決定一項標準，接著就要問標準之下的這些想法如何連接並進而支持中心點。每一個句子都是一個聲明，而且應該具有意義。一個好的論證過程就像是鐵鏈中的環節，連接得很好沒有任何中斷。因此，對於每一個句子所形成的連結要謹慎地檢查才能發現辯詞中的缺點。

To prevail in an argument, an attack must be placed on the analysis rather than the conclusion held by the other side. The reason is simple. The reason is to persuade and the reasons are the foundation upon which a conclusion is built. Once the foundation is shaken, the conclusion will collapse. For this reason, the reasoning process used by the opposite side must be examined closely.

要在辯論中獲勝，我們必須攻擊對方的論理而不是結論。理由很簡單，要說服靠的是論理而不是結論，而且結論是建立在論理之上。一旦基礎動搖，整個結論就會土崩瓦解。爲了這個原因，我們必須嚴格檢驗對方所採用的分析過程。

In addition, if we agree that the training of critical thinking is necessary in college education, then we have to ask ourselves how we can help our students to improve their ability on critical thinking. Critical thinking is a journey of exploring for a standard to be used for judging and evaluating. The setting of a standard is an essential step for training of critical thinking, as Mr. Robert Boostrom has mentioned.

此外，如果我們同意在大學教育批判性思考訓練是必須的話，那我們就必須問自己如何幫助我們學生增強他們的批判性思考。批判性思考是尋找判斷標準的一個過程。確立標準是訓練批判性思考重要的步驟，如同 Robert Boostrom 教授所說到的。

Once a standard is selected, we can apply the cause and effect structure to build our framework for constructing an argument and we can use the same approach to examine our opponents' arguments. There is one important question to ask at this stage, why it is this standard chosen over the others? The standard chosen will seriously affect reasoning and this will change the whole conclusion. The reading of numbers would be different if you apply a different ruler to measure the same object. Different standards applied to the same facts will result in a completely different conclusion. For example, if a school lowers the passage standard from B to C, then more students are able to pass the test. Or if the standard for reading air pollution has been drastically lowered, then a highly polluted city could be regarded as a clean city. The result will vary according to the standard chosen. Therefore, in international trade, the stronger nations build up the rules for other smaller states to follow. Whoever makes the rules is the winner in this game.

一旦標準選定了以後，我們就可以使用因果關係的結構來建立我們辯論的架構，並且使用相同的方法檢驗對手的辯詞。這裡有一個重要的問題，爲什麼是這個標準而不是另一個標準？選定的標準，會嚴重影響論理過程，進而對於結論會有重大的改變。同一件物品使用不同的尺度衡量的話，讀數也會不同。相同的事實使用不同的標準會導致不同的結論，比方說一個學校如果把及格的標準從 B 變到 C 的話，那會有更多的學生通過考試。或是政府改變空氣汙染的標準，那一個高度汙染的城市就可能可以變成一個乾淨的城市。標準不同，結果就不同。因此，在國際貿易中大國制定規則讓小國尊崇。誰制定了規則，誰就是贏家。

In examining an argument, the following questions must be considered:

- A Find the conclusion.
- B Find the reasons to support the conclusion. Pay attention to the examples or analogies used.
- C Spot the issues.
- D Find the standard applied.
- E The standard could be based on an assumption. If so, what is the assumption as the basis for his argument?
- F Is there any other reasonable possibility?

在檢驗一項辯詞應該要問下列的問題：

- A 找出結論。
- B 找出支持結論的理由。注意所使用的例子或是比喻。
- C 找出爭議點。
- D 找出所適用的標準。
- E 標準可能是建立在假設之上。如果是如此的話，什麼是它的假設？
- F 有沒有其他合理的可能性？

8 Finding the standard to apply

A fact is always a fact. A fact, as long it is verified, relevant and sufficient, cannot lie and therefore will help to build up the creditability of a case. However, a fact standing alone cannot lead to a conclusion unless being evaluated with an interpretation, as we have observed from the two prior cases regarding an airline's on-time rate and the one on the Coke-coffee consumption. To evaluate, a standard must be selected and applied. In the airline case (the airline is the best choice for business travelers because of its number one on-time rate), the on-time rate is used as the standard. Since the on-time rate is the standard selected and applied, the airline as the best choice will be the only conclusion that can be drawn. In other words, such a conclusion will be reached as a definite result as long as the on-time rate as the only standard is chosen. As some readers have noticed probably, the argument seems intentionally leaving out other important criteria for evaluation of an airline such as safety, probably the most important, flight fares, convenience for transfer, service, etc. When all criteria are put into consideration, the airline probably will not be the best choice for all business travelers. We have no such information. Simply speaking, the whole conclusion is based on ONE ASSUMPTION as the standard for evaluation, WHILE INTENTIONALLY EXCLUDING THE OTHERS, that the on-time rate is the only standard that business travelers should consider! To destroy the argument, instead of arguing on the conclusion, we have to spot the assumption used as the foundation on which the conclusion is based with a counter-attack by introducing other possibilities. Once the assumption is spotted and other possibilities introduced, the whole conclusion will collapse accordingly.

8 找出適用的標準

事實總是事實。事實只要它是經過驗證、具有相關性以及充分性，是不會說謊的，事實因此可以幫我們建立一個案子的可信度。但是單純的事實沒有辦法得出一項結論，除非透過解釋進行檢驗，就像我們在前面看到兩個關於航空公司準點率以及可樂與咖啡消費的例子。進行檢驗事實的時候，我們必須選擇適用的標準。在航空公司的案例中（該家航空公司對於商務客人是最好的選擇，因爲它第一名的準點率），準點率用來當作標準。因爲準點率是被選擇的標準，因此我們只能得到這間航空公司是最佳選擇的結論。換句話說，這樣的結論是必然，只要準點率是唯一的標準的話。就像有些讀者可能注意到了上面的說法似乎特意遺漏評斷一家航空公司的標準，例如：安全、機票價格、轉機的方便性、還有服務等等。當所有標準都列入考量的時候，這家航空公司可能就不是最好的選擇。我們的手上並沒有這樣的資訊。簡單來說，整個結論是建立在一個假設之上，而特意遺漏了其他的考量，而這個假設就是準點率，是商務客人唯一要考量的因素！要打破這樣的辯詞，我們必須要找出達到這個結論的假設，並且要找出其他的可能性，對這樣的假設進行攻擊。如果我們找出假設而且證明有其他的可能性，那整個的結論就會崩解。

Similarly, regarding the second example, that people drink less Coke but more coffee as age increases is a fact. To claim that consumption on coffee will thus increase because of a higher population of older people in the future is an interpretation. The conclusion is of course to call for more investment in coffee. The assumption here is that no new baby will be born and no older people will die in the future. The conclusion will stand if the assumption is true. But it is not true. In reality, we will have more births of the younger generation and the elderly will pass away, so will be their consumption of coffee. Once other possibilities are introduced, the assumption will fail, so will the conclusion.

同樣的，在第二個例子中，人們年紀愈大喝的可樂愈少，喝的咖啡愈多是一項事實。因此聲稱將來咖啡的消費會愈來愈多，因爲在未來我們會有愈來愈多的老年人口則是一個解釋。結論當然就是要求對於咖啡進行的投資。這裡的假設就是在未來沒有更多嬰兒會出生，也沒有更多年老的人會死亡。如果這個假設是正確的話，那結論就會站得住。但這並不正確。事實上，我們會有更多新的一代，而老人以及他們對咖啡的消費也會逐漸凋零。一旦其他可能性被找出來的時候，這樣的假設就會不攻自破，結論也是一樣。

We may again apply the above technique to a common case regarding commercials given by a telecommunication service company. For example, an ABC telecommunication company states that they offer the best choice for the users in the market because their rate is the cheapest. Such statement regarding being the cheapest, though true, is probably predicated on a belief that the rate is the only concern by all customers while intentionally neglecting other factors such as the quality of service on communication and some other promotional activities (e.g. a bundle of service with mobile phones at a special rate). Students in dealing with such cases must be aware of the assumptions on which the whole conclusion is built and what other factors or possibilities that are being excluded.

我們可以把上面的技巧用在一個大家常常看見的電信公司的廣告上。例如：ABC 電話公司聲稱他們的公司對於用戶來說是最好的選擇，因為他們的費率是最低的。關於費率最低這一部分可能是事實，這樣的說法是建立在費率是消費者唯一的考量，但卻忽略了其他的因素，例如：通話品質，以及其他銷售活動（將服務與手機以特別的價格綁號），學生們在處理這類案件時必須要了解到整個結論所依賴的假設，還有其他被排除的可能性。

Simply speaking, to rebut a statement, it is not wise to focus on the conclusion. Attention shall be given to locating the assumption it is based on and the standard that is applied together with other explored possibilities. Once both are located, the introduction of other possibilities will certainly crumble the whole argument and crush the final conclusion.

簡單來說，在反駁對方的論點上，不值得在對方的結論上下工夫。注意力應該放在找出假設以及所適用的標準，還有探索其他的可能性。一旦找出所適用的標準以及假設，所帶進的其他可能性就會讓辯詞以及結論土崩瓦解。

To summarize the above, in examining an argument, an approach as follows can be considered.

A What is the conclusion?
B What facts are the reached conclusion based on?
C How are the facts interpreted?
D What is the issue?
E What is the assumption?
F What is the standard used for making the judgment?
G What are the other possibilities?
H How will the other possibilities affect the conclusion if introduced?
I Have all the relevant facts been revealed and considered?

The above steps is an algorithm to examine the soundness of the reasoning process leading to a conclusion. In fact, an argument should be written with such an analysis in order to effectively establish a well-connected causal relation between all the events and ideas.

綜上所述，檢驗一項辯詞的時候應該考量下面的因素。

A 什麼是結論？
B 達到結論所依據的事實是什麼？

C 事實是怎麼被詮釋？

D 什麼是爭議？

E 什麼是假設？

F 判斷的標準是什麼？

G 什麼是其他可能性？

H 其他的可能性如果列入考量的話，如何影響結論？

I 是否所有相關事實都有揭露並考量過？

上述的步驟，是檢驗一個達到結論的論理過程是否健全的一種公式。事實上，也可以使用這種分析方法，建立所有事件與想法之間的因果連結，寫出一個具有效果的辯詞。

9 Practice on the GMAT essay questions

Debating skills form the foundation of negotiation. This is because a skillful and experienced negotiator should always expect possible confrontations in a negotiation and confrontations require skills on debating to expose the weakness of the other side so that our bargaining power can be increased. Without such skills, negotiation at best is nothing more than aggressive chatting. This practice, as the most important part of this book, offers training on the debating techniques and the skillful use of these skills will help readers to gain spontaneity in locating an opponent's weakness in his statement and effectively and efficiently demolish his whole argument in gaining a better bargaining power to your advantage in a negotiation.

9 GMAT 寫作測驗練習

辯論的技巧是談判的根本。這是因爲具有技巧與經驗的談判者都知道，在談判中可能會有對抗，而對抗需要辯論的技能來突顯對方的缺點，藉此增加我們的談判實力。沒有這樣的技巧，談判充其量僅僅只是具有侵略性的聊天而已。這部分的練習是本書最重要的部分，提供了辯論的技巧訓練，對於這一部分的熟悉可以幫助讀者找出對方說法上缺點的本能反應，而且可以有效地而且即時性打破對方所有的說法，以便在談判協商當中取得優勢的談判地位。

In the past years of teaching, GMAT argumentative essays seem to be an effective tool to improve the students' critical thinking. It also works well on the training of writing. GMAT essay questions usually present a statement describing a set of facts upon which a conclusion is consequently drawn. The facts in the statement generally are subject to neither argument nor dispute. Therefore, the conclusion closely following the undisputed facts seems to create an impression on a learner's mind that the conclusion cannot be challenged either. The purpose of that question is to test a learner's logical ability on spotting the weakness shown in the reasoning process by finding the assumption on which a standard is based and, by this standard, the facts are evaluated. The same set of facts, when evaluated by a different standard, can lead to a completely different conclusion. The following demonstrations will show how to examine an argument and how to break it up.

在過去幾年的教學中，GMAT 辯論式的題型對於學生批判性思考的訓練是非常有效的工具。他在寫作上也有很大的幫助。GMAT 辯論式的問題通常在問題的說明中描述了一組事實，並且在這事實之上建立了一個結論，這個聲明中的事實通常無法爭議。因此，在這無可爭辯所建立的結論，在初學者心裡創造出一種印象，也就是這個結論不可以被挑戰。這一種問題的目的在於測試學習者發現論理過程中弱點的邏輯能力，也就是找出假設，而這假設產生了評斷所陳述事實的標準。同組事實透過不同標準進行評斷的時候，會產生完全不同的結論。下面的例子會顯示出如何檢驗一項辯詞並且如何打破這項辯詞。

Apply the following questions, a form of algorithm, to examine the examples presented.

A Find the conclusion.

B Find the reasons to support the conclusion.

C Spot the issues.

D Find the standard applied.

E What is the assumption based on?

F Is there any other possibility?

G What is the standard chosen for evaluating this argument?

在下面的例子中，以數學公式的方式透過如下的問題進行檢驗：

A 找出結論。

B 找出支持結論的理由。

C 找出爭議點。

D 找出所使用的標準。

E 什麼是假設？

F 有沒有其他可能性？

G 這個辯詞使用什麼標準進行評斷？

Question 1

The following appeared in an article in a travel magazine.

"After the airline industry began requiring airlines to report their on-time rate, Taiwan Airlines achieved the number one on-time rate, with over 95 percent of its flights arriving on time each month. And now Taiwan air is offering more flights to more destinations than ever before. Clearly, Taiwan air is obviously the best choice for today's business travelers."

Discuss how well the reasoning is ... etc.

Discussion

To examine a claim like this, we first must locate the conclusion and find out what the reasons are to support this conclusion.

Conclusion: Taiwan airline is the best choice for today's business travelers.

Reason: Taiwan air has the number one on-time rate with 95 percent of the flights arriving on time each month.

The issue presented here is: Is the number one on-time rate the only factor for an airline to be considered as the best choice for business travelers? The answer is obviously negative because the on-time rate is only one of the factors. There are other important factors to be taken into account such as safety, security, service, convenience, flight fare, etc. This statement clearly sets as a standard the on-time rate while excluding the consideration of other factors. In other words, the whole conclusion is established on one assumption that all business travelers only care about the on-time rate while excluding the other considerations. Once other important factors such as safety and flight fare are introduced, the assumption on which the conclusion is based will prove highly doubtful. Therefore, the following approaches should be used in examining an argument:

- A Find the conclusion.
- B Describe the reasons supporting the conclusion.
- C Locate the assumption.
- D Point out the issue.
- E Introduce other possibilities.

The above approaches are very effective in examining an argument and expose its weakness, even an advertisement. A reader should constantly practice as many such type of questions as possible and try to answer the questions suggested in the above approaches to gain familiarity and spontaneity in finding a weakness, that is, an assumption. Apply this technique to any statement that you observe and find which standard the assumption is based, introduce other possibilities, and raise questions to cast doubt on the statement.

問題一

下面的說法出現在一本旅遊雜誌上。

「當所有的航空公司被要求要揭露他們的準點率，臺灣航空以每個月 95% 的準點率名列第一，現在臺灣航空要提供更多的航班到更多的目的地，很顯然，臺灣航空是今日商務旅客的最佳選擇。」

請討論這說法的合理性。

討論

要檢驗這樣的說法，我們必須先找出結論，再找出支持結論的理由是什麼。

結論：臺灣航空是今日商務旅客的最佳選擇。

理由：臺灣航空每個月都有高居第一的 95% 的準點率。

這裡所呈現的爭議點是，對於今日的商務旅客而言，航空公司的準點率是不是唯一考量的因素？答案很顯然是否定的，因爲準點率只是商務旅客所考慮的眾多因素之一。其他的重要因素包括飛航安全性、服務、方便性以及機票價格等等都是。而這個旅行雜誌的說法，僅僅只把準點率當作唯一的標準而排除其他重要的因素。一旦其他重要的因素像是安全以及機票價格列入考量的話，這個結論所依賴的假設就會被高度的懷疑。因此，檢驗對方說法的時候，必須要考慮下列事項：

A 找出對方說法的結論。

B 陳述一下支持結論的原因。

C 找出假設。

D 指出爭議點。

E 帶進其他可能性。

上面的方法在檢驗一項說法，甚至包括廣告詞，在暴露其弱點的功能上是非常的有效。讀者應該儘量練習這種題型，並且按照上述所建議的方法回答問題，以便熟悉而且可以本能地找出弱點，也就是假設回答這一類的問題。將這種技巧應用在你所觀察到了的所有的說法上，找出他們說法上的假設和基於該假設所建立的標準，帶進其他的可能性，而且提出質問，將疑問丟在對方的說法上。

Question 2

The following appeared in a memorandum from the president of a company that makes shampoo.

"A widely publicized study claims that ABC, a chemical compound in our shampoo, can contribute to hair loss after prolonged use. This study, however, involved only 500 subjects. Furthermore, we have received no complaints from our customers during the past year, and some of our competitors actually use more ABC per bottle of shampoo than we do. Therefore, we do not need to consider replacing the ABC in our shampoo with a more expensive alternative."

Discuss how well the reasoning is ... etc.

Conclusion of this statement: There is no need to consider replacing the ABC in our shampoo with a more expensive alternative.

Reasons:

A No complaint from our customers was received during the past year.

B Our competitor uses more ABC per bottle than we do.

Assumptions:

A No complaint from our customers will be received in the following years.

B Our competitor receives no complaint.

Introduction of other possibilities:

Ⓐ No complaint has been received in the past years does not necessarily mean that we will receive no complaint in the following years because hair loss is caused after prolonged use. As time goes by, more complaints can be expected.

Ⓑ Our competitor uses more ABC per bottle does not mean that they receive no complaints. What if their complaint letters have piled up like a mountain?

Readers can see that the conclusion that we don't need to change our formula is based on these two assumptions. If the assumptions were true, the conclusion will highly likely be possible. To refute this statement, attacks must be placed on their two assumptions. The best approach is to introduce other possibilities. As long as the other possibilities are reasonably acceptable, their conclusion will collapse. For this reason, the examination should be focused on locating the assumption instead of arguing on the conclusion.

問題二

下列的說法出自於一家生產洗髮精公司的總裁。

「一份大量發行的研究聲稱 ABC，一種洗髮精中的化學物，在長期使用之後會造成掉髮。然而這個研究僅僅只有 500 個對象。更進一步，我們在過去一年當中沒有收到來自於我們顧客的抱怨，而且我們的對手當中，有些在每一瓶洗髮精當中使用更多 ABC 的成分。因此，我們不需要考慮以其他更昂貴的替代品來取代我們洗髮精中的 ABC。」

請討論這說法的合理性。

這個說法的結論：我們沒有必要考慮以更貴的替代品來取代我們洗髮精中的 ABC 成分。

理由：

A 過去一年沒有收到我們顧客的抱怨。

B 我們的競爭者在每一瓶洗髮精中使用更多的 ABC。

假設：

A 在未來的幾年我們顧客一樣不會有抱怨。

B 我們的競爭者沒有收到任何的抱怨。

其他可能性：

A 我們在過去幾年沒有收到抱怨，並不代表我們在未來的幾年也不會收到抱怨，有人長期使用洗髮精之後可能造成掉髮。隨著時間愈來愈久，我們可以期待有更多客户的抱怨。

B 我們的競爭者在每一瓶洗髮精當中使用更多的 ABC，並不代表他們沒有收到任何的抱怨。如果他們的抱怨信堆得像是山一樣高呢？

讀者們可以看到，總裁這樣不需要改變我們洗髮精的成分的結論是基於兩個假設。如果這兩個假設都是對的，那結論很可能就成立了。要反駁這樣的説法，我們的攻擊就必須放在他們的兩個假設上。最好的做法就是帶進其他的可能性。只要其他可能性很合理的被大家所接受，他們的結論就會瓦解。為了這個理由，檢驗應該放在找出假設而不是在結論上進行辯論。

Question 3

The following is from a campaign by Worth Boards, Inc., to convince companies in Mountain City that their sales will increase if they use Worth Boards billboards for advertising their locally manufactured products.

"The potential of Worth Boards to increase sales of your products can be seen from an experiment we conducted last year. We increased public awareness of the name of the current national women's bicycle champion by publishing her picture and her name on billboards in Mountain City for a period of two months. Before this time, although the champion had just won her title and was receiving extensive national publicity, only three percent of 10,000 randomly surveyed residents of Mountain City could correctly name the champion when shown her picture; after the two-month advertising experiment, 50 percent of respondents from a second survey could correctly give her name."

Discuss how well the reasoning is ... etc.

Conclusion: Worth Boards billboards can effectively increase sales for advertisements.

Reasons: Public awareness of the bicycle champion, according to the survey conducted, increased from three percent of the residents in Mountain city to fifty percent within a two-months experiment.

Assumption: Billboards was the only access for the residents in Mountain City of the information regarding that bicycle champion.

Other possibilities: The information was available from other sources such as TV, radio, internet, newspaper, magazines, etc.

Statements like this skillfully used a fact (public awareness increased from three percent to 50 percent) to support the conclusion that billboards are an effective and efficient tool to increase public awareness. A fact always speaks better and it is hard for an untrained mind to challenge. Actually, the fact here is NOT the exclusive reason that the public awareness was raised from 3% to 50%. Without the billboards, the residents still have other access to gain such information. The billboards only serve as one of the reasons. However, a well-trained mind should spot the issue immediately and introduce other possibilities to collapse the conclusion.

問題三

下面是來自於廣告公司的宣傳活動，他們希望說服城市裡的公司，如果使用他們的看板，可以增加都市公司所製造的貨品銷售量。

「我們的看板增加促銷你們產品的潛力，可以從我們去年所做的實驗看得出來。我們把一個女子腳踏車冠軍選手的相片以及她的名字放在我們的看板上二個月，我們增加她的知名度。在這個時間之前，雖然這一個女子冠軍剛贏得了她的頭銜而且獲得廣泛全國性的知名度，但是在這一個城市，10,000 個受訪問的對象只有 3% 可以正確的說出她的名字，但在兩個月的廣告實驗之後，有 50% 的人可以正確的說出她的名字。」

請討論這說法的合理性。

結論：大看板因爲它們在廣告上的效果，可以增加公司在產品上的銷售。

理由：根據民意調查的結果，在這個城市裡大家對於自行車的冠軍認識的程度，在兩個月內從原來 3% 增加到 50%。

假設：大看板是這個城市裡唯一可以取得這個自行車冠軍有關消息的途徑。

其他的可能性：這樣的消息也可以從電視、收音機、網路、報章雜誌等等途徑取得。

大看板公司這樣的說法，很巧妙地使用了一個事實（大眾的認識程度從 3% 提升到 50%）來支持大看板是很有效率的工具，大幅增加大眾的了解程度。用事實說話比較具有可信度。對於沒有受過訓練的人說，比較不容易挑戰。實際上，大看板並不是使得公眾認識程度從 3% 到 50% 的唯一途徑。沒有大看板，這個地方的居民依然有其他的途徑可以得到這樣的消息。大看板只是其中的一種工具。然而一個受過訓練的人，應該很迅速地找出這一點並且帶進了其他考慮的可能性，而推翻這樣的結論。

Question 4

The following appeared as part of an article in a popular science magazine.

"Scientists must typically work 60 to 80 hours a week if they hope to further their careers; consequently, good and affordable all day child care must be made available to both male and female scientists if they are to advance in their fields. Moreover, requirements for career advancement must be made more flexible so that preschool-age children can spend a significant portion of each day with a parent."

Discuss how well the reasoning is ... etc.

Conclusion of the statement:

A Good and affordable all day child care should be provided to scientists.

B Requirements for career advancement should be made more flexible.

Reasons:

Scientists must work between 60 to 80 hours per week and they do not spend enough time with their preschool-age children.

Assumptions:

A All scientists have preschool-age children.

B Both parents are scientists.

Introduction of other possibilities:

A Not all scientists have preschool-age children. They could have no children or have children that already reached maturity. In either case, they have no need for all day child care.

B Not all parents in this case are scientists.

This example again uses the working hours between 60 to 80 hours per week as a fact to support the conclusion. Facts can hardly be denied. Therefore, the conclusion reached accordingly seems reasonable. However, the conclusion could be correct only if the assumptions are true, that is, all scientists have preschool-age children and both parents in this case are scientists. In that case, all day child care should be seriously considered.

In reality, that is not true. Once other possibilities are introduced, the conclusion fails.

問題四

以下出現在一份非常有名的科學雜誌上的一篇文章。

「科學家在每一周一般都必須工作 60 到 80 個小時，如果他們希望有所升遷的話。因此，優質且大家付得起的全天幼兒照顧，應該提供給男性與女性的科學家，如果他們希望在他們的專業當中有所提升。更進一步，專業上的升遷標準應該變得更有彈性，這樣，學齡前的兒童每一天才能有足夠的時間與父母的其中一個在一起。」

請討論這說法的合理性。

本篇說法的結論：

A 優質且負擔得起的全天幼兒照顧，應該提供給所有的科學家們。

B 科學家們的升遷標準應該更有彈性。

理由：

科學家們每一周必須工作 60 到 80 個小時，而且他們沒有花足夠的時間陪伴他們學齡前的孩子。

假設：

A 所有的科學家都有學齡前的小孩。

B 兩個雙親都是科學家。

其他可能性：

A 並不是所有的科學家都有學齡前的小孩，他們可能沒有小孩或是小孩已經成年了。不管哪種情況，他們並沒有全天兒童照顧的需要。

B 本案當中並不是兩個雙親都是科學家。

這個例子使用了科學家每周必須工作 60 到 80 個小時當作事實來支持結論。我們很難否認事實，因此，按照這個事實所達到的結論看起來很合理。但是正確的結論繫於正確的假設，而這裡的假設是所謂的科學家都有學齡前的小孩，而且父母雙親都是科學家。只有在那種情況之下，全天的兒童照顧才需要被嚴肅地考慮。

實際上這並不正確，一旦考慮其他的可能性，這樣的結論就倒下來了。

Question 5

The following appeared in the editorial section of a local newspaper.

"The profitability of ABC Company recently restored to private ownership is a clear indication that businesses fare better under private ownership than under public ownership."

Conclusion of the statement: Businesses fare better under private ownership than under public ownership.

Reason: ABC Company has made a good profit and the company recently restored to private ownership.

Assumption: The company made their profit when in private ownership.

Introduction of other possibilities: The company has just restored to private ownership, which means, its profit was earned while in public ownership.

This statement is short and simple. When a statement is made short, it generally omits some facts in forming the causal links. In this case, this statement creates an impression that the company earned a profit when in private ownership. But that is not true. This company has just been restored to private ownership, which implies that it was in public ownership in the past. A trained mind should immediately find this missing crucial fact by placing all the information into a logical sequence.

問題五

下面的說法出現在當地報紙的評論當中。

「ABC 這家公司最近恢復成了私人企業，而它的獲利能力是一個很清楚的指標，也就是公司在私人企業之下要勝過公營企業。」

結論：私人企業的經營要強過公營企業。

理由：ABC 公司已有良好的收益，而他們也在最近恢復成爲私人企業。

假設：這家公司是在私人企業的情況之下獲利。

其他可能性：這家公司剛剛恢復成爲私人企業，這表示他們應該是在公營事業的時候獲利的。

上面的說法很簡短，當一個說法很簡單又很簡短的時候，通常省略了一些事實。在這裡，上述的說法創造了一個印象，也就是公司是在私人企業的時候獲利的。但這並不眞實，這家公司剛剛才恢復成爲私人企業，也就隱含著它過去是一個私人企業的事實。一個受過訓練的讀者，可以按照邏輯順序的先後，將所有的資訊排列，就能夠迅速找到所特意省略的重要事實。

Question 6

The following appeared as part of a business plan recommended by the new manager of a musical rock group called ABC.

“To succeed financially, ABC needs a greater name recognition. It should therefore diversify its commercial enterprises. The rock group XYZ plays the same type of music that ABC plays, but it is much better known than ABC because in addition to its concert tours and four albums, XYZ has a series of posters, a line of clothing and accessories, and a contract with a major advertising agency to endorse a number of different products."

Discuss how well the reasoning is ... etc.

問題六

下面的說法出現在 ABC 樂團的經紀經理所推薦的商業計畫。

「要能夠在財務上面成功，ABC 必須要有更高的知名度，因此它必須將企業多元化。XYZ 樂團玩著同樣的音樂，但是它比 ABC 樂團有更高的知名度，因爲除了它的巡迴演唱以及四張紀念專輯外，還有一系列的海報、服裝、配件，以及跟主要經紀公司的經紀契約來背書多項不同的產品。」

討論這說法的合理性。

Conclusion: ABC should follow what XYZ has done to win a greater name recognition.

Reasons: XYZ is much more renowned than ABC and XYZ has concert tours and four albums, a series of posters, a line of clothing and accessories, and a contract with a major advertising agency to endorse a number of different products.

Assumption:

(A) ABC already has the same fame as XYZ to engage in same

activities to sell their products.

B ABC has as many resources as XYZ for those activities.

Introduction of other possibilities:

A ABC does not have the same fame as XYZ to make a similar promotion for good sales.

B ABC does not have as many resources as XYZ for those activities.

For any product, if people do not know the brand, little consumption can be expected. To make a successful sale, public awareness of the brand is necessary and such awareness depends on a good promotion. To make a good promotion, public awareness of XYZ's fame is certainly helpful. On the contrary, ABC does not have the similar fame. In other words, ABC's name has not reached public awareness. Therefore, ABC needs a promotion of their name rather than proposed sales of their products. Without public awareness of their brand, no good sale of their product is possible. The business manager mistakenly believes that ABC has the same fame as XYZ to make a good sale.

Besides, concert tours and four albums, a series of posters, a line of clothing and accessories, etc. all require investing a good amount of money, of which ABC is short of, as well as having a good fame which ABC does not have either. Therefore, the suggestion proposed in this business plan is not feasible.

結論：ABC 應該模仿 XYZ 所做的，來贏得更高的知名度。

理由：X Y Z 比 ABC 更有名，而且還有巡迴演唱以及四張專輯、系列海報、衣服、配件，還有主要經紀公司的合約來背書他們的多項產品。

假設：

Ⓐ ABC 已經有 XYZ 相同的名聲來從事一樣的活動，來銷售它們的產品。

Ⓑ ABC 有跟 XYZ 一樣的資源來從事這些活動。

其他可能性：

Ⓐ ABC 並沒有 XYZ 相同的名聲來從事一樣的活動，來銷售它們的產品。

Ⓑ ABC 並沒有跟 XYZ 一樣的資源來從事這些活動。

對任何產品，如果消費者沒有聽過這品牌，銷售會非常的困難。貨品要能成功的銷售，大眾必須知道這品牌，而這有賴於好的行銷。大眾對於 XYZ 的名聲的熟悉，對於他們貨品的銷售當然有幫助。相反的，ABC 沒有這樣的名聲。也就是說大家並不熟悉 ABC 的名聲。因此，ABC 需要行銷的是他們的名聲，而不是銷售他們的產品。如果大家沒有聽過他們的名字，要能成功銷售他們的產品是不可能的。這個經理錯誤地相信 ABC 和 XYZ 一樣的有名，可以成功地銷售貨品。

除此之外，音樂會以及四張專輯、系列海報、衣服、配件等等，都需要金錢的投資，而他們資金並不充分，他們也並不有名，因此這個建議並不可行。

Question 7

The following appeared as part of an article in a trade publication.

"Stronger laws are needed to protect new kinds of home-security systems from being copied and sold by imitators. With such protection, manufacturers will naturally invest in the development of new home-security products and production technologies. Without stronger laws, manufacturers will cut back on investment. From this will follow a corresponding decline not only in product quality and marketability, but also in production efficiency, and thus ultimately a loss of manufacturing jobs in the industry."

Discuss how well the reasoning is ... etc.

問題七

下列說法出現在一份貿易刊物上。

「我們需要嚴格的法律來保護新的家庭防盜系統不受仿造者的仿冒販賣。有了這樣的保護，製造商自然會投資在新的家庭防盜產品的發展，以及生產技術的提升。沒有這樣嚴格的法律，製造者會降低他們的投資。這樣，產品數量還有市場性以及產品的效能，都會相對的降低，因此，最後導致在這個行業裡面的製造工作機會的喪失。」

請討論這說法的合理性。

Conclusion: Stronger laws are needed to protect new kinds of home-security systems from being copied and sold by imitators.

Reasoning: With such protection, manufacturers will naturally invest in the development of new home-security products and production technologies.

Assumption: Sale of home security system depends on the protection of law rather than a sound security function.

Introduction of other possibilities: A well-designed function of a home security system is good enough to defeat any purpose involving imitation ones.

The purpose of a home security system is designed to prevent any burglary and intrusion into our dwelling place. Successful imitations of a home security system have indicated that the function of that security system against burglary and intrusion has failed. A failed home security system cannot make good sales and it cannot be cured by any stronger laws. This is because no consumer will be interested in buying a home security system which fails in its function and a stronger law cannot help sales of a home security system which has failed in its basic function against burglary and intrusion in this case.

結論：我們需要較嚴格的法律，保護新的家庭防盜系統不受仿冒者的拷貝及販賣。

理由：有了這樣的保護，製造商自然而然會投資在新的家庭防盜系統產品以及生產技術的發展。

假設：家庭防盜系統的販賣是依賴法律的保護，而不是健全的防盜功能。

其他可能性：一個設計良好的家庭防盜系統，是能夠達到防盜目的不受仿冒的。

家庭防盜系統的目的，是防止闖空門以及進入我們所居住的地方。一個成功的仿品表示原來防盜的功能已經失敗。一個失敗的防盜系統沒有辦法有良好的銷售，而這個問題也沒有辦法透過嚴格的法律來挽救。那是因爲消費者不會願意花錢購買失去功能的防盜系統，而這個問題並不是嚴格的法律可以幫忙解決的。

Question 8

The following appeared in the opinion section of a national newsmagazine.

"To reverse the deterioration of the postal service, the government should raise the price of postage stamps. This solution will no doubt prove effective, since the price increase will generate larger revenues and will also reduce the volume of mail, thereby eliminating the strain on the existing system and contributing to improved morale."

Discuss how well the reasoning is ... etc.

問題八

下列的說法出現在一個全國性新聞雜誌的意見欄。

「要翻轉郵政系統日漸惡化的情況，政府必須提高郵資，這樣的解決方式，毫無疑問是很有效的，因爲價格的提升可以增加利潤，而且同時可以降低郵件的數量，因此，能夠降低現有制度的壓力並且對於提高士氣會有貢獻。」

請討論這說法的合理性。

Conclusion: The government should raise the price of postage stamps.

Reasons: The price increase will generate larger revenues and will also reduce the volume of mail, thereby eliminating the strain on the existing system and contributing to improved morale.

Assumption: The price increases will generate larger revenues and, at the same time, will also maintain the volume of mail.

Introduction of other possibilities: If price increases, volume cannot be expected to rise.

This statement claims that increase of price can bring in more profit and decrease the volume at the same time and thereby eliminating the strain on the existing system. The truth is that, once price goes up, the cost of mail will increase. When cost increase, volume can be expected to go down. The two cannot exist at the same time.

結論：政府應該提高郵資。

理由：因爲價格的提升可以增加利潤，而且同時可以降低郵件的數量，因此能夠降低現有制度的壓力，並且對於提高士氣會有貢獻。

假設：郵費提高可以增加利潤，但同一個時間也會增加郵寄的數量。

其他可能性：如果郵費提高，我們無法期待數量會上升。

這個說法聲稱郵費的增加會帶來更多的利潤，而且同時降低數量，因此能夠減輕現有制度的壓力。眞實情況是，如果費用一旦增加，那郵費的成本也會增加，當費用增加的時候，數量會減少。這兩者無法同時存在。

Question 9

The following appeared in an article in the health section of a newspaper.

"There is a common misconception that university hospitals are better than community or private hospitals. This notion is unfounded as the university hospitals in our region employ 15 percent fewer doctors, have a 20 percent lower success rate in treating patients, make far less overall profit, and pay their medical staff considerably less than do private hospitals. Furthermore, many doctors at university hospitals typically divide their time among teaching, conducting research, and treating patients. From this it seems clear that the quality of care at university hospitals is lower than that at other kinds of hospitals."

Discuss how well the reasoning is ... etc.

問題九

下列的說法出現在一份報紙的健康專欄上。

「大學的教學醫院要比社區或是私人醫院來得更好是一種誤解。這種想法是沒有根據的，我們地區的大學醫院僱用的醫生少了15%，在醫治病人的成功率也少了20%，獲利明顯較少，付給他們員工的薪水也比私人醫院少很多。而且教學醫院的許多醫生通常將他們的時間分配在教學、研究還有醫治病人上。從這裡看來，很明顯地，教學醫院的醫療品質比其他種類的醫院來得差。」

請討論這說法的合理性。

Conclusion: The quality of care at university hospitals is lower than that at other kinds of hospitals.

Reasoning: The university hospitals in our region employ 15 percent fewer doctors, have a 20 percent lower success rate in treating patients, make far less overall profit, and pay their medical staff considerably less than do private hospitals. Furthermore, many doctors at university hospitals typically divide their time among teaching, conducting research, and treating patients.

Assumption: All hospitals are established for the same purpose with same function and should be evaluated by the same standards together, such as the number of employed doctors and success rate of treated patients, the salary and profit earned.

Introduction of other possibilities: The university hospitals are established for different functions such as training of future doctors as well as researching the more difficult illnesses which are quite different from that for the community and private hospitals.

The university hospitals carry a different function from that of private hospitals. The doctors in the university hospitals, as explain in the statement, have to divide their time among teaching, conducting research, and treating patients. In other words, profit from treating patients is only one of their purpose. They also focus on research and teaching. The conclusion in this newspaper has set a standard that hospitals should be evaluated by the number of employed doctors, the success rate of treated patients, the salary and profit earned as the standard for evaluation.

結論：教學醫院的醫療品質比不上其他種類的醫院。

理由：我們地區的大學醫院僱用的醫生少了 15%，在醫治病人的成功率也少了 20%，獲利明顯較少，付給他們員工的薪水也比私人醫院少很多。而且教學醫院的許多醫生通常將他們的時間分配在教學、研究還有醫治病人上。

假設：所有的醫院爲了相同目的而設立，並且有著相同的功能，都應該被相同的標準檢驗，例如：醫生的數量、病人的治癒率、薪水以及總體的獲利。

其他可能性：教學醫院爲了不同的功能而設立，例如：訓練未來的醫師以及對於複雜的病症進行研究，這些都與社區以及私人醫院設立的目標不相同。

大學的教學醫院與其他私人醫院承擔的功能不相同。教學醫院的醫師，就像這份報紙所說的，必須將他們的時間分配在教學研究還有醫療上。換句話説，在病人的治癒率以及醫院的獲利只是他們的目的其中之一，他們也致力於研究和教學。這份報紙專欄的結論設立的一個標準，也就是所有的醫院都應該以醫生的數量、病人的治癒率、薪水還有醫院的整體獲利來做衡量的標準。

Question 10

The following appeared in the editorial section of a local newspaper.

“If the paper from every morning edition of the nation’s largest newspaper were collected and rendered into paper pulp that could be reused, about 5 million trees would be saved each year. This kind of recycling is unnecessary, however, since the newspaper maintains its own forests to ensure an uninterrupted supply of paper."

Discuss how well the reasoning is ... etc.

Conclusion: Recycling is unnecessary.

Reasons: The newspaper maintains its own forests to ensure an uninterrupted supply of paper.

Assumption: Recycling of newspaper is only to ensure the uninterrupted supply of paper.

Introduction of other possibilities: Recycling is not only for the supply of paper but also for the environmental needs.

This statement again uses a fact (the newspaper maintains its own forests to ensure an uninterrupted supply of paper) to speak for its conclusion. A reasoning process based on a fact generally seems more convincing. In that case, we have to examine if the fact referred to is complete or twisted. If there is no problem on the fact mentioned, then we have to examine the reasoning process. Here we can see the assumption on which the reasoning process is based, that is, recycling is only to ensure the uninterrupted supply of paper. This might be one of the reasons but it is not the only reason because a forest of five million trees may serve as an important habitat for all kinds of creatures in that region. To destroy a forest of that size is to kill those creatures. Therefore, a forest of five million trees is not limited to the supply of paper for the newspaper.

問題十

下列說法出現在一份地方報紙的評論中。

「如果全國最大報紙都可以回收而且轉變成可再次使用的紙漿，每一年大概可以省下 5,000,000 棵樹木。但是這樣的回收是不需要的，因爲這家報紙有他們的樹林，可以確保紙漿源源不斷地供應。」

討論這說法的合理性。

結論：紙張的回收是不需要的。

理由：這家報紙有它自己的森林來確保紙漿的供應無缺。

假設：回收報紙只是爲了確保紙張的供應無缺。

其他可能性：回收不只是提供紙張，而且是爲了環境保護的需要。

上面這個說法再一次使用一個事實（這個報紙保有了它自己的森林來確保紙張的供應無缺）來支持它的結論。一個建立在事實上的論理過程，通常看起來是比較具有說服力的。在這個案子裡，我們必須檢驗所提到的事實是否完整或有沒有經過扭曲。如果事實部分沒有問題，接著我們必須檢驗這個論理過程。這裡我們看到論理過程是建立在一個假設上，也就是回收只是爲了確保紙漿的供應無缺。這可能是眾多的原因之一，但這絕對不是唯一的原因。因爲一片 5,000,000 棵樹木的森林，可以當作在那個區域所有生物的重要的棲息地。毀滅了這樣面積的森林，就等於傷害的全部的生物。因此，這片森林並不是僅僅止於對於報社紙張的供應。

Question 11

The following appeared as part of an article in a popular arts and leisure magazine.

"The safety code governing the construction of public buildings are becoming far too strict. The surest way for architects and builders to prove that they have met the minimum requirements by these codes is to construct buildings by using the same materials and methods that are currently allowed. But doing so means that there will be very little significantly technological innovation within the industry, and hence little evolution of architectural styles and design merely because of the strictness of these safety codes."

Discuss how well the reasoning is ... etc.

Conclusion: The strictness of these safety codes has seriously limited technological innovation within the industry, and hence little evolution of architectural styles and design.

Reasons: The surest way for architects and builders to prove that they have met the minimum requirements by these codes is to construct buildings by using the same materials and methods that are currently allowed.

Assumption: No innovation can be made by using same materials and methods.

Introduction of other possibilities: Innovation in designs and styles does not depend on the materials and method but on the ideas and creativity. This is especially true in the field of art works, fashion and cooking because materials and methods used are basically the same while the result may vary from person to person. Same materials in the hands of a great painter as Picasso will be made into a great piece of treasure, while in the untrained hands of ordinary folks, only become as a piece of junk. The fashion and cooking businesses are roughly the same. It is the idea and creativity rather than the materials that increase the value of a work.

問題十一

下一段話出現在一個非常受歡迎的藝術以及休閒雜誌上。

「建造公共建築物的安全法規變得太過嚴格了。對於建築師還有營建業者最保險的方式，就是證明他們已經滿足了這些法規的最低要求，也就是使用現今法規所准許使用的相同的材料和方法來建造建築。但是這樣做，表示在這行業裡很少有工程創新，也因此在建築式樣以及設計上，只有很少的進步，這都是因爲這些法規的嚴格性。」

請討論這說法的合理性。

結論：嚴格的法規已經嚴重的限制工業的創新，因此在建築式樣以及設計上只有很少的進步。

理由：對於建築師還有營建業者最保險的方式，就是證明他們已經滿足了這些法規的最低要求，也就是使用現今法規所准許使用的相同的材料和方法來建造建築。

假設：使用相同的材料方法是沒有辦法創新的。

其他可能性：在設計與式樣上的創新並不依靠方法以及材料，而是想法以及創造力。這在藝術、風潮以及食物料理的領域裡特別眞實，因爲使用的材料和方法都差不多，但結果卻因人而異。一樣的材料在偉大的畫家畢卡索的手上，就變成了一幅偉大的寶藏，但是在一般沒有受過訓練的人手裡，只是一片垃圾。流行和廚藝也是一樣的，是想法以及創造力而不是材料和方法讓事物的價值提升。

The above examples have shown the approaches used in the examination of any statement, whether written or spoken, on any occasion tinged with confrontation, though it be a business transaction, mediation, an internal meeting for a raise or for a promotion or editorials from a newspaper, etc. To summarize again the approaches for examination:

- A What is the conclusion?
- B The conclusion reached is based on what facts?
- C Are the facts mentioned complete or twisted?
- D Have all the relevant facts been provided?
- E How are the facts interpreted?
- F What is the assumption?
- G What is the standard for judgment?
- H What are the other possibilities?
- I How will the other possibilities affect the conclusion if introduced?
- J Bear in mind that, a standard, similar to rules of laws, is necessary for making a judgment of an argument.

For a negotiation class, the training on examining any statement is necessary, especially as a requisite. The reason is simple. You cannot avoid confrontation in a negotiation. When in confrontation, debating skills are necessary because debating may expose the weakness of the other side and thus give your demand a stronger bargaining power. For this reason, it is fair to say that the skills of debating are fundamental to a good negotiator. Of course, a good negotiator should know the art of "give and take", that is, compromise v. confrontation.

上面例子所使用的方法，可以檢驗任何帶有對抗性質場合（例如：商業談判、和解、內部加薪或是升遷的會議、或是報紙的評論等等）所出現的說法，不管是書面或是口頭的。再一次將檢驗的方法作爲下列摘要：

A 什麼是結論？

B 基於怎樣的事實而達到這樣的結論？

C 所使用的事實是否完整或是經過扭曲（例如部分事實而已）？

D 所有相關的事實是否都已經提出？

E 事實如何被詮釋？

F 什麼是假設？

G 什麼是判斷的標準？

H 什麼是其他可能性？

I 其他可能性如何影響所做成的結論？

J 要記得，一個標準就像是法律的規則一樣，是判斷對方的辯詞所必須的。

檢驗他人說法上，這樣技術的訓練是必須的，特別對於一個談判課程來說，更是一個必備條件。原因很簡單，因爲在談判中，你沒有辦法避開對立。既然有對立，在這裡，當中辯論的技術是需要的，因爲辯論能夠將另外一方的缺點顯露出來，因此，給予你的要求更強而有力的談判力量。基於這個原因，可以很公平的說，對於一個好的談判者，辯論的技術是談判的根本。當然一個好的談判者也需要知道給與拿的藝術，也就是妥協與對抗之間的拿捏。

10 Method used in reasoning

Induction

Inductive reasoning is a process of reasoning by which a general conclusion is drawn from a set of premises, either facts or information from experiences or experimental evidences. The conclusion goes beyond the information contained in the premises, and does not follow necessarily from them. Thus an inductive argument may be highly probable, yet could lead from true premises to a false conclusion.

Inductive reasoning does not begin with a conclusion but with premises. Plenty examples can be found on the application of induction such as advertisements regarding why some products/ services are superior, states more civilized, companies are better, and even criminals convicted on circumstantial evidence. For example, a man was killed in that house probably at 2 o'clock in the morning. Jerry was seen leaving that house around 2 o'clock in the morning with blood on his T-shirt. He looked in a panic and in a rush. Therefore, Jerry could be a killer from the circumstantial evidence provided. In a situation like this, none actually witnessed Jerry committing a murder. However, from the indirect evidence shown, a reasonable man can conclude that Jerry is a suspect possibly committing a crime.

Other examples:

He always likes jogging around 5 o'clock on Saturday afternoon in the New Park. It is Saturday and now is 5 o'clock. You should be able to find him there.

Two years ago, over 90% of baby trolley manufacturers in Taiwan made a good profit. Tom has had a company in Taiwan in a manufacturing business on baby trolley for over five years. Therefore, it is likely that Tom's company has made a good profit.

10 論理的方法

歸納法

歸納法是種論理的過程。透過這個過程，我們可以從一組前提中得到結論，而這個前提，可能是從經驗或是實證所得出的事實或是資訊。所得到的結論會超越前提所包含的訊息，而且並不必然跟隨著這些前提。因此，歸納的辯論言詞是具有高度可能性，但有可能從眞實的前提導致出一個錯誤的結論。

歸納的論證方式是從前提開始，而不是從結論開始。有許多的例子是應用歸納法，例如一些產品或是服務的廣告，一些國家比較文明，甚至是一些依照間接證據將嫌疑犯定罪的情況都是，例如：一個被害者在早晨兩點被殺害。大約在早上兩點的時候，傑瑞被人看到離開那個房子，身上的衣服全是血跡。他看起來神情慌張而且行蹤匆忙。因此從間接證據顯示傑瑞可能是殺人犯，沒有人眞的有看到傑瑞殺人。但是從間接情況顯示，一個理智的人，可以下出這樣的結論，傑瑞可能殺了人。

其他的例子：

每到星期六下午五點的時候，他總是在新公園慢跑，今天是星期六而且是下午五點，你應該可以在新公園找到他。

兩年前，在臺灣 90% 生產嬰兒推車的製造商都賺了大錢。湯姆在臺灣有生產嬰兒推車的工廠已經超過五年了，因此，湯姆的公司可能賺了大錢。

Deduction

Deduction is the process of reasoning typical of mathematics and logic, whose conclusions follow necessarily from their premises. The most commonly seen example is the syllogism. For example: All men have to die. Socrates is a man. Therefore, Socrates has to die.

Other examples:

In mathematics, if A=B, and B=C, then A = C.

All birds have feathers. An eagle is a bird; therefore, eagles have feathers.

All tigers eat meat. Tom's pet is a tiger. Tom's pet eats meat.

演繹法

演繹法是數學與邏輯的典型推論方式。結論從前提而來，最常見的是三段論法，例如：所有人都會死，蘇格拉底是人，所以他會死。

其他例子：

在數學上，如果 A=B，B=C，那 A=C。

所有的鳥都有羽毛，老鷹是鳥，因此老鷹有羽毛。

所有的老虎都吃肉，湯姆的寵物是老虎，湯姆的寵物會吃肉。

11 How to form a framework for a debate

Debate is an argument on different opinions. Quite different from speech, a mere stating of opinion is not enough. Opinions given in debate will be subject to challenges. Speakers are required to defend their position. In addition, speakers must also refute the opposing opinion to establish his creditability, proving that his reasoning is strong enough to withstand all challenges. Therefore, a sound framework for an argument should be established.

11 如何建立辯論的架構

辯論是對不同意見的爭執。與演說不同，單純的陳述意見並不足夠。辯論中的意見是會被挑戰的。演說者必須防禦他的立場。此外，辯論者必須證明對手的意見是錯的，以便建立他的可信度。並且要證明他的論理過程可以承受任何的挑戰。因此，我們必須建立健全的辯論架構。

In the preceding section, we have learned how to organize a sentence sequentially and a short form essay under a cause and effect structure. We also learned how to examine an argument to find flaws. Now we will discuss how to build a framework for an argument.

在上一章節中，我們已經學習了如何使用因果架構來組織單一句型、連續句型和短文。我們也學習如何檢驗一個辯詞來找到缺點，現在我們必須討論如何建立一個辯論的架構。

Debate deals with issues. Issues are problems from our daily lives. Problems demand solutions. Debate therefore seems to find solutions. Interestingly, debate does not necessarily entertain a purpose to find a solution. If finding a solution is the only purpose entertained, then debates in most circumstances cannot achieve that purpose because debates can only find flaws through examination of an opponent's argument with no guarantee to solve the issues presented. For this reason, the purpose of a debate is to persuade the listeners, and our main goal is to show our ability to be seemingly correct by proving our opponent to be wrong. As Socrates has noted, he did not know the answer. He only proved that those who claimed wisdom did not have the wisdom they claimed to have.

辯論主要是處理爭議。爭議是我們日常生活中的問題。有了問題就尋求答案。辯論因此看起來似乎是尋找答案。很有趣的，辯論並不必然抱著一個尋找答案的目的。如果尋找答案是目的的話，那在大多數情況之下的辯論，並沒有辦法達到那個目的，因爲辯論只是透過檢視對手的辯詞來找到對手的問題，而並不保證對問題的解決。因此，辯論的目的是在於說服聽衆，主要的目的是在於透過證明對方是錯的，並同時顯示我們自己看來是對的。就像蘇格拉底所說的，他不知道答案是什麼，他只是證明那些聲稱自己有智慧的人並沒有他們所說的那些智慧而已。

Issues come to our attention from problems from our daily life and make us think. When we think, we have opinions. Opinions originate from either facts or other opinions and are a form of a conclusion. A conclusion is simple with either a positive or negative result (yes or no) as an answer, similar to flipping a coin with either heads or tails as a conclusion. For the purpose of training and proving merit, a conclusion is not important because anyone can make a conclusion. It is the analysis process to persuade and to change society as those contributions that are made by many lawyers in the U.S. through their legal system.

來自於我們日常生活中的問題，吸引到我們的注意而且思考爭議。當我們思考的時候，我們就有了意見。意見來自於事實或是其他的意見，意見本身就是一種結論。結論很簡單，是或否而已，就像是丟擲一個硬幣，結論不是正面就是反面。對於訓練以及證明價值而言，結論並不重要，因爲每個人都能下一個結論。說服以及改變整個社會是要透過分析的過程，就像美國律師透過他們的法律體系一樣。

How to build a framework?

Establishing a framework for an argument is not that different from that of a short form essay. All debates involve issues. Issues will be decided on by the standards adopted and followed with supportive reasoning, explaining why this standard should be adopted, and how this standard is applied to a specific case. Both the standard and reasoning components form a part of the analysis. Reasoning requires facts and the interpretation of facts. Facts must be relevant to the issues or they carry no value at all. These facts together with their interpretation should be laid out in a logical sequence to explain the cause and effect so that all listeners and readers can easily grasp the understanding of the main theme. Challenges are expected. Therefore, the arguments and examining questions that may possibly be raised by the opponents must be researched as well, including their causal links of ideas, logical sequence of cause and effect, issues, the standard used, and the assumption made as a basis for the whole argument—all these must be closely examined. All these are required in any occasion where one is expecting an argument on certain issues, including all of the business and academic worlds.

如何建立一個架構呢？

建立一個辯論架構與寫一篇短論文並沒有太大的差異。所有的辯論與爭議有關。爭議會由所選擇的標準來決定，隨後加以理由上的分析，解釋了爲什麼要選擇這個標準，以及這個標準如何應用在一個特定的案件上。標準和論理的過程，形成分析的一部分。論理的過程需要事實以及對於事實的詮釋。事實與爭議必須相關，否則它們沒有任何價值。這些事實以及詮釋必須按照邏輯順序展開，用來解釋因果關係，好讓讀者與聽衆輕易了解整個主軸。我們可以預見對手的質問挑戰。因此，對方所提出的辯詞以及詰問也必須先研究，包括他們想法上關係的連結、因果關係的邏輯順序、爭議點、所使用的標準，以及作爲立論的假設基礎，都必須嚴密的被檢驗。不論在商業界或學術界，對於任何可能產生爭議辯論的場合，都必須要考慮到使用上述的原則。

Under a cause and effect analysis, we explore causal links between all ideas. Naturally, we will trace back to the origin of the issue. A thorough research on a topic should be covered information related to the topic. What is the problem? What is the factual background of this problem and how did that problem happen? What are the reasons behind that new problem? How does the current system see that problem and why? Why is there a dispute and what is the point of controversy? What are the strengths and weaknesses of the current status/system? Why should a change be considered? What kind of change are we looking for? Is the proposed change what we need? What are the cost and benefits for this new proposal? Can the goal envisaged be fulfilled by this new proposal with new benefits being received and the old evil terminated? Is there any other alternative leading to the same goal but with a better effect and less cost? Always bear in mind that the most important part here is what the issues exactly are between the two arguments because the issues will decide the direction of all reasoning.

在一個因果分析之下，我們會探詢想法之間的因果連結。很正常的，我們會追溯到一個爭議點的源頭。對於主題的研究應該涵蓋與主題相關的資訊。什麼是問題？什麼是問題的事實背景？問題如何發生？問題背後的理由是什麼？現有的系統如何看待這樣的問題？他們爲什麼這樣看待？他們在吵什麼？什麼是爭議點？現有的狀態或是系統優劣點是什麼？爲什麼要考量一個改變？我們希望什麼樣的改變？所提出來的改變是我們所需要的嗎？新的提議的成本是什麼？好處又是什麼？我們所懷抱的目標能夠被新的提議所完成嗎？進而得到新的利益而避開舊的邪惡？是否有其他替代方式能達到同樣的目標？但效果更好花費更少？總是要記得在這一部分最重要的，是這兩個不同的說法中爭議究竟是什麼？因為爭議會決定整個論理的方向。

12 Importance of a Summary and the Introduction of IRAC

To write always make you think. Briefing legal cases is good training on the students' ability to make a summary. A good summary requires students, subsequent to their reading of voluminous materials, to make a description of the necessary and essential information in a simple, concise and succinct form under a clear framework. In a business world, the ability to make a good summary is extremely important, especially for top management. Original documents including contracts and all correspondences regarding a specific case can pile up over hundreds, sometimes thousands of pages. A report presented to management therefore requires a concise and succinct summary made with only a few pages in a good logical sequence covering the description of relevant and important facts and all important issues raised from the analysis of the facts and rules. A good summary can only be made after a clear framework has been established. A clear framework can only be established subsequent to a good understanding to the whole case. A good understanding to the whole case cannot be achieved unless issues have been correctly discerned and spotted. Issues cannot be correctly discerned and spotted unless all relevant and important facts have been revealed and understood. Facts in this case must be placed under a clear cause and effect structure to show the connection of ideas among which relevancy and importance can be found.

12 摘要的重要性以及 IRAC 介紹

寫作總是幫助我們思考。把法律案件進行濃縮是對學生非常好的摘要能力訓練。一份好的摘要要求學生在他們閱讀大量文件之後，在一個清楚的架構之下，做出對於必要以及基本訊息以精簡扼要的描述。在商業世界，特別對於高階主管，好的摘要能力極度的重要。關於一個案件的原始文件，包括契約還有來往信件可能高達百頁甚至千頁。提交給高階主管的報告，因此要求只能有幾頁精簡扼要的摘要，內容以邏輯順序做成，包括相關重要事實的扼要陳述以及從事實與規則分析而得的重要爭議。一個好的摘要需要一份好的架構；一份好的架構需要對一個案件全盤的了解；對一個案件全盤的了解，需要明白而且找出爭議點；要明白而且找出爭議點，必須要知道並且了解全部相關而且重要的事實；事實則必須放在一個清楚的因果關系架構之下檢驗，顯現出想法之間的連結以及其中的關聯性和重要性。

A legal case is mainly composed of two parts, facts and application of the law to the facts. In reality, many disputes are centered on the factual issues regarding evidence. Once the disputes on facts have been ascertained, then the rules of law can be applied through an analysis. Therefore, a discussion on a business dispute is generally written with facts at the beginning, followed by a discussion with references to a contract, purchase order or mutual correspondence as the analysis, finally leading to a conclusion. The following are some simple examples for illustrating the aforementioned principles regarding analysis (that is, consecutive sentences with ideas connected, cause and effect structure, standard applied, etc.) used in making a summary including a brief description of a fact with the issues spotted and rules applied through analysis followed consequently by a conclusion. This format can be used in a business dispute involving a transaction.

一個法律的判決主要是由兩個部分構成，事實以及適用法律於事實上。在現實生活中，許多的爭議是集中在與證據有關的事實爭議上。一旦事實確定之後，法律的條文就可以透過分析應用於爭議的解決。因此商業爭議的討論，都是以事實為開始，接著是對於，例如契約、訂單或是雙方之間書信來往的討論以及分析，而最後引導出了結論。下列是一些簡單的例子，以摘要的方式，包括事實扼要描述、爭議點的提出，以及透過分析適用規則而達到結論，作為上述有關分析原則的示範（也就是，前後句子將所有想法連接，表達出因果關係的架構，還有所使用的標準等等）。這種格式可以使用在商業糾紛。

Demonstration of IRAC

BLYTH v. BIRMINGHAM WATERWORKS CO.

Court of Exchequer, 1856.

11 Exch. 781, 156 Eng. Rep. 1047.

[Defendants had installed water mains in the street, with fire plugs at various points. The plug opposite the plaintiff's house sprung a leak during a severe frost, because the connection between the plug and the water main was forced out by the expansion of freezing water. As a result, a large quantity of water escaped through the earth and into plaintiff's house, causing damage. The apparatus had been laid down 25 years ago, and had worked well during that time. The trial court left the question of defendants' negligence to the jury, which returned a verdict for plaintiff. Judgment was entered on the verdict, and defendants appealed.]

ALDERSON, B.— I am of opinion that there was no evidence to be left to the jury. The case turns upon the question, whether the facts proved show that the defendants were guilty of negligence. Negligence is the omission to do something which a reasonable man, guided upon those considerations which ordinarily regulate the conduct of human affairs, would do or doing something which a prudent and reasonable man would not do. The defendants might have been liable for negligence, if unintentionally, they omitted to do that which a reasonable person would have done, or did that which a person taking reasonable precautions would not have done.

A reasonable man would act with reference to the average circumstances of the temperature in ordinary years. The defendants had provided against such frosts as experience would have led men, acting prudently, to provide against and they are not guilty of negligence, because their precautions proved insufficient against the effects of the extreme severity of the frost of 1855, which penetrated to a greater depth than any which ordinarily occurs south of the polar regions. Such a state of circumstances constitutes a contingency against which no reasonable man can provide. The result was an accident for which the defendants cannot be held liable.

IRAC 的示範

BLYTH v. BIRMINGHAM WATERWORKS CO.

Court of Exchequer, 1856.

11 Exch. 781, 156 Eng. Rep. 1047.

〔被告在街道上安裝水管，並在好幾處定點上安裝消防栓，在原告住處對面的消防栓在一場濃霧中爆破，起因是水管與消防栓間因爲結凍的水導致水管爆裂，因此造成大量的水湧出且噴向原告住處而造成損害。這個設備在二十五年前就設置了，且在這二十五年間都正常運作。一審法院將爭議點被告的過失侵權責任送至陪審團決議，原告之訴被撤回重審。在陪審團評決中判決出爐，被告不服上訴。〕

ALDERSON, B.—我認爲沒有證據上的問題需要陪審團來決定。這案件有賴於是否有事實能夠證明被告是否有過失侵權責任。過失是沒有去做一件合理的人，在考慮過通常規範人世間的事務的指導之下，會做的事情，或是做了件一個合理的人不會去做的事情。被告也許需爲過失侵權負責，若非蓄意，他們疏忽了一個理性自然人應做的事，或做了應注意而未注意的事。被告可能要爲過失負責，縱然不是故意的，他們省略了去做一個合理人會做的事，或是做了一個合理的人不會去做的事。

一個合理的人他會參考在一般正常年代平均的溫度而行動。被告已經根據經驗採取合理的人所能防範這低溫的措施，因此他們並沒有過失，縱然因爲他們所採取的措施被證明是不足以防範 1855 年的極寒，而這極寒穿透了平常極圈之南所能穿透的深度。這樣的情況構成了合理的人無法防範的情況，這樣的結果是被告所不能負責的意外。

Brief of this case

Facts: The plaintiff sues the defendants for negligence on the damage to the plaintiff's house caused by the water that escaped from the leak of the water main due to the expansion of freezing water in a severe winter. The apparatus had been laid down 25 years ago, and had worked well during that time.

Issue: Had the defendants provided against such frosts as experience of a reasonable man would have led men, acting prudently, to provide against and they are not guilty of negligence, because their precautions proved insufficient against the effects of the extreme severity of the frost of 1855.

Rule of law: A reasonable man, when acting prudently with reference to the average circumstances of the temperature in ordinary years, is not negligent in damage caused by a contingency that he cannot prevent.

Analysis: The defendants are not negligent in their insufficient precaution against extreme severity of the frost in 1855 as a reasonable man is incapable of doing.

Negligence is the omission to do something which a reasonable man would do or doing something which a prudent and reasonable man would not do. A reasonable man would act with reference to the average circumstances of the temperature in ordinary years.

In this case, the defendants are not negligent because they had acted with prudence as a reasonable man. They had acted with prudence as a reasonable man because they had referred to the average temperature in the ordinary years in their work and the water main has worked well in the past twenty-five years regarding the average circumstances of the temperature. The extreme severity of the frost of 1855, which penetrated to a greater depth than any which ordinarily occurs south of the polar regions is not the average circumstances of the temperature in ordinary years.

Conclusion: Defendants have acted as a reasonable man and are not negligent in their insufficient precaution to prevent damages caused by the extreme severity of temperature from frost.

本案的摘要

事實：原告控告被告過失侵權，因爲原告埋設的水管在非常寒冷的冬天膨脹造成爆裂，而漫出的水造成原告房子的損害，該水管在二十五年前設置，在這期間當中運作正常。

爭議：被告是否已經根據合理的人經驗，採取謹愼措施防範這低溫，使得他們並沒有過失，縱然因爲他們所採取的措施被證明是不足以防範 1855 年的極寒。

法律：一個合理的人應該參考一般年代裡正常情況的溫度，對於他所不能預防的突發事件所造成的損害，並不負過失責任。

分析：被告並不由於他們對於 1855 年嚴寒的冬天不足的注意，就像合理的人無法注意一般，而有過失。

過失是沒有去做一個合理的人會做的事情，或是做了一件合理的人不會做的事情。一個合理的人會參考一般年代一般環境之下的溫度。

本案，被告並沒有過失，因爲他已經行使了合理人所會行使的注意。他行使了合理人會行使的注意，因爲他的工程參考一般年代之下的一般溫度，而且水管在過去二十五年一般正常情況之下的溫度運作得很好。1855 年的低溫穿透了極地之南正常情況能夠穿透的溫度。

結論：被告已經行使了合理人的注意，並不因未有足夠注意以防上極度的低溫所造成的損害而有過失。

KIRKSEY v. KIRKSEY.

Supreme Court of Alabama, 1845

8 Ala. 131

The plaintiff was the wife of defendant's brother, but had for some time been a widow, and had several children. In 1840, the plaintiff resided on public land, under a contract of lease, she had held over, and was comfortably settled, and would have attempted to secure the land she lived on. The defendant resided in Talladega country, some sixty, or seventy miles off. On the 10th October, 1840, he wrote to her the following letter:

"Dear sister Antillico—Much to my mortification, I heard, that brother Henry was dead, and one of his children. I know that your situation is one of grief, and difficulty. You had a bad chance before, but a great deal worse now. I should like to come and see you, but cannot with convenience at present ... I do not know whether you have a preference on the place you live on, or not. If you had, I would advise you to obtain your preference, and sell the land and quit the country, as I understand it is very unhealthy, and I know society is very bad. If you will come down and see me, I will let you have a place to raise your family, and I have more open land than I can tend; and on the account of your situation, and that of your family, I feel like I want you and the children to do well."

Within a month or two after the receipt of this letter, the plaintiff abandoned her possession, without disposing of it, and removed with her family, to the residence of the defendant, who put her in comfortable houses, and gave her land to cultivate for two years, at the end of which time he notified her to remove, and put her in a house, not comfortable, in the woods, which he afterwards required her to leave.

A verdict being found for the plaintiff, for two hundred dollars, the above facts were agreed, and if they will sustain the action, the judgment is to be affirmed, otherwise it is to be reversed.

ORMOND, J.—The inclination of my mind, is, that the loss and inconvenience, which the plaintiff sustained in breaking up, and moving to the defendant's, a distance of sixty miles, is a sufficient consideration to support the promise, to furnish her with a house, and land to cultivate, until she could raise her family. My brothers, however think, that the promise on the part of the defendant, was a mere gratuity, and that an action will not lie for its breach. The judgment of the Court below must therefore be, reversed, pursuant to the agreement of the parties.

KIRKSEY v. KIRKSEY

Supreme Court of Alabama, 1845

8 Ala. 131

原告是被告的兄長之配偶，她成爲寡婦已有一段時間了，她還帶著幾個孩子。在 1840 年，她在有租約的情況下居住於公有土地，她延長了租約，安穩地居住於此，並嘗試保有她居住的此塊土地。被告居住於塔拉迪加市，距原告大約六、七十英哩遠的地方。在 1840 年 10 月 10 日，她寫給了原告一封信，內容如下：

「親愛的大嫂，我感到非常的羞愧，我聽說了哥哥亨利和他一個孩子過世的消息了。我知道你的處境非常難過又困頓。你以前就過得不好了，但現在更糟糕了。我應該要去探望你，但我現在實在不方便。我不知道你是不是喜歡你居住的地方。如果是的話，我會建議你保有這份情感，把土地賣了離開故鄉，因爲我知道那裡不健康，社會情況也不好。如果你下來看我，我會讓你有一個地方能夠維持生計，且我有比我所能管理的更多的未開發土地。考慮到你的情況，和你的家人，我希望你和你的孩子們都能過得好。」

在這封信件簽收後的一或兩個月後，原告放棄了她的財產，也沒有做任何處理，就搬到了被告的居住地，被告將她安置在一棟舒適的房子裡，且給她土地耕種兩年。在被告通知原告搬離的最後期限裡，他將原告安置在一間不舒適的木屋，之後要求原告從那搬離。

陪審團給原告的判決出爐，賠償金額 200 元，以上的事實皆被承認，如果他們足以支持訴訟，判決就會被確認，反之判決就會被推翻。

ORMOND, J.—就我的想法而言，那些在原告處理過程中的損失和不方便，以及搬遷 60 英哩至被告居住處的事實，都是支持履行承諾的充分考量，讓原告有住處，且有土地能耕種，直到她可以肩負家庭生計，然而，我法院的同事弟兄們卻認爲，被告的部分承諾僅僅只是個恩惠，這樣違反不構成訴訟的理由，因此，根據雙方的協議，必須推翻原法院判決。

Facts: The plaintiff was the wife of the defendant's brother. The defendant, after his brother passed away, wrote to this sister-in-law that she could move to his land, a distance of sixty miles, to take care of her children. Upon receiving this letter, the plaintiff abandoned the land in her possession and moved into comfortable houses the defendant prepared. After two years, she was put by the defendant in an uncomfortable house in the woods and finally was required to leave.

Issue: Were the loss and inconvenience, which the plaintiff sustained in breaking away, and moving to the defendant's place, a distance of sixty miles, a sufficient consideration to support the defendant's promise to furnish her with a house and land to cultivate, until she could raise her family?

Rule of law (limited to Justice Ormond's opinion): The loss and inconvenience, which the plaintiff sustained in breaking up, and moving to the defendant's, a distance of sixty miles, is a sufficient consideration to support the Defendant's promise to be enforced.

Analysis: The defendant's promise is valid and is enforceable. His promise is valid and is enforceable because there is sufficient consideration given in exchange for the defendant's promise. There is sufficient consideration because the loss and inconvenience suffered by the plaintiff do give sufficient value to enforce the defendant's promise.

Conclusion: The defendant's promise is valid and is enforceable because it is supported by a sufficient consideration.

事實：原告是被告兄弟的妻子。被告在他的兄弟過世之後，寫信給這位寡婦，也就是他的大嫂，告訴她可搬到他的土地上，大約60英哩的距離來照顧她的孩子們。原告收到這封信之後，拋棄了她原本占有的土地，然後搬進了被告所準備舒適的住屋。兩年之後，被告把她放到森林中一個不舒適的房子，最後她被要求離開。

爭議：原告因離開原來的地方而搬到60英哩之外被告的地方，所承受的損失和不方便，是否足夠的對價來支持被告的承諾，也就是提供給她一棟房子還有可耕作的土地用以支持她的家庭嗎？

法律（限於ORMOND大法官的意見）：原告因爲被告的承諾而搬到60英哩之外被告的地方所承受的損失和不方便，可以成爲執行被告承諾的足夠的對價。

分析：被告的承諾是有效，而且能夠被執行。他的承諾是有效也能夠被執行是因爲有足夠的對價。這裡有足夠的對價是因爲原告所承受的損失還有不方便產生足夠的價值來執行被告的承諾。

結論：被告的承諾因爲有足夠的對價，所以是有效而且能被執行。

Why training on making a summary is necessary?

Making a summary of a piece of writing or of a speech requires a student to put ideas read or heard in consecutive and logical sequences under a cause and effect structure in a succinct form with plain language so that the readers can grasp the correct understanding effectively and efficiently of the writing or speech. A good summary requires a good organization by a student of the words read or heard, even if the writer or the speaker is not clear about the organization in his own works. By making a summary, a learner will quickly spot both the strength and the weakness of that writing or speech. Thus, practice on making a summary is excellent training for a student to acquire the ability to logically organize. To acquire the ability to logically organize will give rise to a correct analysis. Making a summary is also an important training for improving the students' reading and writing abilities because their understanding is required of the writing read or the speech heard, probably including the implication thereof, and therefore his ability to brief in his own words will improve.

爲什麼我們要練習做摘要？

對於一份寫作或是一場演說做成一份摘要，是要求學生將所聽到的或是所讀到的想法，按照前後以及邏輯的順序，在一個因果關係的架構之下，以簡單扼要的形式以及簡單語言表達出來，好讓讀者能夠在短時間之內很有效的了解所聽到或是讀到的內容。一份好的摘要，需要學生們對於讀到或是聽到的話語，具有良好的組織能力與整理，縱然作者或是演說者可能對於他自己所說或是所寫的缺乏良好的組織。製作摘要的時候，學習者能夠很快地找到寫作或是演說的優點與弱點。這樣的練習，是對學生邏輯組織能力非常良好的訓練。好的邏輯組織會產生正確的分析。摘要訓練對於提升學生的閱讀能力與寫作能力來說也是非常重要的，因爲可以測試學生對於所閱讀的文章或是聽到的演說了解的程度，並且以自己的話簡單扼要表達出他所讀過的或是所聽到的話語，包括其中可能衍生的意義。

In addition, the correct understanding of another person's words through logical organization and analysis can also help interaction with others because such understanding will bring about appropriate responses to the other person's words. This is because good interaction requires an appropriate response. An appropriate response requires true understanding of the other person, that is, empathy. Logical organization and analysis of the other person's words can bring about a good and correct understanding. Fair to say, a correct understanding of the other person's words is like locating a target in a hunting game before aiming or shooting can be initiated, the very first lesson in training of a good hunter. Correct understanding, once established, will also help students to develop their ability in making inferences from the other person's words and reading the implication thereof.

除此之外，透過邏輯組織以及分析來正確了解別人的話語，也能夠幫助我們與其他人的互動，因爲這樣的了解能夠帶來對別人話語的正確回應。一個正確的回應需要正確的了解，也就是同理心。把別人的話語以邏輯組織的方式進行分析，可以帶來正確的了解。持平而論，正確了解別人的話語，就像是在一個打獵活動當中找到目標，那是訓練一個好的獵人的第一個功課。一旦建立起正確的了解，也能夠幫助學生們發展他們從別人話語當中進行推論的能力，以及注意到這些話語當中隱含的意思。

Introduction of IRAC

The summary of the two legal cases are briefed in a form called "IRAC" for analysis and persuasion, which is widely used in the training of all law schools across the United States and the memorandums prepared by their legal practitioners. IRAC is an acronym which stands for issue, rule of law, analysis, and conclusion. The issue is stated subsequently from a summary of a set of facts, followed by a rule of law clearly indicating the standard to be used in evaluating the facts. The analysis explains why and how the rules are applied to the facts. Please note that issue spotting is the most crucial part of an argument as we have seen on those GMAT questions. Once the issues are decided, the whole framework for an argument can be established, standards can be ascertained, and a counter argument can be prepared. Therefore, issue spotting is extremely essential to a student's training on debate, critical thinking, and his future ability on problem solving.

IRAC 的介紹

上面兩個法律案件的摘要，是以「IRAC」的方式進行濃縮，而這種方式是整個美國的法學院以及他們的執業律師所使用的分析與說服方法。IRAC 是一個縮寫，代表了爭議、法律規則、分析以及結論。先陳述事實，接著提出爭議，而後是法律規則，表明了判斷事實所使用的標準。分析部分解釋了爲什麼法律規則可以用在這些事實上以及應該如何應用。要注意，找出爭議點是在辯論中最重要的部分，就像我們在 GMAT 中看到的問題一樣。一旦找出問題後我們可以建立整個辯論架構，也可以確立標準，進而準備駁斥反方的說法。因此，找出爭議點對於學生在辯論、批判性思考，以及他未來在解決問題能力上是非常重要的。

To find an issue from facts, a careful review of all facts and information including the opinions from the opponent's side is necessary for locating the main ideas and concepts. To search for a possible cause and effect relation between facts and ideas could require reading hundreds of pages, sometimes thousands, which is often quite strenuous with no positive result guaranteed. However, the devoted effort can help to nurture a students' ability on summarizing a set of complicated facts concisely and succinctly with issues being precisely spotted. Such ability is highly desirable in any business field.

要從事實中找到爭議點，我們必須很謹慎地檢視所有的事實與資訊，包括對手的看法，這樣才能找出主要的想法與概念。在找出事實與概念之間的可能因果關係，需要閱讀大量的資料，幾百頁或是上千頁，這通常是非常繁重的工作，而且不保證有正面的結果。但是所投入的努力可以培養學生對於複雜事實以簡明、具有效率的方式濃縮成爲摘要，並且展現正確的爭議點，這樣的能力在任何商業部門都是極需要的。

The section on analysis probably will be slightly difficult for a Taiwan student to follow because we simply do not offer such kind of training in our educational system. Analysis basically serves as a bridge between a proposition and a possible answer. It is a step by step reasoning process and each sentence is often carefully linked by the magical term "because". "Because" is used for explaining the relationship between a subject and an object. In an analysis process, an object in one sentence often serves as a subject in the next sentence with a new object followed as illustrated in the preceding section. By this process, an inference can be made through a sequence of logical reasoning that establishes the causal links between sentences and paragraphs that leads to a final conclusion, as we have elaborated on in the prior sections with some examples that were used for the learners' understanding.

關於分析的部分，對於臺灣學生來說可能比較困難了解，因爲在我們的教育體系之下並沒有這樣訓練。分析基本上是問題與可能答案之間的橋梁。它是一個一步一步的論理過程，而每一個句子通常都是由這樣的字眼「因爲」所連結起來。「因爲」是用來解釋兩個事件之間的關係。在一個分析的過程中，一個句子的受詞通常會變成下一個句子的主詞，然後在銜上一個新的受詞，就像我們在前段所說明的一樣。透過這個程序，我們可以經由邏輯推論的過程得到一個推論，然後建立句子之間以及段落之間彼此的因果關係，最後達到結論，就像我們在前面章節所示範的一樣。

13 Memorandum for argument

In an article with a nature of a commentary or a memorandum prepared for an argument, for example, an academic thesis or business documents dealing with disputes, it is good to start with a fact as an example to raise a question or a set of questions. This is because questions demand answers and thus create a need for exploration. A true case will give readers a rough picture on the factual background explaining what, when, where, how and why things happen and between whom. Facts in a true case refer to something that happened in the past and therefore form a story. A story generally can intrigue the listeners' interest easier and help them remember better, and the facts mentioned can hardly be rebutted. On the level of persuasion, facts should be used often as long as the message is clear. In a matter of debate, facts provided from the opposite side should be complete rather than partial, because facts will decide what the issues are and the issues will affect the standards adopted and thus carry an influence on the analysis and, consequently, the conclusion reached.

13 辯論備忘錄

在一項評論文章或是具有辯論性質的備忘錄當中，例如學生論文或是處理商業糾紛的文件，以事實上的例子來提出問題或一系列的問題，是很好的開始。這是因爲有問題就產生了探索的需要。一個實際的例子會給讀者們在事實的背景上有大概的了解，也解釋了事件是什麼、何時、何地、如何以及爲什麼發生，而且是在誰之間發生的。而在眞實案例中的事實，提到的是過去所發生的事情，因此也是故事的一種形式。故事總是能夠激發聽眾的興趣，而且也能方便他們記憶也記得清楚。況且既然是事實，也很難被反駁。在說服這個階層來說，應該常常使用事實，只要所包含的訊息夠清楚的話。在辯論上，對方所提供的事實必須完整的，而不是片面，因爲事實會決定什麼是爭議，而爭議會影響到標準的選用，因而進一步的影響到分析以及最後的結論。

Once issues are spotted and raised, the standard will be adopted and applied. In a business world, the standard usually refers to provisions in a contract or something that both sides have agreed on. Past practices or general customs in the business course are often referred to as well. For example, defective products generally are non-conforming products and will make a seller liable for a breach of contract. To decide if the products are non-conforming, we have to refer to, for example, the purchase order and mutual correspondence to see what specifications that both sides have agreed on. If the products are all made according to the specifications required by the purchase order, then the products are not non-conforming though they might be defective (because the specifications in the purchase order from the buyer is defective in design and, in this case, the buyer should be liable for the defective products). Therefore, the issue here is NOT if the products are defective but rather non-conforming. It is always important to ascertain the issue at the beginning. The standard can be decided only if an issue is ascertained. Once a standard is ascertained and adopted, then the analysis can be made accordingly by applying the standard to the facts. Analysis is a form of discussion and should cover the pros and cons. In other words, a counter argument from the opposite side should be prepared and examined. In dealing with a business dispute, an argument from the opposite side should be read carefully. Examination under the approaches suggested in the prior section will show their weakness. Try to place their argument in a consecutive sequence with a logical order. Such arrangement will show their weakness in an argument. Once our argument has been prepared and delivered, our experienced manager should be able to foresee the possible reaction and response from the clients in complaint after their reading of our argument, and he will know how to respond. This approach of writing starting from the facts stated, the issues obtained, the adopted standard, and ending in a conclusion is quite similar to the old Chinese writing style 起承轉合 (beginning, elaboration, contrary view, analysis and synthesis as a conclusion) which has been in prevalent practice among traditional Chinese intellectuals. This format can be used in a memorandum prepared in a debate in school or in the real business world.

一旦找出爭議點並且提出，接著就會選擇而且適用標準。在一個商業世界裡，所謂的標準，通常是指契約的規定或是雙方所同意的規則。雙方過去的做法還有業界通常的做法，也可以當作參考。例如，有瑕疵的產品通常都是不合規定的產品，會使得賣方負擔違約的責任。但是要決定產品是不是不合規定，我們必須看一看，比方說訂單，還有雙方往來的通信來發現究竟什麼是雙方共同同意的規格。如果產品都是根據訂單上的規格進行生產，那這些產品就是符合規定的，雖然產品可能是有瑕疵的（例如訂單中的規格本身在設計上可能就有瑕疵，這種情況下，訂單的買方自己就要負責）。因此這裡的爭議點，就不是產品是不是有瑕疵，而是他們是否符合規定。所以，在一開始就找出爭議點是非常重要的事情。標準只有在爭議點找到之後才能決定。一旦標準決定之後，分析就能夠完成，也就是將規則應用在事實上，應用的情況就如同在前面法律摘要所看到的情況一樣。而分析是討論的一種形式，應該包括正反的論點。換句話說，我們應該要知悉對手相反的論點並且進行檢驗。在處理商業糾紛，對方的說法應該仔細的研究，按照先前所建議的方法來進行檢驗。也就是試著將他們的說法，以邏輯規則安排在先後順序上。這樣的安排會顯現出他們說法上的弱點。一旦我們發出我們的說詞的時候，一個有經驗的經理人可以很快預見到對方在收到我們的說法後，所可能有的反應以及他們的回覆，並且知道我們應該如何做出應對。這一種方法從事實的陳述，爭議的提出，標準的採用，分析的完成以及最後的結論與中國知識分子所經常使用的起承轉合非常類似。這類的格式可以廣泛的應用在學校寫作以及商業文書處理上。

A movie recommended for learning debates

"Thank you for smoking" is an excellent movie to demonstrate some skills used in a debate. The protagonist is a spokesman for a big tobacco company and his job is to defend the company. He has to face all challenges in any occasion as that on TV or hearing from any individual or organization who are against smoking. However, he is able to manage the pressure because he likes what he is doing. People think that he is spinning the truth. As he says, if you can do tobacco, you can do anything. Readers of this book are highly advised to watch that movie, probably a few times while taking some notes. You are guaranteed to receive your payoff for your time and effort. There is no need for me to explore the details at the current stage. However, there are some interesting notes worth our attention. One interesting note from a conversation between the father and his son in the movie is worth mentioning. The father claimed that, as a debater, you only need to prove the other side is wrong. But his son replied that you didn't prove that you were right! His father said that he only needed to prove the other side was wrong because it was an audience that he was going after. This is true essence of a debate. In a debate, it is highly likely that no one really knows an answer, as admitted by Socrates. Debate is only a process to remove the impossible in a journey searching for the possible.

一部在學習辯論上，值得推薦的電影

《銘謝吸菸》在示範一些辯論技巧上是非常好的一部電影。男主角是一個大型菸草公司的發言人，他的工作就是爲公司說話。他必須在各種場合，例如電視或是公聽會，面對來自於那些反菸個人或團體的挑戰。就如同他所說的，如果你能夠爲菸草辯護，你就能夠爲任何事情辯護。我強烈建議本書的讀者們欣賞這部影片，也許欣賞個幾次甚至記下筆記。你所花的時間跟精神一定會得到回報的。在這個階段，我們不需要討論這些細節。但是有幾點値得我們注意。其中有一場父子之間的對話値得我們提一下。父親說到，身爲一個辯論者，你只需要證明其他人是錯的就足夠了。但是他的兒子回答，你並沒有證明你是對的！他父親說，他只需要證明對手是錯的，因爲他所訴求的是群衆。這就是辯論的精華。就像蘇格拉底所承認的一樣，一場辯論中非常有可能沒有人知道什麼是答案。辯論只是藉由把不可能的移開，進而尋找可能答案的旅行。

To rebut an argument, the most effective is to locate the standard used for making an evaluation. As mentioned in the preceding section, the same set of facts, if judged under different standards, will result in a different conclusion. This rule can be applied to smoking. In terms of hazards caused to health, smoking should be banned. However, if the standard is changed from health to personal choice, then smoking should be allowed. Changing the standard of course changes the conclusion even if the facts stay the same. That is what the spokesman in the movie is talking about. Debate connotes the idea of a judgment and a judgment requires a standard. In any matter related to a judgment, find out what the standard is that is being used and examine the standard to see if there are any other possibilities. Once other possibilities are introduced, the shield from which your opponent is hiding could be well removed. Once the weakness is exposed, a defense will be difficult for the opponent.

要反駁一項說法，最有效方法就是找出他所判斷的標準。就像在前面所提到的。相同的事實，如果在不同的標準之下會產生不同的結論。這個規則也可以應用在抽菸這件事情上。如果判斷的標準是對健康的傷害，那應該禁止抽菸。但是如果標準從健康變更爲個人選擇的自由，那抽菸就可以被准許。辯論本身就帶有評斷的性質，而評斷一定會有一個標準。任何事情與評斷有關的話，那就應該先找出標準是什麼，然後檢驗那個標準，看看是不是有其他可能性。如果一旦有其他的可能性，那你對手所賴以掩護的盾牌就會被移開。一旦弱點暴露，你的對手就很難進行防禦。

Summary of Debate Techniques Used in the Movie "Thank You for Smoking"

Ⓐ Take a firm and clear position, even if you are making a defense on behalf of a tobacco company. He who doubts is like a wave on the sea, blown and tossed by the wind.

B Convince with facts.
C Challenge the authority. Hold neither fear nor hesitation when making an argument.
D Cast doubt BUT not necessarily a denial on an opponent's argument.
E Use language, examples and analogies on the level consistent with the people you talk to so that your words are within their understanding.
F Try to persuade the listeners with an analogy from a common experience (e.g. chocolate was used as an example when speaking to kids on issues relating to their free choice on smoking).
G Understand human nature (e.g. greed).
H Prove your opponent's position is possibly tainted because of self-interest involved in his position (e.g. the anti-smoking group possibly profiting from the death of smokers).
I Avoid arguments on a public known fact such as harm caused by smoking.
J Question the expertise of an opponent.
K Question the standard used in an opponent's argument.
L Apply the same standard used by the opponent to all other similar acts or products to see what other possible consequences might result.
M Argue correctly and you will never be wrong. For example, building your argument on a widely accepted value which may be used as both a shield for defense and spear for attack

(e.g. using free choice, a concept of liberty and widely accepted value, to claim a right for or against smoking and probably for and against abortion as well as other issues that currently exist).

N Shifting the focus of an audience from your vulnerable position to a weakness of your opponent's, for example, avoid an attack on the harm caused by cigarettes by drawing the public's attention to the opponent's possible pecuniary interest in anti-smoking campaigns.

O Apply the standard used by the opponent to judge the opponent's own argument (e.g. evaluating the harm caused by cheese on a heart problem under the same standard as that used against that by cigarettes).

P Relevant examples and facts help to buildup creditability.

Q Be confident about your words and always smile.

R Stay clam even when the whole world is against you.

電影《銘謝吸菸》所使用辯論技巧的摘要：

A 立場必須堅定而明確，即使你在爲香菸公司做辯護。心中有懷疑的人就像海上的波浪，受強風吹襲而且翻滾。

B 用事實來進行說服。

C 挑戰權威。進行辯論的時候，不要有恐懼也不要有遲疑。

D 對於對手的辯詞提出質疑，而不必然全盤否定。

E 使用與你說話對象層次符合的語言、例子以及比喻，好讓聽衆了解你的話語。

F 利用相同的經驗舉例來說服聽衆，例如：「使用巧克力當作例子，當跟小孩子談論對於抽菸自由選擇權利的時候。」

G 了解人性，例如：「貪婪」。

H 證明你對手的立場可能因爲自我利益的影響而顯得不純正（例如：反菸團體可能從吸菸者的死亡而獲得利益）。

I 避免爭論一個大家都知道的事實，例如：吸菸所造成的傷害。

J 質問對手的專業性。

K 質問對手辯論中所使用的標準。

L 將對手所使用的標準適用在其他事件或產品上，看看有何可能後果。

M 使用正確的辯論方法，你永遠不會錯。例如：將你的辯詞建立在大家所接受的價值觀上，因而當作盾牌來防衛及刀槍來進行攻擊。例如；使用自由選擇的權利，一個自由的概念以及廣泛接受的價值觀來聲稱對於抽菸或是墮胎的權利。

N 將群衆的注意力從你的弱點移轉到對手的弱點，例如：「將群衆對於香菸所造成傷害的攻擊，移轉到對手對於反菸活動上金錢的利益。」

O 使用對手的標準來評斷對手的辯詞（例如：以香菸所造成傷害的標準來評斷起司所造成的心血管疾病）。

P 使用相關的例子或是事實來建立可信度。

Q 對於所說的話要有自信，而且要面帶笑容。

R 縱然全世界都反對你，也要保持冷靜。

14 Preparation and practice on topics for debate

In debate training, those who challenge the current system take the affirmative side while the supporters of the current system should take the negative. For example, the death penalty is in a current practice in our legal system, therefore the affirmative will challenge and argue against the current practice while the negative will support and defend the maintenance of the death penalty. On the issue of homosexual marriage, the affirmative will challenge and argue against the current practice which refuses to recognize such marriage while the negative will support the status quo and forbid homosexual marriage. Students who participate in this competition may follow the suggestions given with respect to statement making and cross-examination.

14 辯論題目的準備與實踐

在訓練辯論，挑戰現有制度的是正方，而支持現有制度的則是反方。例如死刑是我們現行的法律制度，因此正方必須要挑戰而且反對死刑，而反方則要支持以及防衛目前的實行制度。在同性戀婚姻方面，正方要挑戰而且反對目前現有制度，而反方則是要支持現有制度並且主張禁止同性戀婚姻。學生參加這個比賽可以參考下面所建議大綱製作以及問題的方式。

Consideration on two debate topics regarding capital punishment and homosexual marriage.

關於死刑以及同性戀婚姻作爲辯論題目的考量之點。

Considerations on establishing a framework for capital punishment:

In a debate discussing whether capital punishment should be abolished, the students may follow the below advice for preparation.

Ⓐ Historical background of capital punishment.

Ⓑ Current legislations in the various countries of the world.

Ⓒ When did the voice of abolition of capital punishment come out? What are the reasons?

Ⓓ What is exactly the evil that such proposal attempts to curb? What is the evolution?

Ⓔ How many countries in this world follow this policy in their legislation? Why? In the countries following the abolition, is evil curbed? What is the cost if any?

Ⓕ Are there any international conventions on this issue? What do they say? What is the policy behind it?

Ⓖ Why do some refuse to follow this policy and still keep capital punishment? If capital punishment is kept for certain reasons or effect, can that effect be achieved by any other alternative?

Ⓗ What are the issues presented on capital punishment?

Ⓘ What are their arguments and what are their weaknesses and strengths?

對於死刑問題建立架構的考量因素：

在討論死刑應該被廢止的辯論中，學生可以考慮下面的建議來進行準備。

Ⓐ 死刑的歷史背景。

B 現今世界上不同國家的立法。

C 廢除死刑的聲音什麼時候出現？理由是什麼？

D 這樣一個提案是想遏止什麼樣的問題？它的演進過程如何？

E 現在世界上有多少國家是尊崇這樣政策？爲什麼？在那些廢除死刑的國家，這樣的罪惡是否有被遏止？代價是什麼？

F 對於這個問題，世界公約是不是有所規範？他們說了什麼？後面的政策理由又是如何？

G 爲什麼有些國家拒絕遵守這樣政策繼續保持死刑，如果繼續保持死刑是爲了達到某些效果，我們可以透過其他替代方式達到這樣效果嗎？

H 死刑的爭議點是什麼？

I 他們的論點是什麼？他們論點的弱點跟強項又在哪裡？

After examining all the facts and reasons, the abolition side (the affirmative), for example, may argue that the death penalty serves no purpose but revenge, e.g. "an eye for an eye, a tooth for a tooth". To execute people is cruel, inhumane and thus barbaric. Besides, there is an alternative to separate the murderer permanently from society, e.g. life imprisonment with no parole. For the above reasons, the death penalty should not be accepted by any civilized nation.

在檢驗事實與理由之後，廢止死刑的一方可以辯稱死刑沒有其他目的，只是報復而已，例如：以牙還牙，以眼還眼。處決人犯是很殘忍的、不人道的，而且野蠻的。除此之外，也有其他替代方法將殺人犯永久跟世界隔離，例如：不得假釋的終身監禁。爲了上述的原因，死刑不應該被任何文明國家接受。

The other side, which supports capital punishment, may defend their position by arguing that the true purpose of the death penalty is on preventing future murders in order to maintain public security and social order. To achieve that goal, the punishment must be serious enough, of course, compared with the degree of harm caused to society. Murder is illegally taking a human life. To execute a murderer is cruel but is fair in light of the cruelty imposed on the victims by the murders and is effective in preventing future killings. Besides, punishment by life imprisonment without parole cannot serve justice because the murderer's life can be spared but the victim had to die. Therefore, to protect the general public and serve justice, capital punishment must be preserved.

支持死刑的另外一方可以辯稱，死刑眞正的目的，是在防止未來的凶殺案以維持公共安全以及社會秩序。要達到上面的目標，懲罰必須夠嚴重，當然要與殺人在社會造成的傷害程度相符合。謀殺是非法取人的生命。執行死刑很殘忍，但是考量殺人犯加諸於被害者的殘忍度，那是公平的而且可以有效遏止謀殺。此外，不可假釋的終身監禁沒有辦法達到公平正義，因爲殺人犯的生命可以得到保全，而被害者卻非死不可。因此，要保護公眾而且滿足公平正義的需求，死刑必須保留。

Arguments from both sides clearly present a conflict between the two sides here, the controversy between individualism (e.g. cruelty and barbarism) supported by the abolition side and collectivism (e.g. public safety and social order) by the other side. Both are concerned with human rights and the difference is based on the standard, either individualism or collectivism. The same facts, if judged under a different standard, will change a conclusion completely. Remember that key issues are the very crucial factors in deciding the consequence of the controversy and must be spotted and studied.

兩邊的說法都提出一個爭議點的衝突性，也就是廢止死刑個人主義的觀點（例如：死刑太過殘忍以及野蠻），與集體主義的觀點（應該要維護公共安全與社會秩序）。兩者都與人權有關，而他們的差異就在於標準，或者從個人主義或者從集體主義來看這件事。同樣的事實，如果採取不一樣的標準，會完全改變結論。要記得在決定一個爭議的時候，主要爭議點是非常關鍵的，一定要找出來且詳細研究。

Another example is the issue on whether homosexual marriage should be legalized. Students may follow the advice as suggested above to conduct a study on all levels regarding marriage including historic background, especially from religious and cultural perspectives, reasons for such a change, and the process of evolution shown from legislations adopted by some individual countries in legalization and, of course, the reasons from the opposite side why some countries refuse to recognize homosexual marriage. Supporters of homosexual marriages challenge the current system on the reason of equality, a concept as well-reserved in the fundamental human rights and they claim that their love through marriage should be protected as any of heterosexual marriage.

The opposite side who stands against homosexual marriage may argue that such marriage should not be allowed because the law protects family with expectation of maintaining the human race through sanctity of marriage. Since homosexual couples cannot reproduce, therefore they are not equally situated with heterosexual couples. Equal protection only protects those who are similarly situated. Therefore, homosexual marriage should not be recognized. Again, once the main themes from both sides are found, an analysis should be made step by step.

另外一個例子，就是關於同性戀婚姻合法化的問題。學生們可以參考前面的建議，在各個層面對婚姻做個研究，包括歷史的背景，特別是從宗教還有文化的角度，改變的理由以及同意同性戀婚姻個別國家的立法演化的過程，當然還有反對同性戀婚姻國家的理由。支持同性婚姻者，以基本人權的平等概念作爲理由，挑戰現有的制度，他們聲稱他們的愛情，應該像其他異性戀者的愛情一樣透過婚姻獲得保障。

反對同性婚姻的可能主張，這樣的婚姻不應該被准許，因爲法律透過婚姻的神聖化保障能夠繁衍種族的家庭。同性戀者沒有辦法生育，因此他們與異性戀者並不應該站在平等的地位。平等保護原則應該只保護那些地位相同的，因此同性戀婚姻不應該被准許。一旦找出兩邊的主軸，分析就可以逐步完成。

Demonstrations

The following shows a research process with pros and cons discussed on the topic regarding capital punishment as well as a sample writing on an argument in support of capital punishment. To establish a framework for research on capital punishment, there are some possible points to be explored in this research such as:

History of capital punishment:

What acts were subject to capital punishment?

When did it start?

Why have it?

How to enforce it?

Why some countries abolished capital punishment?

Where and when did the abolishment start?

Are there any common characteristics that are shared among those countries which abolished capital punishment? What policies are behind it?

Why should capital punishment be maintained?

Why should capital punishment be abolished?

Does abolishing capital punishment lead to a low crime rate or vice versa?

示範

以下顯示出在死刑的議題上，關於正反意見的研究過程同時提出支持死刑的示範文章。要建立關於死刑研究的架構必須探討以下幾點，例如：

死刑的歷史爲何？

什麼行爲是可以判處死刑？

這個刑罰什麼時候開始的？

爲什麼要有這樣的刑罰？

如何執行？

爲什麼有些國家廢除死刑？

廢除死刑從哪裡開始？何時開始？

這樣的廢止死刑的國家有什麼共同性？廢死政策的理由是什麼？

爲什麼應該維持死刑？

爲什麼應該廢止死刑？

死刑的效果是否降低犯罪率或是反而提升？

Reasons taken by the supporting party (supporting capital punishment):

- A Historic, religious and cultural relics.
- B Justice required for punishment of wrongs and maintaining social order.
- C Illegally taking a human's life is a serious crime.
- D Appeasing the victim's family.
- E Murderers, if unpunished, may conduct future killings again.

Ⓕ A warning of threat to the whole society to prevent such potential crimes from happening again.

Ⓖ Waste of taxpayer's money to keep murderers alive.

反方的理由（支持死刑）：

Ⓐ 歷史、宗教以及文化上的傳統遺留。

Ⓑ 懲罰惡行以及維護社會秩序的正義。

Ⓒ 非法殘害人類的生命是一個殘忍的罪行。

Ⓓ 安慰受害者家屬。

Ⓔ 謀殺犯如果不處罰會導致他將來犯更多的罪。

Ⓕ 對於整個社會潛在犯罪者的警告，防止未來的犯案。

Ⓖ 維持犯罪者的生命根本是浪費納稅人的錢。

Reasons taken by the opposing party (opposing capital punishment):

Ⓐ Capital punishment is cruel and uncivilized because of taking a human life. If people deplore killings, why do they engage in this activity?

Ⓑ An eye for an eye was an old practice which had been barred for a long time from modern societies of all civilized nations in Europe.

Ⓒ Liberty is equally important to life. Punishment by permanent deprivation of a man's liberty is as serious as that by capital punishment.

Ⓓ Capital punishment is only maintained for revenge and serves as the evidence of human cruelty as a last ancient remnant.

E Modern trend of psychology and criminology.

F Life carries serious meaning and is more valuable than what money can measure.

G No conclusive evidence can show the absolute causation between capital punishment and a decreased murder rate.

H Possibility of a wrong execution can never be redressed by any means.

正方的理由（反對死刑）：

A 死刑要剝奪人的生命，非常殘酷而且不文明，如果人們痛恨殺人，爲什麼他們還要從事這樣的行爲？

B 以牙還牙，以眼還眼，是一種舊時代的做法，許多歐洲的文明國家已禁止一段時間了。

C 自由與生命同等價值，永久剝奪一個人的自由跟死刑一樣的嚴厲。

D 死刑只是爲了復仇的原因而存在，而且只是人類自古代所留下殘忍的遺跡。

E 現代心理學與刑事學的理論趨勢。

F 人的生命有非常深遠的意義而且不是金錢能夠衡量。

G 沒有證據能夠顯示死刑的執行與犯罪的降低有絕對的因果關係。

H 死刑的誤判與執行完全不能事後補救。

Writing sample on capital punishment

Justice, a scale with two pans balanced

"If rewarding an act of vileness with mercy, then what should you reward an act of mercy with?" thus said Confucius.

死刑寫作範例公義，二邊平衡的天平

「以德報怨，何以報德？」—孔子

Two pans on a scale can be balanced only when the weight on each side is the same. A scale is therefore regarded as a symbol of equality and fairness on which justice is laid. Last month, five convicted inmates were executed in one day by the Justice Ministry of Taiwan. The European Council immediately loudly reprimanded Taiwan for such executions by voicing to cancel visa exemptions granted not long ago to Taiwan tourists. Last week, a junior high girl in Yunlin County was raped and murdered by a repeated sex offender who was recently freed from imprisonment in spite of, prior to his release, all the psychological evaluations conducted which had unanimously indicated a high possibility of the offender's propensity to re-commit sex crimes. Such a shoddy justice administration caused a great uproar in Taiwan's society. The Taiwan president soon made a declaration that Taiwan will continue to follow its penal code to enforce capital punishment. Currently, there are over forty convicted of murder in the Taiwan jail queued to be executed and the upcoming executions have intrigued a great concern from the European Council. Nevertheless, as weight is added on one pan of justice to balance another tilted one, loud and urgent voices from a great majority of the Taiwanese is calling for justice in punishing criminals, especially capital punishment for all cold-blooded murderers.

天秤的兩邊只有在重量相同時才能平衡。天秤也因此被當作平等與公平的象徵，而這正是正義的基礎。前一陣子臺灣的法務部在一天之內處決了五名犯人。歐洲商會立刻大聲的譴責臺灣，並且威脅要取消給臺灣觀光客的免簽待遇。上一週，一個雲林縣的國中女生被一個強暴的連續慣犯強暴之後並且殺害，而這個強暴犯最近才被釋放出來，雖然在他釋放之前所有的心理測試都一致顯示他再犯的可能性。這樣草率的司法在臺灣社會造成了很大的憤怒。臺灣的總統迅速宣示臺灣會繼續遵守刑法並且執行死刑。現階段在臺灣的監獄裡有超過四十個已經定罪並且等待處決的犯人，這也引起了歐洲議會的強烈關注。雖然如此，就像是失去了平衡，傾向於一邊的正義天秤一樣，臺灣廣大的群眾發出強烈並且急迫的聲音，要求正義處罰犯人，特別是對那些冷血的殺人犯應該處以極刑。

Capital punishment has always existed in Chinese society. In ancient times, the Chinese people, whether the autocracy or the general public, who believed that strict punishment should be imposed especially during the times of turmoil replete of crimes. For the autocracy, capital punishment was especially considered as the most effective and efficient tool to curb murder, robbery, rebellion or any crime with a serious nature, thus, the social order, the people's lives and property, government authority and the security of an empire could be maintained. For the common folks, anger could be vented upon a criminal with revenge as "an eye for an eye" for justice. To execute a murderer can also set up a powerful exemplar of punishment to educate the public and to deter further crimes. Such belief is still embedded nowadays in the hearts of the great majority with the prevalent practice in the judicial systems of both Taiwan and China. These beliefs and practice in fairness have a long historical origin and therefore have become implacable as part of the Chinese culture.

死刑一直存在中國社會。在古代中國人不管是貴族或是一般的平民百姓，相信治亂世用重典。對於統治階層而言，死刑被認爲是遏止殺人、搶奪叛亂，或是任何嚴重判刑的有效工具，也因而社會秩序、人民生命財產、政府的權威、人民的安全可以得到維持。大部分的平民百姓對於犯罪者可以「以牙還牙，以眼還眼」的方式進行報復，因而滿足正義的要求。處決一個犯人也可以達到教化群眾的目的，因而阻止未來的犯罪。這樣的信念一直到了今天還存在於大部分中國人的心中。相信這樣公平的信念和做法，在中國文化當中有著淵源已久而且不易變動的歷史根源。

A few months ago, then minister of justice in Taiwan, Ms. Wang Chin-feng, resigned from her position because of her refusal to sign and enforce the death penalty. Her resignation received applause from the general public of Taiwan and the approval from the Taiwan president. This phenomenon confirms once more the belief in the capital punishment among Taiwan society as penicillin for curing social infection of increasing murder rate.

幾個月之前，臺灣的法務部長王清峰，由於拒絕簽屬執行死刑的命令因而辭職，她的辭職獲得總統的准許還有臺灣民眾的掌聲。這個現象確認了在臺灣社會對於死刑的信念，也就是死刑是解決社會日益增加犯罪的良藥。

Two month ago, a scandal broke out and stunned the whole Taiwan society. This case is related to a soldier who was sentenced to death in 1997 for the crime of raping and murdering a young girl. The soldier was soon executed accordingly, but then recently the person who committed the said crime was arrested and made a confession. Thus, such case proved to be a wrongful execution committed in the name of the state. It was alleged that the high ranking military officials then were under great pressure from society to find the murderer and therefore coercion was imposed on the suspected soldier in order to obtain his confession. This wrongful execution case indeed arouses a great concern and protest from the anti-capital punishment groups as well as foreign organizations.

兩個月前，在臺灣社會爆發一個醜聞而且震撼了整個社會，這個案件是關於一個士兵強暴以及殺害一個年輕女孩因而被判死刑。這個士兵很快被槍決，但是一直到了最近，眞正的犯罪者才被逮捕而且做了自白。這樣的案件，證明了以國家名義執行了錯誤的死刑。有報導指出當時的高階軍官在社會壓力之下，要迅速地找到這個謀殺者，因而對於嫌犯嚴刑逼供取得他的自白。這樣的錯誤，導致廢死團體以及外國組織強烈的關心和抗議。

The anti-capital punishment groups argue that capital punishment is a murder committed by humans who tend to make mistakes, and is condemned by a state which is not omniscience like God. The current judicial system can render no impeccable judgment. Mistakes once made leave no room for restoration of the innocent lives lost. The group further argues that it is not necessary to deprive life in order to ensure that social order is maintained because such purpose could be served by permanent imprisonment of the convicted without parole. The only purpose of execution only serves as revenge which is cruel, blood thirsty, uncivilized and full of mistakes ensuing a permanently indelible stain. These arguments are made with merit to a certain extent and are acceptable by a good deal of the western civilized nations.

廢止死刑的團體聲稱，死刑本身就是以國家民意所做的謀殺，而國家並非上帝，只是會犯錯誤的個人而已。現有的司法體系沒有辦法給一個完美的判決。錯誤一旦發生，無辜的生命沒有辦法挽回。廢死團體更進一步宣稱社會秩序的維持並不需要依靠剝奪生命，終生監禁不得假釋，一樣可以達到目的，執行死刑的唯一目的只是報復，這是殘忍的、嗜血的、不文明的，而且充滿錯誤，因而留下不可磨滅的陰影。這樣的說法具有相當部分的價值，而且被相當多數的西方國家接受。

Many countries in Europe have either abolished capital punishment or postponed its enforcement. Few, such as the U.S., still reserve this penalty. We cannot possibly deny that no judgment rendered by a human is impeccable. Yet man-made mistakes can be reduced to the minimum level by a well calculated design of a judicial mechanism. All decisions giving the death penalty should be reviewed with strict scrutiny by the highest judicial level on both the substantial and procedural levels. When in doubt, no capital punishment can be enforced. As an old Chinese aphorism goes, "We do not stop eating simply because we choke sometimes." Similarly, airplanes do not stop flying merely because crashes happen sometimes.

許多歐洲的國家已經廢止死刑或是延緩死刑的執行。有些國家像是美國依然保有死刑。我們沒辦法否認人類的判斷是不完美的，但是人爲的問題可以透過對於司法運作的精心設計降到最低。所有死刑的判決都應該由最高司法單位在實體與程序上以嚴格的標準進行審核。當有懷疑的時候，死刑不應該執行。就像中國古語所說的：「我們不可以因噎廢食。」同樣的，我們也不可以因爲空難的發生而不搭飛機。

On the level of logics, the purpose served by capital punishment in terms of securing social order may arguably be achieved through the permanent separation of the convicted murderer by life imprisonment while leaving no room for the family of the victim to vent their anger. The mind of the general public might not be appeased as such a question is echoed constantly, "Why does the innocent have to die while the life of a murderer should be spared?" Justice is a scale with two pans balancing. Capital punishment is by no means an ancient remedy. It is a fair treatment to those who have inflicted death on others. Once an intentional murder is committed, the murderer has voluntarily submitted his claim to the right of survival to the state and subject to a forfeited future.

在邏輯的層面而言，社會秩序的維持可能可以透過終生監禁，但是被害家屬的憤怒無法得到宣洩。群眾的心裡依然會有這樣的疑問：「爲什麼無辜的人必須要死，而殺人的人可以存活？」正義是天秤的兩邊必須要平衡，死刑並不是一個古代留下來的遺跡而已，對於謀殺者，這是一個公平的待遇。一旦殺人是故意的，謀殺者自願將他生存的權利交給了國家，並且有被沒收的可能性。

Pans on a scale can only be balanced when the weight on each side is the same. Equality and fairness are the prerequisites to justice. To keep the scale of justice balanced, the anti-capital punishment groups should come up with better argument for the maintenance of equality and fairness by the abolishing of capital punishment. "If you reward an inflictor with mercy, then what do you reward those who show you mercy?" as said by Confucius.

天秤的兩邊只有重量相同的時候才能平衡。平等與公平是正義的前提。要保持正義的天秤的平衡，廢死團體應該給出更好的理由，如何透過廢死達到維持平等與公平。「以德報怨，何以報德？」孔子如此說。

Questions prepared by the party in support of the death penalty against the abolition side:

A Do you agree with the definition given by Wikipedia regarding "CHILLING EFFECT": conduct is suppressed by fear of penalization at the interests of an individual or group?

B Is it fair to say that the rules of the criminal code in our social system generally carries a penalty for those violators?

C Is it fair to say that we punish violators for their wrongdoings because we want them to know there is price to pay either in the form of liberty or money so that they won't commit the same act again?

D That means, we want them to have fear and respect to the criminal code, correct?

E Do we also want others to know that those who commit the same offense will be subject to the same penalty so that they won't follow other criminal acts?

F In other words, does punishment of one violator under our criminal code have the effect of preventing other offenses?

G Do you agree that capital punishment should be enforced against those who commit serious crimes, usually involving the murder of others in our society?

H Should such murders be stopped and prevented?

I If a person has fear of losing his freedom or money by committing the regular crimes, should he have more fear of losing his life?

J Do you agree that a balanced scale is a symbol for justice and fairness?

K The scale is unbalanced if the murderer does not have to die but the victim must die.

關於支持死刑一方在交互詰問中，準備質詢對方關於廢止死刑的問題：

A 你同意關於「寒蟬效應」的定義嗎？也就是行爲可能因爲對於個人或團體利益上的懲罰而發生恐懼因而被遏止？

B 我們是否可以這樣說，我們社會的刑法上的條文通常對於犯罪者是加以懲罰？

C 可否這樣說，我們懲罰那些犯罪者，是因爲我們希望他們知道他們必須付出自由或是財產上的代價，之後他們不會再犯罪？

D 那也就是說，我們希望他們對於刑法的規定抱著敬畏的態度，正確嗎？

E 我們希望其他的人知道，犯下相同罪行的人會有一樣的懲罰，所以他們不至於跟隨著那些犯罪者的腳步犯罪？

F 換句話說，按照刑法懲罰一個犯罪者有遏止其他人犯罪的效果？

G 你同意死刑是處罰那一些犯了嚴重罪行通常牽涉到謀殺其他的人？

H 我們是否應該阻止以及預防這一類的謀殺？

I 如果一個人對於失去他自己的自由或是財產感到恐懼，那他是否對於失去生命會更覺得害怕？

J 你同意平衡的天秤是公平正義的象徵嗎？

K 殺人者可以不必死，但是被害人一定要死，就像是不平衡的天秤，這並不公平。

Each question for examination is connected in a logical sequence, from the first to the last, with a goal expecting a positive answer (yes) from the opponent in order to reveal the weakness in the argument for abolition, that is, failure in preserving justice (unfairness) and in prevention of future crimes.

The abolition side can follow the same approach and argue that capital punishment can serve no purpose but revenge with cruelty and barbarism as their core value because there is an alternative to achieve the goal on justice and prevention of future crime. The death penalty is not the only access to justice and fairness. The abolition side may prepare similar questions in a similar logical sequence in their cross-examining of the supporting side.

每一個質詢的問題，都以邏輯排列先後順序的方式，進行連結，從第一個到最後一個，目標是期待對手給予正面答案（必須回答，是的），因而能夠顯露他們在廢死立場上的弱點，也就是沒有辦法保存公平正義（也就是不公平）以及防止未來的犯罪。

廢止死刑的一方也能夠比照一樣的做法，然後辯稱死刑沒有其他的目的，就只是以非常殘忍和野蠻的報復作爲他們主要的價值而已，因爲有其他替代的方法可以達到公平正義以及防範未來犯罪的方法。死刑並不是唯一的方法可以達到公平正義。廢死的一方也可以準備類以邏輯排列順序的問題來質問贊成死刑的一方。

The following considerations can be taken into account by the abolition side (the affirmative) in preparation for the questions directed to the party in support of death penalty (the negative):

A Killing is cruel.

B If killing is cruel, why should a killing conducted in the name of a state be allowed?

C A murderer should be responsible for what he has done; does such concept on the culpability denote fairness or revenge?

D What is the difference between fairness and revenge?

E What is the consequence for executing an innocent person?

F It takes quite a few years for a murderer to be convicted. What if during this time, the murderer has totally changed to a brand new person. Assuming he has totally changed to a much better person, willing to repent and even turn himself into a saint, should society still execute a saint, for the act he has committed ten or twenty years ago? If we have to execute, is revenge the only motive for such execution?

廢止死刑的一方可以參考下列幾點，來準備對於支持死刑一方的問題質詢：

A 殺人是殘忍的。

B 如果殺人是殘忍的，爲什麼以國家名義可以殺人？

C 一個殺人犯應該爲他所做的事情負責，這樣的刑事責任是公平還是一種報復？

D 公平和報復的差別在哪裡？

E 處決無辜的人後果是什麼？

F 一個死刑犯的案件確定需要好幾年的時間。如果在這段時間內，殺人者完全變成一個嶄新的人，假設他完全變成一個很好的人，願意悔改，甚至將自己變成一個聖人，社會是不是需要爲了他十年或是二十年前所做的事情，處決這樣的聖人？如果我們必須處決他的話，報復難道不是死刑執行的唯一動機？

Questions prepared by the abolition side (the affirmative):

A Do you agree that killing is cruel?

B Do you agree that killing conducted in the name of a state is still cruel?

C Would you say that a murderer should be responsible for what he has done?

D Would you say the execution of such felon is the enforcement of fairness and justice?

E Would you agree that it takes quite a long time, generally quite a few years for a murderer to be convicted?

F Are you aware that some felons have totally changed to brand new persons as reported in some public media?

G Assuming a murderer has totally changed to a much better person, willing to repent and even turn himself into a saint, should society still execute a saint for the act he has committed ten or twenty years ago?

H If we have to execute such a saint, will you agree that revenge is the only motive for such execution?

I Would you say that such execution of a saint is still enforcement of justice and fairness? Or simply revenge?

廢止死刑的一方質詢問題準備：

A 你同意殺人是殘忍的嗎？

B 你同意以國家的名義處決這樣的犯人是一樣的殘忍嗎？

C 你認為一個殺人犯應該為他所做的事情負責嗎？

D 你同意通常一個死刑犯的定罪要花很久的時間嗎？

E 你了解有一些罪犯完全變成全新的人，就像一些媒體所報導的嗎？

F 假設這個殺人犯在幾年之後已經變成全新的人，願意悔改甚至變成一個聖人，整個社會是不是還應該為他很久以前所做的事情而處決這個聖人呢？

G 處決一個聖人，這樣的情況你還被認為是執行公平正義？或只是一種報復而已？

H 如果我們要處決這樣的聖人，你同意這樣的處決僅僅是為了報復嗎？

I 你還會說這樣處決一個聖人，是實現了正義和公平，或者只是報復而已？

Demonstration

Sample Writing for an argument against homosexual marriage

Keys with no lock

A lock can shut a luggage tight and it needs a key to open it. It requires both parts working together in performance of the function. Two keys alone cannot carry that function and would thus frustrate the user's purpose. Similarly, it seems normal and reasonable that from the shape and utility of reproductive organs of both genders', a man should unite with a woman for either procreation or for pleasure. Thus, it has been a long time in history that marriage is confined by law and religion to a unity between a man and a woman rather than that between the same sex, though sex among the same gender has been existing for a long time since the Old Testament time.

示範

反方寫作示範

沒有鑰匙的鎖

一個鎖可以將行李箱關緊，需要一個鑰匙才能打開，我們需要鎖與鑰匙才能完成這樣的功能。兩個鑰匙沒有辦法行使這樣的功能，而且會使使用者的目的受挫。同樣的，如果從兩性生殖器官形狀而言來看，男人跟女人必須相結合，才能達到繁衍生殖或是愉悅的目的，是十分正常而且合理。在歷史上有很長的一段時間，婚姻被法律以及宗教定義，是男人與女人而非同性的結合，雖然同性之間的性關係遠從舊約時代就存在了。

Marriage in human society has been long been defined as a form of relationship by unity between man and woman and has been sanctified by many different cultures and religions throughout history. The Bible says that a man should leave his parents to unite with a woman, that is, his wife, and it is always a blessing from God that a family can grow to become numerous as stars in the sky. The belief that marriage is between a man and woman is followed as well by the Muslim world.

人類的婚姻關係，自古以來就被定義成爲男人與女人的結合，而且在歷史上一直被不同文化和宗教視爲神聖。聖經上說男人應該離開自己的父母親與女人相結合，那也就是他的妻子，而且一個家族可以繁衍到有如天上的繁星一樣，總是一種來自上帝的祝福。回教世界也是相信婚姻是男人與女人的結合。

Chinese tradition also regards as a great blessing a great number of offspring. Since the latter part of the Zhou dynasty, the political system had been hereditarily monarchy until the Ching dynasty ended approximately 100 years ago, not even to mention the inheritance of property nowadays as a practice among the lineal descendants. Relations in human society have always been decided firstly by blood where the last names show the origins of families. For any individual, the genes of a blood-related family member can be identified. Hereditary diseases can be passed to the next generation, so are strong genes. Such relations by blood originated from marriages which have been granted with sanctity by many religions and all legal systems, whether the civil or common law system, in order to maintain the stability of family relations ranging from duty and privilege of parents toward children to the apportioning of property accordingly as well as avoiding incest.

中國傳統把子孫眾多視爲一種極大的祝福。從周代晚期開始一直到清代政治體制，是屬於世襲的帝制，遑論今天財產的繼承是在有血緣的關係上。人類社會的關係首先決定的是血緣，以姓氏表明了家族的來源。對於很多個人家族分子的基因是可以被確認。遺傳性的毛病可以傳到下一代，強壯的基因也是一樣。透過婚姻血緣的關係被許多宗教及法律視爲神聖，不論是大陸法系或是習慣法系，那是爲了要維持家庭關係的穩定，從父母對子女的權利義務以及根據這樣的關係決定財產如何分配，也同時避免了亂倫。

Respect to the bond of blood may be revealed from languages of different cultures. A western aphorism such as "blood is thicker than water" indicates that family relations are stronger than any others. A Chinese saying that "only blood-related brothers of a family can fight together against a tiger" carries a similar meaning. It is quite clear that the basic unit in human society is a family where members are originally born and united together through marriage as its very foundation. Abomination of behaviors which may interfere with the stability of a marriage such as adultery has been found either repugnant in the religious tenets or even guilty in the modern legal systems such as the penal code in Taiwan. However, this long held custom of unity between a man and a woman as a perquisite for marriage has been undergoing a great challenge in the past few decades and has experienced some drastic change.

對於血緣的尊重可以由不同文化之間的用語決定出來，西方用語說：「血濃於水。」表明了家庭關係強過於其他的關係。中國成語說：「打虎需要親兄弟。」有著相類似的意義。人類社會基本的單位很清楚的就是家庭，家族成員以婚姻爲基礎而產生並結合。在宗教上或是現在法律制度痛恨打擾婚姻穩定性的行爲，例如：婚外情在臺灣甚至是違法的。但是這樣認爲理所當然以男女爲前提的婚姻制度，在過去幾十年受到很強大的挑戰，也經歷了許多改變。

In the past few decades, the voice for homosexual marriage has been getting vociferous. To challenge the traditional image for a family, Denmark took the lead and was the first country to pass the legislation to recognize homosexual marriage, followed by Holland, Belgium, state of Massachusetts, Spain, Canada, South Africa, state of Connecticut, Norway, state of Iowa, Sweden, state of Vermont, state of New Hampshire, Washington D.C, Mexico City, Portugal, Iceland and Argentina. Even the Supreme Court of the US has ruled that the fundamental right to marry is guaranteed to the same sex partners. It seems that within a decade, homosexual marriage has become popular with western cultures.

Homosexual supporters claim with a tenor that homosexual marriage should be protected equally as heterosexual marriage. They allege that being gay is sex orientation rather than sex preference, which has been existing in their genes rather than their choice. Being gay is more like being a racial minority in a homogeneous society, such as a person being born as a black in a white community, with no possibility to change his/her skin color. They further assert that, on the level of equal protection, any person should not be treated with contempt or prejudice simply because of his skin color. For this reason, they are entitled to the right to have a marriage because of their love as any other heterosexuals.

過去幾十年支持同性婚姻的聲音變得大聲。挑戰了傳統家庭的角色，丹麥是第一個立法同意同性婚姻的國家，接著是荷蘭、比利時、美國的麻塞諸塞州、西班牙、加拿大、南非、康乃狄克州、挪威、愛荷華州、瑞典、美國佛蒙特州、新坎度夏州、華盛頓特區、墨西哥市、葡萄牙、愛爾蘭，以及阿根廷。而美國最高法院也判決同性戀的婚姻是合法的。看起來好像十幾年間，同性婚姻在西方文化裡面立刻受得了歡迎。

同性戀婚姻的支持者的論調是同性戀婚姻應該跟異性戀婚姻平等的受到保護。他們聲稱一個同性戀是一個傾向而不是性上面的喜好，這存在於他們的基因而不是他們的選擇。成為一個同性戀者像是在社會的少數民族一樣，就像在白人環境的黑人，他們不可能改變他們的膚色。他們更進一步的宣稱在平等保護之下，任何人不該因他們的膚色受到輕蔑或是歧視。爲了這個原因，他們應該如同其他異性戀者因爲相愛而有婚姻的權利。

The concept of equal protection originated from the very basic premise that any person in a similar situation should be treated similarly. To grant a homosexual marriage a status similar to that of a heterosexual marriage, the question should be asked: Is a homosexual marriage a similar situation as a heterosexual marriage? To answer that question, we have to ask why does a human society need to sanctify a marriage.

平等保護原則的概念來自於一個基本的前提，也就是任何人處於相似的地位應該有相似的對待。對於給予同性與異性婚姻相同地位，我們要問的問題是：同性與異性婚姻眞的是屬於相同地位嗎？回答這樣問題我們必須問到：爲什麼人類社會將婚姻神聖化？

The law never protects romance or love between lovers regardless of what commitment given to each other through their words. One side can't sue another simply because of the failure to fulfill a promise to get marry. A few decades ago, the state of New York even abolished the heart balm act to prohibit the suit for revoking an engagement. It has never been the intent of the law to protect romance between lovers. The rationale seems simply that law cannot force a person to love someone that he/she has no feelings for.

法律從來不保障兩個戀人之間的羅曼史，不管他們曾給對方什麼承諾。任何一方不能控告對方僅僅因爲他沒有履行婚姻的承諾。幾十年前紐約州就已經廢止了心靈療癒法案，禁止因爲取消婚約所帶來的訴訟。法律從來沒有保障兩個戀人之間的愛情，這個理由很簡單，法律沒有辦法強迫一個人去愛另外一個他已經沒有感覺的人。

However, the law does protect the integrity of marriage by punishing those who have interfered with another's marriage. The Taiwan penal code still carries a penalty of imprisonment for those who commit adultery. Why does the law not protect the romance but a marriage? The reasoning seems quite clear that, in most cases, marriage is followed with procreation which may create a family someday and increase the population. The relations between family members and all their relatives are defined clearly with all rights and duties provided, including the penalty against incest and the rules regarding inheritance. The civil law system even goes further to make any "disinheritance" of lineal descendants null and void. The family value is therefore emphasized and, in many traditional teachings, its stability ensures the society of its security and stability. For this reason, both the legal systems and religious tenets honor and sanctify the marriage from which all domestic relations are originated.

但是，法律確實懲罰那些妨礙別人婚姻的人以達到保障婚姻完整性的目的。對於妨礙家庭的臺灣刑法依然科以刑責。爲什麼法律不保障愛情但卻保障婚姻？理由看起來很簡單，絕大部分的情況結婚之後就是生育，這可以使一個家庭將來人口眾多。家庭成員以及他們的親戚們的關係是被定義得很清楚，包括他們的權利義務，這同時也包含了禁止亂倫以及關於繼承的規則。大陸法系的民法甚至規定，禁止直系卑親屬的繼承是無效的。因此家庭的價值是被強調的，而且在很多的教導中説明家庭的穩定確保了社會的安全與穩定。爲了這個理由，法律的制度以及宗教的教義尊崇婚姻並將其神聖化，而婚姻是一切家庭概念的開始。

Homosexual groups argue that not all heterosexual marriages can reproduce. Some couples are infertile. Why can't they get married because of their love? They even go further to claim their right to procure children through a surrogate or to adopt.

同性戀團體聲稱並不是所有的異性戀婚姻都可以生育。有些人是不孕的，他們爲什麼不可以因爲彼此相愛而結婚呢？他們甚至更進一步的聲稱，他們可以透過代理孕母或是收養的方式得到小孩。

While it is true that not all heterosexual couples may procreate, a general situation is that most couples do procreate if they choose to. Some don't probably because of their choice or being barren due to a physical condition (either age or illness). Simply speaking, it is not a regular situation. In the homosexual situation, the nature of their unity totally forbids their procreation so that they have to completely rely on a surrogate or even adoption. A child grows in this family won't be able to know what roles their parents play, paternal or maternal? It is needless to emphasize the importance on the psychology of a child that a model should be recognized and followed so that he may understand his identity when growing up. The research shows that a child who grows up in an environment where one parent speaks two different languages interchangeably will confuse the child's recognition and learning of a language and will hinder his/her language ability later in life. Is it possible that a child who grows up in such a homosexual family will suffer the pains of recognizing his sex orientation? Besides, allowing homosexuals to adopt children may also bring forth some serious problem such as incest which may happen unintentionally and cause great damage to future generations. It is inappropriate for homosexuals to adopt any child. Homosexuals are not similar in their situation as heterosexuals in terms of marriage.

確實有些情況異性戀是不能生育的，但是絕大部分的情況，他們如果願意的話是可以生育的。有些不能夠那是因爲他們的選擇或是身體的情況（年紀或是生病）。簡單來說，那不是經常性的情況。在同性戀的情況下，他們的結合完全禁止他們的生育，所以他們必須絕對依賴代理孕母或是收養。一個小孩在這樣的家庭長大，沒有辦法知道他們的雙親扮演什麼角色，父親或是母親？我們不用再強調確認一個模範對於一個小孩子的影響，好讓他在長大的時候了解自我。研究顯示，一個小孩子在成長的過程中，父親或是母親一個人說著兩種不同的語言，很容易混淆這個孩子在學習語言上的能力。同樣的，在一個同性戀家庭下的小孩，將來在自我對於性向的認知會不會混淆？除此之外，准許同性戀收養小孩也可能帶來亂倫之類嚴重的問題，對於下一代產生嚴重的影響。同性戀者收養小孩並不適當。以婚姻而言，同性戀者與異性戀者並不在同一線上。

Another important issue raised in a homosexual family is on their formation of domestic relation between parents, children and siblings. Such domestic formation in a homosexual family is created by law rather than by their blood bond. They are not related by blood at all. Once it is created by the law, it could certainly be changed by law as long as there is consent. This is because such domestic relation is not formed by blood bond but by consent. Simply speaking, such domestic relation is subject to change by mutual consent. Bonds between parents and siblings could be released and changed to another relation including that between a husband and a wife, even between siblings of same gender.

在同性婚姻家庭產生另外一個重要的問題就是，他們父母子女以及兄弟姐妹家庭關係的形成。同性婚姻家庭關係的組成是靠法律而不是靠他們的血緣。他們彼此之間的血緣並沒有任何的關係。一旦是法律上擬制的，只要雙方同意就可以改變法律上的關係。這是因爲這樣的家庭關係不是靠血緣，而是依同意所產生的。簡單來說，這樣的家庭關係只要經過同意就可以改變。父母與兄弟姐妹之間的關聯可以被解除，而且也可以改變成爲另外一種關係，包括夫妻之間以及兄弟姐妹之間甚至同性的兄弟姐妹之間。

Marriage has been sanctified by law and religion in human society for thousands of years throughout history. The very purpose for recognizing a marriage with sanctity is to provide stability for a family to ensure the interest of the future generation in our society. Homosexual marriage is not similar in their situation as the heterosexual marriage. This is so because homosexuals can never reproduce. They have no such ability. There might be romance or so-called love between them, but it is never an intent of law to protect romance. They may choose to live together. It perhaps seems wiser to incorporate a new concept such as a "civil union act" to accommodate the homosexual marriage as a new relation into our social system.

在人類數千年的歷史上，婚姻被法律以及宗教所尊崇，承認婚姻主要的目的在於維持家庭的穩定，確保未來世代的利益。同性戀婚姻與異性戀婚姻地位並不對等。這是由於同性戀者無法生育。他們沒有這個能力。他們之間或許有愛情，但是法律的目的不在於保障愛情。他們可以選擇住在一起。看來比較適當的做法是採用新的觀念「市民結合法案」，把同性戀結合當作新的關係納入到我們的社會制度裡面。

Cross-examination directed at the argument in support of homosexual marriage:

A Will anyone be punished because he/she refuses to fulfill his/her engagement vow?

B Does the law enforce an engagement vow between a man and a woman?

C Is it fair to say that romance is not what the law intends to protect, whether homosexual or heterosexual?

D If heterosexuals are not entitled to protection of their love, then there is no reason for a homosexual to claim the protection for their love.

E Is it fair to say that the unity between a man and a woman may produce in a NATURAL way an offspring? and thus form a family?

F Is it fair to say that reproduction and the raising of an offspring are important to maintain the human race?

G Is it fair to say that a family is the basic unit in society?

H Is it fair to say that generally the BOND BY BLOOD since

ancient times is a key factor to an inheritance of property among private citizens and even for an inheritance of a throne for a kingdom?

I Is it fair to say that the reason the law protects marriage rather than an engagement vow is because the law intends to maintain the bond of blood in a family, the very basic unit of all societies?

J Is it fair to say that healthy families are the most important foundation on which stability and security of a society are laid? For this reason, is it fair to say that observance of sanctity of marriage will help to keep the harmony of a family and is important for the maintenance of a stable society?

K Are homosexuals able to reproduce in a natural way?

L Can a homosexual, after adopting a child, be identified in a natural way as one of the parents of the opposite gender, paternal or maternal?

M Do homosexuals intend to have a legalized marriage to protect either of their liberty (free choice) or romance, to which the heterosexuals are not entitled, and therefore, gaining unfair advantage over heterosexual romances?

N Can the property issued between homosexual couples be solved by the law on civil partnership?

O If so, why do they insist on gaining the status of a marriage?

P Equal protection connotes that anyone situated similarly

should be treated similarly. Homosexuals are NOT situated similarly with the heterosexual ON THE ISSUE REGARDING MARRIAGE and adopting children.

Q Is it fair to say that the domestic relation in a homosexual family is created by law rather than by blood?

R Is it possible that the domestic relation in a homosexual family created by law be changed by mutual consent subsequently?

S If so, is that possible that the relation between a parent and a child or that between siblings in a homosexual family is terminated by mutual consent and later change into a marital relationship?

T Is that possible to forbid such transformation by mutual consent of domestic relationship in a homosexual family with legislation?

對於支持同性戀婚姻的交互詰問：

A 任何人會因爲違反他／她的愛情誓言而受到法律處罰嗎？

B 法律保障男女之間的愛情誓言嗎？

C 不論對於同性戀者或異性戀者，我們可以說愛情並不是法律所要保障的對象嗎？

D 我們可以說如果異性戀的愛情並不獲得保障，也沒有必要對於同性戀的愛情保障嗎？

E 我們可以說一個男人跟女人的結合可以正常的產出他們的後代嗎？因此組成一個家庭？

F 我們可以說生產與養育後代對於維持人類的生存是很重要的

一件事嗎？

G 我們可以說家庭是社會的基本單位嗎？

H 我們可以說自從古代開始，血緣的關係在人民當中對於財產的繼承很重要嗎？甚至對於一個王位地位的繼承也很重要嗎？

I 我們可以說爲什麼法律保障婚姻而不是愛情，是因爲法律要保障家庭的血緣關係嗎？家庭是所有社會最基本的組成觀念？

J 我們可以說正常的家庭是社會穩定與安全最重要的基礎嗎？基於這個原因我們可以說注重婚姻的神聖性可以幫助維持家庭的和諧以及一個穩定的社會？

K 同性戀能夠以自然的方式生產嗎？

L 一個同性戀者在收養小孩之後可以以自然的方式辨別出他究竟是父親還是母親嗎？

M 同性戀者需要一個合法的婚姻保障他們的愛情或是選擇上的自由，而這樣的愛情保障卻是異性戀所沒有的，如此是否不公平的享有了超越異性戀對於愛情在法律的權利？

N 同性戀伴侶之間財產的問題是否可以以法律或是市民法案解決？

O 如果可以的話，同性戀者爲什麼堅持要一個婚姻的地位？

P 平等保護原則說明了任何地位相似待遇也應該相似。關於婚姻以及收養小孩問題上，同性戀與異性戀並不相等。

Q 我們可以很公平的說，多元家庭的內部關係是法律所擬制的而不是眞正有血緣關係？

R 這樣的法律擬制的關係是否可於其後依雙方合意改變嗎？

S 是否有可能在多元家庭父母以及兄弟姐妹之間的關係可以雙方合意停止，之後變成婚姻關係？

T 是不是可能立法禁止，多元家庭透過雙方合意改變彼此家庭關係？

The above two essay samples are written in a style of advanced writing and can be summarized with an outline as a memorandum for a debate.

前面兩篇評論的範例是以高級寫作的方式寫出，並且可用摘要的方式當作辯論的備忘錄。

The beauty of a debate lies in cross-examination. Cross-examination is the essence of a debate. As shown in the GMAT argument questions, once assumption is found, a simple introduction of other possibilities can collapse the whole statement. Without a cross-examination, a debate is not that different from a speech. If challenged without a duly organized cross-examination, the whole debate will be more like a dog fight.

辯論的美妙之處在於交互詰問。交互詰問是辯論的精華。就像我們在 GMAT 辯論問題上所看到，一旦找出假設，我們只要找出其他的可能性，整個辯詞就會崩解。沒有交互詰問，辯論與演說並沒有什麼不同。如果不用組織良好的交互詰問方式質詢對方的話，整篇的辯論只會變成像是吵架而已。

A successful cross-examination requires that complete facts are provided, crucial issues are spotted, a full understanding to the issues presented, good analytical ability to build a sound framework as well as high intelligence in spotting any weakness during the time when the opponent is stating his argument. Time is of essence in a debate. The ability on cross-examination is the core of the very essence of a debate. Therefore, it is fair to say that good questions asked can prove your competency for your position because good questions can help to procure important information dispositive on your decision, to expose your opponent's weakness and thus consequently help to gain a stronger bargaining power. For this reason, training on cross-examination is crucial for any business manager on their improvement of their persuasive powers and management of business disputes. On the contrary, do not ask bad questions if unprepared. Bad questions not only waste time, both yours and others, but also earn contempt from others, tarnishing your image, especially among those who don't know you well or in a situation where confrontation can be expected. Your questions show your level of knowledge, intelligence and training.

一個成功的交互詰問需要完整事實的提供、重要爭議點的定位、對於所提出爭議完全的了解、以良好的分析能力建造出健全的架構，以及當對方正在陳述他的辯詞時，聰明地立刻找出弱點。及時的反應非常的重要。交互詰問的能力是辯論最重要部分的精華。因此持平而論，能夠問一些好的問題可以證明你有足夠的能力應對職位上的要求，因爲好的問題可以幫助你取得商業判斷上的重要的資訊，也能夠暴露出你對手的缺點，最終取得強而有力的談判籌碼。爲了這個原因，詰問的訓練對於所有的商業經理人在增進他們說服力以及對於商業糾紛的控管上是迫切需要的。相反的，如果沒有準備的情況之下，不要問一些不好的問題。問題問得不好，會讓別人輕視你的能力，形象上大打折扣甚至鬧出笑話。這特別是在跟不熟的人或是與洋人打交道的時候要特別注意。所以在沒有準備的情況之下，不能隨意發問，特別是在面對不熟的人或是有潛在對立情況的時候。你所提問的問題，反映出你在知識、聰明度以及訓練上的程度。

Cross-examination in a debate generally refers to a process of examining an opponent's argument with questions prepared in advanced. Immediate questioning an opponent's argument is difficult, demanding ability on quick understanding and precise issue spotting. Whoever can do a good cross-examination can do well on research, issue spotting, analysis, and statement elaboration. One thing should be noted here is that debate is not the same as a speech. During debate training, more emphasis should be placed on issue spotting and cross-examination. Many debate competitions in Taiwan emphasize the importance on the utterance and manner in the statement given rather than on questions in cross-examination. Some competitions do not even include cross-examination as a part in their evaluation. Without cross-examination, stating of an opinion with reasoning, in a debate is a speech in essence and can confound the listeners with two opposite views only. As to the presenting of an argument, the training is rather similar to that in a speech and generally will not help much on critical thinking, especially on the defense of your own opinion and exposing the opponent's weakness.

辯論中的交互詰問，通常就是針對對手所提出的辯詞的檢驗程序。當下立即的質問是很困難的，那需要快速了解對手所提出的辯詞以及精確找出問題的能力。能夠做好交互詰問，也能夠在資料研究、爭議點的定位、分析以及論點說明上面做得很好。這個地方要說明一點，辯論與演說不同。在訓練辯論當中，我們會強調找出爭議點以及交互詰問能力。臺灣很多辯論比賽強調了演說以及表達的方式，而不著重於交互詰問的問題。有些比賽在計分的時候並不包括交互詰問，沒有交互詰問而只有提出意見以及理由的辯論，本質上只是一場演講而已，使得聽眾對於兩種不同看法產生困惑。至於提出辯詞部分，這一部分訓練與演說大致相同，通常對於批判性思考幫助不大，特別是在於防衛自己的意見和顯現出對手的弱點方面。

Other Topics for Debate Exercises

Six topics listed as follows are appropriate for debate exercises and should be practiced under guidance of a teacher.

A Corporal punishment should be forbidden.

B Surrogate motherhood should be allowed.

C Abortion should be legalized.

D Rape charge should be initiated with the victim's consent.

E Prostitution should be legalized.

F Gambling should be legalized.

其他辯論的題目

下列有六個適合的題目，可以在老師的指導下進行練習。

A 校園的體罰應該禁止。

B 代理孕母應該合法化。

C 墮胎合法化。

D 強暴最應該改成告訴乃論。

E 性產業應合法化。

F 賭博合法化。

Samples for demonstrations

Topic: democracy under a relative majority should not be the only standard to judge if a nation is not civilized.

Claim: U.S. has repeatedly claimed that democracy is a universal value and should be practiced by all nations in the world. The rationale is that the ruler should procure the consent of the ruled. In a democracy, the government has obtained the consent through a majority vote. Therefore, a democracy should be a universal value among all civilized nations. China does not have a democratic regime. Therefore, China does not accept universal value and cannot be regarded as a civilized nation. Please rebut.

範例

主題：相對多數決的民主政治不應該是文明國家的唯一指標。

聲稱：美國不斷強調民主是普世價值，而且世界各國都應該採行這樣的制度。立論的基礎就是統治者應該取得被統治者的同意。在一個民主制度中，一個政府已經取得了多數人的同意。因此民主應該在所有文明國家是一個普世價值。中國並沒有民主政體。因此中國並不接受普世價值，不能夠被視爲一個文明國家。請反駁。

Rebuttal: What is democracy? Democracy is probably best represented by the idea based on the check and balance consequent in the separation of powers, presented by Montesquieu and was incorporated subsequently into the US constitution in the late 18th century. No doubt the check and balance represented by the separation of powers is a form of confrontation to prevent the concentration of powers. By confrontation through separation of powers, no power will be concentrated so that any authoritarian or even totalitarian government can be avoided. Confrontation is not a common practice in a society built on collectivism which emphasizes harmony and cooperation where a group such as a family rather than an individual serves as a unit. Confrontation originated from raising a doubt in an individual's mind and is therefore embedded in individualism. To claim democracy as a universal value is to claim that individualism is superior to collectivism.

反駁：什麼是民主？民主最佳的呈現就是權力制衡所發展出來的三權分立。這是由法國學者孟德斯鳩所提出來，在十八世紀晚期納入美國憲法當中。毫無疑問的，三權分立所代表的權力制衡，是以對抗的方式來防止權力的集中。透過三權分立所採取的對抗，沒有權力會過度集中，因此專制政體政治，甚至集權政治因而被避免。對於一個以群體、強調和諧與合作的集體主義社會，對抗並不是常見的方式。對抗來自於個人心中的懷疑，因此是深根於集體主義上。聲稱民主是舉世價值，也就是主張個人主義優於集體主義。

Besides, the rule with consent from the majority in democracy only means procuring a consent of 51% of the electorates who vote. People who actually vote are probably only slightly higher than 60% in many western nations. In other words, in democracy with a bipartisan system, the consent of the majority could only stand for consent of 30% of the electorates. To rule with consent of 30% of the whole electorates (i.e. another 70% who do not show their consent) can hardly be called the rule by majority. If that is a majority, it is a relative majority. In fact, a great majority probably do not accept the ruling authority in an election.

除此之外，民主制度的多數決只是意味著取得投票人數 51% 的同意。在西方國家眞正投票的人也許只有 60%。換句話說，在一個兩黨政治的民主政治，所謂的多數決只是整個選民的 30% 的同意而已。以所有投票人口整數 30% 來進行統治（其餘 70% 沒有同意的人）很難說這是多數決。如果那是所謂的多數，那它只是僅僅相對的多數。

Most of all, the term "civilized nation" explicitly refers to nations with civilization. Civilization is defined by the Oxford dictionary as "the condition that exists when people have developed effectively ways of organizing a society and care about art, science, etc." or "a particular well-organized and developed society." China's political regime since almost two thousand years ago has a strict selection process firmly embedded in the Confucius philosophy "selecting people with talents and choosing capabilities to rule". The whole society has always been well-organized and developed with great care on art and science. It seems that People's TALENTS rather than their CONSENT are much closer to the definition on civilization. To sum up, China is a nation managed by a group of capable intellectuals with a great majority as philosophers, artists chosen by emperors under the strict process to rule.

For the reason stated above, democracy by a relative majority is not a standard to judge whether a nation is civilized or not.

最重要的這個字眼「文明國家」，很明白的是指那些具有文明的已開化國家。文明按照《牛津字典》的定義就是：「人們發展出很有效果的方法以組織的一個社會，而且重視藝術與科學的狀態」，或是「一個特別良好組織跟發展的社會」。中國的政治制度有將近兩千年的歷史，以基於孔子哲學有著非常嚴謹的選拔過程，選賢與能對國家進行統治。整個社會是有相當的制度而且高度發展，非常重視藝術與科學。而且看起來，是人們的才能而不是他們的同意，更能接近文明的定義。總之，中國是由一群有能力的知識分子，而且他們大部分是哲學家與藝術家，並且由皇帝以嚴格的制度所選拔進行統治。

基於上述原因，相對多數的民主制度不應該是判斷一個國家是否文明的唯一標準。

The above demonstration is a short summary on arguments made by both sides, followed by an issue centering on the difference in views regarding the administrations between the rule by consent and rule by talents supported by reasoning. In fact, the analysis reveals a question, that is, is it appropriate to connect civilization with form of political regime if the term civilization is defined as a society well organized and developed with care on art and science? It seems that People's TALENTS rather than their CONSENT are much closer to the definition "the condition that exists when people have developed effectively ways of organizing a society and care about art, science, etc." or "a particular well-organized and developed society."

Readers can feel free to try to write down reasons placed in a logical sequence to support your own view.

上面的示範是正反雙方辯詞的簡短摘要，爭議點在於對文明政府的看法究竟應以人民的同意進行統治，或是以能力統治爲判斷的標準，以及所持的理由。事實上，這樣的分析也顯示出一個問題，也就是把文明跟政府的型態連結在一起，是不是適當？如果文明這個字眼是被定義爲一個有良好組織與發展，並且特別注重藝術與科學的社會。而且看起來，是人們的才能而不是他們的同意，更能接近所定義的「人們發展出很有效果的方法以組織的一個社會，而且重視藝術與科學的狀態」，或是「一個特別良好組織跟發展的社會」。

讀者們可以練習，以邏輯順序自由地寫下你支持哪一方的理由。

Demonstration

Being tough, good or bad?

An eye for an eye, a tooth for a tooth and an arm for an arm, as the old saying goes. A form of revenge implies a sense of justice. Then what's wrong with enforcing justice? Therefore, being tough seems a good choice for all. But the Bible says, those who kill with the sword shall die by the sword. You will be treated in the same way as you treat others. When you play tough with others, people treat you tough as well. What would you say if you lived in a world that treats you tough every moment?

示範

強悍好還是不好？

「以眼還眼，以牙還牙，以手還手」，古老的諺語這樣說。報復的形式意味著正義。那執行正義有什麼錯呢？因此，強悍對於所有的人來說，看起來應該是個好事。但聖經上這樣說，那些動刀的必死於刀下。你如何對待別人，別人也會如何對待你。你以強悍的方式對待別人，別人也會以強悍的方式對待你。如果你活在一個凡事對你表現強悍的世界，你的感受會是如何呢？

Rebuttal (by Guo Wenqian)

Ⓐ According to the theory of evolution, it is always the fittest, the toughest that survives.

Ⓑ This theory not only can be applied to nature but also to our society.

Ⓒ No success in our society can be easily achieved without unshaken determination.

Ⓓ In the work place, tough people are usually aggressive and strong-minded. They are more determined when it comes to realizing their goals, and stick to their principles.

Ⓔ Therefore, in most cases, tough people can adapt themselves to fierce competitions and defeat their comparatively weaker counterparts.

Ⓕ Some Chinese philosophers in ancient times believed that being tough is not a wise way to respond to challenges. In Confucianism, conquering the unyielding with the yielding is widely believed. They used water as an example, claiming that a constant drip wears away a stone even though water is regarded as being very weak, while stone is seen as being tough.

Ⓖ However, they fail to notice that the reason that a rock can be worn through by water is from the result of the constant dripping of water. One drop of water is weak, whilst the constant dripping of water generates a strong strength, which is even tougher than rocks.

Ⓗ Therefore, even in this case, the ultimate cause of water

wearing through a rock is being tough.

反駁（郭文倩）

A 根據進化論，適者生存。

B 這樣的説法不僅適用自然界，而且也適用人類的社會。

C 在我們社會沒有成功是可以不靠堅定的意志能達成的。

D 在工作場所強悍的人通常比較具有侵略性而且意志堅定。當談到實現他們的目標以及堅持原則的時候，他們有更強的決心。

E 因此，在絕大部分的情況下，強悍的人會調整他們適應激烈的競爭，而且打敗相對較弱的競爭者。

F 古代中國的一些思想家相信，強悍的方式面對挑戰並不適合。儒家相信以退爲進，他們用水當作例子，聲稱滴水穿石，雖然水看起來是非常柔弱而石頭非常堅硬。

G 但是，他們沒有注意到爲什麼水能穿石的理由。一滴水可能很柔弱，但是長時間持續性的滴水，會有很強大的力量。

H 因此，就算在這個例子裡，水能穿石就是因爲水很強悍。

To rebut the student's rebuttal: According to this statement, only the strongest is the fittest that can survive in the world full of competitors, the so-called rule of evolution. Therefore, in order to survive, for example, in a work place, we have to stay strong probably in the form of toughness to face the challenges encountered so that we can excel over others to survive or to receive a promotion.

The whole statement is premised on the assumption that others who are competitors will NOT get tougher in respond to the toughness encountered. In other words, if you are trying to survive or even to succeed by applying toughness, others will surely apply the same rule against you. If they are weaker, by applying the rule of evolution, they might unite their weakness together against your toughness, as the example shown in your statement regarding the constant dripping of water. Stone is tough, but water drops, as you may find, are even tougher.

Therefore, you cannot always rely on your toughness to excel because you can always see others who are stronger.

反駁學生的意見：根據這個命題，只有最強的人才是在這個充滿競爭的世界最具有競爭力的人，因此能夠生存，也就是所謂的進化論。因此爲了要生存，例如一個工作場所，我們必須以強悍的方式保持強壯來面對可能遇到的挑戰，因此能超越別人達到生存，或是晉升的目的。

所有的說法是建立在一個假設上，也就是其他的競爭者在遇到強悍的事情的時候，不會以更強悍的方式回擊。換句話說，如果你希望藉由強悍的方式達到生存的目的，其他的人也會使用相同的規則攻擊你。如果他們是屬於較弱的一方，在進化論的規則下，他們可能結合起來共同對抗你的強悍。就如同上面所談到滴水穿石的例子。石頭是很強悍的，但是持續的滴水可能更加的強悍。

因此，你無法依靠你的強悍來超越別人，因爲你總是會看到更強的一群。

Practice of IELTS essay questions

IELTS written tests generally demands a discussion of a topic with different views supported by reasons. It seems a matter of choice. A choice requires a comparison of the pros and cons, advantages and disadvantages, or the cost and benefits regarding certain issues. This writing training also serves as a good training of a debate because it involves an argument with an explanation on the reason "why".

IELTS 作文練習

IELTS 作文測試通常要求以不同看法加上理由來討論一個主題。看起來好像是一個選擇的問題。一個選擇要求對於特定議題正反的比較、有利支點與不利支點的比較，以及成本與利益的比較。寫作的訓練也是一種很好的辯論訓練，因爲它包含了對於辯論言詞的解釋，並提出「爲什麼」的原因。

Demonstration

Many people believe that a formal "pen and paper" examination is not the best method of assessing educational achievement. Discuss this and give your own opinion.

示範

許多人相信紙筆考試並不是最好的方法來評量教育的成果。請討論並且說出你的意見。

Sample answer

"Pen and paper" examination requires students to put his answer on the paper for evaluation. In that case, nothing but the answer sheet serves as the only evidence to assess the merit of the student tested. Therefore, the question here is whether the content of the answer sheet ALONE can fairly speak for the student's achievement or his full knowledge on the subject matter? The answer seems probably in the negative.

範例答案

紙筆考試要求學生將答案寫在紙上進行評量。在這樣的情況之下，只有答案紙是衡量受測試學生程度的唯一證據。因此這地方的問題就在於，單純一張答案紙的內容，是不是可以很公平的顯現出學生的成就及對主題的了解，答案看起來似乎是否定的。

Most schools still rely on the "pen and paper" examinations because, whether in multiple choices or in essays, the students' knowledge on the subject can be effectively and fairly evaluated. The writing test now held serves as the best evidence because the writer's usage of vocabulary and grammar, issue spotting ability, and his framework upon which the arguments are built together with his reasoning process can speak best for his writing level and can be fairly judged by an experienced examiner within a short time. Besides, "pen and paper" tests are still prevalent in most schools in Taiwan, the U.S., and many parts of this world. It's fair to say that these facts prove that most schools believe in a fair assessment made by the "pen and paper" examination of a student's achievement.

絕大部分的學校依靠紙筆考試，因爲不論是選擇題或是申論題，學生對於科目的知識可以很有效而且公平的被測試。現在所使用的筆試也可以用來當作學生學習的最佳證據，因爲學生所使用的字彙與文法，找出爭議點的能力，辯詞的架構與説理的過程，可以眞實的表達出他寫作的程度，並且能夠在很短的時間由老師進行評價。除此之外，紙筆考試在臺灣、美國絕大部分的學校依然普遍。這事實證明了，大部分的學校相信紙筆考試在測試學生學習程度的公平性。

However, certain merits cannot be ascertained by the "pen and paper" examination. For example, a student's performance in certain courses such as speech, debate and negotiation relate to utterance (i.e. oral expression), process of persuasion, act performing or even mind playing that are often seen in a real business world which cannot be evaluated by a piece of paper alone. This is because an evaluation in this situation requires an observation of the interaction and communication between the student being tested and his counterpart. A pen and paper can neither faithfully nor vividly record the real process of utterance and persuasion. Other courses, such as experiments in science, will have a similar problem if no actual experiment is conducted. Mere memorization of data or equations will not build up a student's ability unless he is actually engaged in the practice. Another phenomenon that we should also take notice to is that many schools now require students to do an internship as part of their college curriculum. Obviously, schools and businesses are already aware of the insufficiency of the book knowledge which stands for the weakness of the "pen and paper" examinations.

但是，紙筆考試沒有辦法衡量一些學生的學習程度。例如學生在一些科目上的表現，像是演説、辯論以及談判，這些與表達「口語表現，説服過程，動作表演，甚至是商業場上的鬥智」，都無法以紙筆測驗來進行。這是因爲這種情況下的評量要求對於受測試學生與他同伴互動的觀察。紙筆測驗沒有辦法很忠實地記下表達與説服的過程。其他在科學上實驗科目也有類似的問題，如果不進行實地操作的話。僅僅對於資料以及方程式的強記並不能夠建立學生的能力，除非學生進行實地的操作。另一個現象我們應該要注意的是，現在許多學校要求學生實習當作學分之一。很明顯的，學校和商業界已經了解到不足，這也是紙筆測試很大的缺點。

In conclusion, it is fair to say that the "pen and paper" examination is an effective process of evaluation and is still prevalent in most schools in this world, but there is certain training where merely the "pen and paper" examination cannot make a full assessment because a student's merit cannot be fairly assessed within the four corners of that answer sheet. Therefore, the "pen and paper" examination is not the best assessment of a student's educational achievement because it cannot fully test a student's merit.

總而言之，我們可以很公平的說，紙筆測試是評量很有效的方法，而且在絕大部分學校很盛行，但是很多是無法用紙筆測驗進行的，無法用紙筆測驗進行評價。

Demonstration

You should spend about 40 minutes on this task.

Write about the following topic:

Some people prefer to spend their lives doing the same things and avoiding change. Others, however, think that change is always a good thing.

Discuss both these views and give your own opinion.

Give reasons for your answer and include any relevant examples from your own knowledge or experience.

Write at least 250 words.

示範

你有四十分鐘完成這個工作。

針對下列題目進行寫作：

有些人喜歡做相同的事情不願意改變，有些人則認爲改變是一件好事情。討論一下這個看法，對於你的意見寫出理由，包括你本身的經驗寫出例子，至少二百五十字左右。

Change has always happened during the thousands years of human history, from civilization to civilization, empire to empire, and dynasty to dynasty. Rarely anything could last over hundreds of years. Bygone civilizations were replaced by the new as old empires were defeated by the young. In Chinese history, almost no dynasty could last over 300 years at best regardless how hard the emperors tried to lay the foundation for their heirs to maintain power. It seems that nothing can stop change in human history. Whether we like it or not, change is always on the corner waiting for all of us.

在人類幾千年的歷史中，改變不斷的發生，從文明到文明，帝國到帝國，朝代到朝代，很少有事情可以保持幾百年的時間，消失的文明可以被取代，就像是古老的帝國被新的帝國取代一樣。在中國歷史上，幾乎沒有朝代可以存活三百年，不管帝王如何處心積慮為他的後代立下根基以維持權力。人的歷史看起來好像是不能停止改變的，不管我們喜歡與否，改變似乎總是在角落等著我們。

Regardless whether changes constantly happen, some people prefer no change at all. This is because changes exact a great price coupled with the risks of failure for an unknown future. If change happens for the better with little cost, then most, if not all, will welcome such a change. If for the worse, then none will like it. Twenty-five years ago, I worked for the foreign ministry holding a position as a specialist in the legal department. It was a position of prestige with stability but slow in promotion because the seniority is the priority in consideration for a promotion, a form of bureaucracy so to speak. I was young then and eager to make a breakthrough. My dream at that time was to acquire a full professional legal training in the U.S. and become a New York attorney. My father held a completely different view. For a man who had experienced WWII, nothing was more important than stability and security which a government job of course could duly provide. I still remember my conversation with him that evening. I told my father, "You are 60 years old now and if everything still remains the same 10 years from now, you will be happy." Obviously, the same answer could not satisfy my need because I wanted to be a lawyer in the U.S. I wanted a change in my future.

儘管改變如此頻繁的發生，有些人並不喜歡改變。那是由於改變對不可知的未來伴隨著因爲失敗所要付出的嚴重代價。如果改變的發生是朝向更好的未來而所付的代價極少，那絕大部分的人會希望這樣的改變，即使不是全部。如果是變得更糟，那沒有人喜歡這樣的改變。二十五年前，我在外交部調解法律室工作擔任專員。那是一個穩定性很高而且有身分的工作，但是升遷緩慢，因爲年資很重要，一種行政官僚。我那時候很年輕而且希望能夠有突破，當時的夢想是希望能在美國取得完整的法學專業訓練，以及成爲一位美國紐約律師。我的父親抱持著另外一種完全不同的看法。對於一個曾經經歷過二次世界大戰的人，沒有什麼工作可以比公職所能提供的穩定和安全性來的重要。我仍然記得那天傍晚跟他的對話。我告訴我的父親，你已經六十歲，如果每一件事在十年之內跟現在都一樣，你會很高興的。很明顯的，相同的答案沒有辦法滿足我的要求，因爲我想成爲一名美國律師。我希望未來能夠有一個改變。

So, who prefers change? I have no hesitation to say that those who like to have a better future want change. No one likes change for the worse. Therefore, to encourage a person to make a change, we must give him/her a hope for a better future.

所以，誰喜歡改變呢？我會毫不遲疑的說，那些想有更美好的未來的人會想有改變，沒有人會希望變得更壞。因此，要鼓勵一個人願意改變，我們必須給他對於美好未來的希望。

Demonstration

Aristotle said the best activity of the soul is Eudaimonia (happiness/joy/the good life), which can be achieved by living a balanced life and avoiding excess by following a middle way between excess (too much) and deficiency (too little). Do you agree with the above statement? Please state why.

示範

亞里斯多德說，靈魂最快樂的活動是「快樂喜悅的美好生活」，而這些是可以透過一個平衡的生活，避免過度，遵循在過度與貧乏中間的中庸之道，你同意上面的看法嗎？請解釋。

A plane will fall on the ground if losing balance in the sky. A ship will sink into the ocean if losing balance on sea. No machine without stability can serve its purpose. Once balance is not maintained, then there will be no stability and the consequence will be disastrous. Balance resulting in stability therefore seems important in the regular operation of a machine. Balance is having equal power on all sides without excess on any. Where there is balance, there is stability.

飛機在天空如果失去平衡的話會失事；船隻如果在海洋上失去平衡的話會沉沒。失去穩定性的機器沒有辦法達到它應該有的目的。如果平衡不能維持的話，那就不會有穩定，後果不堪設想。對正常運作的機器來說，保持平衡帶來穩定是非常重要的。平衡就是在各個角度、在各方面有相等的力道，並沒有過之與不及。有了平衡就會有穩定。

Balance in life seems as important as that in a machine. Wine can help to relax and savor life with taste. An alcoholic who indulges too much in liquor cannot stay sober with a clear mind often end up in trouble (e.g. involved in an accident or violence). Work can help to make money and earn a sense of achievement. A workaholic who has spent too much time and effort in work to earn money and promotion could result in losing health and endearment time with his family. A man who has too much excessive greed for money observes no need for any friendship will most likely end up with a lonely life. We all love to earn money, enjoy good friendship, and a close family relationship. These goals cannot be achieved if we exhaust our time and effort on one end while ignoring the other. To keep a balance in life, we must apply equal power on all sides of our life. The Bible seems to take a similar approach. As Proverb puts it, "Let me be neither poor nor rich but give me my daily bread lest I either curse or forget God." Both poverty and riches in this context are in excess in a life led by a Christian. For a non-Christian, what exactly is an excess? How to decide?

平衡對於生活就跟機器一樣重要。美酒可以幫助我們紓壓以及給生活帶來品味，但是一個喝了太多酒的酒鬼沒有辦法保持清醒，通常帶來很多麻煩（例如：車禍或是暴力行爲）。工作可以賺錢以及得到成就感，一個爲了賺錢與升遷而花了太多時間以及精力的工作狂，可能會失去他的健康以及與家人相處的時間。一個人如果只在乎金錢而不在乎友情，很可能過著非常孤獨的生活。我們希望賺錢享受美好的友誼以及親密的家庭關係，我們如果花了太多時間及精力在某一項，就沒有辦法達到這樣的目標。爲了保持平衡的生活，我們必須對生活的各個角度保持均衡。聖經上看起來也採取相同的看法。就像箴言所說：「不要讓我太窮，也不要讓我太富有，但是供應我每天需要的麵包，這樣我才不會詛咒或是忘記上帝。」對於基督徒來說，貧窮與太過富足都是在生活中太過分的一件事。對於非基督徒來說，什麼是過分呢？如何來決定？

The answer seems rather easy. A man can try many things for enjoyment even though they may not always be beneficial to his interest. When such enjoyment, for example, in liquor, cigarettes or gambling, cannot either be controlled or stopped, then it becomes an addiction causing harm to both health and wealth including harm to others too. An addiction is surely an excess in life which will bring a man away from his happiness because he is constantly forced to engage in the same harmful acts.

答案看起來很簡單，一個人爲了快樂可以嘗試很多事情，但不必然對他有益。當享受快樂，例如：飲酒、抽菸、賭博無法被控制或停止的時候，這就會上癮，對健康跟財富甚至其他的人造成傷害。上癮在生活中就是一件逾越的事情，會將一個人帶離他的快樂，因爲他不斷被迫從事具有傷害性的行爲。

As to deficiency, especially that in severity, no one likes it because needs cannot be satisfied and the right to choose is severely limited. When there is no such balance between need and satisfaction in life, there can be no stability, as we often see in some poor areas in cities infested with crime. However, some with courage and determination will regard deficiency as a form of a challenge to prove a person's value and merit and to make a balance resulting in a better future. People in poverty would like to move from deficiency to a more balanced life if they can.

至於不足，特別是嚴重的不足，沒有人喜歡，而且選擇的權利嚴重的受限。當生活中需要與滿足不能維持平衡的時候，那就沒有所謂的穩定。就像我們在市區貧困的地方所看到充滿犯罪的地方一樣。但是有一些具有勇氣與決心的人，會將不足當作一種挑戰，用來證明一個人的價值達到平衡，並且有個完美的未來。貧困中的人們希望脫離不足達到一個平衡的生活，如果他們能夠的話。

In conclusion, to keep a balance in life with neither excess nor deficiency is to have stability leading to happiness and joy. Without such balance, life could lose control, ending in troubles or tragedy beyond our imagination.

總而言之，保持生活中的平衡，無太過與不足，就必須維持穩定，以達到快樂和喜悅。沒有這樣的平衡，生活會失控，導致超過我們想像的麻煩和悲劇。

Demonstration

Some think that a diploma is important while others don't. What is your view and state why.

示範

有些人認爲學歷很重要，有些人認爲不重要。你的看法爲何？請解釋。

Evidence is essential and dispositive in any judicial process on a trial especially those of criminal cases. Any statement, if not corroborated by evidence, remains mere words only which carry no validity to affect a court's subsequent decision. Many suspects, for example the suspect in the O.J. Simpson's murder case, have been acquitted because of insufficiency of evidence. Therefore, it is fair to say that the evidence presented will tell how far a case can go and further decide the merit of a judgment rendered by a court.

在法律審判特別是刑事案件中，證據是非常重要的，而且具有決定性質。任何的證詞如果沒有證據，那就只是言詞而已，不具有影響法院後來判決的效果。許多嫌犯，例如辛普森案，由於證據不足而獲得釋放。因此我們可以說，所提出的證據可以決定一個案件究竟可以走多遠，並且決定法院判決的效果。

Similarly, a diploma is a certificate issued by a school to recognize a student's knowledge and skill received in a school after successful completion of the requirements for academic works. In the old times, education was built on an apprentice system and the quality of education could be affected by many factors such as a teacher's ability on his profession and a learner's intelligence and attitude, etc. which may vary from case to case. The modern system imposes a minimum standard on accredited schools to assure the basic quality of education. In fact, all school nowadays issue not only diplomas but also transcripts probably even with class rankings attached to show the evaluation of the extent and degree of a student's knowledge and skill in comparison with that of his/her classmates so that the general public may understand where is the student situated in their professional training. That is why many employers placed great emphases on the reputation of the degree and the class ranking that an applicant has.

同樣的，一個學校所發出的學歷就是一個證明，承認學生在學校完成學業之後所學得的知識與技能。在過去教育依賴學徒制，教育的品質被許多因素所影響，例如老師的專業能力，學生的智力與態度等等。每個案件都不相同。現在體系在所獲得承認的學校加諸了最低標準以確保教育的品質。事實上，現在所有的學校不只發出學歷證明，而且附帶具有班上排名的成績單，顯示對於學生知識與技能程度的評價，並且與他的同學們做比對。好讓大眾了解這一個學生在他的專業訓練中處於什麼樣的地位。這就是爲什麼很多雇主特別重視學校的名聲，以及應徵者班上的排名。

Of course, there is still something that the four corners of a diploma cannot evaluate such as integrity, morality, creativity, etc. However, a diploma has won much recognition in society for evaluating the merits of an applicant in a job market as evidence, just as the evidence that can decide the fate of a suspect in a criminal case, whether you like it or not.

當然，很多事情是單單的一紙文憑無法評斷的，例如品格、道德感，以及創造力等等。但文憑在整個社會於評斷應徵者的能力方面已經廣泛被承認，就像刑事案件中的證據一樣，不管你喜歡與否。

Demonstration

People who have original ideas are of much greater value to society than those who are simply able to copy the ideas of others well.

To what extent do you agree or disagree with this statement?

示範

具有原創性想法的人，比起那些只能拷貝別人想法的人，對整個社會來講價值更大。

在什麼樣的範圍內，你同意或不同意這個說法。

Many people do think that those who have original ideas are of much value to society than those who are good at copying ideas of others. Is that really so?

許多人們認爲，那些有原創性想法的人，比起那些只能拷貝別人想法的人，對整個社會來說有更大的價值，但眞的是如此嗎？

Plants produce pollens for reproduction but it is the insects that deliver them to achieve that purpose. Without insects as a medium, pollen stays as a seed only. While recognizing the importance of a plant's ability to bear pollen, we must admit the insects' contribution in the growth of a forest. Obviously, the function of insects cannot be ignored in the plants' reproduction.

植物爲了繁衍產生花粉，但是也是要依賴昆蟲來完成這樣繁衍的目的。我們承認植物產生花粉的重要性，但我們也承認昆蟲對於整個森林形成所做的貢獻。很顯然的，在植物的繁衍上，昆蟲的功能不能被忽略。

People who give original ideas are very much like plants which bear pollen. Ideas are like pollen, which may in the future be adopted and applied in many fields resulting in a variety of products serving our welfare. Any idea, regardless how great it is, if not adopted and applied, will surely remain unknown with no utility as if it has never existed.

有原創性想法的人，就像是那些產生花粉的植物。那些原創性的想法就像是花粉，在未來可以在許多方面被採納而且應用，因而產生了很多產品，增進我們未來的福祉。任何想法，不管多麼偉大，如果沒有被採納以及應用，那就永遠不爲他人所知，也沒有辦法產生任何效能，如同從來不曾存在一樣。

Take a telephone as an example. It is in public use in these modern days to serve the great interest of the whole human race, which is very essential in our daily life, so to speak. If the invention by Mr. Bell had never been adopted and produced by manufacturers, such invention would always remain as an idea, and we could not enjoy the convenience brought by his invention. Similarly, cars, airplanes, movies, computers, internet, medicine, and any works of art that offer great comfort, convenience and pleasure to our daily lives all start from ideas as pollen of plants requiring insects as a medium. People who copy such an idea well are a medium to facilitate the application of ideas to our real life. Therefore, we should also recognize the contribution given by those who actually adopted the idea and put it into application in addition to that given by those who have original ideas. Without their effort, we cannot enjoy the fruits born from their inventions.

以電話為例，現今電話的使用，服務了大眾的利益，可以說，電話是我們日常生活的必須。如果貝爾先生的發明從來不獲製造商的採納以及應用，那這樣的發明，就僅僅只是一個想法，我們沒有辦法享受這個發明所帶來的便利。同樣的，可以為我們日常生活帶來舒適、方便、樂趣的汽車、飛機、電影、電腦、網路、醫藥以及藝術品都像是植物的花一樣，需要昆蟲當作媒介。善於拷貝想法的人們，就像是把想法加速應用到我們日常生活的媒介。因此，除了那些有原創性想法的人，我們也需要承認那一些實際上採納並且應用想法的人的貢獻。沒有他們的努力，我們沒辦法享受發明所帶來的果實。

For the reasons stated above, in terms of improving public welfare, people who are able to copy the ideas of others well are of same value to society as those who have original ideas.

基於上述原因，在增進未來的公共福祉上，那些能夠完善拷貝別人想法的人，與那些具有原創性想法的人，對於整個社會來講，一樣重要。

Demonstration of a Student's work

By Guo Wen-qian

Why do we follow the crowd? Are we afraid of being different?

學生作業示範

郭文倩同學：

為什麼我們跟隨群眾的腳步？我們害怕不一樣嗎？

Successful commercials and salespersons are good at taking advantage of people's fear. For a sales person, the threat sometimes works better than flattery. In cosmetic shops, words of warning can often be heard. If you don't really take good care of your skin, the condition will soon get much worse than you can expect. You will look older than your friends of your age. However, our products can save you from this tragedy. These sale talks successfully exploit the fear of a woman who is afraid of getting older, looking worse than their friends of the same age. Products are sold not because of flattery but because of the fear that is voiced.

成功的廣告還有銷售員，非常懂得怎麼利用人們的恐懼。對一個推銷員來說，這種恐懼有的時候比諂媚他人更為有效。在一個化妝店裡面，我們可以常常聽到警告的話語，「如果妳再不好好的照顧妳的皮膚，情況會比妳現在更糟糕，妳會比妳同年紀的朋友看起來更蒼老，但是我們的產品可以讓妳避免這樣的悲劇。」這一些行銷的術語，很成功地利用一個女人對於看起來比她同年紀朋友更為蒼老的恐懼。產品能夠賣得出去，並不是由於諂媚顧客，而是造成恐懼的言語。

Similarly, people have the same fear in choosing their future careers. There are some professions that seem to lead toward a bright future. Some departments in colleges always seem more popular than others. Students in business management, finance, computer science, electrical or mechanical engineering are often more optimistic about their future. The reason is simple. They are likely to have better opportunities to receive better payoffs once they graduate. The term "popular" has been connoted as a choice made by a great many. The question deserving our consideration here is that do they really make their choice out of their love or out of their fear?

同樣的，人們在選擇未來的職業時，也有相同的恐懼。有一些行業看起來可以有著光明的未來；一些大學的系所總是比其他系所更熱門；商業管理、財務、資訊、電機或是機械科系的學生，通常對於他們的未來感到樂觀。理由很簡單，他們可能在畢業的時候有比較好的機會回收他們的付出。「受歡迎」這個字眼，就有了眾多人選擇的意涵。這裡所呈現值得我們思考的問題就是，他們的選擇，究竟是因爲他們的喜愛還是他們的恐懼？

Yesterday I came across an answer in Quora on why we follow the crowd. It says: As "herd animals", we have established a social norm to encourage a herd behavior while, at the same time, discouraging against those who deviate from the flow. By doing so, herd animals protect themselves from predators by hiding in the crowd. If one is in a herd, and it sees a lion, it doesn't have to run faster than the lion, it just needs to beat the next guy in its speed. That is how a weak animal can survive among all dangers and find its own security. Any deviation could end up in a disaster.

爲什麼我們要跟著群體，我昨天在 Quora 上無意中找到了答案。作爲群居動物，我們建立了一個社會體系鼓勵群體的行爲，而且也同時不鼓勵那一些與眾不同的人。這樣做的時候，群體動物們隱身於群眾當中，保護自己不受掠食者的攻擊。如果隱身在群體當中，當他遇到獅子的時候，他不需要跑得比獅子更快，他僅僅需要跑過他隔壁的同伴就好。這就是爲什麼一個弱者在所有的危險當中依然能夠生存，而且可以找到他的安全感。與眾不同，就可能遇到災難。

If you are weak, find your herd and make sure you can always beat the next guy in speed. By then you should be able to survive and find your own safe haven. After all, being in a herd is only for survival, so to speak.

如果你很軟弱，那就找到跟你同類的群體，然後確信你永遠可以在速度上打敗另外一個同伴，這樣你就能生存，而且找得到你自己的避難所。畢竟，可以這麼說，隱身在群體當中究竟只是爲了生存。

A corner in a classroom

A conversation exchanged with a student who graduated five years ago regarding his question on comments from his supervisor and his co-workers on his professional writing. He is currently a manager in a multinational company.

教室的角落

一段與五年前畢業學生的對話，關於他所詢問有關他主管跟同事對他業務上專業寫作的評語。他現在是一家跨國公司的經理。

"After working for a few years, my writing has recently been commented on by my supervisor and co-workers as "good but distant". I am wondering how to manage my professional style in writing which, as I have already been well aware of, might take a long period of training."

「幹業務也有一段時間了。近期常被評價爲『很會寫文章，但也因爲如此很有距離感。』文章的設計、拿捏才是這個工作該具備的專業，這又是一個很花時間跟精力的訓練。」

Answer

My answer: According to their comments, the problem does not seem to be on the content, but with the style.

回答

我說：應該不是內容的問題，而是表達方式產生的距離感。

His comment: Accuracy of the content is indubitably fundamental. What outweighs it is the way the messages are delivered. In most cases, poor delivery only leads to anger and refusal. It can even go worse from being misunderstood to redundant clarification, and then it ends up falling into a vicious circle. Axiomatically, different levels of formality are appropriate in different situations. The statement should be designed to talk, rather than to LECTURE.

他說：內容的準確性毫無疑問是非常重要的，但是訊息傳達的方式更重要。在絕大部分的情況之下，不好的傳達只會造成生氣還有拒絕。甚至更糟糕的是，從誤解再帶來不必要的澄清而使情況變得更壞，而最後變成惡性的循環。明顯並正確地說，比較適合的是，針對不同情況而使用不同程度的格式。說法應該要有對話而不是訓話。

My answer: Debate aims at issue spotting followed by an analysis to consequently find a solution. Negotiation aims at reaching an agreement. A solution is not equivalent to an agreement. An agreement is a solution acceptable to others, in this case, your coworkers.

我說：辯論的目標在於找出爭議之後，進行分析而最後找到答案。談判主要是達成協議，而解決方案的提出並不等於達成協議。達成協議是大家都能接受你的解決方案，在你的情況下，也就是你的主管還有同事能接受你的解決方案。

Remember, the key word here is "acceptable". Bearing this in mind, you will see what problem you are talking about here.

要記得這個地方的關鍵字是「能接受」。把這個記在心裡，你就會知道你的問題在哪裡。

His comment: Precisely! The standard here is to be "acceptable" in order to judge whether the solution is valuable or not.

他說：中肯啊！能不能「被接受」才是有效／無效的指標。

15 Common Mistakes Made in Writing

Writing is more like driving a hand-shift car and it takes skill to drive it smoothly. Too many sharp curves and jerks by a newly unskilled driver will make the passengers miserable, vomit, or even cause an accident. Skill can be built up through the accumulation of years of experience on this practice. Mistakes can't be avoided during the learning process but should be confined to the minimum. In other words, students are advised to follow the most effective and efficient fashion for reaching their goal.

15 寫作上常犯的錯誤

寫作就像是開著一部手排檔的車子，需要技巧才能夠平穩的駕駛。不熟練的新手駕駛缺乏經驗，太多的大轉彎還有抖動，會讓乘客感到不適、嘔吐甚至造成意外。技巧是靠著多年的經驗，透過不斷的練習。在學習的過程中，沒有辦法避免錯誤，但是應該限定在最少的代價。換句話說，建議學生們以最有效的方式達到他們的目標。

The most common problems on student writings that I have encountered in the past few years are:

First, neither purpose nor any concept is found in the writing. We may assume that all writings are made with a purpose. It is to my surprise that students often have no idea to the topic they are writing about, not even to mention what the reasoning or interpretation is. A writing by anyone who has no idea (or purpose) on a topic is like scribbles made on the computer screen. It simply makes no sense at all! So many times I have to act like a detective at a crime scene, putting together all the broken bodies, a time consuming task. Only then can I make a rough guess what the victim originally looked like (i.e. what the writers are trying to say)! In other words, when writing is more or less deemed as a game of puzzles, no one can easily read it with pleasure. Such writing fails at the beginning as to its primary purpose.

在過去幾年中，我在學生寫作上最常看到的問題是：

第一，整篇文章沒有目的，也沒有提出概念。我們假設所有的寫作都是具有目的性，有的時候我感到很意外，學生對於他們所寫的主題並沒有任何的想法，還不用提有什麼解釋或是闡述。任何不具有想法或是目的的寫作，就像是電腦螢幕上的亂碼一樣，不具有任何意義。非常多的時候，我必須像是在一個犯罪現場的偵探一樣，把所有支離破碎的身體重新組合起來，非常耗時的工作。只有如此，我才能夠大概的猜測原來的被害人看起來像是什麼樣子（也就是作者想說什麼）。換句話說，當寫作只是像拼圖遊戲一樣的時候，沒有人可以對閱讀感到樂趣。這樣的寫作不能達到任何目的，在一開始就是非常失敗的。

Second, the purpose should be supported by some ideas, concepts, basic principles, or some examples laid out in a logical format. Even if they are able to grasp an idea sometimes, they still have problems with the process of presenting the ideas to the readers. The question to contemplate on in this phase is: how to present an idea in a logical format acceptable to the readers. Writers in this circumstance, of course, should remember the purpose of their writing and understand who their readers are. Style and choice of vocabulary for presenting their purpose may vary. Regardless who their readers are, what remains important is that writing should be logical, clear and easy for the readers' understanding of their purpose. The most common mistake made in this phase is the flaws made with reasoning, that is, students simply do not know how to make an analysis. Analysis is essential in supporting the idea. Without a sound analysis (i.e. reasoning), the readers can only see many adjectives arbitrarily and capriciously used, consequently jumping to a conclusion. Students should bear in mind that each conclusion can only be reached by reasoning. Many times I have seen a statement shown in the conclusion without being reasoned out in any prior paragraph. Many times also I have seen a few conclusive statements in the first few paragraphs without any subsequent analysis. No logical process is found in their writing but jumping from one idea to another. Such skipping or omitting any logical process renders the whole writing broken and unreadable. Readers do not know how the conclusion was reached. That is like the sharp turns and jerks made by a newly unskilled driver I was referring to in the beginning. It is a great pain to read those writings. Students at this age might only observe the level of vocabulary and style that are used to reflect the purpose of this writing. For example, in a business occasion, a piece of writing should be formal rather than casual with a concise content. A sound framework and careful usage of terms will show that the writer is well trained for the task that is being undertaken. Reading good writing is more like enjoying a smooth ride in a beautiful country side by a very experienced chauffeur.

第二，目的應該要有一些想法、概念、基本原則以及例子或事實以邏輯陳列的方式來支撐。學生們縱然有的時候能夠抓住一些想法，他們依然對於如何將想法呈現給讀者的過程有疑問。這個階段的問題，就是如何以邏輯排列的方法呈現一個讀者所能夠接受的想法。作者在這樣的情況之下，應該要記得你的寫作目的以及了解你的讀者是誰。呈現目的的風格和用字遣詞，有的時候不相同。不管你的讀者是誰，寫作中很重要的是，必須要有邏輯，要很清楚，然後很容易讓讀者了解你的目的。這個階段最常見的問題，就是在論理方面的瑕疵，也就是學生們不知道如何進行分析。分析在支持想法上是非常重要的事情。沒有一個好的分析（也就是論理過程），讀者們可能會看到缺乏事實上的依據，充滿恣意而用的形容詞，而驟下的結論。學生們應該要記得，一定要透過論理的分析才能達成結論。有許多次，我看到結尾出現一些之前完全沒有經過分析的結論；也有很多次，我看到前面幾段就直接出現結論，之後根本沒有任何分析。在他們的寫作中，沒有任何邏輯性的過程，就直接從一個想法跳到另外一個想法。這樣的跳躍或是省略，使得整篇文章支離破碎而且很難閱讀。這就是我前面一開始所說，不熟練的新手駕駛開著手排車時候的快速大轉彎，以及不正常的震動。閱讀這些作品是很痛苦的事情。學生們也應該注意到字詞和風格應該反映寫作的目的和他們專業的程度。例如，這一個商業場合，一封書信應該內容精簡，語體正式。健全的作品架構以及謹慎的用字遣詞，顯示作者受過良好的訓練。閱讀一篇好的作品就像在美麗的鄉間乘坐受過良好訓練的司機所駕駛的轎車，享受非常舒適的旅程。

A few minor points need to be noted are that 1. students are too eager to use the new vocabulary they are learning. They often neglect the definition of the term and apply it in a wrong context. I would suggest for them to refer to a dictionary regarding the definition and usage in light of the context. 2. Students are tempted to write a sentence in a complicated structure. A complicated structure is generally used when many different ideas, concepts, and causations of events are expressed in one sentence. It requires great skill and an inexperienced writer generally makes a good deal of mistakes regarding this. In other words, a complicated sentence, if used inappropriately, can obviously reveal your status as a foreign writer attempting to tackle an approach but unskillfully. Use of simple sentences are strongly advised in this situation.

另外有一些該注意的：1. 學生們很急切想要使用剛剛學習到的新單字。他們通常忽略那個字眼的定義，而做錯誤的應用。我會建議他們應該參考一下字典以及上下文關於定義還有用法。2. 學生有時傾向以複雜的結構寫下句子。複雜結構通常是用一個句子表達有許多不同想法、概念、諸多事件的因果關係。這一種使用需要高度的技術，一個沒有經驗的作家在使用複雜句型的時候，通常會犯很多錯誤。換句話說，如果不適當的使用一個複雜的句型，可以很明顯的表示出，你是一個希望使用這種表達方式的外國作者，但是不熟練也不成功。所以，強烈建議使用簡單句型。

To explore these problems further: My observation indicates that many students are quite fluent with their English both on a conversational and writing levels. Their proficiency is at the level with native speakers if plain English is used. However, in their process of learning, they will try to practice the new vocabulary they just learned as mentioned above. This is probably because they have been encouraged by their teachers in high schools or cram courses to earn extra credits by using difficult vocabulary for their exams. Problems sometimes ensue when the new vocabulary are inappropriately used because of their misunderstanding of the definition. Such misuse on application is probably caused by using an English-Chinese dictionary, because some true and original “flavor” is easily lost in the translating process, and thus the language equivalency cannot be found. Simply speaking, students are too busy on memorizing definitions without referring to a dictionary regarding their usage in a sentence. In addition to the misuse of vocabulary, awkward application of grammar on its complicated structure has obviously identified the writer as a foreigner who is not familiar with this language and sometimes renders his writing unreadable. To avoid this common problem, my advice is to use an English-English dictionary and also to try to use the new vocabulary after referring to the usage in a dictionary.

我們再進一步的探討一些問題：我的觀察顯示出，許多學生的英文，在會話以及寫作上相當的流利。如果他們使用平易的英文，流利程度跟本土人士相當。但是在他們學習的過程中，他們試圖練習剛學到的字眼。可能是由於高中或是補習班老師們的鼓勵，使用困難的單字可以在考試的時候得到額外的分數。但是由於對定義以及用法都不熟悉，導致使用上的不恰當。而這樣誤用的情況，可能是由於他們使用英漢字典翻譯的緣故，因為在翻譯的過程當中，容易失去原味，因此找不到語言上的平等性。簡單來說，學生們通常只集中在記住單字的定義而不參考字典關於單字在句型中的用法。錯誤的使用單字再加上奇怪的複雜文法句型，讓人立刻明白文章的作者，是不熟悉英語的外國人，有的時候甚至讓整篇文章無法閱讀。要避免這些問題，我的建議是使用英英字典，然後參考字典上的句型。

A rule of thumb for examining your writing is: ask your classmates to read your writing to see if they understand clearly what you are saying. If your writing is subject to different interpretations, then you know that you are not clear and need to re-clarify your meaning again. If possible, ask a native speaker to see if they can tell that this is written by a foreign hand? If so, ask why? Advice from a native speaker may help you to understand your problem on your choice of terms, usage of grammar, style, examples or metaphors used, etc. Another rule of thumb for judging your writing is: leave your writing in a corner of your drawer and come back to read it again after a period of time. If you do make progress on your English, you will see your own improvement.

在檢驗你的寫作的一個概略規則就是：請你自己的同學讀一下你的文章，看看他們是否很清楚地了解你要說什麼，如果他們對你的文章有不同的解釋，那你就知道你的內容並不清楚，需要把那些懷疑重新做個釐清。如果可能的話，問一下英語爲母語的本國人，看一看他們是不是可以看得出來，這是不是外國人的文章？如果是的話，爲什麼？本國人的建議，可以幫助你了解你的問題所在，像是你的用字遣詞、文法的使用、風格、例子，甚至是隱喻的使用等等。另外一個概略的規則，就是把你的文章放在你抽屜裡面，過一陣子後再回來看看。如果你真的進步了，你就會很清楚看到你自己的進步。

Finally, I would say at this moment that Chinese writing should be no different from English on a professional level where good reasoning is always required. Good writing, if aimed at persuasion, must use many facts to be interpreted with good reasoning. There should not be any difference on this point on any writing. Therefore, the approach to issues should be made with sound organization backed with logical reasoning that is acceptable in other professionals.

最後我要說，在專業上對於好的論證的要求，中文的寫作跟英文沒有什麼差別。一個好的文章必須以好的論證方式對於事實進行詮釋。任何文章在這一點上沒有差別。因此，應該以很健全的組織與邏輯性的論證處理爭議點。

國家圖書館出版品預行編目資料

關鍵60秒：菁英式說服力／鄭家捷著. --
初版--. --臺北市：書泉, 2019.11
面； 公分
ISBN 978-986-451-172-3（平裝）

1.說話藝術 2.溝通技巧 3.人際關係

192.32 108017027

3M52 職場專門店045

關鍵60秒：菁英式說服力

作　　者 — 鄭家捷（381.5）
發 行 人 — 楊榮川
總 經 理 — 楊士清
總 編 輯 — 楊秀麗
副總編輯 — 劉靜芬
責任編輯 — 林佳瑩、黃麗玟
封面設計 — 姚孝慈
出 版 者 — 書泉出版社
地　　址：106台北市大安區和平東路二段339號4樓
電　　話：(02)2705-5066　傳　　真：(02)2706-6100
網　　址：http://www.wunan.com.tw
電子郵件：shuchuan@shuchuan.com.tw
劃撥帳號：01303853
戶　　名：書泉出版社

總 經 銷：貿騰發賣股份有限公司
電　　話：(02)8227-5988　傳　　真：(02)8227-5989
地　　址：23586新北市中和區中正路880號14樓
網　　址：www.namode.com

法律顧問　林勝安律師事務所　林勝安律師

出版日期　2019年11月初版一刷
定　　價　新臺幣580元